MANAGING RETAIL CONSUMPTION

MANAGING RETAIL CONSUMPTION

Barry J. Davies and Philippa Ward

Cheltenham and Gloucester College of Higher Education

JOHN WILEY & SONS, LTD

Other Wiley Editorial Offices

John Wiley & Sons, Inc., 605 Third Avenue,
New York, NY 10158-0012, USA

Wiley-VCH Verlag GmbH, Pappelallee 3,
D-69469 Weinheim, Germany

John Wiley & Sons Australia, Ltd, 33 Park Road, Milton,
Queensland 4064, Australia

John Wiley & Sons (Asia) Pte Ltd. 2 Clementi Loop #02-0 1,
Jin Xing Distripark, Singapore 129809

John Wiley & Sons (Canada) Ltd, 22 Worcester Road,
Rexdale, Ontario, M9W ILL, Canada

Library of Congress Cataloging-in-Publication Data
Davies, Barry J.
  Managing retail consumption / Barry J. Davies, Philippa Ward
    p. cm.
  Includes bibliographical references and index
  1. Retail trade—Management. 2. Consumer satisfaction. I. Ward, Philippa. II. Title.
HF54289.D3344 2001
658.8'7—dc21

                                                                                2001046622

British Library Cataloguing in Publication Data

A catalogue record for this book is available from the British Library

ISBN 0-471-489123

Typeset in Palatino by Deerpark Publishing Services Ltd, Shannon, Ireland.
Printed and bound in Great Britain by Antony Rowe Ltd., Chippenham, Wiltshire.
This book is printed on acid-free paper responsibly manufactured from sustainable forestry in which at least two trees are planted for each one used for paper production.

CONTENTS

Part 2 – Management of the Arena of Retail Consumption

Part 4 – The Retail Future

Preface

Reasons for writing

This book has been written to provide those studying retailing with a text that explores some of the area's more specialized issues. In doing this, it breaks away from the nature of much of the traditional retail literature that takes a necessarily instructional perspective. This book, though, stems from a much more interdisciplinary viewpoint; and, rather than primarily focusing on the retailer, considers shopping from both the customer's and the retailer's perspectives.

Without understanding its customers' attitudes and involvement with the shopping experience, it would, at best, seem difficult for a retailing organization to provide an engaging and appropriate offer. Although, as a core tenet of marketing, this would seem an obvious notion, as far as we are aware, there has been little attempt to provide material that brings both perspectives together.

This book therefore also represents the authors' belief that there is a gap between the existing retail literature, with its managerial slant, and the consumption literature, which - being based in the socio-cultural tradition - often ignores those organizational issues of concern to retailers.

In bridging these divides - which are clearly related - the book's focus is on the store as a point of interaction, where retailers and customers create and play-out the retail encounter in all its forms.

Because of this focus on the store as a physical meeting point, the book does not explore Internet-based retailing provision in any great depth - although many of the issues discussed here are as relevant in a virtual context as they are in a concrete setting.

The notion of retailing as a meeting point for customer and retail provider - both in a social context and in terms of fulfilling the needs of both parties - is central to the book, and provides a constant thread that links the individual issues considered. This thread is further enhanced by using the Servuction model and dramaturgy as conceptual mechanisms to emphasize the depth and diversity of the customer-retailer relationship.

Intended audience

It must be stressed that this is not intended as an introductory text to the subjects of either retailing or consumption. In writing this book, we have assumed that the reader will already have attained a certain level of knowledge in these areas, as well as in related topics such as marketing and business management. We envisage that this volume will be of most use to those in the final years of an undergraduate retail degree, or those studying retailing at a postgraduate level.

We are also certain that this book is not an end in itself; and, where possible, we have given sources of additional information and pointers to areas worthy of further investigation. This book we hope, though, will provide those interested in retailing with a sound basis for exploring the issues raised in greater depth, and, by doing so, help create a more detailed understanding of this rich area of study.

For Miles

Introduction

About this Book

This book explores retailing primarily from the customers' viewpoint – from their experiences and their interpretations. It is therefore about the *consumption* of goods, services and the totality of the retail experience – of the creation and use of 'symbolic value' in the retail setting. As this value is co-produced – involving a combination of the consumer, the retailer, the manufacturer and society – the activities of consumption are examined within a broad context, and not simply as 'consumer behaviour'. In the space of one book, however, it would be impossible to cover each of these co-producers' contributions in depth; and we therefore focus on those of the customer and the retailer – and especially their interplay.

The distribution of goods and services through a retail mechanism is therefore viewed as a 'productive' task – a task that creates or adds value *for the customer*. In doing so, retailing becomes intrinsically linked to the 'classical' Marxian sphere of production, particularly in the case of the retailing of goods; yet at the same time can be seen as conceptually distinct. Retailing can itself add or create value linked to the goods sold, but it also creates a 'consuming' experience; and in so doing, deserves to be seen as separate from classical production.

The Economics of Production

The majority of concepts of retail development are grounded in the literature of the economics of production, and build on the theoretical construct elaborated by Marx (1904) as 'the sphere of circulation'. Each of the three related spheres described by Marx – production, circulation and consumption – overlaps in a way that creates and adds cumulative value.

However, in Marxian analysis, the real value is seen as being created in the sphere of production. Shifts in later writing, though, have tended to emphasize and elaborate the mechanisms by which value is created, sustained and shared in the two other spheres – those of circulation and consumption.

Retailing is clearly not located in the production sphere: but can be seen as a major component of that essential link between production and consumption – the sphere of circulation. To understand the nature of retailing within this sphere, therefore there is a need to understand what actually constitutes retail activity.

Retailing as a Distinct Entity

There are a considerable number of definitions of the concept of retail or retailing, developed in the academic literature related to the study of the discipline, as well as in allied subject areas such as marketing and sociology. However, the core concept remains simple:

> Retail – the sale to the public of goods in relatively small quantities, and usually not for resale.
>
> The New Shorter Oxford English Dictionary, 1993

> Retailing – the process of selling goods and services to ultimate consumers, or those buying on behalf of such consumers, particularly when carried out through store outlets… mail order etc.
>
> Baron et al., 1991, p. 163

These definitions appear simple, but the processes they define and describe can be complex – arising as they do, historically, from the range of activities undertaken by retailing organizations.

This development, while not linear, can be generalized as starting with relatively simple historic retail archetypes and 'progressing' to a system characterized by its extended and multi-faceted nature. If viewed as a continuum, it starts with ancient forms of retailing, such as the informal market, and ends at present with hypermarkets and e-tailing. Implicit in this notion of a continuum is the idea of increasing complexity – both of the retail organization and of its goods and services – created as they are through a continual and incremental change process. Such a view of retail institutional development, and its variants, have been embodied in linear, cyclical, conflictual or environmental models; and these constitute the greater part of the retail change literature (Brown, 1988, 1995).

Traditionally, there has also been a tendency to consider the role of retailing organizations within contemporary society in a purely *economic* context. However, if retailing as an activity itself is examined, then there is a need not only to consider the economic, but also the broader, social aspects. This is reflected in Campbell's (1995) argument that the treatment of consumption relies in practice on two broad strands of influence:

- The economic-materialist; and
- The psychological-cultural.

Our Approach

In this book, these two strands are both central. The specific role of retailing itself is also examined, within a perspective that is largely historical, by putting the principal forms of retail enterprise in context in terms of their time of appearance, and then relating them to the consumption behaviour of the population of that time. We do not explicitly consider the mechanisms for retail change, nor consistently employ any one theory of change. However, these are obviously implicit themes throughout. Instead, the forms of enterprise are identified and located in time (and sometimes also spatially).

There are, of course, huge geographical dimensions to the appearance, spread and domination of specific markets by particular retail forms. These aspects of the development of retail provision are not neglected, but they are not the prime focus of this book. Our perspective is to view retailing as the essential mechanism through which the consumption needs of more developed post-tribal societies are met. The thematic concerns of the text are:

- Consumption and the creation of identity;
- Style and consumption;
- The increasing role of retailers in designing and specifying both the spaces and the merchandise within it; and
- The need for explicit management of all elements that contribute to the complex retail offer of today.

How This Book is Structured

The book is in four parts. The first – introduction and context – sets out the historical background. The second part deals with the retail arena and its management; the third, the broader contexts of retail enterprise. The concluding chapter draws together the issues raised in the other sections and offers some prognostications for the future.

Part 1 – Introduction and Context: the Role and History of Retail Consumption

Chapter 2 – Retailing History

The concept of retailing is introduced as one of the defining characteristics of our type of society. The development of retail formats and offers is also discussed. A number of key points are raised in this chapter:

- As economies develop:
  - The individual produces less and purchases more;
  - Therefore an increasing percentage of consumers' requirements are met through retailing; and
  - The arena for exchange becomes increasingly formalized and elaborate and is subject to more regulation and increased managerial control.

- This 'progress' is illustrated through the provision of a diverse range of examples both historical and geographical, including:
  - Markets and fairs, the classical world, and souks;
  - The birth of modern retailing in the eighteenth century;
  - Its apogee in the nineteenth century; and then
  - A more detailed discussion of the trends evident in the twentieth century: the rise of multiples, the growth of non-store retailing (including the Internet), internationalization, shopping centres and malls.

The chapter stresses the importance of the non-merchandise dimensions of fairs, markets and other 'public' retail offers. It also emphasizes the increasingly 'leisured' orientation of retail provision based on that tradition.

Chapter 3 – The Birth of Modern Consumption

Without consumers, it would be impossible for retailing to exist. Here, the growth of the consumer-based culture within developed economies is examined. Therefore, the culture of consumption and its growth is also reviewed.

- The development of consumption as a productive and creative act is investigated; as is the rise of the symbolic.
- The question is asked: how do we find ourselves in societies where consumption has such a central role to play in our lives?
- Some of the events that have brought us to this position are examined, and suggestions made for the growth of consumption as a means of expressing who we are.

Chapter 4 – Consumption, Signs And Symbols

As the symbolic nature of some goods is one of the features of life today, then in such a situation, consideration of these symbols has a cultural dimension. Given this proposition, the following issues are examined:

- Expressiveness and its relationship to consumption;
- The development of this symbolic nature, as a result of the roles of producer, retailer and consumer;
- The interplay of relationships and the creation of new reality. Consideration of how retailers now have to manage this complex relationship to create a piece of theatre where consumption can take place to create self;
- The massification of theatricality in consumption, and the development by many consumers of the ability to create a persona; and the
- Creation of community and the feeling of the hyper-real through retail provision.

Part 2 – Management of the Arena of Retail Consumption

Chapter 5 – A Dramaturgical View – Elements of the Drama: a Question of Perspective

The 'creative' elements of retailing are further explored in this chapter, but using dramaturgy – the explicit and formalized study of plays, dramatic composition and the dramatic art. Here, dramaturgy is used as a theory that interprets individual behaviour as the dramatic projection of the chosen self.

The chapter begins to draw together some of the themes and topics introduced in the preceding chapters by applying this theory; it also facilitates an operational approach that starts to address and explore the processes of retail-based interaction and the management tasks concerned with that interaction.

This chapter focuses on issues including:

- The theatre metaphor;
- Text and discourse;
- Character and actor;
- Aesthetic questions; and
- Staging.

Chapter 6 – The Servuction Model and its Extensions

This chapter introduces the Servuction model and its extensions. This model provides a conceptualization of retail interaction that focuses structure and content by considering the service experience from the customer's viewpoint. By applying this perspective, the line of visibility – dividing the world of the retailer into backstage and front-of-house concerns – is created; as is the notion of a bundle of benefits being extracted by individual users as an outcome.

Here, the emphasis is placed on front-of-house as an arena for retail exchange and theatre; and the elements that constitute front-of-house are explored:

- The inanimate environment and the concept of 'servicescapes';
- The importance of both service personnel and other customers;
- The continuing impact of technology; and
- The potential for the customer's mood and time availability to influence their 'reading' of the retail experience is highlighted.

Chapter 7 – The Physical Environment

The physical environment for retailing is a multi-layered phenomenon. For the purposes of this book, we concentrate on two particular layers:

- The upper layer, concerned with the centre of shopping (the high street, precinct, mall, and other facilities).
- The lower level, concerned with the specifics of the retail unit itself.

At both levels, the same broad approach can be employed; although there may be holistic effects at the higher level, which exhibit systemic properties (i.e. the effects in relation to centres of shopping are not simply linear combinations of the effects of individual units). Both levels require managing, in order that an appropriate space for retail consumption is created. Such a managed space provides the stage on which retail performances can be enacted, leading this chapter to consider:

- The twin threads of mass consumption and the privatization of public space – the rise of ever larger private spaces dedicated to activities associated with consumption;
- Environmental cues;
- Sensory modalities;
- Orienting factors; and
- Environmental objects.

Chapter 8 – Merchandise

In a retail setting, merchandise obviously has a central place. Its role is essential in many retail exchanges, and as such, it has an importance greater than that which might be attached to the props in a stage play. However, there is a sense in which any type or item of merchandise may have a symbolic value or meaning attached to it by the purchaser. Thus, a major task in this area is for the retailer to ensure that the selection and display of merchandise reinforces the messages sent by the physical environment, in such a way as to ensure that the intended customers are able to easily read the script.

Given these concerns, and those that stem from the organization, such as the creation of profit, this chapter examines:

- Retail buying and merchandise selection;
- Merchandise management and display;
- Space-planning; and
- Locating merchandise within the benefit bundle.

Chapter 9 – Atmosphere and Image

Whilst the notion of retail image has had currency since the late 1950s, the image attributes that have been identified often relate to functional aspects of the store. The cognitive and affective ways in which a more generalized notion of retail image influences consumer actions is therefore presented.

The importance of store image may lie in the need to expand on merely economic or geographic predictors of store attractiveness; and image has been shown to be related to store loyalty and patronage. In such circumstances, the manipulation of controllable elements to create positive image, and thus 'liking', is a major component in a retailer's ability to differentiate its offer from that of its competitors. This leads to an examination of:

- Atmosphere and ambience;
- Branding and differentiation;
- Liking and image; and
- Patronage motives.

Chapter 10 – The Social Dimension

In the social context of the larger setting for retailing, e.g. the mall, there are two principal groups:

- People present for the same purpose – users; and

- Those visiting for other reasons – visitors.

Within this larger setting there are also two staff groups:

- Those who are attached to the general venue; and
- Those associated with a particular retailer.

In a particular retail setting, there are users and service personnel who may be involved in a directing or facilitating role. As these actors are placed within a setting that has a particular socio–cultural character, this must also be considered in any detailed analysis of the overall social *milieu* – aspects of which give rise to feelings of liking, belonging, understanding and safety. These feelings may be strengthened through the particular content of any interaction that the individuals may have, as well as the extent to which they perceive themselves as having behavioural control. The elements of the social nature of retailing must be understood and explored:

- Other users;
- Visitors; and
- Venue staff; and
- Directing and facilitating retail staff.

Chapter 11 – The Temporal Dimension

There are a number of aspects related to time, within the context of retail interactions, that can have a particular impact on the way in which an individual engages with a retailer. The pattern of engagement may itself vary over time.

It is within this complex web of time-based factors that relationships may develop; that usage may produce liking; that demands made by a given user may vary over time and from occasion to occasion. This issue of time is one that retailers have increasingly considered as an element of the retail management task and can be explored in relation to a number of factors:

- Extended interchanges versus brief exchanges;
- The temporal dimension and the development of relationships;
- Time-rich versus time-poor;
- Time availability; and
- Orientation – past or future.

Chapter 12 – Customers' Psychological State

Each of the various factors introduced in the arena for retail drama can be seen as having an impact on consumer's psychological state. Each consumer, of course, enters the retail drama in a particular psychological situation, or antecedent mood state, that can impinge on his or her reaction to any interaction. Understanding the importance of the following can provide the retailer with rich insights for the creation of an 'appropriate' retail drama:

- Pleasure, arousal and dominance;
- Planned intention;
- Previous experience;
- Risk; and
- Decision-making.

Part 3 – The Retail Enterprise in Context

Chapter 13 – The Strategic Context

Retail strategy is the process of creating the desired broad retail climate and appropriate consumer expectations. The retail strategy process is therefore a balancing and blending of running stores for efficiency and effectiveness.

As the book focuses on consumer-related aspects of retailing, there is less attention paid to those aspects that occur behind the line of visibility. However, this chapter emphasizes the retailer's opportunity to manage for efficiency in these areas.

This chapter therefore considers a mix of the relevant 'customer-visible' and 'customer-invisible' areas:

- Logistics;
- Sites and location;
- Design and merchandising;
- Personnel;
- Organization; and
- Image.

Chapter 14 – Service Characteristics and Context

This chapter introduces the role and extent of services in the developed economy; and the four characteristics of services:

- Intangibility;
- Inseparability;
- Heterogeneity; and
- Perishability.

The operational and marketing consequences of these characteristics for service firms are briefly considered. The consequences of intangibility are explored in some detail, as they are held to be the core distinguishing feature of services as products. The evidence shows merchandise retailers to be within the definition of services, but not to have featured strongly in the analyses provided by some key authors. The intangible nature of the total retail service highlights the need for careful consideration of customer requirement and service delivery management.

The use of typologies and classification systems as aids to management are discussed. Quality measurement and management propositions from a range of sources are compared and contrasted. These propositions form the basis for the use of particular techniques designed to measure quality. The approach to measurement of quality in a retail setting is shown to be contingent on a number of factors. In particular there are component effects due to factors arising from the:

- Phases in purchase;
- Merchandise type;
- Market position; and
- Other factors.

Chapter 15 – The Locational Context

In a treatment consistent with the other areas of the book, concern here is with the two selected levels of locational context:

- The store itself (pico-level); and
- The upper layer, concerned with shopping (micro-level).

Brief consideration is given to two further aspects:

- The network and area questions (meso-level); and
- The region and the particular development of international retailing (macro-level).

Based on this selected approach, the following elements of the locational context are touched upon:

- Managing the urban retail drama:
  - Retailers;
  - Developers;
  - The audience;
  - Planning authorities;
  - Ancillary service providers; and
  - Other provision.

- Research strands from geography, marketing and consumption studies
- Shopping malls and town centre management.
- Location studies and trade area assessment.
- Retail internationalization.

Chapter 16 – The Social and Ecological Context

The focus of concern here is on those broader aspects of retail policy – effectively beyond management's control (albeit subject to some influence) – which embed the firm in its environment:

- Political;
- Economic;
- Social;
- Technical; and
- Legal.

However, these are used only to place the following issues in context:

- Retailer responsibility, and the consideration of the social consequences of firm-level activity – the politics of choice;
- Ethical retailing and fair trade;
- The ecological impact of retail decisions; and
- Considerations of corporate ethics.

Part 4 – The Retail Future

Chapter 17 – Conclusions and Prognosis

This chapter provides specific consideration of a number of emerging themes identified throughout the book, and that can be discerned as operating in much of retailing. The merchandise and services that western consumers need, want and desire, are placed in the context of both developments in retailing, and in consumption. The following, sometimes competing, themes are highlighted:

- The diverging of retail into pleasure-oriented centres of consumption and utilitarian loci of supply – a division, however, not solely based on the ability to pay, as it was historically.
- The prospect of the return of manufacturing to the site of retail – against the clear trend of retailing attached to manufacturing (such as factory outlets).
- Retail internationalization and consumption convergence.
- Identification through material wealth – the limits of sustainability, and the rise of the spiritual (post-materialist?) consumer.

Central Theme

Before beginning this journey through retail consumption, it is necessary to clearly state that in writing this book a particular view is taken towards consumption itself. It has been suggested that cultural consumption is at best a form of manipulation of the masses (see Storey, 1999, for a fuller discussion) – a creation of 'false wants' – with an implicit view that industry in general, and large corporations, in particular, are 'bad'. This is *not* the perspective taken in this book.

As Storey's (1999) work contends, there are both implicit and explicit problems with the consumption-as-manipulation model. In support, he cites cultural critic John Docker's response to the suggestion that mass culture is a disabling influence, as being "preposterous, ludicrous" (1994, p. 41).

Storey concludes in the final pages of his book that…

> …people *make* culture from the repertoire of commodities supplied by the cultural industries. Making culture – 'production in use' – can be empowering to subordinate and resistant to dominant understandings of the world. But this is not to say that cultural consumption is always empowering and resistant. To deny the passivity of cultural consumption is not to deny that sometimes cultural consumption is passive; to deny that the consumers of the commodities produced by the culture industries are not cultural dupes is not to deny that the culture industries seek to manipulate. But it is to deny that the culture of everyday life is little more than a degraded landscape of commercial and ideological manipulation, imposed from above in order to make a profit and secure social control (pp. 168–169).

His conclusion is our beginning, providing the underlying assumptions that influence all that follows:

- That consumption rests on the *interplay* of manufacturer, retailer and consumer;
- That these relationships – in parallel with the spheres of production, circulation and consumption – are *interlocking* and *not linear*; and
- That consumption is a creative and expressive act (for all concerned), which, rather than being *imposed* on consumers by manufacturers and retailers, *strengthens* the relationships involved.

References

Baron, J.S., Davies, B.J. and Swindley, D.G. 1991. *Macmillan Dictionary of Retailing*. London: Macmillan Press Ltd.

Brown, S. 1995. Postmodernism, the wheel of retailing and will to power. *The International Review of Retail Distribution and Consumer Research*, 5(3), 387–414.

Brown, S. 1988. The wheel of the wheel of retailing. *The International Journal of Retailing*, 3(1), 16–31.

Campbell, C. 1995. The Sociology of Consumption. In Miller, D. (Ed.). *Acknowledging Consumption. A Review of New Studies*. London: Routledge, pp. 96–126.

Docker, J. 1994. *Postmodernism and Popular Culture*. Cambridge: Cambridge University Press.

Marx, K. 1904. *Critique of the Political Economy*.

Storey, J. 1999. *Cultural Consumption and Everyday Life*. London: Arnold.

The New Shorter Oxford English Dictionary (4th Ed.). 1993. Oxford: Oxford University Press.

Part 1

Introduction and Context: the Role and History of Retail Consumption

RETAILING HISTORY

The concept of retailing is introduced as one of the defining character-istics of our type of society. The development of retail formats and offers is also discussed. A number of key points are raised in this chapter:
- As economies develop:
  - The individual produces less and purchases more;
  - Therefore an increasing percentage of consumers' requirements are met through retailing; and
  - The arena for exchange becomes increasingly formalized and elaborate and is subject to more regulations and increased manage-rial control.
- This 'progress' is illustrated through the provision of a diverse range of examples both historical and geographical, including:
  - Markets and fairs, the classical world, and souks;
  - The birth of modern retailing in the eighteenth century;
  - Its apogee in the nineteenth century; and then
  - A more detailed discussion of the trends evident in the twentieth century: the rise of multiples, the growth of non-store retailing (including the Internet), internationalization, shopping centres and malls.

The chapter stresses the importance of the non-merchandise dimen-sions of fairs, markets and other 'public' retail offers. It also emphasizes the increasingly 'leisured' orientation of retail provision based on that tradition.

Introduction

This history is partial, selective and brief. There is too much to encompass in a single chapter on the history of so widespread a phenomenon as retailing. This chapter therefore takes a broad perspective, aiming to highlight important issues and trends. The aim is to demonstrate that retailing – and, in particular, the fixed, managed retail space – is not a modern phenomenon. It is also important to establish that other forms of retailing are still with us, e.g. the 'hawker', but what has altered is the relative balance between the forms of retail enterprise.

Retailing has evolved in terms of both the balance between formal and informal provision, and in the increasing sophistication of what retailers aim to provide. This rise – e.g. the increased attention on aesthetic issues – is not simply focused on the late twentieth century, but has roots that extend much earlier; this begins to demonstrate that there is no simple and straightforward pattern of development, with clear-cut periods that focus on one specific issue. It also means that providing a chronology of retail development is not a simple matter. So, rather than develop a strict chronology, retail development is considered on a more thematic basis.

Given the complexity of retail development, the chapter also cannot hope to provide a detailed discussion of retail history and the associated theory. However, it is important to identify the chief forms of formal retailing systems and structures. This helps to ground the discussion and examination of retailing provided in the rest of the book. This is also supported by considering – in this chapter, within the modern era – the mechanisms through which the activities of retailers are seen to have had an impact on individual consumers, and, more generally, on society.

The Rise of Formal Retailing

Retailing arises in two chief ways. The first is through the growth in the trade of goods over considerable distances. The transportation of merchandise requires the development of an infrastructure to support merchants – an infrastructure containing:

- Designated routes (e.g., roads and sea-lanes);
- Hotels and livery stabling;
- A ready means of exchange; and
- Storage, wholesaling and retailing facilities.

Within this situation, there are two types of merchandise groups:

- Those which were being transported, which were often 'luxury' items; and
- The 'everyday necessities', often sold along the route to support transportation, e.g. food, equipment and clothing.

Examples of this pattern of trading can be found in the ancient societies of the Middle East and Asia, where camel trains and sea routes grew, as did trading 'hubs' along these channels. Here, the trader or the sailor could not only enter into the sale or exchange of their 'cargo', but also engage in the purchase of items for their own consumption or to assist in their journey.

The second manner in which retailing growth was stimulated is through the increasing size of human settlements. In societies where settlements occur, and there is a move to urbanization, space dedicated to retailing always seems to be found. Here, growth is again associated with a ready means of exchange, but it is also contingent upon the attainment of economic surplus and post-subsistence living.

When these conditions are met at the lowest level, barter was often seen as an informal system of retailing. With increasing sophistication and urbanization, and the advent of money (or another easy form of exchange), the formalization of retailing moves ahead. Those spaces dedicated to retailing – which we would recognize as shops or market places – become established; as perhaps did the role of the 'shop-keeper'.

Such conditions can be seen in Mesopotamia as early as 3500 BC, where archaeologists have found clay shapes depicting a wide range of material objects from animals to cloth. It has been suggested that these items provided an early form of 'bookkeeping', that facilitated trade and coincided with the rise of urbanization in the area. Pierre Amiet even hypothesized that trade and retailing provided the impetus for the development of a formal written language, which was then later used to record a great deal more than just simple 'account' information.

Conditions for Retail Development

Given the two ways in which retailing's development has been stimulated, it would seem that there are a number of conditions that need to be met to provide an appropriate environment for the growth of formal retailing:

- Economic surplus;
- Settlement (and ultimately urbanization); and
- Money (a ready means of exchange).

The issue of settlement is, perhaps, for many, the most surprising characteristic necessary for the development of formal retailing. There are, of course, nomadic societies where fixed location is not a central element of the lifestyle adopted. However, the development of formal retailing within such societies is somewhat different. Nomads that are involved in a subsistence economy do not themselves seem to develop a retail sector. Such societies, depending on their particular circumstances, may well engage in trade with outsiders. However, the impetus for such trade may well come from those external societies. In the case of nomadic peoples who move to provide subsistence for their flocks, there is greater evidence for an engagement in trade. In this case, there may be economic surplus produced (e.g. more wool than is needed by the 'tribe' itself), and this may be actively traded with outsiders. Such trade may well take place at specific locations, and these may be either permanent settlements, or established points of trade at identifiable locations. For such groups, although they themselves do not have a fixed settlement, there is still often a link between trade and retailing and the concept of a 'fixed' geographic point.

The other 'nomad' in the world of retailing is the pedlar. Ubiquitous and ever-present…

> …they filled in the gaps in the regular channels of distribution, though mostly in villages and hamlets. Since the gaps were plentiful so were the pedlars and this too was a sign of the times.
>
> Braudel, 1983, p. 71

Given the complexities of their distribution networks, pedlars still needed a fixed point of wholesale and supply. So, even in this context, there is an element of settlement. The pedlar's role is sometimes seen as being synonymous with lower levels of economic development, but they are still present in developed economies today, where they often form part of the informal retail structure.

A distinction can therefore be made between formal and informal types of retailing. Informal retailing occurs when the activity is an adjunct of an individual's (or economic unit's) usual range of activities. For example, car-boot or yard sales; sporadic retail sales by a wholesaler or manufacturer; or by a merchant on route whilst transporting wholesale quantities (off-the-back-of-a-lorry). Formal retailing however occurs where the primary economic purpose of the individual or organization is to sell to the ultimate consumers, or where continuing spatial or temporal provision is made for retail sales. The thrust of this chapter is to examine formal retailing, with a particular emphasis on shop-based forms. But we begin with an ancestral form, the market.

The Market

If this elementary market… (of trestles, a canopy to keep off the rain, stall-holders, each with a numbered place, duly allotted in advance, and to be paid for as authorities or landlords decreed; a crowd of buyers and a multitude of petty traders – a varied and active proletariat) …has survived unchanged down the ages, it is surely because in its robust simplicity it is unbeatable – because of the freshness of the perishable goods it brings straight from local gardens and fields. Because of its low prices too, since the primitive market, where food is sold 'at first hand' is the most direct and transparent form of exchange, the most closely supervised and the least open to deception.

Braudel, 1983, pp. 28–29

Braudel goes on to argue that this very ancient form of exchange had existed for centuries or millennia – it was practised in classical Rome, in ancient Greece, in classical China – and that "The origins of the markets of Ethiopia go back into the mists of time" (p. 29). The organized markets of the classical world, of Africa and the Middle East stand, in their antiquity, between the formal and informal sectors of the economy. Such markets are formal, in that they are organized, controlled and regulated; but they have characteristics that are often found in the informal sector of the economy – "less stable, more oppressed and fragile, and sometimes impermanent" (Dewar and Watson, 1990). This impermanence was often a feature, with designated days being 'market days', rather than trading taking place on a continuous basis.

Markets also often serve in particular the poorer members of a community. In consequence, the economic stability of traders supplying these poorer sections of a community is itself compromised. Poorer members of the community have often tended to develop unregulated (often roadside) markets themselves. These unregulated markets serve to provide a medium for the sale of home-produced goods or the sale of articles surplus to household requirements. These 'unofficial' markets may exhibit some of the characteristics of more formal markets: particularly when larger numbers of unofficial traders site themselves together. When larger numbers congregate, aspects of permanency may develop.

A wide range of options exists about the degree to which externally provided shelter, infrastructure and services are provided in markets. At one end of the continuum, nothing is externally provided; at the other, almost everything is externally provided (this may take the form of a market building with a full range of infrastructure).

Dewar and Watson, 1990, pp. 12–13

It is within this general panoply that the term 'market' is to be understood. The issue of permanency is what begins to distinguish markets from the more transitory 'fairs'.

Fairs

Fairs, however, had their own 'rhythm', were impermanent, and were distinguished by being rich, large and gaudy. They had a festival or carnival aspect that made them 'more than a market' in their feel and importance. In much of Europe, fairs are associated with religious festivals in their origins, and were frequently held in the grounds of churches. For many fairs, this provided a scheme of regulation, which gave rise to the 'peace of the church'; and where disturbing that peace was seen as an offence that was seriously dealt with. The existence of that peace made fairs an attractive place to trade, and, partly as a consequence, assumed national or international significance, even as early as the thirteenth century. By 1450, St. Bartholomew's fair in London was 'policed' by three hundred men, and was a well-established international event – as were many other such fairs – as illustrated by this extract from Piers Plowman:

> Barons and burgesses and bondsmen too
> I saw in this assembly as you shall see later
> Bakers and butchers and brewers galore,
> Weavers of wool and weavers of linen
> Tailors and tinkers and tax-collectors,
> Masons and miners and many other craftsmen,
> Cooks and their kitchen-boys calling 'Hot Pies!'
> Geese and good gammon! Get a good dinner!
> Advertising taverners told the same tale
> With a white Alsatian wine! Red wine of Gascony!
> Rhenish and claret give relish to a roast!
> All this I saw sleeping and seven times more!
>
> Coghill, 1949, p. 40

This popular participation benefited from the huge range of activities – parades, musical interludes, gambling, tumblers, juggling – which were evident at many fairs. The core business of the fair was, however, wholesale trade. As fairs concerned the trade between dealers, their other principle function was to provide a mechanism for the settlement of debt owed between dealers, and the creation of new credit.

The Decline of the Fair

By the seventeenth century, the position of the fair in the commercial life of nations – at least in Europe – was decreasing. This occurred as a result of sellers increasingly choosing to sell by sample, rather than at fairs; the rise of the 'bourse', where bills of exchange could be circulated, and the increase in urbanization and the concomitant growth of *fixed* retail provision. These changes meant that the traditional roles of the fair were superseded, and fairs either began to die out or changed in their nature.

Hodson (1999) points out that "the preoccupation of business historians and economists with innovation, growth and scale has focused work on the more obviously dynamic aspects of the retail sector: the multiplication of fixed shops and the rise of the department store" (p. 94). This admonition serves to remind us that markets and fairs are always with us – they cannot be considered an historical remnant, or merely a precursor to more 'modern' forms of retailing. As her work shows, there is the possibility (also high-lighted by Dewar and Watson) for the market form to have a high degree of structure and substance. This, in itself, is not new.

Examples of the building, the regulation, the granting of specific privi-leges in relation to trade to designated markets (or bodies deemed entitled to hold them) are to be found in many societies throughout history. This is as true of the souks of the Mahgreb and the Middle East, as it is of European nations. Those very advantages described by Braudel, however, led to law and regulation at an early stage.

The Rise of the Guild

The move away from feudalism in many European societies had, as an impor-tant component, the rise of the town. In England this was the renaissance of the town. In Roman Britain the town had performed a major role. They were developed as centres for defence and for administration, but subsequently became a focus for trading activity. Under the feudal and manorial systems, towns were often bound by obligations to their overlord. Chief among these was the requirement that grain was milled at the lord's mill and bread baked in the lord's oven. "In addition to manorial obligations, all trade conducted in the mediæval towns was subject to tolls and customs, payable in part the lord and in part to the crown" (Roberts, 1948, p. 21). The towns sought charters of the crown to release them from these taxes and to enable them to manage their own affairs, which was obtained through the payment of an annual fee. Once 'free,' the towns could regulate trade within their 'borough'. This led to the development of 'guilds' that provided a system for the organization of craft activity and the sale of goods.

Each craft activity became the subject of a separate guild, e.g. the shoemaker's guild and the mercer's guild, and as crafts proliferated through the increasing specialization in production, so did the number of guilds. The guild played an important role in regulating the retail activity of its members and any visitors that they permitted to trade. This can be seen in the following instructions taken from the shoemaker's guild of Beverly (cited in Davis, 1966):

> They shall have and keep their tables for selling shoes in a lane called Shoemaker lane, standing in order on the south side of the said lane on market days and other markets and fairs... and every shoemaker shall stand in his priority as he entered the craft, beginning at John Danby's shop...
>
> Davis, 1966, p. 40

The craft guilds were also often involved in determining the price at which goods could be sold: this prevented individuals being under-cut by fellow guild members. This created a strong sense of fixed prices for both the seller and the buyer in relation to the products of many trades.

However, it was not just the market that enjoyed this degree of official sanction and regulation in early times. The creation of specific shopping spaces also has an extended history – reaching back, at least, to classical Greece.

Shops and Shopping Spaces

The 'agora' of ancient Greece served as a public meeting place, and was surrounded by public buildings. Where they were surrounded by colonnades, these spaces are likely to have included shops. Thus, the agora could be seen as the shopping mall, as well as marketplace of an ancient Greek city. For example, in Hellenistic Athens, what today might be described as shopping malls, were a feature of city planning. Here, a row of permanent retail units contained with the Stoa of Attalus, which was an elaborate two-storey colonnade that was more than a hundred metres long, was a feature of city life.

As the Roman Empire developed, the agora was adopted and regularized to create the forum. These urban spaces also came to provide a concentration of shops that were under some form of public management. In both the agora and the forum, not only shops were present: it may have been that permanent booths for merchants, as well as more temporary structures used for periodic markets, were a familiar element in the townscape. From Athens to Corinth, from Rome to Pompeii, the place of shops in the townscape is clear. The shop therefore cannot be seen as a simple evolution of the market. These forms of retailing have long and established histories, which for many societies run in parallel. However for some the shop, and not the market, provides the mainstay of early retail provision.

> According to travelers, Szechwan, that is the upper basin of the Yangtse–Kiang, which had been reoccupied in force by Chinese colonization in the seventeenth century, was a zone of scattered settlements isolated from each other, whereas in China proper, the population was concentrated in centres. Yet in this area of low population density, groups of small shops, yao-tien, were set up in the middle of nowhere, and played the role of a permanent market. Again according to travelers, the same was true of Ceylon in the seventeenth century: there were no markets, but there were shops.
>
> Braudel, 1983, p. 60

The Speciality Retailer

In the main, early forms of retailing seem to have specialized in one line of trade. As towns and cities grew in size, trades were often concentrated in particular streets and districts. In Venice in the mid-fifteenth century, for example around the Rialto, each street contained shops of a particular speciality – one street for spice and another for precious fabrics and silks. Early shops may well have sold a variety of goods, but followed one of two patterns of early store-keeping:

- That of the artisan producer/retailer – who *manufactured and sold* goods on the same site: e.g. tinsmiths and shoemakers; or
- That of the merchant – who only *sold* goods, which were often 'luxury' or imported products: e.g. perfume.

This pattern of store-keeping types is one that persisted (and still does to some extent to this day). However, the proportion of each type has undergone considerable change – with the merchant becoming the principal form.

The rise of the merchant can, in part, be connected to the guild system. Over time, the guilds led to the emergence of 'masters of their craft' who amassed considerable wealth, and who were well-placed to become merchants in the modern sense – manufacturing could be undertaken by others. This, in turn, meant that the guilds themselves were undermined, and eventually died out. The guilds, therefore, played an important role in retail history: particularly in terms of the establishment of a *merchant class* involved principally in retailing and wholesaling.

Increasing levels of demand and supply were also an important factor in the rise of the merchant as the predominant type of shopkeeper. It was the re-growth of the town in Europe that led to increasing concentrations of population, and thus demand. Such concentrated populations detached from the agricultural basis of economic life, provided a pool of demand that stimulated the growth of differentiated retail supply. Within an environment that stimulated retail trade, guild members were provided with increased opportunities to prosper. Some, who became the merchants, accumulated wealth and became capitalists.

> As a rule, everywhere one group of merchants sought to set itself above the rest…. In Italy, and in the free cities of Germany, the distinction (between merchants and small traders) was even more clear: the wealthy merchants in fact became an aristocracy, a patriciate: they formed the government of the great trading cities.
>
> Braudel, 1983, p. 68

The inability of the artisan trader to continue to meet increasing demand; the widening range of merchandise carried in a single shop, and the emergence of credit and the function of the retail store as a meeting place, requiring greater space, further meant that it was the merchant that began to predominate. These reasons also helped the fixed shop begin to gain supremacy over the market in terms of its ability to meet the continuing requirements of households.

(It is worth noting that the periodization of retail history is certainly not 'smooth' or continuous in terms of format and size of operation; nor is it contiguous in terms of geographic areas. For example, take the notion of fixed prices as a practice seen in only modern retailing. It can in fact, be witnessed as prevalent in London in the eighteenth century, or even in some trades under the control of medieval guilds).

The Emergence of Modern Retailing

The Initial Phase: Urbanization and Specialization

The 'birth' of modern retailing coincides with the slow growth of urban centres in Europe in the sixteenth and seventeenth centuries. Of more significance in this period is the coalescing of major centres of population in the capitals and major ports of Europe. This led to what seemed to be an explosion in the number of shops – as Lope de Vega said of Madrid in 1606, "all has turned into shops" (cited in Braudel, 1983, p. 68). The rise in population and its concentration were compounded by the growth of new trades such as tobacco, tea and clocks, which saw further development of new kinds of retail provision.

It is impossible that Tea, Coffee and Chocolate can be so enhanced in their consumption without an eminent increase in those trades that attend them, whence we see the most noble shops in the City taken up with the valuable Utensils of the Tea-table.

Defoe, 1713 (cited in Davis, 1966)

Two contrasting tendencies may be noted from the commentators of the time. Firstly, the rise of the luxury establishment – glazed and gilded at great expense. Secondly, in contrast, is the financially precarious nature of much shop-keeping business. The period shows interplay between these tendencies, with the former very clear in the large cities and the second predominant in smaller, secondary centres. There was some commonality, irrespective of the nature of the business, in particular the scope of goods sold. These tended to be restricted, and could be expressed by a descriptive single name. For example: a milliner, a glover, a hatter, a silversmith, a cobbler, or a tailor.

Shops in city centres up until the 1830s tended to be highly specialised. Their turnover was relatively slow; margins were high and overheads heavy. Not surprisingly prices were high in such establishments, with a clientele to match.

Lancaster, 1995, p. 8

These specialized shops also had another common feature. They were typically owned by a single proprietor, and the store traded under the owner's name. The branding of the store was therefore personalized; so the corporate fascia that is prominent on the contemporary high street was not particularly evident.

One facet that needs to be emphasized is that retailing developments form a 'mosaic'; local, regional and national factors interplay. Retailing is essentially a localized phenomenon and local factors can therefore predominate. However, an important feature of modern retailing is the presence of large numbers of retail chains. It is not clear when such enterprises originally appeared (they may have been present in the pre-classical world).

In this early phase of modern retailing, retail chains are not prominent. What does come into prominence is the growing sophistication of individual outlets, especially in major urban centres, e.g. in terms of display, stock and merchandise range, pricing approaches and customer service, as witnessed in Defoe's comments on London and its retail trade. Additionally, there was the use of advertising and sales promotion within retailing in this period (Fowler, 1999). What was also distinctive was the offering of personal, store-based credit – this has almost disappeared in much of modern retailing.

The period also saw a rise in the opulence of retailing to such an extent that it received attention and comment from writers of the time, whose work is still readily available to us today. These records provide a strong sense of practice still found in 'modern' retailing. But to assume that this period saw the rise of what would be considered modern is perhaps an oversimplification. We do not have the number or depth of records to assess the prevalence of modern retail practices before this time, but we cannot dismiss out-of-hand the notion that they would not have been present. However, as Alexander and Akehurst (1999) note: "...modern retail systems may be seen to have their origins in the late eighteenth century and early nineteenth century" (p. 5).

The Second Phase: Massification and the Reduction of Risk

This period saw further movement towards what might be considered modern retail practice. The first notable shift is the growth and success of the proto-department store.

> The key to this success was that such stores took the fear out of shopping for the new lower middle class and the better-off working-class housewife. Clearly-marked prices, that were never present in the specialist shop, facilitated budgeting and also took away the dread of showing your moderate circumstances and unrefined taste. Yet, these new stores were neither palaces of temptation nor arbiters of taste. Many of the items on offer still required the labour of the housewife or a seamstress for conversion into finished products; the furniture and household goods on offer were sturdy but plain. Similarly, display methods were primitive, and selling techniques unsophisticated. The truth of the matter was that up until the mid-nineteenth century – and indeed for some years later – demand reflected the plain and simple needs of the lower middle class (Lancaster, 1995, pp. 13–14).

It is worth bearing in mind that, in terms of this emerging mass market, a distinction between food and non-perishable goods must be made. Food still tended to be purchased from markets (Davis, 1966). This means that consumers experienced two very different environments – that of the 'unstructured' street market, and that of the 'ordered' store. This is well-illustrated by Davis' (1966) comment that markets "were in every way more important in the scheme of things, as well as more tumultuous, more urgent, more disorderly, more often a battle of elbows as well as a battle of wits" (p. 255). The market may therefore be seen to represent a riskier arena for purchase than the shop.

In common with the developments elsewhere in retailing – such as the introduction of fixed pricing – the risk of market shopping was reduced with the introduction of the municipal market hall. These large structures that began to appear in the first quarter of the nineteenth century, particularly in the growing industrial towns of the north of England, were an attempt to contain the unruly mass of the market. They were often a response to the problems generated by the collision between market traders and their customers and the increasing populations seeking to throng the thoroughfare. (It is worth noting that the concerns of the Victorian city fathers may have been little different from those of their predecessors in Hellenistic Greece). These halls also became important symbols of civic pride and rivalry (Hodson, 1999).

The municipal market hall of England, the galleria of Italy and the mercardo of Spain, typified Victorian confidence in the future and a desire for display through the concrete and tangible. These new buildings echoed the general striving for efficiency and progress that characterized many developed societies in this period. Progress in gas lighting and plate glass availability, for example, contributed directly to the further development of the form of the fixed shop. As the century progressed, the development of railways, of canning technology and of refrigeration, all began to impact the availability of perishable food stuffs. These technical developments in the supply chain permitted food retailing to enter the path that durable goods retailing was already following.

Limited Liability

The principle of limited liability and its availability to entrepreneurs and retailers was probably another important factor in facilitating size of individual stores and the growth of retail chains. Limited liability had been a doctrine in English law since the fifteenth century, but it was originally applied to guilds, universities and boroughs. Later in England (and elsewhere), the 'chartered company' was often a licensed state monopoly, mixing the functions of business and the state. The Dutch East India Company, founded in 1602, was granted a trade monopoly between Africa and the Straits of Magellan. The company was also given the right to maintain armed forces, conclude treaties and administer territories. Such powers are typical of those granted to various chartered companies from this time onwards by a number of governments. Such companies were formed increasingly in the seventeenth and eighteenth centuries.

Over time, the function of these companies came to focus more on the commercial than the political. The bridge to the fully commercial corporation of today was in the form of increasing numbers of the companies chartered to run infrastructure projects: such as building ports, harbours, turnpikes and waterworks. New York was one of the first states to allow for modern incorporation methods, when in 1811, a State act provided that businesses could be incorporated with the provision of articles and memorandum of incorporation. Similar developments spread across the rest of the United States and Europe – albeit a little later. Commercial trading risk could be moved away from the individual, and capital raised, making both start-up and growth easier. This can be seen in retail operators in the nineteenth century, for example both Heal's and Harrods became limited liability companies during this period, and both realized extensive growth; but this was yet not the norm for the retailer.

The latter half of the nineteenth century saw the development of the first full department store in a modern sense – originally in France with the opening of the Bon Marché in Paris, but then later in London and Chicago. These stores drew on the expanding range of building technologies to provide increasingly elaborate and exotic shopping environments. These department stores also spilled over the boundaries of merchandise assortment that had restricted the individual shopkeeper. They provided a catalogue of taste for the new middle classes, and built on the practice of fixed pricing by introducing clear price marking. This was possible partly because such stores displayed stock openly for inspection, and made use of new types of fixtures and lighting. This also meant that customers had to neither haggle nor ask the price: thus providing a mechanism by which clients could assess both the goods and their own ability to afford the merchandise, without potential embarrassment. Additionally, the department stores began to introduce innovative promotional techniques that also often had a core element of entertainment and spectacle. Roberts of London had a Christmas grotto in 1888, replete with live Santa Claus and Cinderella (Lancaster, 1995). Such techniques also sought to tempt the passer-by into the store, as well as making the store a destination for leisure activity.

Smaller retailers also sought to attract passers-by by using window displays and the distribution of advertising in the form of handbills. This signalled a move away from their reliance on loyal customers (Davis, 1966) and further underlines a shift in the nature of the customers served towards an urbanized waged population. Fawcett (1992, cited in Fowler, 1999) claims that the introduction of retail warehouses at the end of the eighteenth century further indicated the beginning of mass-marketing techniques. This rise of the mass market provided retailers with additional opportunities to extend successful trading formats by opening further branches – beginning the rise of the retail multiple.

Retail Networks

The establishment of a branch network was the next great innovation in the development of retailing: occurring at a similar time on both sides of the Atlantic. In America, the Great American Tea Company, later to become the A&P Grocery Company "is often considered to be the prototype of the chain store.... Starting in New York City in 1859 it spread... reaching a total of some 100 units in 1881" (Walsh, 1994, p. 13). In England, in 1856, the Rochdale Pioneers (established as a consumer co-operative society in 1844) opened their first branch store. They rapidly developed their network, alongside a wholesale department. "These two innovations, both the work of the Pioneers, were nothing less than the keys to large-scale trading" (Davis, 1966, p. 280).

These early developments in the food trades were paralleled in other sectors. Vertical integration was an essential factor in food, as well as in other areas. The Singer Sewing Machine Company developed vertical integration, as did other manufacturers; but in other areas it was advances in production and distribution technology that sustained these developments. In much of Continental Europe, the development of the chain store was inhibited by the actions of small shopkeepers, who were successful in having such operations outlawed.

These branch networks, established by what were, in the main packaged goods and grocery retailers, began to increasingly sell fresh produce, such as bread and morning goods, dairy and fresh fruit and vegetables. This diversification of range brought the early grocers a little closer to the modern supermarket; but the stores were yet neither large enough to be considered comparable, nor were they self-service. One notable exception to this pattern was Sainsbury's, which began as a dairy, selling butter, milk and eggs; but, after opening its first branch in 1873, expanded its range to include meat and cheeses and other 'counter' goods. However, it was not until later that groceries were added to the range of goods sold. What is illustrated is the merging of fresh food and grocery retailing – a trend that eventually would have a profound effect on the structure and format of food retailing.

This development was also paralleled somewhat in the household goods market. Here, a new type of store began to appear that catered for the growing affluence of the working classes – the variety store. It utilized two techniques to promote its success. Variety stores often applied low fixed price-points across the merchandise they sold and they employed an early form of self-service selection. Such stores were exemplified in the late nineteenth century by Woolworth in the US and Marks & Spencer in the UK. Both retailers were highly successful, but Woolworth attained higher branch numbers in the latter half of the century. By 1895, it had 25 stores, and in the five-year period to 1900 this had increased to 57, with a sales turnover of $5 million (Walsh, 1994). The trading practices of the variety stores led to a pre-occupation with "achieving an ever-increasing high volume of turnover at relatively low margins on the one hand, and sourcing and creating products of high quality to be sold at relatively low prices on the other" (Tse, 1985, p. 16).

These concerns further highlight a move towards what might be considered modern retailing. These retailers not only sourced products for sale, but also increasingly sold such goods under their own brand. The quality of merchandise and relationship to price was keenly considered, as was the relationship between market, margin, turnover and profit. Entering the twentieth century, such retailers had built on earlier foundations to create operations that were well-placed to grow. Many of these stores can still be seen on the modern high street.

The Rise of the Multiple and the Public Limited Company

The early twentieth century saw an increase in the number of retailers that were developing branch networks. Davis (1966) notes that this was accompanied by two inter-related trends. The first she cites as being the growth of the 'shopkeeping organization' that turned retailing into big business. For example, by 1926, the New York department store Macy's employed approximately 12,000 people; which swelled to 20,000 during the Christmas season (Graham, 2000). Macy's also began to pay increasing attention to both 'scientific management' and industrial psychology, using Lillian Gilbreth (wife of Frank Gilbreth) as a consultant to aid the development of 'more efficient work systems' (Graham, 2000). Retailers were not only increasingly using modern management techniques, they were also becoming public limited companies, enabling further access to capital and "whose names are household words from one end of the country to the other" (Davis, 1966, p. 277). Here, it is clear that such retailers had developed wide geographic coverage, and this necessitated that they pay even closer attention to the issues of warehousing and distribution on a much larger scale.

In the UK, the Co-operative Societies would eventually come to have over 4,500 stores; and Woolworth would have over 1,000 within the limited area of the UK's shores (Baren, 1996). Such numbers needed a vast support system to ensure that individual outlets could trade. The growing retail organizations began to command considerable power; and began to set the pace, style and standards of retail practice. This enabled them to occupy prime locations at the expense of other shops; and, in so doing, there began a concentration of the retail sector. In the UK grocery market, this was to reach tremendous proportions with four companies – Tesco, Sainsbury's, Asda (Wal-Mart) and Safeway – controlling over 70% of the total market (Mintel, 2000). It was not only the UK grocery sector where such companies would predominate; the growth of the large multiple retailer has led to the 'homogenized high street', with each town and city featuring many of the same stores.

The development of these retail giants was also aided by the second trend that Davis (1966) highlights – that of increasing 'simplicity' of the retail trade. Here, she focuses on the further rise of the manufacturer and their associated brands. This became possible through mass-production, the growth in the range of manufactured goods, and the increasing use of advertising as a means of stimulating consumer awareness and demand. This Davis saw as leading to the retailer only having a passing familiarity with the products that they sold. (This is an oversimplification in many retail contexts, especially where goods are produced specifically by or for the retailer. Even where this is not the case, it overlooks the importance and potential difficulties of assortment selection and management.) The fast-moving consumer goods manufacturers were set to become powerful forces in the retail sector. The power struggles that occurred between them and the large multiple retailers had a profound impact on retailing in the latter half of the twentieth century.

Retailers have become, in many instances, corporate giants in their own right, and the numbers of independent retail operators have decreased. In the grocery sector, these giants took on the role of the specialized food seller: providing fish, deli and butchery counters, as well as in-store bakeries, pizza preparation and even roast chicken rôtisseries. Such provision has led to one-stop shopping patterns and the demise of the local butcher, fishmonger and fruiterer. There has, to a small extent, been some resurgence in the consumer's interest in 'speciality' shopping; but the impact of this has not significantly been felt in turns of a rise in independent or small multiple store numbers. The public limited multiple retail chain has become the predominant organizational form in Western society: both in terms of presence and power on the high street. The store and other forms of fixed retail provision are not however, the only areas that have seen development.

Non-Store Retailing

Retailing has not only significantly changed in its physical complexity and organizational form – there has been a growth and divergence in what might be termed 'non-store retailing'. Both store-based and market-based provision has some fixed element, be it physical or temporal. The pedlar, however, with neither fixed location or set time, has been joined by a number of other non-store formats that have further developed the range of possibilities.

It would seem appropriate to consider first the transformations that have occurred to the oldest non-store retail provider – the pedlar. The term, for many, conjures up an antiquated nineteenth-century picture – epitomized in the scene from the film *Oliver*, where the flower girl and the milkmaid ask "Who will buy?". The pedlar would appear to be an echo of Victorian, or perhaps, even earlier times. This is a misleading notion, as the pedlar is still a feature of western retailing, even if no longer a main element of its provision, but rather "a curiosity on the fringe of retail trade…" (Davis, 1966, p. 247).

Many people are still called upon by 'pedlars' selling anything from household cleaning products to double-glazing and paving. These experiences may not be frequent; but perhaps the most striking change in such encounters is that of the terminology used to describe those involved, particularly when considering the latter two examples. Such traders are often described as selling 'door-to-door', and here, the presence of backing from a corporation provides a sense of formalization. These door-to-door traders often represent an established organization, and there is usually a well-known brand-name involved. These characteristics have in some way, erased the description 'pedlar' from such callers – although they may still be seen as a nuisance! Those to whom the term pedlar might still be applied however, are the 'individual' sellers standing on the doorstep with a bag of small inexpensive goods for purchase. Here, the lack of formalization perhaps leads us not to view them as retailers at all: but just someone that called trying to sell something. Such sentiment can also be extended to the hawkers present in many city and town centres – selling cigarette lighters, small novelty items and posters, for instance. The lack of formalization displayed leads to little thought being given to them as retailers, but perhaps more likely as street traders. This description may extend as far as ice-cream sellers and hot-dog vendors.

Where there is again some divergence is when such traders are backed by corporations, for example the street-based seller of Häagen–Dazs ice cream. In such instances, the street trader becomes an extension of the organization, and as such is viewed as formalized. The nature of the pedlar has therefore changed, and in some degree become bipolar – the individual seller not viewed as a retailer in the modern sense, in parallel with the corporate representative who co-incidentally stands on your doorstep or in the street. These corporate representatives are also to be found in the form of the party-plan organizer and catalogue-based order-taker – such as the ubiquitous Avon lady.

Catalogues

This last example perhaps highlights a more important element of modern non-store retailing – the catalogue. The use of the catalogue as a mechanism to show goods has an established history in retailing. The catalogue probably first appeared in relation to clothes and furniture. Catalogues may also have been used to display different styles and options, or to act as an advertisement for a particular store. However, the epiphany of the catalogue was in its use as a mechanism for enabling retailing at a distance – through mail order. This type of retailing is dependent on there being a reliable form of distribution, often facilitated by the established postal system. The use of catalogue-based shopping in Europe can be traced back to 1870 in Germany, where linen manufacturers used catalogues to sell their products. Mail-order was particularly important in America in the late nineteenth century, where much of the population still lived in rural locations. Montgomery Ward had established a catalogue offering some 10,000 lines by the 1880s (Walsh, 1994). His success was followed by others, and catalogue shopping was firmly established as an alternative to the store. Such patterns were also (at different times) to be seen in Europe, where retailers such as IKEA also provided catalogues as did UK-based Littlewoods. Many catalogues came to carry a prodigious range of merchandise – everything from lawnmowers to lingerie. 'Specialist' catalogues covered a particular merchandise category: e.g. the French children's clothing specialist Vertbaudet.

Catalogues in the UK in particular, also used an additional element in the distribution of goods – the agent. Often, these *women* gained a 'commission' on the goods that they sold. Agents also facilitated the extended credit terms offered by many catalogue retailers by collecting customers' payments.

The agent system did not, however, remain in place for long. The facility for buying on credit (even though there were often high interest rates) made catalogue shopping in the UK particularly popular with those in the lower social classes (McGoldrick, 1990). Catalogue shopping therefore came to have a relatively down-market image, and it was not until the 1980s that there was a significant change in such perceptions. This was stimulated by catalogues such as the first Next Directory (for which a charge was made), which began to provide a much more highly 'designed' and 'produced' feel – both in terms of the merchandise range itself and the nature of the catalogue. It also saw the beginning of 'specialogs' such as ScrewFix (providing woodwork fastenings and tools) and Frederick's of Hollywood (selling lingerie).

The penetration of mail-order shopping is vastly different in various countries – with mail order trade reaching over 5% of total retail sales in some places. As such, it is now an important element of the retail landscape. Otto Versand is the world's largest consumer mail order retailer, with a turnover of over $18.6 billion in 1999. The company, although mail-order only, is also one of the top thirty retailers in the world.

Direct-Response Retailing

Closely associated with catalogue mail order is direct-response retailing, which often relies also on postal distribution. Here however, rather than a catalogue, there is an advertisement or a mail-based vehicle that is used to provide a means of presenting goods for sale. There is also often the heavy usage of databases to both provide mailing lists and manage customer data. This type of direct-response retailing is used to sell a wide range of merchandise – from wine to tapestry kits and garden furniture.

There has been a further extension to the formats through which non-store-based home shopping is offered, in the shape of the Internet. Here, retailers are able to offer a virtual, interactive catalogue without the difficulties, costs and delays of distributing a paper-based one. The Internet provides a new medium for the retailer to extend its reach: enabling the provision of additional services that are not facilitated by static paper-based mechanisms.

There are also however new complexities and difficulties that need to be overcome in Internet retailing. Such difficulties concern both the development of websites and the servicing of customers. This extended use of technology is perhaps the latest advance in retailing. It has been suggested that it has the potential to significantly alter the nature and structure of western retailing, providing a paradigm shift in retailing (Dawson, 2000).

The Rise of E-Tailing

As Dawson (2000, p. 136) comments: "One of the greatest unknowns over the next five years is whether or not e-commerce will become a significant force in satisfying consumer markets and so make electronic retailing a serious competitor to fixed store retailing". E-commerce in total has certainly grown significantly in terms of sales – from a few million dollars in 1995 to an estimated 36 billion dollars in 1999 (Boston Consulting Group, 1999). There has also been a rise within the UK, Europe and America in online retailing in terms of both spending and the frequency of purchase (Boston Consulting Group, 2000a,b). However, the pattern of growth is not consistent across all product categories, company types, or, indeed, between companies based in different countries.

Within the UK, four retail sectors provide the mainstay of online shopping: computers, travel, books and food and wine. In total, these sectors account for 83% of the market (Boston Consulting Group, 2000a). This pattern is reproduced for e-tailing across most countries. Categories such as clothing, home and garden and toys are represented on the Internet, but sales in these sectors are significantly smaller. Nevertheless, online retailing is clearly growing in general terms, and part of the reason for this increase can be attributed to the perceived benefits that have been ascribed to the medium.

For example, online shopping seeks to provide customers with greater utility in comparison to traditional formats: specifically facilitating extended product search and the comparison of facilities and delivery (Kolesar and Galbraith, 2000). These elements are seen as coalescing to generate time-saving and increased convenience, whilst reducing the risk of post-purchase dissatisfaction as a result of the enhanced ability to search for product information (Alba et al., 1997). There is also a range of potential benefits that accrue to the retailer (Rowley, 1996):

- Extended reach;
- Reduced entry costs;
- Reduced costs associated with the running of stores; and
- Elimination of the costs connected with other direct retail formats such as catalogues.

Doherty et al. (1999) also suggest that direct communication can be considered a potential benefit. However, as Rowley (1996) also indicates, there are potential problems related to online retailing for both the retailer and customer:

- Finding the e-retail site;
- Security – in particular, concerns regarding divulging financial information such as credit card details; and
- Adding value to the experience.

The balance between the benefits and problems of Internet shopping is one explanation for the behaviour of some customers when shopping online. As Kolesar and Galbraith (2000) highlight, there are those shoppers who will use the Internet as a search mechanism, but do not actually buy online. This presents e-tailers with a substantial behavioural problem, which can perhaps be solved by providing information and reassurance; developing a positive reputation, and eventually generating brand loyalty.

The growth of Internet retailing is also bound-up with the customer's willingness to become a 'partial employee': as in the online retail context, the customer is responsible for 'delivering' the service. The online retailer provides the backdrop for the service, but if navigating the experience is too difficult, too slow, or overly complicated, then it is unlikely that the customer will either complete the transaction or return to the same site – in effect, the amount of 'work' demanded is too high.

For traditional retailers, Internet-based retail provision, whilst providing a new distribution channel and new opportunities, as is often the case, also provides a number of potential threats and problems. Doherty et al. (1999) suggest that these can be classified as:

- Logistics – the issues associated with providing adequate fulfilment and delivery of goods purchased online. For many traditional retailers, although they have well-developed in-bound supply chain management, the issue of out-bound distribution has never been addressed. This link between retailer and customer has been vested in the store, with the customer providing distribution between store and home. Therefore, those retailers that have developed direct retail systems, such as catalogue-based operations, have an easier task of adapting their distribution systems to meet the needs of servicing an online offer. Equally, those traditional retailers that have the necessary capital to invest in such enlarged logistics operations might also be better placed than those operators that do not.

- Disintermediation – the ability of the Internet to facilitate product distribution without the need for the retailer to be present in the channel. The traditional skills and locational advantages that retailers have enjoyed in the distribution channel are also somewhat obviated by the Internet, as it has the potential to facilitate manufacturers offering products directly to the customer. However, manufacturers may be reluctant to adopt such a pattern of delivery, as it would necessitate moving their core business away from production, and encompassing retail-related activity. This does though, present opportunities for vertical integration – manufacturers effectively 'buying in' the necessary skill and systems to augment their core business.

- Virtual merchants – the Internet has also provided an additional (and it has also been suggested 'easier') arena for the entry of new retail competitors in the form of 'pure-play' operators (those based solely in virtual space). Such operators have included Amazon, ClickMango and eToys. However, Barsh et al. (2000) suggest that, for pure-play retailers, the competitive dynamics of Internet retailing make it impossible for such operations to be profitable – unless they grow to a significant scale, such as that of Amazon (and even then, there are no guarantees). Booz Allen & Hamilton (2001) support this suggestion, and contend that many pure-play retailers will cease to exist – either going out of business, or being bought out by traditional retailers – thus providing the physical retailers with online presence.

Many traditional retailers have tried to combat some of these problems by developing their own presence on the Internet. This 'clicks-and-mortar' approach has itself presented a number of strategic problems. Many of these issues stem from the decision to run the two channels – clicks *and* mortar – as one business, as two separate operations, or as some kind of hybrid. Gulati and Garino (2000) suggest that if...

- The brand extends naturally to the Internet;
- Management have the necessary skills and experience to operate on the Internet;
- The company is willing to apply different evaluative criteria to measure the success of an Internet operation;
- Distribution systems can be altered to provide appropriate delivery on promise;
- Current information systems act as a solid foundation for an Internet-based approach; and
- Either channel constitutes a significant competitive advantage...

...then an integrated strategy is a viable choice.
　However, if...

- Different segments will be targeted by the two channels;
- Different pricing strategies will be applied;
- Conflict is likely;
- The Internet provides a fundamental threat;
- The necessary management skills are lacking and cannot be attracted;
- Additional outside funding is required; and
- Success of the Internet channel is reliant on a 'partner'...

...then, adopting a strategy of separation is more viable (Gulati and Garino, 2000).
　The Internet and its associated benefits, problems, opportunities and threats have provided an additional issue for modern retailers to consider. However, Nilsson (1999) concludes: "Ultimately, the fact is, technology may change the outward appearance of the playing field, but the game remains the same" (p. 12).

Internationalization

One of the ways that the Internet has changed the retail playing field is by providing an additional means of reaching an international market: helping to make the growth of internationalization an essential feature of retailing in the twentieth century and beyond. Hence, it is the expansion of retail operations into a different country that is crucial, rather than the trading of goods between countries. Such international retail first began to take place on a larger scale at the beginning of the century, when retailers – including Frank Winfield Woolworth, who brought his variety store format to England in 1909 – began to trade beyond their domestic markets. Hollander (1970) also identified US and European retailers being active in Latin America at the same time as Woolworth was expanding in the UK.

This early retail internationalization focused on taking an established retail format to another country, where, ostensibly, it was replicated. These early attempts at retail internationalization were not however commonplace. In Europe, C&A – from its beginnings in the Netherlands where Clemens and August Brenninkmeyer opened their first store in 1841 – started its international trading in 1910. However, even though shops opened under the name of C&A, these new international stores were owned and operated by other members of the family. This pattern of operation enabled C&A to continue its international expansion across Europe; and in 1922 the first C&A was opened in London (Baren, 1996).

There is unfortunately a lack of detailed consideration of much of the early patterns and timings of retail internationalization. Shaw et al. (1999) note in their consideration of the structural and spatial trends in British retailing, that such lack of deliberation is perhaps due to the small number of "historical studies [that] have addressed this theme in an empirical manner… perhaps because of its requirements for extensive research at the firm level" (p. 81). It is therefore difficult to provide a detailed account of the chronology and organizational composition of early retail internationalization.

What is apparent though, is that these early attempts at internationalization were not extensive, but were surprisingly varied in nature. For example, in 1938, UK-based Black and White Bars were opening outlets in France, and Whiteaway Laidlaw reported increasing profits from its department stores in the Far East, South America and Africa (Davies et al., 1992). However, Akehurst and Alexander (1999) note that retail internationalization in the second half of the twentieth century had become more extensive and received greater academic consideration. In fact, they suggest that internationalization did not see dramatic development until the 1960s and 1970s, especially in Europe. This interest in cross-border operation was in part stimulated by sustained economic developments in domestic markets and an accompanying desire for continued growth potential. These factors led retailers to look for new opportunities in foreign markets, especially those that were trading in home conditions that had become increasingly concentrated. Not only were some retail firms seeking cross-border expansion, many had now developed an organizational structure and associated processes to support such activity.

Table 2.1 Top 30 international retailers – ranked by sales volume[a]

Rank	Name	Country	Sales (€M) 1998
1	Wal-Mart	USA	144,920
2	Metro EG	Germany	46,884
3	Kroger	USA	41,425
4	Sears, Roebuck	USA	36,704
5	ITM Entreprises	France	35,000
6	Albertson's	USA	34,492
7	Ahold	The Netherlands	33,369
8	Carrefour	France	32,395
9	Kmart	USA	32,378
10	Dayton Hudson	USA	29,761
11	J C Penny	USA	29,284
12	Home Depot	USA	29,056
13	Rewe	Germany	28,990
14	Tengelmann	Germany	27,504
15	Edeka	Germany	26,587
16	Tesco	United Kingdom	26,397
17	Aldi	Germany	26,092
18	Safeway Inc	USA	26,048
19	Ito-Yokado	Japan	26,020
20	Costco	USA	22,914
21	Auchan	France	22,562
22	Centres Leclerc	France	22,105
23	Daiei	Japan	20,001
24	Jusco	Japan	19,638
25	Promodes	France	19,620
26	IGA	USA	17,308
27	Otto Versand	Germany	16,873
28	Karstadt Quelle	Germany	16,837
29	Federated Department Stores	USA	16,757
30	Pinault Printemps Redoute	France	16,514

[a] Source: adapted from PricewaterhouseCoopers (1999b).

These later attempts at retail internationalization also began to use a much wider range of mechanisms to facilitate cross-border trading. The 'simple' method of replicating a successful format in a foreign market was augmented by a range of other approaches including franchising, the building of strategic alliances and takeovers.

Franchising

Franchising has provided a successful mechanism for a wide range of cross-border retail activity. This is demonstrated in the wide range of examples provided by Bailey et al. (1999) which includes Benetton, The Body Shop, Toys 'R' Us, Vision Express and, of course, McDonalds. They also highlight the growth of in-store concessions, by those such as Sears; the rise of joint ventures, including those of Marks & Spencer and Next; and the growth of multiple alliances such as NISA – which itself is a member of European-based EMD. International retail has become big business, epitomized by Wal-Mart, the world's largest merchandise retailer in terms of sales (reaching €144,920 million in 1998 from its global operations (Pricewaterhouse-Coopers, 1999a)). However, although the number of international players in retailing has increased, it is striking that most come from a limited number of countries. Using the list of top 30 international retail companies ranked by sales volume, it is clear that US retailers have become the largest international operators (Table 2.1).

The Americans are followed by the Germans and then the French. There are further representations from a number of European countries, as well as the Japanese. Given the limited dispersion of home countries, it appears that although the number of retailers generating sales in overseas markets has grown, there is a clear core of operational bases from which these companies emanate. This generates a further level of retail concentration at the international level. Here there is a clear trend and according to Flickinger (1999), seven major industrialized countries act as base of operations for companies that in total account for 70% of international retailing business.

An additional layer of distinction has been added to the retail landscape – no longer are there independents and multiples, there are now the national and international players with distinct organizational forms and goals.

Shopping Centres and Malls

There has been a further shift within retailing in the rise of the shopping centre and mall. The development of this superordinate retail form is not a straightforward one. At the beginning of this chapter, when considering early retailing, the existence of the arcade or galleria was established. These single architectural structures, which housed multiple retail providers were not uncommon, and this type of 'definition' of the shopping centre could even be extended to include the 'market halls' of northern England.

What is perhaps distinct about the twentieth century centre or mall, is the scale and wider scope of provision that has become a hallmark of such destinations. Walsh (1994) contends that the growth in this form was stimulated primarily by the increasing 'personal automobility' of the consumer. This indeed provides the means for customers to access the shopping centres and malls that are located away from either their home or town centre. She goes on to suggest that the movement of retail provision to these 'remote' locations was additionally stimulated by the patterns of site location instigated by grocery retailers. The rise of the supermarket – with its wide-range, self-service format and increasingly large free car parks – necessitated that retailers look for larger development plots. This was also tempered by the need to consider the high volume/low margin approach adopted by many grocers, which also meant that there was close attention to issues such as site costs.

These twin strands led to grocers increasingly locating new supermarkets in edge- or even out-of-town locations, to provide the largest sites possible at a reasonable cost. McGoldrick (1990) suggests that this pattern of movement was replicated by retailers in other sectors seeking similar economies and potentials of growth at limited cost. These out-of-centre stores proved popular, and continued the trend towards self-service retail and wide merchandise selections.

Malls

In America, these single out-of-town centres began to 'group' together to provide a strong draw, and in some cases an easily accessible and convenient alternative to in-town retail. In 1945, there were only eight shopping centres in the US; but by 1960 extensive growth had taken place, and there were 3840 (Walsh, 1994). However, this pales in comparison to the expansion that occurred in the subsequent decade, when shopping centre numbers in America reached over 10,000. These centres attracted a wide range of retail providers, including department stores and other 'magnets', which left their traditional sites to become 'anchor' stores within the shopping centres. Shopping centres also began to incorporate services such as cinemas, restaurants and cafés, and hairdressing. These – coupled with controlled temperature, lighting, easy store access, bright interiors and piped music – created a 'complete' shopping environment that provided as much a social space as a commercial base.

The shopping centres in Europe, as well as displaying a clear trend towards out-of-town locations that incorporated additional service provision, also developed as an entity in many major city and town centres. Here, the shopping centre continued on the trajectory laid down by its ancestral forms. In the UK, some of the earliest centres were developed as 'replacements' for the traditional central shopping district and in fact, provided the mainstay of retail provision in these locations – the shopping centre in Blackburn, Lancashire being one such example. The shopping malls that developed within city and town centres were often confined spatially in comparison to their out-of-town counterparts. This, alongside other factors, leads to the identification of four main types of shopping centre (McGoldrick, 1990, p. 50):

- Speciality centres: which house mainly small independent stores that carry specialized merchandise aimed at distinct markets such as tourists. These include Covent Garden in London.
- District centres: covering between 100,000 and 300,000 sq. ft. using a supermarket as an anchor store, but also often housing retailers selling routine durable consumer goods.
- Retail parks: these are a confluence of retailers – originally providing relatively utilitarian products, such as those related to home improvement through warehouse-style stores – based around a unified site. These 'parks' have steadily improved in the aesthetics of their built environment and through the provision of additional service and leisure offers.
- Regional centres: have at least 500,000 sq. ft. of floor space that is primarily devoted to comparison retailing provision. Such locations also increasingly offer leisure and service facilities in the form of food courts, cafés and restaurants, cinemas, bowling alleys, crèches and fun fairs. Such centres include the West Edmonton Mall in Canada and Bluewater in England.

One of the most significant alterations to the retail landscape as a result of shopping centre development is that the infrastructure for such provision is privately managed. Therefore the roles of shopping centre developers and managers become increasingly important, as they can begin to shape the scope of the overall retail offer delivered.

Non-Formal Retailing

Whilst in general terms, retailing provision has become increasingly formalized and organization-centred, there is still a strong thread of either informal, or at least less-formal, retail. This can be seen in the increasing occurrence of:

- Car-boot sales (Williams and Windebank, 2001; Stone et al., 1996);
- Garage sales (Zinkhan et al., 1999);
- Farmers' markets (Grocer, 2001);
- Flea markets (Sherry, 1990); and
- Swap-meets.

There has also been a rise in the number and diversity of slightly more formal retailing, in the shape of second-hand stores (Williams and Windebank, 2001) and charity shops (Horne and Broadbridge, 1995). Alongside the growth of these less formal types of retail provision, there is still a strong element of 'traditional' informal retailing – e.g. the street market (Zinkhan et al., 1999). This presents the consumer with a wide-range of options when considering where to make a purchase. Their choice will ultimately be driven by their motivation in relation to the individual shopping experience, task, product and personal factors that are present.

It is therefore unsurprising that consumers shop at these locations for a variety of reasons. These range from the functional, e.g. access to choice, freshness, and low prices (Williams and Windebank, 2001; Zinkhan et al., 1999; Stone et al., 1996; Sherry, 1990) to the experiential and hedonistic e.g. for fun, social contact, and the pleasure of browsing and 'rummaging' (Zinkhan et al., 1999; Stone et al., 1996; Sherry, 1990) – and, in fact, often combine a number of motives. However, whatever the customer's motivation, access to a diversity of retail provision is seen as being a positive factor. Given this, it is unlikely that the number of retail formats will diminish, and it is rather likely to proliferate, providing consumers with a complex set of consumption alternatives (Berry, 1995). The pattern of retail formats is therefore set to become even more diverse; with retail provision increasingly pluralistic in its nature.

Conclusions

Retailing has not undergone a clear pattern of evolution from one form to another, or from one set of concerns to another. Rather, the history of retailing is populated by parallel lines of development, whose history can be traced back to the very earliest civilizations. Even those actions which are often viewed as 'modern' – e.g. the current focus of much retailing on aesthetics and environment can be seen to have precursors in the rise of the shop in the sixteenth and seventeenth centuries. What is distinctive about the modern retail form however, is its organization and scale. Contemporary retailing in western societies has become increasingly the province of the public limited company that operates multiple stores. Some of these multiple operators have also internationalized, beginning to create a group of 'Über-retailers'. Even within national boundaries the predominance of multiple operators has led to increasing concentration, and it could be suggested that this has left consumers with a homogeneous high street, irrespective of where they may be.

Retail companies in western societies have become highly organized institutions. They have sought to develop product range diversity and depth; the physical shopping environment; the provision of spectacle, and the overall sophistication of their retail offer. These shifts in retail practice have paralleled movements in the broader social and economic environment that have necessitated retail change. It is these changes in consumer patterns and culture, and their influence in creating the modern role of retailing as a highly-developed sphere of distribution, that are examined in the following chapter.

References

Alba, J., Lynch, J., Weitz, B., Janiszewski, C., Lutz, R., Sawyer, A. and Wood, S. 1997. Interactive home shopping and the retail industry. *Marketing Science Institute Report Summary*, 97–105.

Akehurst, G. and Alexander, N. 1999. The Internationalisation Process in Retailing. In Akehurst, G. and Alexander, N. (Eds.). *The Internationalisation of Retailing*. London: Frank Cass, pp. 1–15.

Alexander, N. and Akehurst, G. 1999. Introduction: the emergence of modern retailing, 1750–1950. In Alexander, N. and Akehurst, G. (Eds.). *The Emergence of Modern Retailing, 1750–1950*. London: Frank Cass, pp. 1–15.

Bailey, J., Clarke-Hill, C. and Robinson, T. 1999. Towards a taxonomy of international retail alliances. In Akehurst, G. and Alexander, N. (Eds.). *The Internationalisation of Retailing*. London: Frank Cass, pp. 25–41.

Baren, M. 1996. *How It All Began: Up The High Street*. London: Michael O'Mara Books.

Barsh, J., Crawford, B. and Grosso, C. 2000. How e-tailing can rise from the ashes. *The McKinsey Quarterly*, 3, 98–109.

Berry, L.L. 1995. Stores with a future. *Arthur Andersen Retailing Issues Letter*, 7(2), 1–4.

Booz Allen & Hamilton. 2001. *Crash of the E-Tailers: a Fire or a Phoenix*. Insights: US Retail Interest Group, March, 1–8.

Boston Consulting Group. 2000a. *The State of Online Retailing in the UK: Getting Started*. London: The Boston Consulting Group.

Boston Consulting Group. 2000b. *The Race for Online Riches: E-Retailing in Europe*. London: The Boston Consulting Group.

Boston Consulting Group. 1999. *The State of Online Retailing*. Boston, MA: The Boston Consulting Group.

Braudel, F. 1983. *The Wheels of Commerce*, (S. Reynolds, Trans.). London: Book Club Associates and William Collins and Sons. (Original work published in 1979.)

Coghill, C. 1949. *The Vision of Piers Plowman*.

Davies, B.J., Jones, P. and Pal, J. 1992. Spokes in the wheel of retailing. *International Journal of Retail & Distribution Management*, 20 (2), 35–38.

Davis, D. 1966. *A History of Shopping*. London: Routledge and Kegan Paul.

Dawson, J. 2000. Retailing at century end: some challenges for management and research. *International Review of Retail, Distribution and Consumer Research*, 10(2), 119–148.

Defoe, D. 1713. *The Review, 8th January*.

Dewar, D. and Watson, V. 1990. *Urban Markets: Developing Informal Retailing*. London: Routledge.

Doherty, N.F., Ellis-Chadwick, F. and Hart, C.A. 1999. Cyber retailing in the UK: the potential of the Internet as a retail channel. *International Journal of Retail and Distribution Management*, 27(1), 22–36.

Fawcett, T. 1992. Bath's Georgian warehouses. *Costume*, 26, 32.

Flickinger, B. 1999. Retail industrial complex. (*http://reveried.com/reverb/retsiling/flickinger/flickinger2.html*).

Fowler, C. 1999. Changes in provincial retail practice during the eighteenth century, with particular reference to central-southern England. In Alexander, N. and Akehurst, G. (Eds.). *The Emergence of Modern Retailing, 1750–1950* London: Frank Cass, pp. 37–54.

Graham, L, 2000. Lillian Gilbreth and the mental revolution at Macy's 1925–1928. *Journal of Management History*, 6(7), 285-305.

Grocer, 2001. Spur to renewed local produce buying. *Grocer*, 224(7487), 10.

Gulati, R. and Garino, J. 2000. Get the right mix of bricks and clicks. *Harvard Business Review, May–June*, 107-114.

Hollander, S. 1970.

Kolesar, M.B. and Galbraith, R.W. 2000. A services-marketing perspective on e-retailing: implications for e-retailers and directions for further research. *Internet Research: Electronic Networking Applications and Policy*, 10(5), 424–438.

Hodson, Deborah. (1999) 'The municipal store': adaptation and development in the retail markets of nineteenth century Lancashire. In Alexander, N. and Akehurst, G. (Eds.). *The Emergence of Modern Retailing, 1750—1950*. London: Frank Cass, pp. 94–113.

Horne, S. and Broadbridge, A. 1995. Charity shops: a classification by merchandise mix. *International Journal of Distribution Management*, 23(7), 17–23.

Lancaster, W. 1995. *The Department Store: a Social History*. London: Leicester University Press.

McGoldrick, P.J. 1990. *Retail Marketing*. Maidenhead: McGraw-Hill.

Mintel, 2000. *Food Retailing Review (August)*. London: Mintel International Group Limited.

Nilsson, R. 1999. Perspectives Retailing: confronting the challenges that face bricks-and-mortar stores. *Harvard Business Review, July—August*, 1–12.

PricewaterhouseCoopers. 1999a. A snapshot of the international retail scene. (*http://www.agri-business.asn.au/statistics/food%20industry_retail%20sector/top50inter.htm*)

PricewaterhouseCoopers. 1999b. *Food for Thought*. Special insert 30(1).

Roberts, D.W. 1948. *An Outline of the Economic History of England (5th Ed.)*. London: Longmans, Green and Co.

Rowley, J. 1996. Retailing and shopping on the Internet. *International Journal of Retail and Distribution Management*, 24(3), 26–37.

Shaw, G., Alexander, A, Benson, J. and Jones, J. 1999. Structural and spatial trends in British retailing: the importance of firm-level studies. In Alexander, N. and Akehurst, G. (Eds.). *The Emergence of Modern Retailing, 1750–1950*. London: Frank Cass, pp. 79–93.

Sherry, J.F. (Jr.) 1990. A sociocultural analysis of a midwestern American flea market. *Journal of Consumer Research*, 17(1), 13–32.

Stone, J., Horne, S. and Hibbert, S. 1996. Car boot sales: a study of shopping motives in an alternative format. *International Journal of Retail and Distribution Management*, 24(11), 4-15.

Tse, K.K. 1985. *Marks & Spencer: Anatomy of Britain's Most Efficiently Managed Company*. Oxford: Pergamon Press.

Walsh, M. 1994. The organization of American consumption. In Thompson, G. (Ed.) *Markets: the United States in the Twentieth Century*. London: Open University/Hodder and Stoughton, pp. 7–33.

Williams, C.C. and Windebank, J. 2001. Acquiring goods and services in lower income populations: an evaluation of consumer behaviour and preferences. *International Journal of Retail and Distribution Management*, 29(1), 16–24.

Zinkhan, G.M., de M. Fontenelle, S. and Balazs, A.L. 1999. The structure of Stildeao Paulo Street Markets: evolving patterns of retail institutions. *Journal of Consumer Affairs*, 33(1), 3.

The Birth Of Modern Consumption

Without consumers, it would be impossible for retailing to exist. Here, the growth of the consumer-based culture within developed economies is examined. Therefore, the culture of consumption and its growth is also reviewed.

- The development of consumption as a productive and creative act is investigated; as is the rise of the symbolic.
- The question is asked: how do we find ourselves in societies where consumption has such a central role to play in our lives?
- Some of the events that have brought us to this position are examined, and suggestions made for the growth of consumption as a means of expressing who we are.

Introduction

The possessions that surround most people in western societies, and the services and experiences that they choose to consume, are a significant, if not primary, means of self- and social-expression. This phenomenon, although now an intrinsic part of many people's lives, has not been constant (in the way we interpret it now) in post-industrial western life. However, Douglas and Isherwood (1979) suggest that goods provide, and have always provided, a language for self-expression, that connects both 'tribal' and 'modern' cultures, by providing a means of constructing identity. They also note that those in western societies have so many more possessions, and question why this contrast exists. They suggest that such 'extended ownership' is a direct result of the expansion of both the size and intensity of western culture, which necessitates the use of new symbols – and, by implication, new goods – to enable us to adequately locate ourselves in such an ever-broadening context. Therefore, it would seem appropriate to consider how consumption has become such an import element of current western life, and is now playing an increasingly significant role in many other societies.

The Roots of Consumption

Bocock (1993, p. 3) defines consumption:

> ...in late twentieth-century western forms of capitalism, ...as a social and cultural process involving cultural signs and symbols, not simply as an economic, utilitarian process.

From this, it is clear that contemporary consumption is intrinsically linked with a modern capitalist economy (Lee, 1993). Consumption is also focused on the use of 'commodities' and the meanings attached to them for the satisfaction of needs and desires (Bocock, 1992). Here, 'use' does not only have a literal meaning, but also encompasses a range of other activities related to commodities. Envisage a trip to the shopping district of a local town. On that trip the consumers may look in a number of shop windows; enter a variety of stores; handle, taste and experience a range of products; see a wide selection of promotional material; observe other 'shoppers'; take a break in a coffee-shop or restaurant, and experience the fabric and features of the overall shopping district – without actually purchasing a single item to take home. Each of these individual activities is part of the wider process of consumption: where it is not only the purchase of goods and services that is of interest, but also the social experiences that surround them.

Consumption has increasingly been outlined as an activity directed towards meeting desires as well as needs in western society (Baudrillard, 1988). These desires manifest themselves in an individual's wish to become a certain type of person; to create, emulate or obtain a certain lifestyle and image. Their desire therefore relates to their attempts to manufacture and express an impression of who they are. This is accomplished through the 'language' of consumption – the signs and symbols that are attached to products and experiences. What impression is expressed by someone who wears an Alien Workshop T-shirt and Lakai shoes; owns a Zoo York skateboard; listens to Goldfinger, and uses Flash animations on their website?

Humans have always engaged in consumption as a means of expression (Firat and Venkatesh, 1995): body adornment, the ownership of tools and other objects provide obvious symbolic meaning and send a message to others regarding status, importance and role. Early forms of consumption, although sharing some of the qualities of 'modern' consumption – particularly in terms of the symbolic messages that surround ownership and use (Sahlins, 1976) – were very different in one key respect: the relationship between the element consumed and its physical production; or, to express it slightly differently, the underlying economic form (Fowles, 1996).

In much of pre-monetary society, consumption and physical production took place within the same context, be it family or community. Those that produced an item would also often consume it; although it must be remembered that there was always an element of trade in most pre-monetary societies. The development of excess production, the application of 'special' skills, or possession of 'special' manufacturing techniques and mechanisms meant that many people would have consumed items that were not produced within their immediate social context. Therefore the balance between those things produced *outside*, and those produced *within* the same context began to favour the latter group.

This balance began to change particularly after the industrial revolution, when a significant separation of production and consumption started to occur. The role of the retailer had been well-established by this point in time (although – while the paths of retail development and consumption are clearly and inextricably linked – providing a full discussion of consumption practices in relation to early retailing is difficult within the confines of a single chapter). These practices no doubt informed later consumption developments that can eventually be traced to modern patterns of behaviour. However, concentrating on what shaped attitudes to consumption around the time of its substantial separation from production, provides a clear conceptual starting point – if not one that is truly historically distinct.

Lee (1993) in fact, suggests that it is the separation of production and consumption that begins to delineate 'modern consumption' as a distinct entity from more traditional forms. He also states that modern consumption can be positioned as "...the final link in a chain of economic activity..." (Lee, 1993, p. 3) that acts as a central element in modern consumer capitalism. Firat and Venkatesh (1995) propose that the separation of production and consumption is also surrounded and connected to a number of other separations – that of workplace and home; of time for work (as embodied by 'job') from time for leisure; of what is public and what is private. They suggest that these separations led to the view that what takes place in private, home-based leisure time is consumptive; but that public, job-related work-time is regarded as production. Mapping the development ofthis separation provides one means of outlining the birth of modern consumption.

From Separation to Modern Consumption

The following discussion provides an overview of the historical context surrounding the rise of modern consumption – it is however, mainly focused on Europe, due to the attention that this location has received as the suggested birthplace of modern consumption. It concentrates on the commentaries supplied by writers on 'classical' consumption, but also attempts to provide a flavour of the events and moods that influenced social development. The aim is to create a sense of how and when key features of the patterns of behaviour that we now experience as consumers began to emerge, and, where possible, suggest reasons for these developments.

1650: Puritanism – a Potential Beginning

Bocock (1993) suggests that the earliest roots of modern consumption can be traced back to the post-Civil War period in England, during the latter half of the seventeenth century. A central element in focusing on this period is the proposed importance of Puritanism, especially Calvinism, and the Protestant ethic of society at the time.

Calvinists attached great value to hard work, thrift and efficiency in the worldly role fulfilled by an individual. The display of these qualities was seen as central in achieving eternal salvation. This was also accompanied by a belief that the good things in life could be enjoyed, but only within limits and whilst ensuring that they did not distract from the goals prescribed by their doctrine. This meant that Calvinists had ascetic values coupled with beliefs that stressed hard work. This gave rise to a group who were disposed to the development of personal economic wealth through labour, and who had an aversion to spending on luxuries or anything deemed extravagant. In England, the Puritans and Protestants became strong groups within early manufacturing, forming companies such as Wedgwood and Cadbury's. Given the values of these companies' founders, the profits created were often reinvested or used to support employee benefits such as pensions, rather than providing the founders themselves with overly affluent lifestyles.

This pattern of Puritan activity led Weber (Parsons, 1930) – a Prussian-born sociologist and political economist, whose mother was raised in Calvinist orthodoxy – to develop the notion that there was a statistical correlation (in Germany) between interest and success in capitalist ventures and a Protestant background. Weber extended this argument in his best-known and most controversial work, *The Protestant ethic and the spirit of capitalism* (1904–1905). Here, he proposed that Protestant – and in particular Calvinist – doctrine created unique, if accidental, psychological consequences in its followers.

This in practical terms, led them to pursue the most rapid accumulation of capital possible. Weber suggested this was the basis for the rise of capitalism, which provides an appropriate environment in which modern consumption can take place.

Weber's theory has been criticized on a number of levels since it was first published (Kent, 1996). Early critics focused attention on the existence of highly-developed capitalist enterprises that existed before Calvinism. Weber did not deny this, but emphasized that what made the relationship between Calvinism and the rise of capitalism significant was that the accrual of wealth was itself a central element of this religious belief system, rather than an activity that received either passive or active hostility from the prevailing religious order. What has however, been the most important and recurrent criticism of Weber's proposition, is that it provides a monocausal explanation of the rise of capitalism.

Tawney (1926) extended Weber's theory, and also provided a multicausal explanation, when he proposed that the prevailing political and social pressures, as well as a strong sense of individualism, were more significant in propagating the rise of capitalism than Calvinist doctrine. However, both Weber's and Tawney's theories focus on the accrual of capital. This, in itself, is only part of the equation – relating only to physical production and the development of economic wealth. For capitalism to flourish, there also needs to be a strong consumptive element, which balances and even perhaps stimulates production.

The Protestants that Weber focused on were unlikely, because of their ascetic ethic, to consume more than made life 'comfortable'. So, as Bocock (1992) asks, who was it that consumed the goods produced – especially those that could be labelled as luxuries? He suggests that the answer included the aristocracy and landed gentry. These two groups shared a very different life view: one that allowed, if not encouraged, a much more pleasure-centred outlook. These two very different approaches to consumption must have developed certain tensions; but their interaction helped to shape the culture that emerged in the eighteenth and nineteenth centuries.

In Europe, Puritanism had a substantial social effect, providing a focus for the development of particular attitudes to work and consumption, some of which can perhaps, still be felt today. However, the Puritan doctrine of asceticism failed to become hegemonic (Bocock, 1992). Equally the attitudes of those with different views, such as the aristocracy, also did not prevail in their entirety; but elements of their ethos of pleasure-through-consumption began to pervade other strata of society – just as the Puritan ethic of hard work and the accrual of economic wealth had made an impact in some countries.

1650–1780: The Rise of the Bourgeoisie, the Fall of Mercantilism, and the Seeds of Industrialization

The most notable impact of this change in attitude was on the growing numbers of European bourgeoisie. This newly wealthy group were concentrated in the growing conurbations of Europe. However, the pace and nature of this change was highly varied across the continent. This variation makes it difficult to provide an account that succinctly describes this growth, and yet is linked to the long-time period that needs to be considered.

The rise of the bourgeoisie in Europe is seen to begin in places such as London, Constantinople, Naples, Paris, Rome and Seville. Given that Calvinism did not have a significant effect in these cities, this also begins to raise questions regarding Weber's propositions. The rise of this new class – incorporating clerics, lawyers, officials, merchants, shopkeepers and master craftsmen – spans the period between 1600 and 1800, depending on specific location. This gives rise to a wide timeframe that overlaps the rise of Puritanism. However, the development of the bourgeoisie does appear to be consistent (albeit not in timing) in its basis on the provision of goods and services to others. (The explosion of shops and shopkeepers in the developing cities is considered in Chapter 2.)

There are a number of other common elements that provided this group with distinguishing features:

- The possession of property and the aspiration and resources to extend this;
- A readiness to work for a living, and
- A view that they were superior to unskilled workers or peasants.

This group became increasingly important in their impact on the development and success of the towns, cities and even countries, that they inhabited.

Perhaps a necessary condition for the rise of this group was the waning of mercantilist theory. This assumed that domestic markets were finite, and that, therefore, to increase trade, it was necessary to find new markets. This is illustrated by the writing of the merchant Thomas Munn (1630):

> we must ever observe this rule; to sell more to strangers than we consume of theirs in value.

Such thinking fuelled foreign trade and helped to elevate the position of overseas traders in the seventeenth and eighteenth centuries – particularly in England, Germany and the Low Countries. It was also coupled to a particular social and moral view – which is also of critical importance. Social mobility and increased spending by a population were seen as signs of social disorder

– not as potential new markets themselves. Mercantilism though, saw maintaining proper status distinctions and the wealth of the state as central. This stemmed from its moral context, which was grounded in medieval precepts such as the city-state, the guilds, and doctrines that included the concept of usury as a sin. Mercantilism had laid the foundations for the elevation of traders. It had also illustrated that wealth could be accrued through such economic activity, but because of its core concepts and its reliance on the granting of exclusive trading rights as well as the regulation of prices and wages, it did not remain the main economic form.

Mercantilists failed to recognize, or value, the rise of the internal consumer, and also failed to see that the rise of such activity meant that the rules and regulations that governed the production and distribution of goods had become inhibiting. This limiting nature meant that mercantilism was replaced. Without its decline, it would have been difficult for the development of the bourgeoisie, with their associated rise in status as a result of their gaining economic wealth. By 1776, the economic society that Adam Smith describes in the *Wealth of Nations* is already somewhat removed from a mercantilist approach, and can be termed 'capitalist' in tenor. It is subject to market forces: in that wages and prices are much more likely to be affected and determined by the interplay of supply and demand; and price and profit are exposed to the effects of competition, not determined by regulation. What led to this shift – and, in so doing, helped to stimulate the rise of the bourgeoisie?

One cause was the influence of Puritan ideologies that were also present at the time; but there was also a movement towards entrepreneurial and enterprise-based activities over a wide region. This shift was accompanied by increasing paid employment; and with that came new attitudes to the management of staff. Artisan-owners began to view the journeymen not as co-workers but as waged labour that they managed. The view that workers were obligated to their employers was displayed with greater regard to hours worked, regular pay for regular work, and a reduction in Saints' Day holidays. Such changes began to pave the way for the development of the factory, mill systems and the industrial revolution.

There were also other concomitant changes that helped to create the groundwork for the birth of capitalism and fuelled the growth of a consumer culture. International trade grew, aided by better navigation and improved transport networks, and in some cases, the abolition of internal customs such as tolls. Retailing also developed further – goods were less and less likely to be made on the premises: creating yet another form of separation. Municipal, private and state banks and lending flourished in certain countries (western Europe also took on the Italian practice of using bills of exchange – freeing credit); joint stock companies became an increasingly common means of spreading risk and attracting investors; newspapers boomed: disseminating not only news but price-lists and discussions of their changes.

Additionally, towards the end of the seventeenth century, the Enlightenment began to make a significant impact. This movement made a significant difference to the way people thought, although there is still some debate about its extent and influence. It provided a focus on liberalism, equality, natural law, and a tolerance that influenced the social landscape of the time. Some of its proponents (such as Morelly, de Mably and Godwin) suggested that the ownership of property was a negative occurrence leading to crime and a lack of benevolence. Such views were not however adopted by the various rulers and regimes of the time. Had they accepted these views, the development of companies would have perhaps been very different and as a result, so too might consumption patterns. However, the ownership of property continued to be of importance, as did the increasing personal ownership of goods, which stimulated growth in various markets.

As internal and external markets grew, the primitive (often domestic) arrangement and output of most manufacturing was no longer sufficient to satisfy them. In England, rather than simply continue to increase the number of people involved in manufacturing, a fundamental shift occurred – the development of the factory. This created a system that was vastly more efficient and capable of producing goods in sufficient quantity for the mass market. It also continued a trend that had been seen in domestic-based manufacturing – mainly as a means of providing some increases in efficiency – the division of labour. This was also accompanied with, if not facilitated by, technical advances that further helped to mechanize and concentrate manufacturing. Such new technology continued the trend towards specialization of labour within production. The economic and social foundations of the mass markets had been established, and many more individuals were becoming increasingly more akin to modern consumers – working for their living and increasingly having to buy items, rather than producing them for their own consumption. This shift in the nature of the productive unit also had an impact on other areas of life.

1780–1850: The Rise of the Industrialist and the Romantic

The development of factories spurred on urbanization – towns and cities growing rapidly, and often based on the manufacturing that was taking place locally. The end of the eighteenth century and the beginning of the nineteenth also saw massive population growth. This helped to break-down the traditional passing-on of skills and land, and saw a rise in the number of people that were seeking paid labour. The towns were supported by the increasing industrialization of agriculture, which helped increase productivity and provide food for the increased population, especially those living in towns and cities. This combination of events provided a solid foundation for the increasing industrialization of production.

Although the industrial revolution was led by Britain, by the mid-nineteenth century much of western Europe had followed suit. There was further expansion of transport networks and the growth of powered forms of transportation. Communication technologies evolved and the introduction of the telegraph enabled much faster exchange of news and commercial information. Manufacturing technology also progressed. This technology however, was expensive and businessmen needed considerable capital to invest in such machines. This capital could be raised through the formation of partnerships, joint-stock companies, or through bank loans. So, although many firms remained small, there began the expansion of the 'business unit', which was based on seeking massification and the spreading of risk (these issues are explored further, in relation to retailing, in Chapter 2). Such growth in size and form was evident in retailing when Bon Marché opened in Paris in the early 1800s. Even smaller shops began to invest in merchandise and also increasingly in the fabric of their stores, as illustrated in the following:

> First one passes a watch-making, then a silk or fan store, now a silversmith's, a china or glass shop. The spirit booths are particularly tempting for the English are in any case fond of strong drink. Here crystal flasks of every shape and form are exhibited; each one has a light behind which makes all the different coloured spirits sparkle. Just as alluring are the confectioners and fruiterers, where, behind the handsome glass windows, pyramids of pineapples, figs, grapes, oranges and all manner of fruit are on show.
>
> Source: von La Roche, 1786, p. 141 (cited in Davis, 1966)

In western Europe, industry in general had progressed significantly towards increasing commercialization and a capitalist model. Social shifts also accompanied the changes in economic systems. Factory workers increasingly found themselves bound by 'shop rules' that stressed good time-keeping and encouraged only 'productive' activity in the workplace. These rules were enforced by foremen who acted as a means of control for the owners – beginning to separate owner from labourer in a very tangible sense. The need for efficiency was stressed, and the pace of work became dictated by the pace of the machine. Agricultural labourers were perhaps not as radically affected, but industrialization did also begin to affect their work with the increased introduction of machinery. These changes put further pressure on those working in these contexts – making time for production for their own consumption even more restricted. This in turn, served to increase their reliance on the purchase of products. These changes in attitude to work, and their resulting effect on consumption, were not however limited to those working in factories or on the land.

This increasing focus on work and efficiency also impacted the bourgeoisie, or middle class. The new work ethic was taken up within this social group: and hard work was seen as a way of bettering themselves. This was even evident in some of the contemporary literature aimed at both adults and children. Authors such as Samuel Smiles wrote stories that depicted poor people achieving financial progress and even social mobility through work-related dedication, perseverance and application; and with this mobility came increasing access to goods and services. Such attitudes and reinforcement meant that the middle classes increasingly scorned laziness. These views – increasingly work-focused and achievement-oriented – also impacted leisure consumption. The growing middle class began to focus on self-improvement and family cohesion as a key element of leisure activity. As a result family reading, learning to play the piano, attending concerts and lectures (that provided information and thoughts about applied science and management) were popular. For this group, work and leisure were clearly separate – if, however, intrinsically linked.

For both agricultural and manufacturing labourers, a shift in the nature of their leisure activities also took place. These groups had only limited time for such activities and traditional pursuits – such as animal contests and festivals – were slowly eroded and replaced by concerts, circuses and 'respectable' family pastimes. This movement did not occur as a result of a new work ethic, but was influenced by the attitudes of the middle class and, perhaps most importantly, by the authorities that saw traditional leisure activities as 'dangerous' – the new urban police forces in Britain spending a considerable amount of their time trying to control behaviour at such events. Drinking, although frowned upon by the middle classes, remained a popular activity, and in working-class areas in the early nineteenth century, bars became commonplace: providing a social venue for men in particular. Work and leisure activities had therefore become clearly delineated. In fact, for male labourers, the separation may have been even more striking.

Not only were work and leisure clearly separated but so, increasingly, were *work* and *home*. This physical, and often geographic separation also helped to stimulate the separation of gender roles. The nineteenth century saw dramatic changes in the nature of the family – women were now seen as central in the family and domestic life (even among the working class, where legislation limited women's working hours, with the aim of protecting their family role; but of course, also helped to reduced their economic opportunities, making them more reliant on the family unit). Children's education was also encouraged, and children's ability to work was again limited by regulation. In middle-class families, there was also a shift to smaller family size, which would later become the dominant pattern across Europe. Through changing roles and attitudes, the position of the family had changed – it had become the focus of consumption, and women were increasingly central in such activity. This pattern would not change for some time. The idea of 'self-identity' was also brought to the fore at this time.

Across Europe, the early nineteenth century also saw the rise of Romanticism. In England and Germany though the birth of this movement could be seen in the late 1700s, and by the beginning of the nineteenth century, it was already well-established. The Romantics were opposed to the rationalism of the eighteenth century, and instead focused on individualism as a central element. Hence, the potential of the individual as creator, as challenging the world and mastering it through ingenuity, were key. Romanticism sought to explore experiences that previous views had neglected: including reality, both external and internal. This led to a freedom of expression and an extended range of subjects for artists – their focus being to explore the boundaries of their own expression rather than to succeed in the formal sense. This helped further bolster the Romantic focus on self-consciousness and identity, which has had a continuing impact on western culture and is explored in relation to consumption by Campbell (1987).

Campbell's (1987) work on the development of the Romantic ethic and its link to individuals seeking pleasure from consumption focuses on English society in the eighteenth century. Campbell suggests that, through the consumption of products, people in this period were able to experience in reality what they fantasized about – to derive pleasure not from the simple possession of goods but from the internal use and manipulation of the meanings attached to them. Such fantasies were fuelled by the growing numbers of novels being published and the inclusion of fictional serializations in newspapers and journals.

Bocock (1992) comments that Campbell's observation underpins the controversial notion that this period saw a movement from biologically-driven or economic consumption towards a more modern view based on the social, psychological and symbolic, which is also echoed by Miles (1998). There is perhaps another interpretation – that Campbell's comments also suggest that possessions not only symbolically displayed who a person was (as they had done for centuries before), but were now used to show who the person *wanted* to be, and were more fluid in their meaning. However, whichever perspective is taken, both lead to the same position – one that is closer to a contemporary view of consumption.

1850–1900: A Whole Host of Isms, and the Victorian Ethic

Romanticism waned under the political and ideological instabilities of the latter half of the nineteenth century – the mood of Europe changed. The hopes of the Romantic period had not been met, and Realism took its place with a focus on what could be easily seen and felt – a search for certainty, not experimentation. This was accompanied by a similar movement in science towards materialism and the analogy of the machine. This was displayed in Darwin's theories of evolution, with its focus on mechanistic selection based on superiority. (Although other reasons for evolution were proposed in Darwin's work, these were largely overlooked and ignored). Such viewpoints coalesced and helped to foster the Victorian ethic with its core of earnestness, righteousness, simple truth and respectability. This can be applied not simply to Britain, but to much of Europe at the time.

The second half of the nineteenth century continued to see the rise of industrialism across Europe – Germany outstripping Britain in terms of economic output by the 1870s. America had also become a major industrial power, and increased efficiency in transatlantic shipping, and new technologies such as canning, enabled it to trade with Europe in foodstuffs. Manufacturing technology also continued to improve: so much so that in some areas the need for skilled operators was reduced, and the semi-skilled worker became the norm. Companies also became larger, partly fuelled by the increases in efficiency, but also helped by the easing of restrictions related to the formation of joint-stock companies. In some countries, these new corporate giants banded together to form cartels: heavily influencing trade in their sectors. These shifts also influenced consumption patterns by facilitating cheaper goods, moderating the effects of seasonality in food provision, and by enabling consumers to store goods, which started to lengthen the intervals between shopping trips.

The social structure was also again shifting. In the industrial towns and cities the working class continued to expand. The growth of shops and larger corporations created a need for clerical and shop staff, which relied on a certain degree of education. These workers were clearly employed in very different activities from those directly involved in production, and this new type of role began to form a new social strata – that of the lower middle class. At higher levels a partial union of the aristocracy and successful businessmen took place – forming a powerful group who affected not only the economic but the political shape of Europe. The general trend across all of society was to increased prosperity: although there were periods of major economic downturn and associated hardship, more people had more access to more goods.

This led to increased living standards. Even within the working class, there were improvements in the food and housing purchased; there was also increasingly some discretional spending that was used to buy additional goods. Crazes such as bicycle riding were seen among the middle classes in the 1880s: with many able to purchase these relatively expensive goods, which eventually were also bought by those in the working class. This pattern of higher spending was also aided by decreasing family size across society, which was a result of lower infant mortality rates and a movement towards children being viewed as an expense.

Workers had become more organized, and sought shorter working hours – many having previously worked a fourteen-hour day. There was a reduction in hours for some workers to twelve, then ten hours per day. In Britain, the break at the end of the week was extended to not only include Sunday, but also Saturday afternoon – providing the birth of the modern 'weekend', which became a focus for leisure activity. Vacation days were also introduced. The middle-class work ethic was tempered, and a wider range of leisure activities became increasingly common. Participation and spectatorship of team games – such as football – increased across classes; and the introduction of stadiums and leagues signalled the beginning of activites still clearly seen today. Such team games were a male preserve; however, women also began to take part in activities such as tennis and bicycling. There was also the growth of public parks and museums, and of theatres and music halls. Excursions to the seaside also became popular. These activities show, in varying degrees, an increase in the desire for escapism and pleasure-seeking in leisure activities across a wide range of social groups – well-illustrated by the rise of entertaining feature stories in newspapers, rather than the more traditional focus on politics. These ideas of escape and pleasure would remain a feature of consumer behaviour.

This period at the end of the nineteenth century provides the backdrop for the work of American economist and social scientist Thorstein Veblen. He sought to apply Darwin's concept of evolutionism to his study of economic life and organizations in this period. His first work – entitled *The theory of the leisure class: an economic study of institutions* (1899) – brought him literary acclaim and a reputation as a social critic: his work was viewed by many of his contemporaries as satire, and not the serious scientific analysis that he had intended it to be. His 'analysis' focused on those who ruled business, or the so-called "…nouveaux riches – the 'new rich'… whose wealth was recently acquired, aped the European aristocracy, or tried to do so in order to win social acceptance" (Bocock, 1992, p. 127). This work – although never perhaps being viewed as its author had intended – did raise various points of interest in relation to consumption, and also coined a number of memorable phrases, such as 'conspicuous consumption', 'pecuniary emulation', and 'to consume vicariously'.

The concept of conspicuous consumption is perhaps central; it restated the idea that goods could provide a symbolic mechanism for expression. But it also focused on the use of a high disposable income, beyond that of many of the population, to provide a means of engaging in patterns of consumption that were intended to impress. Consumption was used as a means of indicating refinement and good taste. The display of this good taste was presided over by the wife, who herself was an object used to display her husband's wealth and success. This was done in a number of ways: firstly, and perhaps most significantly, through the husband's ability to support and provide for his wife (and family), enabling her to stay at home and not be involved in paid work; secondly, through her dress and the leisure activities that she undertook; and, finally, through her ability to decorate and adorn the family home. This positioned consumption within the middle classes as a female-dominated activity. Consumption, and more specifically shopping, as a female pursuit, is a notion that reoccurs as a theme in many considerations of modern consumption.

A contemporary of Veblen's, based in Berlin, who examined the phenomenon of urbanization, was German sociologist Georg Simmel. He focused on the distinctive culture and consciousness that he saw being developed as a result of the growth of the city. This new city culture was characterized by 'over-stimulation' that had the potential to foster a bored – or even blasé – attitude to life. Simmel went on to suggest that city-dwellers could only endure this over-stimulation by creating a façade of individuality through their consumption of goods, and that such individualism created barriers between people in the cities – causing them to be reserved and isolated. Such observations led him to assert that "one nowhere feels as lonely and lost as in the metropolitan crowd" (Corker, 2000).

Simmel's work highlights a further separation – which perhaps became more acute for the 'modern' consumer than it was for those living before 1850 – the separation of the individual from the community and culture in which they are located. This notion was also grounded in the Romantic notion of individualism. Miles (1998) emphasizes that this struggle between individual and community was additionally related to the display of class distinctions – showing membership of one group, but still retaining a sense of self. He goes on the propose that, from Simmel's observations, society can be can be characterized as a compromise between these tensions of conformity and distinction, played out through consumption. The brief but frequent social interactions of the city dweller meant that it was increasingly difficult to portray identity through interaction itself; but that identity was rather established through appearance – emphasizing still further the role of consumption, and, in this instance, of clothing and adornment. Bocock (1992) comments that this separation showed that "the person in the big city consumes in order to articulate a sense of identity, of who they wish to be taken to be" (p. 127).

The city was however, also viewed in a much more positive light – Durkheim declaring the 'great cities' as "...the uncontested homes of progress; it is in them that ideas, fashions, customs, new needs are elaborated and then spread over the rest of the country...". The city, as a social construct, can be seen as a prime focus for the development of modern attitudes and patterns of consumption – its epiphany resulting from the gradual development and interplay of economic and cultural changes.

The latter half of the nineteenth century in Europe saw yet another change of mood, as writers as varied as Baudelaire, Arnold, Adams, Flaubert, Ruskin and Nietzsche, began to comment that society had been debased by progress, and that all that stood out was vulgarity and arrogance; that which had been created was the middlebrow mainstay of the masses. Such views saw a return to more Romantic values, and provided a platform for the developments that led to the beginning of the twentieth century.

In Britain, this period saw the beginning of a movement later to be termed 'Arts and Crafts' – whose central figure, William Morris, was to make a substantial impact on the nature of objects produced for mass consumption. Morris and his six partners formed Morris, Marshall, Faulkner & Company (MMF & Co.) in 1861, with the aim of changing the British public's attitudes to the decorative arts. The company saw some success, but also some difficult trading times, and eventually Morris went on to trade as Morris & Company, having dissolved the earlier partnership. However, both companies sought to produce goods that were beautiful – incorporating visual and manual skills – bringing to the fore the importance of design. Morris was not only a superlative designer, but also an astute businessman and retailer. His shop in Oxford Street, opened in 1877, where his...

> ...creations were displayed in a tastefully fashionable setting... never sold at discount prices, and prompt payment was demanded of all customers, whatever their rank or social standing. Prices were 'for ready-money-payments', and the warning was issued that 'all sums unpaid after one month from the delivery of the account will be charged with interest at the rate of 5 per cent per annum'. This was a distinctly modern feature, the better-off were accustomed to long periods of credit. Another break with convention was that names, dimensions and prices were marked on all items. It was still the normal practice

of high-class shops to avoid labelling although the Morris approach was shared by newer types of retailers such as department stores.

Harvey and Press, 1996, pp. 52–53

Morris also recognized that much of the merchandise that the company produced was beyond the pocket of many. As a result of the interest he perceived in this as yet untapped market, the company developed products such as 'tapestry kits', that enabled a larger group of customers to purchase and display Morris & Company designs in their homes. Morris died before the turn of the century, but his impact on products made for mass consumption was considerable.

1900–1950: The Rediscovery of Design and the Growth of Pluralism

The Arts and Crafts movement, and its reintroduction of a design ethic, stimulated those involved in machine-based production to re-examine the importance of design itself. The twenty years after 1900 saw such producers take on designers and begin to apply 'design principles' not only to their products, but to all aspects of their offer, e.g. packaging and advertisements. The production of these newly 'designed' products was also facilitated by further developments in factory layout, construction and technology.

The importance of design to the development of consumer culture and its implications are considered by Miles (1998). He cites Sparke's (1986) proposition that design is a necessary condition for the development of a capitalist economy, as it provides variation, and in so doing, stimulates consumer demand. Sparke also notes that consumers at the turn of the century were exposed to greater ranges of products, and that these goods became an increasingly important means of displaying 'style' – this itself fuelling further 'product elaboration'. The language of product design and style became a central component of manufacturing – no longer was the quest for productivity enough. Miles (1998) suggests that the role of design has perhaps been underplayed in many considerations of the rise of consumption, and that it deserves serious consideration, given that "design was a business strategy in what amounted to a self-conscious attempt to give consumer goods added-value" (p. 39).

Social change also continued, with the demise of the 'Victorian' ethic. There was a move away from the moral centre of Victorianism, and its concentration on absolutes and unity, towards an increased pluralism, as is seen in the work of Nietzsche, Shaw and Wilde. This move is perhaps first seen in an 'overturning' of the accepted order, and a questioning of assumptions. This manifested itself not only in writing and thought, but also in social action – people divorced; the unmarried lived openly together; contraception was both practised and preached, and women demanded the vote. Styles and tastes changed, and were quickly adopted and disseminated. The years leading to World War I were a period of intense change and continuing growth.

The great wars of 1914–1918 and 1935–1945, and the period between them, obviously signalled tremendous social and political upheaval. Accompanying them were the various depressions – which impeded further dramatic developments in consumption. However, this period saw the rise of women in the workforce and their gaining the right to vote across much of Europe. It also saw manufacturing and technological advances, although, rather than directed at market development *per se*, many were inextricably linked to war.

1950–1970: A Return to Rapid Growth; and the Affluent Worker

As Bocock (1992) states, changes in consumption that took place in the post-Second World War period are best encapsulated in the rise of the 'affluent worker'. The 1950s saw manufacturing begin to grow again, and this was a time of high employment and high wages – especially for skilled workers who were in limited supply. This continued into the 1960s, and, in a study by Goldthorpe et al. (1968), the term 'affluent work' first appeared to describe a 'new man' that emerged in the British working class. This new man was employed in emerging industries such as car manufacture; was much more home and family orientated, and even spent part of his leisure time shopping (perhaps beginning to signal consumption as being less female dominated for this group). This, it was suggested, was a pattern of consumption behaviour distinct from that of the traditional male worker employed in heavy industries. This shift was heightened by the decline in such heavy industry and the concomitant rise in male unemployment in towns based around such work. However, the affluent worker could engage in conspicuous consumption, and Bocock notes that this period saw, for many in the working class, the creation of identity based more on consumption and lifestyle than their work role.

This then begins to mark a further, but vital, separation – in this case one of importance for identity creation. It was suggested that production (in the sense of job role) and consumption begin to have disproportionate weight for members of the working class in expressing who they were (or wanted to be seen as being). This is also reflected in the treatment that consumption has increasingly received from academics – it is no longer simply seen as a by-product of classical production (Miles, 1998), but more as a creative and productive act in itself.

1970–1990: The New Consumer

By the 1970s, a new type of consumer – for whom consumption played a central role – was well-established. They were defined by the 'internal dynamics' of the group to which they belonged rather than by their gender, age, occupation or ethnicity (Bocock, 1993). For many though, the focus on consumption was dented by the global impact of the series of fuel crises, which severely knocked consumer confidence for a considerable period. However, whilst patterns of spending and the availability of goods were negatively impacted, there was also growth. This occurred in a second wave of design diffusion: from its concentration in the 1960s within cities to a much broader geographic basis. This was in part the result of the increased success of department stores and national retailers in providing goods that aped the trends set by those such as clothing designers and the rising celebrities of popular music, television and sport. Design in the 1970s also began to display a stark divergence of 'theme' – on the one hand, the functional, ergonomic and sleek; and, on the other, the playful and colourful (Hiesinger and Marcus, 1993). This was augmented by a new interest in ergonomics and the environment – the latter continuing to be an important consideration for some consumers (see also Chapter 16). These interests were partially related to the increasing impact that technology was having on consumer goods and life in general. This was the period that saw the introduction of the Sony Walkman and the personal calculator. This mix of contradictions, the increasing impact of technology, and divergence of styles, was to have profound repercussions.

The 1980s saw the Thatcherite–Reaganite period: a time of increasing prosperity for many in the North Atlantic economic arena – although by no means all (hence today's increased rebellion against capitalism and commercialism as economic forces). This prosperity led to the rise of the Yuppies (the young upwardly-mobile – or urban – professionals), who brought with them a very obvious resurgence of two historic patterns: the development of a new *nouveaux riches* and the reassertion of conspicuous consumption writ large. This growth and expansion – both in terms of economic and consumption –further fuelled the disaffection felt by many in the countries of the Warsaw Pact. This contributed to the erosion of Communism and a move towards free market practices and consumption patterns. However, many of these 'new consumers' faced a period of huge social, economic and political upheaval. The impact of this upheaval was perhaps made worse by access to western media which promoted a picture of life that was seductive in its imagery.

In fact, this proliferation of global communication and business provided much of the world – not simply those in the ex-Warsaw Pact countries – with the opportunity to view the consumer capitalist lifestyle of the west. This increasing globalization reinforced the dominance of certain brands that were almost ubiquitous – including McDonalds, Coca-Cola, Nike and Levis. Others, although not having such a wide geographic spread, certainly became increasingly international: for example Gap, The Body Shop, Marks & Spencer and Tie Rack.

However, the late 1980s and early 1990s also brought economic downturn and increasing disaffection with the Yuppie 'ideal'. There was an increased interest in environmentalism and with the homogenization of the High Street across much of the world, there was also a rise in the number of consumers that sought variety. For others, such brand imperialization led to a renewed call for the end of capitalism and in particular, anger against global super-brands (Klein, 2000). This range of consumer sentiment heralded the rise of 'the cause'; but alongside it was increased access to an ever-widening range of consumer goods and services.

The 1990s – Present: Seeking Experience

The final decade of the twentieth century saw further pluralism in terms of both the acceptance of various styles, choices and viewpoints. It also saw movements in the provision of goods and services ranging from the organic store and farmers' markets, to increasing prevalence of national, international and global brands. The tensions between the local and global were also highlighted by increased access to the Internet, which enabled global search from home, work, or the increasing number of locations that acted as a 'third space' – a place to be, a place to experience – outside of work and home. This seeking of experience has become one of the defining elements of consumer culture in the late twentieth and early twenty-first centuries (Pine and Gilmore, 1999).

The current state of consumer culture is eloquently described by Feather-stone (1991, p. 86):

> … the heroes of consumer culture make lifestyle a life project and display their individuality and sense of style in the particularity of the assemblage of goods, clothes, practices, experiences, appearance and bodily dispositions they design together into a lifestyle. …The preoccupation with customizing a lifestyle and a stylistic self-consciousness are not just to be found among the young and the affluent; consumer culture publicity suggests that we all have room for self-improvement and self-expression whatever our age or class origins. This is the world of men and women who quest for the new and the latest in relationships

and experiences, who have a sense of adventure and take risks to explore life's options to the full, who are conscious they have only one life to live and must work hard to enjoy, experience and express it.

Conclusion

This abridged history provides a context for the role that consumption now plays in many of our lives. Consumption has become a central element across much of western society; and has increasingly been used by a wider range of people as a means of expressing (and even creating) their identity. Consider, albeit in an oversimplified example, how we introduce ourselves, and how we convey to strangers who we are:

- During the 1600s, it was likely that a person would introduce themselves in one of two ways – either based on their parentage or place of birth e.g. John, son of Edward; or John of Hastings – depending on whom they were addressing.
- As industrialization progressed, such practices faded, and people were increasingly liable to use their job role as a demarcator of position and belonging e.g. John Stephenson, engineer.
- Then, as Simmel suggested, the growth of cities brought about an impersonalization of contact and increasingly, rather than title or job role, it was appearance that conveyed identity.
- Finally, consider the affluent worker – rather than job role, or even appearance, it was their total consumption activities that defined them (both in terms of their own identity and in being a distinctive group within the British working class).

Increasingly, products have been at the centre of these shifts – to the point where they now provide the mainstay of identity creation. This in turn means that larger numbers of products have become ever more symbolic – or at least are seen as carrying symbolic meaning. What (if anything) does always drinking Diet Coke say about a person? And is it different to what always drinking Evian suggests?

Featherstone (1991, p. 121) again succinctly captures this sentiment, and comments that:

> Modern society, then, is far from being a symbolically impoverished mundane material world in which commodities, goods and things are regarded as mere 'utilities'.... Consumer culture produces a vast shifting web of signs, images and symbols....

This chapter therefore briefly maps the development of such consumer culture, and begins to suggest that consumption is not simply a process aimed at the satisfaction of physiological needs, but one imbued with meaning and creative expression. The following chapter seeks to explore perspectives for viewing consumption, and explicitly considers the role that retailers play in creating this "web of signs, images and symbols" in which we all participate.

Note

The invaluable entries in the *Encyclopaedia Britannica* that provided dates and context are gratefully acknowledged.

References

Bocock, R. 1993. *Consumption*. London: Routledge.

Bocock, R. 1992. Consumption and lifestyles. In Bocock, R and Thompson, K. (Eds.). *Social and Cultural Forms of Modernity*. Cambridge: Polity Press/Open University Press, pp. 119–167.

Baudrillard, J. (1988). *Selected Writings*, Poster, M. (Ed.). Cambridge: Polity Press/Oxford: Blackwell.

Campbell, C. 1987. *The Romantic Ethic and the Spirit of Modern Consumerism*. Oxford: Blackwell.

Corker, D. 2000. *http://www.uea.ac.uk/eas/staff/corker/amdoss.htm*

Davis, D. 1966. *A History of Shopping*. London: Routledge and Kegan Paul, Ltd.

Douglas, M. and Isherwood, B. 1979. *The World of Goods: Toward an Anthropology of Consumption*. New York: W.W. Norton.

Featherstone, M. 1991. *Consumer Culture and Postmodernism*. London: Sage.

Firat, A.F. and Venkatesh, A. 1995. Liberatory postmodernism and the reenchantment of consumption. *Journal of Consumer Research*, 22 (3), 239-268.

Fowles, J. 1996. *Advertising and Popular Culture*. Thousand Oakes, CA: Sage.

Goldthorpe, J., Lockwood, D., Bechhofer, F. and Platt, J. 1968. *The Affluent Worker: Industrial Attitudes and Behaviour*. Cambridge: Cambridge University Press.

Harvey, C. and Press, J. 1996. The Businessman. In Parry, L. (Ed.). *William Morris*. London: Philip Wilson Publishers, pp. 49–57.

Hiesinger, K.B. and Marcus, G.H. 1993. *Landmarks of Twentieth Century Design: an Illustrated Handbook*. New York, NY: Abbeville Press Publishers.

Kent, R. 1996. The Protestant ethic and the spirit of marketing. In Brown, S., Bell, J. and Carson, D. (Eds.). *Marketing Apocalypse: Eschatology, Escapology and the Illusion of the End*. London: Routledge, pp. 133–144.

Klein. N. 2000. *No Logo*. London: HarperCollins Publishers.

Lee, M.J. 1993. *Consumer Culture Reborn*. London: Routledge.

Miles, S. 1998. *Consumerism – as a way of life*. London: Sage.

Parsons, T. 1930. (trans) Weber, M. *The Protestant Ethic and the Spirit of Capitalism*. London: George Allen and Unwin.

Pine, J. (II) and Gilmore, J.H. 1999. *The Experience Economy: Work is Theatre and Every Business a Stage: Goods and Services Are No Longer Enough*. Boston, MA: Harvard Business School Press.

Sahlins, M. 1976. *Culture and Practical Reason*. Chicago, IL: University of Chicago Press.

Sparke, P 1986. *An Introduction to Design and Culture in the Twentieth Century*. London: Allen and Unwin.

Tawney, R.H. 1926. *Religion and the Rise of Capitalism*. New York, Harcourt Brace.

von La Roche, S. 1786. *Sophie in London 1786, Being the Diary of Sophie von La Roche*.

4

Consumption, Signs and Symbols

As the symbolic nature of some goods is one of the features of life today, then in such a situation, consideration of these symbols has a cultural dimension. Given this proposition, the following issues are examined:
- Expressiveness and its relationship to consumption.
- The development of this symbolic nature, as a result of the roles of producer, retailer and consumer.
- The interplay of relationships and the creation of new reality. Consideration of how retailers now have to manage this complex relationship to create a piece of theatre where consumption can take place to create self.
- The massification of theatricality in consumption, and the development by many consumers of the ability to create a persona.
- Creation of community and the feeling of the hyper-real through retail provision.

Introduction

The previous chapter provides a brief historical backdrop, which begins to illustrate the central role that consumption has increasingly played in the lives of many in the western world. In doing this, it suggests that consumption is itself an integral part of the culture that underpins our lives. Here culture can be taken to mean the coalescing of a social group's values, ideas and knowledge, which provides a platform of signs and symbols that enables appropriate interaction; or more simply put – culture is the 'social glue' that enables us to function as a community, and as individuals within the group. In this case then, culture is plainly about the everyday – about how we live our lives.

These interconnected issues of culture and consumption gained increasing interest from researchers in a number of disciplines in the 1980s (Lee, 1993). This in turn reawakened and stimulated the discussion of 'why we consume in the way that we do'.

'Why We Consume In The Way That We Do' – Some Theoretical Explanations

A wide range of approaches conceptualizing consumption have been suggested by a variety of commentators. It would be impossible in the space available in this book to undertake a thorough examination of all these propositions. (For those seeking a fuller discussion see Bocock, 1993; Featherstone, 1991; Lee, 1993, and Storey, 1999). What follows is therefore a summary of some of the most widely discussed ideas.

A Marxian Perspective

For Marx (1818–1883), the consideration of consumption was not a primary aim, but rather a by-product of other concerns. In his early work his focus was on what distinguished and made humans unique from other animals. Marx proposed that humanity's uniqueness stemmed from the way in which production was undertaken – the outcome of the activity being first created in the mind and then produced physically (the moulding of natural resources to fulfil this idea) – and that this production was not simply linked to the basic needs of life, but was used to produce far in excess of those needs (Lee, 1993).

It is the marriage of production and its use to satisfy needs that Marx saw as the chief mechanism for achieving human happiness and progress – products being made and consumed to provide 'use-value'. The notion of production, and therefore product, becomes key to understanding humanity, and is seen as a central component in human culture.

Within a capitalist structure however, production and use (or consumption) are separated, and this breaks the link between the two activities. This means that products are not simply made and consumed, but form the basis of a system of exchange: and therefore move from having only use-value to also having exchange-value, where their exchange-value is a measure of one product's worth against another. In this separation and the creation of exchange-value, workers are 'alienated' from the fruits of their labour and are simultaneously "...'forced' to become consumers by buying the products they or their fellow workers have made" (Miles, 1998). The product of their labour is a 'commodity', defined by Marx as an object produced for sale, which is sold to provide profit for those that own the means of production and not the workers (Bocock, 1993). The workers are, in fact, exploited to produce this profit, as they are paid less than the value of the products they make, and yet have to pay that same price to buy the commodities that they need. Marx therefore – although incorporating consumption in his work – saw it as an adjunct to production, and when considering his analysis of workers, as an integral part of an exploitative system.

These views led Marx to see capitalism as a negative structure, which he suggested would be replaced in due course by a 'better' social and economic order. However, this has not yet happened, and modern capitalist societies have continued to increase the range of commodities produced. So much so that Bocock (1993) contends that capitalism has undergone a quantitative shift from the system that Marx studied and could now be considered a distinct form – consumer capitalism.

However Marx's work, although it has been heavily criticized, has proved to be a powerful and influential analysis that has affected much of what has been written about consumption. His ideas of commodity, use- and exchange-value are perhaps key in the context of this chapter, as is the notion of consumption as a dislocating act – one which is secondary to production: as consumption does not create anything of value to society or humanity (Bocock, 1993; Featherstone, 1991).

From a Marxian perspective, workers consume because they are 'forced' to do so by the capitalist system that surrounds them and those that 'control' it. The system also separates them from the objects that they produce – they are denied the means of attaining happiness and progress through their production, and therefore turn to consumption as a means of fulfilment. For Marx this was an inversion of importance and the loss of what distinguished humans from animals (Bocock, 1993). This approach raises issues regarding class and consumption and about consumption as a negative and exploitative act.

The Frankfurt School

The work of Marx informed a number of social commentators, whose work is grouped together in the Frankfurt School of critical theory. One member of this group was Adorno (1903–1969), whose analysis also drew on Freudian theory to examine aesthetic development and stressed individualism whilst shunning authoritarianism. As Featherstone (1991, p. 33) notes:

For Adorno the increasing dominance of exchange value not only obliterated the original use-value of things and replaced it by abstract exchange-value, but left the commodity free to take on ersatz or secondary use-value...

This secondary value was, in part, created by what Adorno and his colleague Horkheimer termed the 'culture industry' (Adorno and Horkheimer, 1979): which seeks to organize leisure time in the same manner that production is organized in the capitalist system. The culture industry (film, television, magazines, radio. advertising – and by extension, retail), seeks to oppress the worker further by promoting dreams of wealth, love and power that divert attention from their exploitation and instil interest in the consumer goods that the system produces (Storey, 1999).

Such thoughts are extended by Marcuse (1968), who suggests that the culture industry promotes 'false needs' and the 'ideology of consumerism'. In providing these needs it prevents consumers from contemplating more 'serious' (and dangerous) thoughts regarding the system in which they live and its effect on them; and, at the same time, masks the drudgery of their lives. So consumerism and increased consumption in the working class is not evidence of progress, but of increasing control of the capitalist system (Lee, 1993).

Those in the Frankfurt School contend that workers consume because they are manipulated by the culture industry (itself a by-product of capitalism) and are seeking escape from their mundane existence (which is also a product of the very same capitalist system). Consumption is seen as a destructive act – as with the Marxian view – purely to 'replenish' the individual for the role that they fulfil in production. This view has been criticized, and, in particular, Docker (1994, cited in Storey, 1999) views the work of Adorno and Horkheimer as nothing short of "preposterous" and "ludicrous", and describes their approach to providing evidence for their theories as "disturbingly casual and even laughable... complacent and...repellent" (1994, p. 41). This said, the view that consumers are actively manipulated and coerced is a recurring theme, but from the outset, this viewpoint does see consumption as a purely passive act.

Not Simply Passive – But Perhaps Creative... Consumption as a Demarcator of Class

The notion of consumption being a passive act was somewhat brought into question by the work of both Veblen and Simmel (whose work was introduced in the preceding chapter). Consumption is viewed rather as a mechanism for communication (of status in particular) and as a vehicle for competitive display. Consumers are not passive but use consumption to express their class. However, both suggest that the display presented by those at higher levels of society is 'emulated' by those below. Simmel in particular saw society as split between passive imitators and the innovative who strive for differentiation (Storey, 1999). Therefore, as those in lower classes imitate the consumption behaviour of those above in an attempt to improve their status, those in classes being imitated seek to change their display to maintain social demarcation. What is therefore presented is an endless cycle of imitation and innovation. Here, class is seen as playing a central role in defining and stimulating consumption and in particular in relation to dress.

However, the views of Veblen and Simmel, in particular that consumption patterns 'trickle down' from those in the highest social class to those in the lowest have been criticized on a number of levels. McCracken (1990) contends that what is actually occurring is an upward motion – not a downward one. He sees those in lower classes actively chasing the consumption patterns of those above them, with the appropriated behaviour being discontinued only as a result of its assimilation by those in a lower class. McCracken also suggests that class may not be the only base for social stratification and that gender or ethnicity may also provide differences where emulation can also be apparent. His final criticism is that to view class as the main motivation for consumption is to ignore the other elements of the social context – such as gender and ethnicity – and in so doing provides only a monocausal explanation. In addition, the class-based perspective is difficult to apply, especially in a modern context, as it assumes that there is one clearly defined and jointly acknowledged class system, which Campbell suggests is not the case (Storey, 1999).

The notion of class and consumption being intrinsically linked is also expressed by Bourdieu (1984). He, however, goes further than suggesting that consumption is a means of displaying class demarcators, but is rather a mechanism for establishing and maintaining class boundaries (Miles, 1998). Bourdieu contends that this means of 'social distinction' is ultimately linked to economic inequalities that give varying access to wealth and varying potential for consumption. The creation of these patterns of distinction is therefore imbued with class 'taste' judgements that act as 'classifiers' of those that make them (Storey, 1999). Bourdieu seeks to draw attention to a range of class tastes – encompassing food, art, leisure pursuits (in fact everything that can be 'consumed') – and he expresses the view that a hierarchy of tastes is produced. This itself leads to mass culture, which stresses function at one end of the hierarchy and 'Culture', that focuses on form at the other.

These two very different perspectives on taste manifest themselves in the development of what Bourdieu termed 'cultural capital'. This concept enabled Bourdieu to explain why class distinctions were apparent between groups who had the same economic capital. As Lee (1993, p. 33) comments

> ...just as economic relations express networks of power, which can be quantified in economic capital, then so too do cultural relations express the differential levels of learned and empowering competences, or cultural capital, as these are relatively distributed throughout the social field. Cultural capital is here defined as the possession of certain cultural competences, or bodies of cultural knowledge, that provide for particularly distinguished modes of cultural consumption and for relatively sophisticated classification of cultural and symbolic goods.

Lee goes on to explain that unlike economic capital that can be accumulated relatively quickly or instantaneously, the gaining of cultural capital is the result of long-term effort, often in the form of education. Bourdieu also adds a third form of capital – social – which is itself affected by the cultural capital that is imbued in the consumed.

These three forms of interconnected capital give rise to a rich and dynamic system of signs and symbols that is used to demarcate social classes (Miles, 1998). This system is not only produced through the underlying economic form and education, but through what Bourdieu termed the 'habitas'. This is a complex construct that he uses to explain the reproduction and change in class-based tastes. Miles (1998) defines the habitas as "a group-distinctive framework of social cognition and interpretation [which] is reproduced between generations and thereby generates the schemes by which cultural objects are classified and differentiated".

Bourdieu builds on a Marxian perspective. He sees consumption as a determining element of social classification that is highly symbolic and draws on economic, cultural and symbolic capital. The points of reference for this symbolic world are learned, reinforced and changed through the habitas, which enables people to at the same time draw lines of distinction and create a sense of shared values and ideas. The consumer, for Bourdieu, is the creator of social strata.

Creation of Shared Identity – but not a Class-Based One

The concepts of the symbolic and the creation of a shared identity suggested by Bourdieu are also found elsewhere. However, the focus is not on class but subculture and in particular, that of youth culture. The views expressed here are based even more firmly on the notion of consumption as a creative act. In 1984, de Certeau proposed that consumers 'read' their own meaning into the products and services that they use – and that this places them in a position of some strength and creates what he terms 'secondary production'.

The language that he uses does however suggest that this 'power' is set against the much greater strength of the organizations that produce these objects and experiences. For example, he talks of consumption as subversion or as poaching, and talks of the appropriation of what is used – the 'act' of consumption – as one of use and manipulation by the consumer, and not the producer.

Such ideas are also seen in the work of Cohen (1980); Hall and Jefferson (1976); Hebdige (1979), and Willis (1978), which examine various aspects of youth culture (Storey, 1999). Hebdige (1979) is the most vocal on the role that consumption plays in youth subculture. He sees it as being a 'foremost concern' of youth groups: who use consumption to delineate themselves form the dominant culture in which they are based. As Storey (1999, p. 55) comments:

> Youth subcultural consumption is for Hebdige consumption at its most discriminating. Through a process of 'bricolage' they appropriate for their own purposes and meanings the commodities commercially provided by the culture industries. Through acts of 'bricolage' products are combined or transformed in ways not intended or envisaged by their producers; commodities are re-articulated to produce oppositional meanings.... Youth subcultures engage in symbolic forms of resistance to both dominant and parent cultures... [but] always move from originality and opposition to commercial incorporation and ideological defusion as the culture industries eventually succeed in marketing subcultural resistance for general consumption and profit.

Consider how elements of 'punk' in the 70s and 80s became visible in high-street fashion collections and how even the most outrageous of club wear influences contemporary trends – the 'hottest hot pants' of the summer of 2000. However there is an important distinction between these two examples. Punk subculture was potentially totally immersive – there were for example definite clothing, music and belief conventions. It was very much a distinctive and easily identifiable subculture – as were its members. The contemporary club scene is different. It is not as concrete a subculture, although those people that participate may share dress codes and some ideas, these are not as defined, or, most importantly, as defining. Subcultures such as punk easily portray the creation of a shared identity that differentiates those that belong to it from those in the parent culture. Consumption is central here, not only in creating social distinction, but also in creating self and social identity. What is seen in the more contemporary 'club' example is not as easily explained using this perspective, and perhaps another viewpoint affords a better basis for exploring this less singularly defining pattern of identity and consumption.

Postmodernism and Consumption

The concept of identity creation through consumption is one of the central themes articulated by theorists that take a 'postmodern' perspective. There has been increasing reference to 'postmodernism' throughout various discussions on a wide range of topics including the artistic, intellectual, and academic (Featherstone, 1991). Postmodernism is described by Firat and Venkatesh (1995) as a move away from modernism, which is the totality of the sociocultural conditions and philosophical ideas that accompany the period in western history from the early sixteenth or seventeenth century to the present (the period briefly considered in the preceding chapter).

They go on to suggest that modernism signifies:

- The rule of reason and the establishment of rational order;
- The emergence of the cognitive subject;
- The rise of science and an emphasis on material progress through the application of scientific technologies;
- Realism, representation, and the unity of purpose in art and architecture;
- The emergence of industrial capitalism; and
- The separation of the sphere of production, which is institutionally controlled and public, from the sphere of consumption, which is domestic and private.

Such elements have informed many of the viewpoints on consumption discussed above, but there has been increasing articulation of perspectives on consumption that are influenced by postmodernism.

Postmodernism emerged partly from a critique of modernism and partly from the development of a contemporary set of world views (Firat and Venkatesh, 1995) that consider current patterns and modes of consumption. What are central are issues of culture, aesthetics, language and symbolic modes; and it is the "micropractices of everyday life, discontinuities, pluralities, chaos, instabilities, constant changes, fluidities and paradoxes [that are deemed to] better define the human condition" (Firat and Venkatesh, 1995).

These elements are key within a postmodern perspective, yet providing a precise definition of the concept is in fact a difficult task. Connor (1992) partly attributes this to the multi-dimensional nature of postmodernism, commenting that many of its aspects are based on unreality and uncertainty, suggesting that postmodernity possesses a commitment to indeterminacy. The ephemeral nature of postmodernism has given rise to criticism of its theoretical 'centrelessness', which according to Rajchman (1987) makes it "the

Table 4.1 Implications of postmodern conditions for market and marketing strategies[a,b]

Postmodern condition	Market implications	Marketing strategies
Openness/tolerance	Communicating (rather than knowing) markets	Flexible marketing
Hyperreality	Constructed (rather than given) markets	Adaptive marketing Thematization
Perpetual present	Consumer preference for simulations 'Here-and-now' markets	Simulation Immersion
Paradoxical juxtapositions	Bricolage markets	Image fragmentation
Fragmentation	Fragmented markets	Image clustering
Loss of commitment	'Touristic' markets	Spectacle marketing
Decentring of the subject	Consumers with fragmented selves	Continual image (re)generation
Reversal of consumption and punctuation (re)constructionProcess marketing	Customizer marketsProducer markets	Market de
Emphasis on form/style	Image (rather than brand) markets	Image (versus brand marketing)
Acceptance of disorder/chaos	Fluid markets	Empowerment

[a] Concepts are positioned in the table for reasons of parsimony and clarity; readers should understand that while we intentionally denote some specific relationships in the table, in fact the concepts, as discussed in the text, are very dynamic and each is related to and impacts all the others.
[b] Source: Firat and Shultz, 1997, p. 202.

Toyota of thoughts; produced and assembled in several different places and then sold elsewhere" (p. 51). However, despite such criticism, it is a viewpoint that has enjoyed increasing currency.

If an encompassing definition of postmodernism is illusive (Brown, 1995), what has been provided in its discussion is a set of conditions that denote the postmodern and the consequences of these factors, which are expressed in Table 4.1.

Jameson (1984) suggests that postmodernism consists of two key themes, which are present in Table 4.1, the transformation of reality into images leading to the subsequent importance placed on form and symbols; and the fragmentation of society leading people to have inconsistent and varied narratives of life. These symbols and this fragmentation are intrinsically linked to consumption. A postmodern interpretation of consumption, in common with the interpretations of those such as Bourdieu, sees it not as a point of destruction but "a moment where much is created and produced" (Firat and Venkatesh, 1995, p. 251). The consumer is a producer of images at each consumptive moment through "fluid movements among different experiences, images and meanings" (Firat and Shultz, 1997, p. 104). Du Gay et al. (1997) suggest that this has been encouraged by the massive explosion in the range of goods available for consumption in modern western society. They go on to comment that consumers use the commodities to become what they wish – "they play with the range of commodities" (p. 104), styling a range of identities for themselves through their consumption practices.

Postmodern Consumption and Identity

It is this concept of a range of identities that further separates the postmodern perspective on consumption from that given above by Bourdieu and others. They talk of consumption for identity creation, but there is an implicit notion that the identity created is a relatively stable one. However, those guided by postmodernity talk of multiple identities and images. Identity is seen as fast becoming:

> fragmented and disconnected, and that the decentred postmodern self... no longer possesses the depth, substantiality and coherency that was the ideal, and sometimes achievement of the modern self.
>
> Baudrillard, 1983, p. 233 (cited in Kellner, 1995)

This new, disjointed self has arisen in response to the acceleration and complexity at which current society operates (Kellner, 1995). This provides even greater scope for the use of goods and experiences in the creation of these fragmented identities.

Costa (1994) suggests that increased societal fragmentation allows the freedom to explore many differing roles and constructions of self. The idea of varied 'narratives of lifestyles', engendered through fragmentation, has fostered an air of accepted 'chaos' where according to Featherstone (1991), there are no rules – only choices. This led Elliott and Wattanasuwan (1998) and Kellner (1995) to propose that such experimentation with narratives of lifestyle through consumer choice can be achieved not only through lived experiences, but also through the consumption of 'media products', and therefore extends experimentation and image creation into the world to imagination and fantasy. This clearly echoes the concept of 'hyperreality' proposed by Firat and Shultz (1997) in the table above, where an individual has the freedom to realize a variety of experiences: past or present – real or unreal. They go on to suggest that simulated realities are permitted through sophisticated means, such as cyberspace, or the simulated worlds of tourist attractions such as Disney World, and even that of the shopping mall. However, Bocock (1993) believes that we are also exposed to more everyday opportunities to live varied realities, such as advertising or soap operas. These forms show products, such as clothes or furniture, in the context of a certain lifestyle or 'dream world'. The purchase of the depicted product becomes a symbolic 'key', allowing access to this world, and providing associated benefits – the product encompassing symbolic value that extends far beyond its functional use.

Postmodernism, in its focus on consumption, therefore also reflects a move away from work role as the central element in people's lives from which they develop their sense of identity (Featherstone, 1991), to one where this sense of 'self' is created through accumulation of possessions, products or experiences. Products or experiences that provide a sense of past: telling 'who we are, where we have come from, and perhaps where we are going (Belk, 1988, p. 160). From the perspective of the postmodernist, consumption is primarily about creating identity – but this identity is not stable and is impacted as much by the hyper-real as by the lived experience – and image is the actual product (Firat and Shultz, 1997).

Postmodern Consumption and Retailing

The postmodern view of consumption can further be distinguished by its consideration of the role of retailing. The perspectives outlined above – other than that of postmodernism – make no reference to the 'sphere of circulation' as a concrete component of consumption. They rather concern themselves with the product (even at times its advertising and depiction in the media) and its 'use'. There are implicit connections, of course, to purchasing and shopping; but the impact of the retail environment is by and large neglected. In clear contrast, the notion of 'shopping as an activity' and the nature of the retail environment are recurring themes in the postmodern consideration of consumption. There are a number of reasons for this, and a range of notable implications for the retailer that are brought to the fore as a result.

Perhaps the strongest recurrent premise is that of the retail environment providing a space for consumer experimentation with various (self) images. (For a more detailed consideration of consuming retail space see Shields, 1992). In many cases, this can also be linked to the concept of the hyper-real and the creation of fantasy, which is often associated with the use of 'theme' within the retail environment.

Firat and Shultz (1997) provide a number of interesting examples. They first talk of Las Vegas as a prototype for 'postmodern space' with its numerous themed hotels – the Luxor with its evocation of ancient Egypt; Caesar's Palace and its aura of the Roman Empire; Treasure Island and its creation of a pirate paradise. They also cite NikeTown and the less well-known Electronic Café International as more obviously retail-based postmodern spaces. (Although, to a certain extent, this element of fantasy has long been present in many retail environments. Just envisage the transformations that occur in a department store at Christmas – not least the provision of that childhood favourite 'Santa's grotto'. And, should we need any further justification of the hyperreality present in retailing consider as an example an episode of the American comedy series 'Ally McBeal'. Here, as part of a claim for unfair dismissal, a 'fat' sacked department store Santa's case rests on the proposition that the Santa of the department store were he worked is the 'real' Santa. And, if the store hired a non-traditional Santa – which would better meet its "shoppers' demographic" – it would in fact be dashing the image of Santa for the city's children. Can you get any more hyper-real than that?)

Firat and Venkatesh (1995) also note a "widespread 'Disneyfication' and/or thematization' of all urban and suburban experiences, from the shopping malls to town centers". The retail arena is very much part of this: Meadowhall and the Trafford Centre projecting, Hogwarts-like, a simulated and changing sky above shoppers in their food courts; and with the recreation of the 'exclusive shopping district' and the 'three-day market' (complete with its artisan-retailer), all under one climate-controlled roof. In doing this, they capture the essence of these retail offers and selectively project an idealized reality or simulation for the shopper to experience.

The creation of this 'fantasy' space has been criticized. Miles (1998) cites Friedberg's (1993) description of shopping malls as a 'contemporary phantasmagoria' that blinds shoppers from the realities of urban blight. Irrespective of such criticism, retail space appears to have become a focus of concern on a number of levels. Alongside the notion of the hyper-real (which might even be extended to the tableau created in window displays, the elegantly styled home that is fashioned or the illusion of the party queen), where as Gabriel and Lang (1995) comment, products become part of fantasies and fantasies about products – there are other propositions that compel us to consider retailing as an integral part of contemporary consumption.

Featherstone (1991) comments on the Metrocentre's "...Antiques Village, fantasy fairytale 'Kingdom of King Wiz', Ancient Roman Forum gallery and general eclectic smattering of symbolism to evoke the myths of a communal past via Christmas card and chocolate-box iconography" (p. 103). This concept of community is one that is also presented by Miles (1998), who highlights the contention that the shopping mall provides a sense of community that may not be present in other aspects of consumers' lives. Such sentiments are also provided by Goodwin (1994), who proposes that 'service places', such as the shop, may provide a sense of 'community', and that this is a reflection of the traditional role of the local store or pub.

Given the focus in the discussion above on the creation of a self-identity in postmodernity, there is the potential for tension with the notion of 'community'. Whilst it is true that from a postmodern perspective, there is a strong focus on the individual (Cova, 1996), there is also consideration of community, particularly as embodied by what is termed neo-tribalism (Cova, 1997). Cova (1996) explains that tribe "refers to the re-emergence of quasi-archaic values: a local sense of identification, religiosity, syncretism, group narcissism and so on". He goes on to note that these postmodern tribes are "inherently unstable, small-scale, affective and not fixed by established parameters of modern society. Instead, they can be held together through shared emotions, styles of life, new moral beliefs and consumption practices". A person is not limited to belonging to one tribe at a time, and this generally nebulous and fleeting attachment to – and the nature of such – tribes means that the term 'neo-tribe' better describes this phenomenon.

The retail environment is presented as a place for the enactment of the rituals of many of these neo-tribes. Cova (1997) relates the example of shopping malls being taken over by 'gangs' of teenagers as their 'tribal' space. This can also be seen in individual retailers, for example those serving the 'surf'-based tribe, where not only are potentially unfamiliar products sold, but if you are outside the tribe, a 'foreign' language is spoken. The retail space becomes central to the 'tribe'. It is then very much their place for expression, meeting and display. These privately-owned environments then become places for public display and the development of 'community'.

This is perhaps an inversion of the traditional pattern of 'public space' – the town hall, the village green, school house or place of worship – being used as centres for the development of community. These have slowly been eroded in many situations as a focus of community, and the retail space, which has always played some part, has been elevated to a primary position. If retail environments can act as a focus for the development of community, then retailers must consider the means and benefits of facilitating such a role for their stores. Miles (1998) provides the example of the Southdale Mall in America as an attempt to create a safe and environmentally-controlled commercial space that seeks to create a modern equivalent of the Roman and Greek marketplace, serving civil, cultural and social needs, as well as commercial requirements.

The idea of commercial space providing a focal point for the development of community is also highlighted by Haslop et al. (1998). They also stress the importance of the space for identity creation. "The 'marketplace' assumes the role of village square, a place for meeting and cultural exchange as well as ongoing creation and negotiation of shared identity" (p. 319). They also go on to note that in these circumstances, the boundary between consumer and citizen are blurred. Consumers become increasingly 'part' of this commercial space, their presence is central to its success – both commercially and as an 'experience'. Malina and Schmidt (1997) comment that it is marketers that 'follow' the lead set by consumers as active 'citizens', and that the creative and innovative management of this 'interaction' by service providers is essential in creating a superior experience. This idea of 'experience' is then a recurring theme itself within postmodern considerations of retailing and service provision.

The use of the term 'experience' begins to suggest a number of different, but connected concerns. The first is illustrated in Campbell's (1997) discussion of shopping as a leisure activity in its own right. The process of shopping is presented as 'experience', irrespective of the act of purchase and use of a product. This is further emphasized by Schmidt et al. (1999), who comment that symbolic cultural capital is only in part expressed through the product purchased, and that it is also associated with process of consumption. They also note in the findings of an exploratory study that for some consumers, there is a shift in importance towards process rather than product. If this is the case, then the retailer's potential importance for this group is elevated – they, and not the goods that they sell, take centre stage.

This concept of experience is also concerned with the provision of 'memorable events' to the customer (Pine and Gilmore, 1998). Here, there is a strong link to the development of themes: with the offerings of those such as Disney and the Rainforest Café being cited as 'experiences'. Here too, more traditional retailers offer experience-based offers – "...NikeTown, Cabella's and Recreational Equipment Incorporated draw consumers in by offering fun activities, fascinating displays, and promotional events (sometimes labeled "shoppertainment" or "entertailing")" (Pine and Gilmore, 1998, p. 99).

The consumption of experience is receiving increasing attention (e.g. Arnould and Price, 1993; Hirschman and Holbrook, 1982; Hopkinson and Pujari, 1999). There also seems to be a strong association between entertainment and the creation of hyperreality. These issues are further discussed in the following chapter, where the potential of retailing to develop both hyperreality and entertainment is explored through the use of the metaphor of the theatre. Therefore, the role of the retailer when considered through a postmodern perspective, has moved. The retailer has become a creator of themes that reflect a particular image; a manager of private space that serves a public purpose, providing a platform for the development of community and yet still facilitating the expression of self, and acting as a medium for cultural symbolic capital.

From the postmodern viewpoint, consumers are not forced to consume – they do so as a creative act: to express who they are (or want to be perceived as being) at any moment in time. They do so at times to belong, but not necessarily to one group. They can be fleeting in their allegiances. What is constant is self-expression through products – "outward[ly] constructing the social world: Social-Symbolism, and inward[ly] towards constructing our self-identity: Self-Symbolism" (Elliott, 1997, p. 2).

What therefore seems clear is that whichever theoretical proposition on consumption is selected, the overall outcome is always related in some way – be it secondary, class-based, shared totality or fragmented creativity – to expressing who we are. How should we then examine this expressiveness?

Expressiveness in Context

Expressiveness by its very nature, cannot exist in a vacuum, but is rather formed within a context. This may be a physical setting, a relationship, or may even be within the individual (when they for example, attempt to understand themselves or others (Kaiser, 1998)). The context is also formed by the attitudes of those involved – the person expressing the message, and those perceiving it – the nature of their relationship, and the setting in which this interaction takes place.

When focusing on consumption, this expressiveness centres on the selection, use and display of goods, services and experiences as a mechanism for the transmitting of messages about the individual. At a broader level, the culture in which these people live and have been brought up, the historic meanings associated with the objects and experiences that they consume, also constitute part of the context in which their expression takes place (as indicated in the various perspectives on consumption explored above).

The study of social expressiveness – and the attempts to understand various aspects of its context – has taken many forms, and has drawn on a number of traditions. The following brief discussion introduces a number of perspectives, and considers the relative contribution made by each. It is worth noting that a number of the perspectives examined here have strong associations with a particular viewpoint on consumption; but a detailed examination of the interplays is beyond the scope of this chapter. (See Storey, 1999 for a fuller discussion).

The Cognitive Perspective

The cognitive perspective centres primarily on an individual's perceptions and how people form impressions of others and to some degree, of themselves. This approach stems from psychology, and therefore focuses on thought processes and how, using the cues provided by consumption, impressions are formed. Consumption and in particular, consumed objects, are viewed as stimuli, which provide information that is used to create an impression about people. The focus is therefore on the use and retrieval of information about individuals and groups of individuals, particularly in relation to personal traits (Kaiser, 1998).

This perspective is based on a number of underlying assumptions:

- Cues presented by stimuli are used to simplify and make sense of social interactions.
- People strive for consistency and continuity in relation to their thought processes.
- Humans seek and use aesthetic stimulation in their environments.
- People are motivated to explain social occurrences or outcomes in terms of causality.

As a perspective clearly focused on the interpretation of impressions, it does not consider the creation of these impressions and the importance of this element in human expressiveness. This has led to the use of other perspectives that begin to address this gap.

Symbolic Interactionalism

Symbolic interactionalism extends the cognitive perspective to consider the creation of an impression as well as its assessment. This viewpoint therefore has a focus that is based on two-way interaction and accordingly, the language and main area of concern moves from stimulus and information to the creation and sharing of meaning. This perspective stems from a sociological tradition, and is firmly grounded in the importance of the social context in which the interaction takes place.

Symbolic interactionalism also centres on the study of social actions and social objects (McCall and Simmons, 1966), and how people weave together their behaviour to enable them to make sense of the world and exist within it. This 'weaving' is achieved through negotiation and the sharing of meanings. For example, sharing with the wearer of a Prada suit an understanding of what that means about them, and any associated inferences in terms of behaviour and relationship that could be drawn from that meaning. Are they smart, fashionable, successful, and someone who is to be considered a peer? Or are they conceited, self-absorbed, superficial and too materialistic? Which meaning is constructed is of course dependent on the individuals concerned, and the social context in which they are located at the time. However, what is being sought is an understanding of one another to enable social interaction to take place. In this instance it could be mutual appreciation and respect, or mutual distrust and animosity. Irrespective of the nature of the shared meaning constructed, this understanding provides a foundation for the actions and reactions of those involved. The response of those interpreting the impression displayed can take a number or forms. As illustrated above, it can be an emotion, a judgement, a sensation, or an expression of taste.

The nature of the jointly-constructed meaning is not necessarily identical, but is perhaps better described as being "approximately the same" (Davis, 1982). These approximations are based on the associations that we develop attachments to objects and consumptive acts. These associations can, for example, relate particular objects and experiences to certain groups of people, particular attitudes or beliefs. The assumptions used may not be totally accurate, but they provide sufficient detail for those involved in the interaction to understand one another's identities, communicate and react.

Symbolic interactionalism also has at its core a number of assumptions:

- Humans create their own realities, partially through their display of objects and their consumption of selected experiences to provide a basis for communication.
- People use symbols to enable them in interact with each other appropriately and develop a sense of their shared social world.
- People's actions and reactions to others is affected in part by the meaning attached to consumption.
- The meanings ascribed to the consumption of particular objects and experiences is a product of shared social interaction. Thus, meaning is not static but context-specific, although it may have elements which provide continuity across both time and situations.
- Once meaning is attributed it continues to evolve through an interpretivist process of feedback, renegotiation and modification.

Symbolic interactionalism holds "that the self is established, maintained and altered in and through communication" (Stone, 1965), and that this communication can be based on the meanings attached to consumption. It therefore clearly moves beyond perception and interpretation – the cornerstones of the cognitive perspective – and includes the creation of meaning. However, although both the cognitive perspective and symbolic interactionalism give consideration to cultural issues, neither uses them an the foundation of their viewpoints.

The Cultural Perspective

Kaiser (1998), in her consideration of symbolic appearance, advocates that a broader cultural perspective be taken to the interpretation and study of expressiveness. Such a perspective places research against a larger cultural framework that focuses on cultural objects and their relation to belief systems from an interdisciplinary stance. Contributions from a wide range of human sciences – including anthropology, consumer behaviour, cultural studies, psychology, semiotics and sociology – are drawn together.

Any object or experience has the potential to take on cultural symbolism, and this is not necessarily achieved through its production, but through its consumption and the cultural meaning attached to that act. An object or experience can be designed to project a certain meaning, but it is those that consume the product and negotiate its meaning that ultimately infer symbolic value. A product can therefore develop a symbolic value that was never envisaged by its manufacturer. It is also equally likely that symbolic meaning attached to an item may vary across different cultures, as the basic values and belief of different cultures may give rise to different interpretations of meaning. This means that careful consideration of culture and its potential impact on consumption and associated meanings needs to be made.

Before such attention can be given, it would seem appropriate, and perhaps necessary, to define what is meant by culture. This is no easy task, as there are a plethora of meanings attached to, and conceptualizations of, culture.

Jenks (1993) suggests that one possible interpretation of culture that is common amongst sociologists and anthropologists is that "it directs us to a consideration of all that which is symbolic: the learned, ideational aspects of human life" (p. 8). Culture can be seen as a means of helping us derive solutions to the problems of living within a community – to known and familiar problems (such as the interaction needed to buy our daily newspaper), and those which are unknown and unfamiliar (such as the interaction needed to select and arrange our first mortgage). Here, culture provides a framework for both thought and action in any situation, enabling the individual to function by facilitating the interpretation and creation of shared meaning – even within an unfamiliar context.

If this is used as a starting point, it would seem fitting to return to the notion of meaning, its construction and its relationship to culture. MacCannell and MacCannell (1982, cited in Kaiser, 1998) consider that culture, from a semiotic perspective, can be an interplay between an historical memory of meaning and social resistance to this. Here, culture is (re)formed and maintained through the potential tension created by historic meaning and people's potential attempts to redefine and alter those very meanings. This viewpoint therefore not only considers the creation of meaning at that instant – as does symbolic interactionalism – but also enables the consideration of meaning over time, helping to show how it evolves.

An element of the shared meaning that is an integral part of culture is derived from exposure to products, their buying, selling and use. Products become cultural objects that are imbued with meaning by the very way people relate to and use them. This process is called 'signification': where certain products come to represent shared meaning becoming a basic element of the cultural perspective. Other inherent assumptions are:

- Cultural values and belief are often perpetuated on a relatively unconscious level by the meanings attached to products.
- People can create their own realities by manipulating products in their own cultural worlds.
- People use cultural codes to decipher meaning and provide 'rules' for the (re)creation of meaning.

The cultural perspective takes a broader view of expressiveness, placing the creation and deciphering of meaning against a backdrop of cultural values and beliefs.

The Contextual Perspective

Each of the three perspectives outlined above takes as its starting point slightly different assumptions; and the use of each viewpoint as a means of interpreting social expressiveness displayed through consumption may lead to different outcomes. However, the perspectives do not have to be viewed as mutually exclusive, and elements of each are combined in what has been termed a contextual perspective (Kaiser, 1998). Such an approach enables the study of how people manage and perceive consumption in everyday life, whilst paying attention to the social, cultural and historical contexts in which they are located. This approach therefore begins to combine both the micro and macro level issues and levels of analysis considered above.

Conclusions

Even though what is presented in this chapter is only a partial selection of the suggested approaches to consumption and expressiveness, it is apparent that these areas have stimulated, and still continue to stimulate, much debate.

Consumption has increasingly been viewed as having as much, if not more, importance in defining who we are than the 'productive role' that we fulfil. The view that consumption is something that we are 'forced' to engage in as a by-product of a capitalist economy has for many lost some of its currency; and the notion that consumption is a mechanism for self-expression has gained impetus. This perspective, which has developed the concept that we have one concrete and stable self to express, has been challenged by those taking a postmodern view. We are depicted as having multiple self-images that we create, change and manipulate through our consumption patterns.

It is also from this perspective that the role of the retailer in this endeavour to fashion self is brought into distinct consideration. The potential for the retailer to be more than a 'simple provider of products' is highlighted. The retailer is seen as having the potential to deliver an experience that may be more important to self-expression than the product that might be purchased. The ability of the retailer to provide such experiences may become even more important if we are to consider McLarney and Chung's (1999) description of the 'post-materialist' consumer who seeks quality of life and experience over materialism. The role of retail space as a centre for the development of community is also illustrated, and perhaps further supports the concept of our seeking more than the material in all our retail experiences.

Given this, it is important to remember that the retailer, as well as providing an environment and mechanism for consumption, does indeed 'assemble' a merchandise range – or indeed specifies goods that are produced. In doing this, they are even further embedded in the cycle of consumption. The retailer has a wide selection of elements that it can manipulate to create a 'stage' for our own creative act of self-expression. It is the concept of stage and 'theatre' that provides the vehicle for further analysis of the potential role of retailer in staging the drama of consumption.

References

Adorno, T.W. and Horkheimer, M. 1979. *Dialectic of Enlightenment*. London: Verso.

Arnould, E.J. and Price, L.L. 1993. River magic: extraordinary experience and the extended service encounter. *Journal of Consumer Research*, 20 (June), 24–45.

Baudrillard, J. 1983. *In the Shadow of the Silent Majorities*. New York: Semiotext.

Belk, R.W. 1988. Possessions and the Extended Self. *Journal of Consumer Research*, 15 (September), 139–168.

Bocock, R. 1993. *Consumption*. London: Routledge.

Bourdieu, P. 1984. *Distinction: A Social Critique of the Judgement of Taste*, (translated by R. Nice). Cambridge, MA: Harvard University Press.

Brown, S. 1995. *Postmodern Marketing*. London: Routledge.

Campbell, C. 1997. Shopping, pleasure and the sex war. In Falk, P. and Campbell, C. (Eds.). *The Shopping Experience*. London: Sage, pp. 387–414.

Cohen, P. 1980. Subcultural Conflict and Working-Class Community. In Hall, S., Hobson, D., Lowe, A. and Willis, P. (Eds.). *Culture, Media, Language*. London: Hutchinson.

Connor, S. 1992. *Postmodernist Culture*. Oxford: Blackwell.

Costa, J.A. (Ed.). 1994. *Gender Issues and Consumer Behaviour*. London: Sage.

Cova, B. 1997. Community and Consumption: towards a definition of the 'linking value' of products or services. *European Journal of Marketing*, 31(3/4), 297–316.

Cova, B. 1996. The postmodern explained to managers: implications for marketing. *Business Horizons*, 39(6), 15–24.

Davis, F. 1982. On the 'symbolic' in symbolic interaction. *Symbolic Interaction*, 5, 111–126.

Docker, J. 1994. *Postmodernism and Popular Culture*. Cambridge: Cambridge University Press.

du Gay, P., Hall, S., Jones, L., Mackey, H. and Negus, K. 1997. *Doing Cultural Studies: the Story of the Sony Walkman*. London: Sage.

Elliott, R. 1997. Symbolic meaning and postmodern consumer culture. In Bromlie, D. (Eds.). *Rethinking Marketing*. London: Sage.

Elliott, R. and Wattanasuwan, K. 1998. Brands as symbolic resources for the construction of identity. *International Journal of Advertising*, 17(2), 131–144.

Featherstone, M. 1991. *Consumer Culture & Postmodernism*. London: Sage.

Firat, A.F. and Venkatesh, A. 1995. Liberatory postmodernism and the reenchantment of consumption. *Journal of Consumer Research*, 22(3), 239–268.

Firat, F.A. and Shultz, C.J. 1997. From segmentation to fragmentation, markets and marketing strategy in the postmodern era. *European Journal of Marketing*, 31(3/4), 183–207.

Friedberg, A. 1993. *Window Shopping: Cinema and the Postmodern*. Berkley, CA: California University Press.

Gabriel, Y. and Lang, T. 1995. *The Unmanageable Consumer*. London: Sage.

Goodwin, C. 1994. Private roles in public encounters: communal relationships in service exchanges. *Proceedings of the 3rd Seminar International de Recherché en Management des Activities de Services*, La Londe les Maures, pp. 311–333.

Haslop, C., Hill, H. and Schmidt, R. A. 1998. The gay lifestyle – spaces for a subculture of consumption. *Marketing Intelligence & Planning*, 16(5), 318–326.

Hall, S. and Jefferson, T. (Eds.). 1976. *Resistance Through Rituals: Youth Subcultures in Post-War Britain*. London: Hutchinson.

Hebdige, D. 1979. *Subculture: the Meaning of Style*. New York: Routledge.

Hirschman, E.C. and Holbrook, M.B. 1982. Hedonic consumption: emerging concepts, and propositions. *Journal of Marketing*, 46 (Summer), 92–101.

Hopkinson, G.C. and Pujari, D. 1999. A factor analytic study of the sources of meaning in hedonic consumption. *European Journal of Marketing*, 33(3/4), 273–290.

Jameson, F. 1984. *Postmodernism: or the cultural logic of late capitalism*. New Left Review, 146.

Jenks, C. 1993. *Culture*. London: Routledge.

Kaiser, S.B. 1998. *The Social Psychology of Clothing (2nd Ed. Revisited)*. New York: Fairchild Publications.

Kellner, D. 1995. *Media Culture*. London: Routledge.

Lee, M.J. 1993. *Consumer Culture Reborn*. London: Routledge.

MacCannell, D. and MacCannell, J.F. 1982. *The Time of the Sign: A Semiotic Interpretation of Modern Culture*. Bloomington, IN: Indiana University Press.

Malina, D. and Schmidt, R. 1997. It's business doing pleasure with you: Sh! A women's sex shop case. *Marketing Intelligence & Planning*, 15(7), 352–360.

Marcuse, H. 1968. *One Dimensional Man*. London: Sphere.

McCall, G.J. and Simmons, J.L. 1966. *Identities and Interaction*. New York, NY: Free Press.

McCracken, G. 1990. *Culture and Consumption*. Bloomington, IN: Indiana University Press.

McLarney, C. and Chung, E. 1999. Post-materialism's "silent revolution" in consumer research. *Marketing Intelligence and Planning*, 17(6), 288–297.

Miles, S. 1998. *Consumerism – as a way of life*. London: Sage.

Pine, B.J. and Gilmore, J.H. 1998. Welcome to the experience economy. *Harvard Business Review*, July–August, 97–105.

Rajchman, J. 1987. Postmodernism in a Nominalist Frame: The Emergence and Diffusion of a Cultural Category. *Flash Art*, 137.

Schmidt, R., Sturrock, F., Ward, P. and Lea-Greenwood, G. 1999. Deshopping – the art of illicit consumption. *International Journal of Retail and Distribution Management*, 27(8), 290–301.

Shields, R. (Ed.). 1992. *Lifestyle Shopping: the subject of consumption*. London: Routledge.

Stone, G.P. 1965. Appearance and the self. In Roach, M.E. and Eicher, J.B. (Eds.). *Dress, Adornment, and the Social Order*. New York: John Wiley and Sons, pp. 216–245.

Storey, J. 1999. *Cultural Consumption and Everyday Life*. London: Arnold.

Willis, P. 1978. *Profane Cultures*. London: Routledge and Kegan Paul.

Part 2

Management of the Arena of Retail Consumption

5

A DRAMATURGICAL VIEW – ELEMENTS OF THE DRAMA: A QUESTION OF PERSPECTIVE

The 'creative' elements of retailing are further explored in this chapter, but using dramaturgy – the explicit and formalized study of plays, dramatic composition and the dramatic art. Dramaturgy is used as a theory that interprets individual behaviour as the dramatic projection of the chosen self.

The chapter begins to draw together some of the themes and topics introduced in the preceding chapters by applying this theory; it also facilitates an operational approach that starts to address and explore the processes of retail-based interaction and the management tasks concerned with that interaction.

This chapter focuses on issues including:
- The theatre metaphor;
- Text and discourse;
- Character and actor;
- Aesthetic questions; and
- Staging.

Introduction

This chapter uses the theatre as a metaphor for retailing – applying a deliberate, constructed device to that arena. Such 'constructed' metaphors however, are typically restricted in scope because as a literary device, the metaphor is often limited to only a single facet of the resembled or comparative entity – for example "if you describe Oxford as a hive of Industry" (Knox,

1999, p. 1756). Such a use is also more or less 'isomorphic', in that it only compares one facet of an object with one aspect of another.

However, this chapter seeks to go beyond the surface level that such a simple application of the theatre metaphor can provide. It considers in more depth concepts drawn from the academic analysis of theatre, its techniques and historical development.

So, What Is A Metaphor?

The metaphor has been described as one of the most powerful and creative devices in language (Crystal, 1997). Partridge (1965) says that "Aristotle in The Poetics went so far as to declare that 'the greatest thing by far is to have command of the metaphor'", and added that "to employ metaphors happily and effectively" it was necessary to have "an eye for resemblances" (p. 184).

The power of the metaphor has led some to debate whether language is itself essentially metaphorical, or whether metaphor is simply an additional ornament. Fowler (1930) wrote that virtually all words "can be traced back to something physical". As such, each word may be seen as some kind of 'natural' metaphor – or as having acquired meaning through the processes of 'metonymy': "in which one thing is replaced by another associated with it, such as 'the Crown' for 'the Queen'" (Collins Gem English Dictionary, 2000, p. 347). However, metaphor is now described by linguists as a core constituent of the manner in which we not only use language to *tell* of our world, but also as fundamental to the ways in which we *interpret* it.

Not only do we understand the world in terms of such conceptual metaphors, but the building blocks – or 'experience essences' – that make up this world can also be described as metaphoric. Such 'essences' are also shaped by their cultural context, both philosophically and historically, and are neither fixed nor eternal, as they undergo continual modification as a result of negotiation and adaptation as the context itself changes (Leddy, 1995). This can be seen in various marketing literatures, where the use of metaphor has been employed for some considerable time. These metaphors have undergone considerable evolution: changing both in nature, and, at times, in the level of their complexity.

The Use of Extended Metaphor in Marketing

In her paper, *A review of the marriage analogue in relationship marketing*, Tynan (1997) uses metaphor as a basis. As well as using the word analogue in the title, there is an extended discussion of the mapping of the terms in one area to the other. The use of these various mappings does, at one level, go beyond the use of a single like-for-like comparison, by using a somewhat multi-layered approach. For example, the article seeks to categorize various business relationships as monogamous, polygamous or adulterous.

This is an extension of the simple 'relationship marketing is marriage' device. The varied nature of marital forms and practices are considered, and the potential of each to provide a mechanism of comparison is developed.

There have been other attempts to use a multi-layered approach to the use of metaphor in marketing. In their contribution to Marketing Apocalypse McDonagh and Protheroe (1996) present a play, and then describe a single element of it as "an analogy" – but there is no explicit recognition that the overall exercise represents some sort of extended metaphor. However, the piece does again begin to go beyond simple literary device, and attempts to use the power of metaphor in a richer and more developed manner. This approach of extending the various points at which metaphor is applied can also be seen in the use of theatre in the study of retailing.

The Metaphor of Theatre in Retailing

When considering the metaphor of retailing and the theatre, there are various elements that provide a basis – cast, script, props, audience – placing a clear emphasis on the physical environment and actors involved in service exchange (Grove and Fisk, 1983). If we wish to better understand retailing by considering the nature of theatre, we must move further than the simple application of certain borrowed terms, more formally considering the processes, structures and concepts underlying this extended usage of theatrical terms.

Thinking of the process as one of 'transappropriation' of terms provides an initial starting point. Such an approach shows that attention needs to be directed to the core concepts involved in the consideration of theatre. Pavis (1998) provides a thematic index to theatre: placing terms in their conceptual context, based on type of approach or critical field. By doing this, he provides a list of 'headwords' that includes:

- Dramaturgy;
- Text and discourse;
- Actor and character;
- Genres and forms;
- Aesthetic questions; and
- Staging.

The established vocabulary of those writing about service delivery and retailing does not cover as broad a range of concepts as provided by Pavis.

Although there is the use of terms such as 'impression management', there is much less explicit consideration of genres and forms, or of text and discourse. In the retail literature, the focus is more on the 'physicality' of provision. However, there is some move away from this in the discussion of experience. MacCannell (1973) talks of staging authentic experience, and Celsi et al. (1993) extend the metaphor still further by discussing dramatic consumption – suggesting that it is not only the service provider and customer roles that can be viewed from a dramaturgical perspective, but also the way in which the service is consumed. Celsi et al., in fact go so far as to suggest that "in our Western Society the dramatic framework is a fundamental lens through which individuals frame their perceptions, seek their self-identities and engage in vicarious or actual behaviours" (p. 2).

Given that drama (or theatre) is an important lens for viewing the way we live, we need to consider the concerns raised by Van den Bulte (1994). The first of these is the need to pay serious attention to the incomplete or misleading nature of metaphor. The second is to offset strengths and weaknesses of one metaphor against another. Within this chapter only the metaphor of the theatre is used. However, in an attempt to address the first of Van den Bulte's concerns, the chapter acknowledges many of the elements of the theatre outlined by Pavis and therefore, the following discussion is structured around the themes he identifies.

The first of these is dramaturgy – the dramatic art – which provides a broad framework for consideration of the theatre and, by inference, retailing.

Dramaturgy

The playwright Bertolt Brecht expounded the notions of 'dramatic' and 'epic' theatre by characterizing theatre in relation to its role in society. 'Dramatic' theatre attempts to stage a performance that mirrors 'reality' and is naturalistic – so that the audience is swept up by the action of the play – concerning itself with the interaction between characters within a simple linear story. However, in 'epic' theatre, the aim is to provide a critique of society. Hence, the performance seeks audience interaction through theatrical devices, such as commentators and narrators, which create a non-linear experience that stimulates a critical response. In this form, the actor 'shows' character, but does not seek to embody it.

Given the use of the theatre metaphor within retailing, it is important to consider which particular conceptualization is appropriate. In doing this, there is a move towards a fuller comparison of the two elements and away from the simplistic use of the theatre metaphor as a basis for 'fun' and 'entertainment' within the retail context.

The potential of the dramatic theatre parallel is seen in the following example. Electrical retailer Comet describes going into one of its megastores as "like being in Disneyland...". The aim is that the store design, staff uniforms and training serve to emphasize that the customer has entered a 'theatrical' arena, where the staging is conscious and the trajectory of the plot leads to a resolution of purchase followed by satisfaction. The reality may be very different – and the experience is in fact nothing like being in Disneyland! In the store the environment *is* staged, but it fails to engage the audience as Disneyland might. The customers (the audience) are not 'swept-up' in the performance. The Disneyland analogy fails and therefore, the underlying theatrical metaphor needs more careful examination. Such examination is however difficult to achieve.

Goodwin (1996), in her thoughtful article on services marketing, argues solely from a 'dramatic' theatre perspective. However, such a simple acceptance of the dramatic form of the theatre is uncritical and looks purely at the surface. Attention also needs to be focused on the 'epic' notion of the theatrical form.

A full consideration of the dramaturgical aspects of the theatre metaphor requires that retailers consider:

- Spectacle and narrative;
- Commentary and interaction; and
- Critique and acceptance.

Both epic and dramatic forms are required. In contrast to the dramatic attempts of the Comet store, the epic retailer of hi-fi would emphasize the store and its non-domestic nature; make clear the difference in performance; provide unedited external criticism of products, and draw attention to the external non-theatrical parameters that the purchasers should consider. The retailer would be distanced from their merchandise, acknowledging the existence of the customer's external world. A visit to such a store may not be considered theatrical in the everyday sense, but would be clearly 'epic' in relation to Brecht's ideas. By including both theatrical conceptions we begin to widen the possibilities of the theatrical metaphor within retailing.

Text and Discourse

These possibilities can be further developed by considering one of the central elements of much theatre – the word and its performance. The traditional, rooted conception of the play has been to focus on the play purely as text. This was described by Pavis as "theatre [being] imprisoned within a logocentric conception" (1998, p. 384). This longstanding tradition has been challenged in the modern era: as the *performance* of these words also became a focus of attention. Such a focus on what, in theatrical terms, is know as 'staging', represents a considerable shift of emphasis.

This modern conception of theatre as both text *and* performance has tended to provide the frame of reference for academics in the retailing and services literature, with both writers and commentators relying on the simple notion of 'text' as incorporating both aspects – turning 'script into performance' (Hornby, 1977). This is clearly seen in Zemke's (1993) comment that "The trainer's role... is to prepare the cast to know their cues, hit their marks, deliver their lines and improvise when another cast member (or someone in the audience) disrupts the *carefully plotted flow of the performance*" (emphasis added) (p. 41). The implication is that there is one simple path that performance must take.

However, theatre studies (dramaturgy) has subsequently moved beyond this straightforward structuralist application of semiology – of signs and symbols – to the narrative (or narratives) of the performance. This movement away from a conception of the play (or retail story) as having only one carefully-plotted direction, is not, however reflected in the use of the drama metaphor within retailing. In providing text-and-performance for retail employees, the emphasis (in the light of this contemporary dramaturgical interpretation) has to be on intention and corporate direction. The purpose, in fact, is not to search for the elimination of gaps and inconsistencies, but to provide a direction for employees to follow whilst giving them scope for improvisation. This begins to introduce the importance of the actor to performance and the interpretation of the retail play and its plot.

Actor and Character

'Actor and character' present the surface structure of the play. They are connected through the working of the plot. Each of the play's surface elements is underpinned by a deeper or discursive structure. As such, the actor is a fundamental conduit through which both surface and deeper elements are presented and intertwined. Actors 'play out' the characteristics associated with more fundamental human qualities: love, courage, evil. These qualities are 'embodied' in the characters. The actors and their characters are the manifestation of these figurative qualities. The plot is a working-out of the action implied by the interplay of these fundamental qualities through the logic of their development.

Thus in Romeo and Juliet, the star-crossed lovers represent romantic love as a quality. Their interaction follows a trajectory in the plot that we would expect from an understanding of the impetuous actions of young love. Their

Table 5.1 Nordstrom rules[a]

Welcome to Nordstrom	Nordstrom rules
We're glad to have you with our Company	Rule#1: Use your good judgement in all situations
Our number one goal is to provide outstanding customer service	There will be no additional rules
Set both your personal and professional goals high	Please feel free to ask your department manager, store manager, or division general manager any question at any time
We have great confidence in your ability to achieve them	

[a] Source: Zeithaml and Bitner (1996, p. 319).

families may be said to represent duty and family obligation and the antipathy that this might generate. These concepts, that may be seen to drive the action of the play, do not constitute a 'statement of the plot'. They are however as much part of our understanding of the play and its meaning as the plot. To work this deeper understanding from the theatre metaphor back into retailing requires a more careful transposition than is often attempted.

Using Nordstrom as an example, the employee 'actors', in their performance, all seek to represent the same underlying quality – that of common sense and 'hospitableness'. This is the overall trajectory of the Nordstrom plot, which is clearly demonstrated in the employee handbook – and action, which underlies plot, is stipulated as good judgement (see Table 5.1).

The language often used to describe situations such as that of Nordstrom frequently abandons the theatre metaphor. Particularly within the services literature, the term 'empowerment' is often used for such behaviour (see for example, Rust et al., 1996; and Lovelock et al., 1999). The use of the word empowerment suggests that power is somehow being given to the employee. This is emphatically not the case. What in fact is being done is the removal of *de-powering* and debilitating constraints.

This network of constraints, or rules may sometimes constitute the only text (or script) given to employees. Even where the script is more formally given, it is usually presented as something again *within* which employees must work (so itself is a constraint). The trouble here is that what is lacking is often an indication of the fundamental qualities and entities that need to be represented to customers.

On top of this, there is a further problem – which is bound up with the fundamental qualities to be portrayed – in that the employee (or actor) is not provided with the context or genre these fundamental qualities should be delivered in. Without an understanding of both context and qualities, there is limited direction for the actor (employee) to deliver an appropriate performance. This can best perhaps be explained by the following illustration.

One of the fundamental qualities present in many forms of theatre is heroism. This finds its expression through the concept of 'hero', embodied in a particular character. The nature of the character and the way that the heroic character acts is bounded by the context of the genre in which they are located. The actions and character of the heroic character in a pantomime are in many ways distinct from those of the heroic character in Shakespearean drama – Jack (and the beanstalk) versus Henry V, for example – although the underlying concept that is being represented is the same. In both contexts, the nature of the genre also impacts the relationships portrayed, the nature of the actions staged, and the operation of the role.

If the retail environment is considered, then service orientation finds its expression through the service provider, which is embodied in a character such as that of service operative. Here, again, the retail context will impact the delivery and actions undertaken. The context of the fast-food restaurant leading the performance in a clear direction towards speed, simplicity and courtesy – compared to that of the up-market ladies apparel store directing the performance of the same character to involvement, discretion and attentiveness. It is only by understanding what is required completely as an actor that the appropriate performance can be rendered.

Within the study of theatre, these relationships between context, character and actor are explored in the 'actantial model' (Pavis, 1998). An adapted version of the actantial model is depicted in Table 5.2. It considers the dialectics between character and action, and the transition of one to the other. Additionally, there is consideration of the overarching mechanisms through which these transformations take place by examining the 'levels of existence' that are present.

When looking at the model, Levels I and II constitute 'deep structure' – the underlying thrust (the performance and its interpretation) – and are the responsibility of management. This deep structure relates to the vision and direction supplied by the organization and its management. Without this clear context and path, it is highly unlikely that employees have the necessary framework within which to develop appropriate performances. These performances are embodied by Levels III and IV, which bring together both text and staging and in so doing, focus on the part to be played by the actor. It is instructive that the position of role within the model bridges deep and surface structure: implying that role is in fact created through the interplay of levels – or partnership between elements in the theatre – and it is not solely in the domain of performance.

Table 5.2 The actantial model[a]

	System of character	Level of existence	Level of action
			Surface structure
Level IV: Manifest structure (performance)	Actor (player)	Relations between perceptible characters	Character perceptible through actor
Level III: Discursive structure (text)	Character in the play ⌐	Motifs, themes	Plot
	Roles └		*Deep structure*
Level II: Deep structure Narrative	Actants (fundamental qualities)	Narrative	Action
Level I: Logic	Logical operators	Elementary structures of meaning	Logical mode of action

[a] Source: adapted from Pavis (1998).

By using the actantial approach, it is clear that simply to apply the term actor to an employee is an extensive oversimplification. There is rather a complex mesh of action and meaning – and therefore, by implication, performance. For a retailer to fully contemplate what it is that it wants its staff to deliver to the customer, attention must be paid to each element within the actantial model and the context profile by differences in retail generics.

Genres and Forms

Within the theatrical context, the concept of genre can be interpreted in two ways – a typology of forms, or a typology of discourse (Pavis, 1998). The first relates to historical attempts to classify works based on a range of criteria that relate to intrinsic similarities or differences between genres, e.g. (simplistically) tragedy or comedy. Other types of genre within such typologies might be thriller, romance, farce. Each type has features in common, relating to the subject matter (e.g. criminal activity) or to audience reaction (e.g. laughter). This is perhaps the most common usage of the word genre – to describe the 'pigeonhole' into which a work may be classified. The weakness of this approach to genre is that the individual 'pigeonholes' are determined by reference to what is within the work. Apart from the simplest of divisions, there is no real sense of the underlying dimensions that could be used for classification. Thus, comedy and tragedy could be interpreted as an opposing pair, but thriller does not stand in opposition to any other single form.

Within retailing classification, retail form (or genre) is also a major issue. Classificatory schemes proposed might rest on features such as merchandise type, size of store, type of location, customer segment served. The weakness of such schemes is that they have been developed to determine a pigeonhole or category in respect to some narrow aspect of the operation or offer – for example, out-of-town and in-town. This leads to a situation where there is no uniform and consistent classification scheme in place. Were such a scheme in place, then it would be possible to classify new retail offerings as they arose, and indeed identify pigeonholes that are empty.

The second uniform and consistent classification scheme is a structural approach that is concerned with developing a universal typology. Such schemes incorporate existing retail forms or genres, whilst allowing for genres that do not yet exist but are theoretically possible. This type of method is the second form of approach identified by Pavis that represents a consistent effort within current theatrical analysis. There is no such consistent attempt or concern to develop a typology of genre or form within the study of retailing.

The identification of a *particular* instance of a retailing format with a general type is less difficult within the study of retailing. Retail management is often able to specify a format in terms of what it 'is' – for example, department store, power centre, and category killer. In this situation, a set of beliefs about what is effective and appropriate within the category or genre may be available. Here though, retail management has the same difficulty as a playwright who knows the rules of writing farce, but is unable to transfer the knowledge to another genre, such as tragedy. The diversity of classificatory dimensions serves to limit the effective transfer of knowledge skills and concepts across genres. For effective skills transfer to take place, the important contingent dimensions within a uniform classification scheme need to be understood. For instance: why has it been difficult for B&Q, a successful UK-based DIY retailer, to apply its knowledge and skills to the management of the UK variety store, Woolworth?

The conceptual difficulty in developing a regular classificatory scheme is one that has not been grasped by academics or practitioners in the field of retailing. There are useful rules of thumb for specifying types that work well enough in very narrow contexts. Similarly, there has been a reluctance to engage with other areas of the retail experience where the challenge of developing an appropriate language and framework is also great. The way 'stores look' and 'why they look good' is another such area.

Aesthetic Questions

Aesthetics is both the science of the beautiful and the philosophy of art. In seeking to be a philosophy or theory, aesthetics defines the criteria on which a work of art should be judged. Theatrical aesthetics can be subdivided into the two areas: production and reception.

> [Production aesthetics] lists the factors that explain how the text is formed (historical, ideological, and generic determinants) and how the stage functions (material working conditions, conditions of performance, acting techniques)…
> …the aesthetics of reception [examines] the spectator's point of view and the factors that have determined his or her correct or incorrect reception, the cultural and ideological horizon of expectations, the series of works preceding this text and performance, the mode of perception (distanced or emotional), the relationship between the fictitious world and the real worlds of the period represented and the spectator.
>
> Pavis, 1998, p. 16

In retailing, there needs to be a consideration of how 'visible' the production aesthetics should be. How obvious should the 'mechanics of theatre' be?

Is the retail space to be obviously 'designed', or the selection of the merchandise assortment appear contrived?

What is difficult for retailers to consider in production aesthetics are those antecedents that underlie the text of the store. Should these antecedents – history, ideology and belief – be made explicit for customers to see? For example, the Harrods food-hall makes an evident play on its past through its decoration, subdivision of space and visual cues. Here, the aesthetics of production are projected into the realm of reception. In contrast, Austin Reed, another long-established British retailer, no longer projects its history and ideology into the realm of reception within its stores. Such choices are conscious decisions regarding production aesthetics on the retailers' part.

However, when making these production decisions, retailers must consider the reception aesthetic of their intended audience, and those factors that affect it. If those that are reading the text (visiting the store) do not have the historical and ideological background that parallels that of the text (store), then they simply rely on a 'literal' reading of what is presented, or devise their own interpretation drawn from their own experiences. To return to the Austin Reed example: envisage a non-British customer who has no concept that this is in fact a well-established clothing retailer and longstanding firm. When entering the store they are presented with cues that generate an image of the retailer as 'modern', and without examining the merchandise, could be as likely to infer that it simply sells jeans.

If, therefore, the theatre metaphor is pursued, the retailer needs to consider explicitly how issues around both production and reception aesthetics are to be incorporated into management decisions. This necessitates that retail managers understand how their text has been generated, and how it is to be read.

Staging

The pattern of development in staging has undergone many characterizations. Each of these, though, has concerned the interplay between text and stage. In contemporary situations, there is the need to consider text, subtext and staging. In the retail sphere, there is a need to consider not only the interplay between store design, visual merchandising and sales-staff scripts, but also the overall composition and trajectory of the drama.

At one extreme it may be sufficient for a retail operator to provide one staging and text, which are not subject to interplay. McDonalds provides an example of such an operation. The customer enters a closely controlled staging with staff working to a tight script to achieve performance effects that are narrowly defined. There is no emphasis on text and intertextual under-standing, or on interplay, and it simply 'tells it as it is'. There is nothing hidden – what is experienced is what is presented ('what you see is what you get') with no subtext or room for differing interpretations.

At the other extreme (or corner, vertex, or apex, as the continuum may not be linear), there are retailers such as Hobbs or Borders, who introduce addi-tional levels of complexity into their staging. They use elements drawn from a domestic or hotel environment to provide areas for creating different forms of interaction. These may not necessarily be merchandise-related, but rather add to the theatricality of the environment. The store visit then becomes an event. The staging created gives rise to what has been termed a 'third space' (Oldenburg, 1989), or a "joint creation of a new service encounter – a... play-space" (Malina and Schmidt, 1997, p. 359).

The concept of space is of particular importance within the context of staging. The very notion of theatre relies on space marked by the division of the gaze (spectator) and its object (the stage). In its simplest form, theatre requires a division into two spaces. The performance on stage is itself supported by the third area, on which the gaze (conventionally) does not fall. This 'backstage' or 'back-of-house' is a location where 'cast and crew' can develop and resource the intended performance. Within the theatre meta-phor, the fourth broad area of space is 'front-of-house'. This is the location where the transformation of passer-by into spectator occurs. The precise forms of these four spaces – and of the distinctions between them are not fixed. The classical western picture may be of the Italian proscenium arch theatre design, but this is only one form of the tradition: any institutionalized space for voyeurism is a theatre.

Conclusions

The metaphor of theatre in retailing provides a much richer and deeper basis for exploration than has currently been applied by many writers. It would seem that the retailing and service literatures have displayed a relatively one-dimensional approach to the use of the device. This is, however, not surpris-ing: as with any area of concern, there is always a period of development and increasing sophistication. One example of such increasing depth of applica-tion is displayed by Malina and Schmidt (1997), who attempt to combine the theatrical metaphor with established perspectives on service – in this parti-cular instance, that of the Servuction model. The model that they develop is displayed in Table 5.3.

Their focus is clearly on the interaction between staff and customers, and on the support mechanisms needed to facilitate what the customer experi-

Table 5.3 A drama perspective of the Servuction system[a]

Backstage	Frontstage
Actors	Actors
Auditioning	Test new performances
Selecting	Document performances
Training	Critique performances
Rehearsals	
Team development	
Tangible evidence	Audience
Design	Select
Evaluation	Train
	Encourage audience participation
	Encourage customer-customer interaction
	Evaluate customer-customer interaction
Planning for new customers	
Market research	
Scripting	
Interaction with suppliers	Tangible evidence
Product development	Experiment with new service-setting designs
Back-up systems	Evaluate degree of consistency/congruity of overall cognitive message
Strategy formation	Evaluate customer interaction with service setting

Bundle of service benefits

[a] Malina and Schmidt (1997, p. 355) (adapted from Langeard et al., 1981 and Fisk and Grove, 1995).

ences. In doing this there is a clear attempt to consider a range of operational issues that benefit from, and are intuitively allied with, the theatrical.

It is perhaps interesting that in the writing and terms developed by Pavis in relation to theatrical studies, there is very little of the operational. He does not consider these issues alongside the more conceptual elements of theatrical analysis. Yet, within the services and retailing literature, it is exactly these operational issues that have been used to extend the theatrical metaphor. However, if the theatre metaphor is applied at a deeper level, there is considerable potential to extend beyond such an application. The theatre metaphor provides the potential to span not only the operational, but also issues related to retail strategy and corporate mission – those fundamental qualities that the retailer is seeking to express.

In doing this, there is a further step to incorporate the theatrical metaphor into those elements of retailing that lie beyond what the customer can directly see, but are no less important in shaping and creating the experience that they have. To fully consider the potential of the theatrical, it is necessary to fully understand all the aspects of the retail context that can affect the customer's perception of the offer with which they are presented. To do this, it is useful to develop a fuller understanding of the 'parts' played by various elements in retail theatre, and to facilitate such an appreciation the Servuction model applied by Malina and Schmidt provides a useful starting point.

References

Celsi, R., Rose, R.L. and Leigh, T.W. 1993. An exploration of high-risk leisure consumption through skydiving. *Journal of Consumer Research*, 20 (June), 1–23.

Collins Gem English Dictionary. 2000. London: HarperCollins Publishers.

Crystal, D. 1997. *The Cambridge Encyclopedia of Language (2nd Ed.).* New York: Cambridge University Press.

Fisk, R.P. and Grove, S.J. 1995. Service performance as drama: quality implications and measurement. In Kunst, P. and Lemmink, J. (Eds.). *Managing Service Quality, Vols. I and II.* London: Paul Chapman Publishing.

Fowler, H.G. and F.G. 1930. *The King's English (3rd Ed.).* London: Oxford University Press.

Goodwin, C. 1996. Moving the drama into the factory: the contribution of metaphors to services research. *European Journal of Marketing*, 30(9), 13–36.

Grove, S.J. and Fisk, R.P. 1983. The dramaturgy of services exchange: an analytical framework for services marketing. In Berry, L.L., Shostack, G.L. and Upah, G.D. (Eds.). *Emerging Perspectives on Services Marketing.* Chicago, IL: American Marketing Association, pp. 45–49.

Hornby, R. 1977. *Script Into Performance: a Structuralist View of Play Production.* Austin, TX: University of Texas Press.

Knox, R.A. 1999. *In The New Shorter Oxford English Dictionary (4th Ed.).* Oxford: Oxford University Press.

Langeard, E., Bateson, J., Lovelock, C. and Eiglier, P. 1981. *Marketing of Services: New Insights From Consumers and Managers.* Cambridge, MA: Marketing Science Institute.

Leddy, T. 1995. Metaphor and metaphysics. *Metaphor and Symbolic Activity*, 10(3).

Lovelock, C., Vandermerwe, S. and Lewis, B. 1999. *Services Marketing: A European Perspective.* Upper Saddle River, NJ: Prentice Hall Inc.

MacCannell, D. 1973. Staged authenticity: arrangements of social space in tourist settings. *American Journal of Sociology*, 79(3), 589603.

Malina, D. and Schmidt, R. 1997. It's business doing pleasure with you: Sh! A women's sex shop case. *Marketing Intelligence and Planning*, 15(7), 352–360.

McDonagh, P. and Protheroe, A. 1996. Making a drama out of a crisis: the final curtain for the marketing concept. In Brown, S., Bell, J. and Carson, D. (Eds.). *Marketing Apocalypse.* London: Routledge.

Oldenburg, R. 1989. *The Great Good Place.* London: Paragon.

Partridge, E. 1965. Usage and Abusage (6th Ed.). London: Hamish Hamilton.

Pavis, P. 1998. *Dictionary of the Theatre: Terms, Concepts and Analysis.* (Trans by C. Shantz) Toronto: University of Toronto Press Incorporated.

6

THE SERVUCTION MODEL AND ITS EXTENSIONS

This chapter introduces the Servuction model and its extensions. This model provides a conceptualization of retail interaction that focuses structure and content by considering the service experience from the customer's viewpoint. By applying this perspective, the line of visibility, dividing the world of the retailer into backstage and front-of-house concerns, is created; as is the notion of a bundle of benefits being extracted by individual users as an outcome.

The emphasis is placed on front-of-house as an arena for retail exchange and theatre and the elements that constitute front-of-house are explored:

- The inanimate environment and the concept of 'servicescapes';
- The importance of both service personnel and other customers;
- The continuing impact of technology; and
- The potential for the customer's mood and time availability to influence their 'reading' of the retail experience is highlighted.

Introduction

The previous chapter focused on the process elements of the retail drama: plot, direction and improvisation. This chapter introduces the Servuction model, which provides a clear description of the structural and content elements of the retail arena. In a sense, process elements are present, but they are reduced to mere schematic representations. The model itself is designed to encompass most forms of service encounter where the customer visits the service provider's facility. Store-based retailing is one major type of such provision.

Before the Servuction model is discussed, it is useful to place it in an historical context – to consider the development of the academic environment and concerns that helped generate its conception.

The Development of the Servuction Model – a Brief Historical Context

Services marketing developed steadily from the 1960s onwards, but its growth accelerated in the mid-1980s. The impetus for its growth derived from dissatisfaction with the dominant marketing conceptualizations of the time. This was reinforced by the increasing dominance of services within developed economies. Two of the chief strands in this development were the extension of the 'classic' marketing mix (Table 6.1), and the development of conceptual frameworks for the analysis of the service arena and the activities within it: e.g. Fisk et al. (1993).

The Marketing Mix and its Origins

As with any area of enquiry and endeavour, the development of underlying paradigms that "consist of values and procedures that control our thinking and behaviour" (Gummesson, 1994, p. 77) is central to the provision of a platform for organizing thoughts and actions. This is no different in either of the spheres of marketing research or practice. In these contexts, the marketing mix has provided an important point of departure for research, and has acted as a means of marshalling its application in business.

The traditionally-accepted paradigm of the marketing mix was introduced by Neil Borden during an address to the American Marketing Association in 1953, although he claimed to have been using the term in his work and teaching since 1949 (Borden, 1964). The concept he proposed was however, based on the idea of the business executive as a 'mixer of ingredients' constructed by James Culliton in an earlier work (van Waterschoot and Van den Bulte, 1992). A number of early writers further developed the notion of the marketing mix to provide a systematic conceptualization (Frey, 1961; Howard, 1957; Lazer and Kelly, 1962; McCarthy, 1960).

However, the marketing mix eventually became synonymous with – and is now embodied by – the 'Four Ps' (product, place, price and promotion) that McCarthy (1960) generated. His classification assumed a dominating – and somewhat unchallenged – position as a cornerstone of marketing within any context (Grönroos, 1997). In doing so, the mix replaced other conceptualiza-

Table 6.1 Elements of the marketing mix of manufacturers (Source: Borden, 1964, p. 3).

1	Product planning – policies and procedures relating to:	a b c	Product lines to be offered – qualities, design, etc. Markets to sell – whom, where, when and in what quantity New product policy – research and development program
2	Pricing – policies and procedures relating to:	a b c d	Price level to adopt Specific prices to adopt – odd-even etc. Price policy – one price or varying price, price maintenance, use of list prices etc. Margins to adopt – for company, for trade
3	Branding – policies and procedures relating to:	a b c	Selection of trade marks Brand policy – individualized or family brand Sale under private label or unbranded
4	Channels of distribution	a b c	Channels to use between plant and consumer Degree of selectivity among wholesalers and retailers Efforts to gain cooperation of trade
5	Personal selling – policies and procedures relating to:	a	Burden to be placed on personal selling and the methods to be employed in: 1. Manufacturer's organization 2. Wholesale segment of the trade 3. Retail segment of the trade
6	Advertising – policies and procedures relating to:	a b c	Amount to spend – i.e. the burden to be placed on advertising Copy platform to adopt 1. Product image desired 2. Corporate image desired Mix of advertising – to the trade, through the trade, to consumers
7	Promotions – policies and procedures relating to:	a b	Burden to place on special selling plans or devices directed at or through the trade Form of these devices for consumer promotions, for trade promotions
8	Packaging – policies and procedures relating to:	a	Formulation of package and label
9	Display – policies and procedures relating to:	a b	Burden to be put on display to help effect sale Methods to adopt to secure display
10	Servicing – policies and procedures relating to:	a	Providing service needed
11	Physical handling – policies and procedures relating to:	a b c	Warehousing Transportation Inventories
12	Fact finding and analysis – policies and procedures relating to:	a	Securing analysis, and the use of facts in marketing operations

tions and approaches to marketing that have passed into marketing's pre-history, and are almost forgotten by many texts: for example, systems theory (Fisk and Dixon, 1967) and institutional approaches (Duddy and Revzan, 1947).

Problems with the Marketing Mix

The rise of the marketing mix approach, and its acceptance by both academics and practitioners alike, focused attention on the management of a narrowly-defined set of elements, which, although perhaps offering a credible and operationally-sound basis for those producing packaged consumer goods, became limiting and even inappropriate to those engaged in other areas of business activity – for instance, retailing and industrial markets – where issues related to service are perhaps more central.

The marketing mix inadequately addresses a number of issues so making its application problematic in business areas that rely heavily on personal contact between provider and customer. The Four Ps focus attention on four intuitively pleasing – if not entirely conceptually distinct – elements (van Waterschoot and Van den Bulte, 1992), making it appear that marketing is an easily delineated task. This, in turn, has led to the suggestion that market-ing then becomes a clearly separate function that is the remit of the 'market-ing specialist', who bears responsibility for the management of the marketing mix elements and, by implication, controls these elements that also constitute the customer interface (Grönroos, 1997).

This 'Four Ps' interpretation of the marketing mix as the mainstay of custo-mer interface management is severely limiting. These limitations stem from the parsimony of this version of the mix and the lack of explicit consideration of the interrelationships between the mix elements. These limitations can in fact, be demonstrated at a number of levels. The lack of integration applies to all of those variables that underlie the mix elements; the elements themselves, and the wider concept of marketing within the organization.

These problems have led to various revisions and modifications of the Four Ps framework. Vignali and Davies' (1994) work has sought to strengthen the consideration given to achieving a cohesive and integrated mix. It focuses on developing a 'mix mapping' approach, which identifies the position of each component or 'variable' within each mix element. They advocate that the relative placements of each variable map onto the overall position desired for the factor. This is achieved through the use of a matrix approach. The aim is to provide a managerially-useful heuristic device. This enables managers to consider each factor of the mix in a more comprehensive manner. Vignali and Davies have concentrated on refining the elements or 'factors' of the mix to provide a more detailed set of concerns for marketing management. The extension to the mix elements that they provide is to add people and service. However, despite its more integrated stance, their work does not address a number of operational issues that lie beyond the Four Ps, and that are key to service-based organizations e.g. service delivery processes.

As Rafiq and Ahmed (1995) show, others have added additional Ps from time to time, ranging from packaging to power. These additional factors have been largely *ad hoc*; and, although providing further material for managers to consider, have never coalesced in a substantive form to provide as popular a model as the Four Ps framework. There is one notable exception – the Seven Ps approach proposed by Booms and Bitner (1981). This influential idea was intended to apply specifically to services.

Rafiq and Ahmed (1995) demonstrate that there is general support for the extended framework. Each of the additional Ps – participants (people), physical evidence and process – however, engenders support in different measure. Rafiq and Ahmed conclude that the Seven Ps framework should replace the Four Ps as the 'generic marketing mix' (p. 14).

In providing their extended services marketing mix, Booms and Bitner (1981) made a major contribution to the continuing development of services marketing thought (see Table 6.2).

The Growth of Services Marketing

The development of services marketing as an academic topic first began to appear as a distinctive area of study in the 1960s (Fisk et al., 1993). This emergence was only partly fuelled by the lack of appropriateness in the more traditional marketing literature. It was also stimulated by the growing service economy (Bateson, 1995), which began clearly to require further consideration of its specific issues and concerns.

This growth in interest was centred in North America and in Northern Europe (Grönroos, 1997). Early work in the area focused on discussions of whether or not there were any significant differences attached to service-based organizations that necessitated a distinct body of literature. Shostack (1977) forcibly presented the case that a broader view was needed, and that concepts that included management of the service environment were required. Her proposition parallels the work of researchers in the Nordic School (Grönroos and Gummesson, 1985), who highlighted the need to reconsider marketing as an element in itself that cannot be separated from overall management. It is interesting to note that the development of such perspectives begins to recapture elements of the early conceptualization of marketing that lost out to the marketing mix paradigm.

Table 6.2 Extended mix

Product	Price	Place	Promotion	People	Physical evidence	Process
Range	Level	Location	Advertising	Personnel:	Environment:	Policies
Quality		Accessibility	Personnel	• Training	• Furnishings	Procedures
Level	Discounts:	Distribution	selling	• Discretion	• Colour	Mechanisation
Brand name	• Allowance	channels	Sales	• Commitment	• Layout	Employee
Service line	• Commissions	Distribution	promotion	• Incentives	• Noise level	discretion
Warranty	• Payment terms	coverage	Publicity	• Appearance		Customer
After-sales			Public	• Interpersonal	Facilitating goods	involvement
service	Customers'		relations	behaviour	Tangible clues	Customer
	perceived value					direction
	Quality/price			• Attitudes		Flow of
	Differentiation			Other customers:		activities
				• Behaviour		
				• Degree of		
				involvement		
				• Customer/		
				customer contact		

Source: Cowell, 1984, p. 70 (adapted from Booms and Bitner, 1981).

MANAGING RETAIL CONSUMPTION

These early services marketing writers identified a clear need for a distinctive body of work that considered the needs and requirements of successful services marketing and management. Their work was further developed and extended by the rise of concepts such as the 'Servuction' model by Langeard et al. (1981). This model considers the potential nature and impact of the service operator's interface on the customer during consumption. It indicates the need for management of supporting elements that the customer may never see. It also begins to address, if inadvertently, many of the criticisms levelled at the traditional concepts of marketing – it is integrative and holistic, and facilitates the wider devolution of marketing responsibility in service organizations, whilst emphasizing that the benefits that a customer takes from the exchange are potentially drawn from more than the narrowly-defined elements of the Four Ps.

The Servuction Model Itself

The notion that customers receive a 'bundle of benefits' from the service experience as a result of their interaction with the visible elements of the service system is a central element of the model (Figure 6.1) (Baron and Harris, 1995).

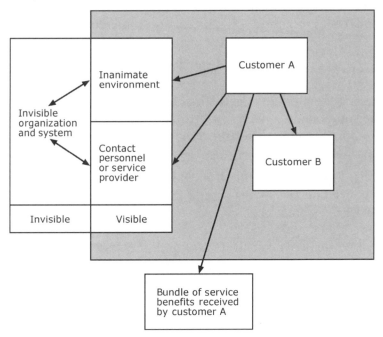

Figure 6.1 Servuction diagram

Source: Langeard et al. (1981).

This concept extends beyond the sphere of services marketing and crosses into mainstream marketing and retailing literature – indicating that this elemental concept is a powerful one. It also begins to suggest that the customer may not simply receive a single clearly-delineated benefit, and that what they actually take with them is a composite derived from various interactions with various elements of the service provider's offer.

This proposition therefore implies that service providers must pay close attention to the management of the various elements that can add to the benefits that the customer can derive. In so doing, the model provides an indication of the management complexity that service providers face – beginning to suggest that the successful management and marketing of a service is itself a complex task.

This implied complexity is further highlighted when the nature of each individual customer's 'bundle of benefits' is considered. The nature of what is derived by a single customer is personalized and externalized (Baron et al., 2000). This suggests that each customer develops an individual bundle of benefits that they take with them into their own 'life-world'. This again adds additional layers of complexity.

Despite this overall complexity, the model depicts the core visible elements within the service arena in a simple but effective fashion (Bateson, 1995) – and it is this combination of functionality and clarity throughout the Servuction model that make it a powerful conceptual and managerial tool.

The Line of Visibility

A key feature of the model is the distinction drawn between the visible and the invisible components – what the customer sees and doesn't see – of the provider's service system. This distinction splits the service organization into two clear components:

- The service arena is identified as the Servuction (service production) system, which constitutes the visible elements of the firm. This is where the experience is created that gives rise to the benefits enjoyed by the customer.
- The invisible elements constitute all the processes and materials that the service provider uses to support the service arena.

One observation that arises from the managerial consequences of the line of visibility is that, in the invisible areas, management may focus on efficiency; whereas, in the visible Servuction system, the focus is on the effective delivery of appropriate experiences.

Creating Benefit

When considering the development of the service and the creation of benefit, the model places the customer *within* the delivery mechanism. By doing so, the model identifies customers as 'co-producers' of their own service experience (Normann, 1991). This further highlights the customer's pivotal role within the Servuction model – not only is the delineator of an element's position within the model set using the customer's 'line of visibility', but the customer is also depicted as an essential component in service production.

The position of the customer's bundle of benefits – placed beyond the service delivery mechanism – also begins to indicate that the customer, as well as being co-producer, is the recipient of the final output of the service and the arbiter of its quality. The centrality and use of the customer viewpoint as a defining focus provides the model with an inherent strength as a marketing construct.

The service arena is composed of four elements which in varying combinations, provide the customer with a bounded set of interactions that may then go on to affect the bundle of benefits that they derive. The visible elements are:

- The inanimate or physical environment;
- The service personnel;
- The individual customer; and
- Other unrelated customers who might be present at the same time within the service arena.

Each of the four discrete elements has its own potential to impact the service experience; and therefore, service marketers need to consider each one both individually and as part of the total service experience.

Inanimate Environment

The inanimate environment – which encompasses all the tangible objects that a customer encounters in the service delivery arena – has received considerable attention as a focus of study: both in terms of considerations of service environment design *per se*, and its effect on customers. The function of the service environment, and its potential to act as a key component in service delivery, is perhaps less well-addressed than the examination of the impact of the service environment on the customer.

There has been a wide range of research considering the implications and effect of a diverse range of physical elements – such as colour, texture, landmarks and smell – on the customer within a service setting (Baker et al., 1994).

Lovelock et al. (1996) also suggest that the service environment can create positive and negative customer impressions, and this element of the Servuction model therefore needs careful management. Bitner's (1992) concept of 'servicescape' explicitly considers the customer's behavioural response to the inanimate service environment, and she identifies three basic dimensions that combine to create the servicescape:

- Ambient conditions (for example: music, noise, temperature and air quality);
- Spatial layout and functionality (encompassing issues such as layout and its ability to impact customer's perceptions of fitness for purpose); and
- Signs, symbols and artefacts (focusing on décor and way-finding, and the potential effect that such elements can have on customers' behaviour and mood).

The potential of the inanimate environment to create a response in the customer is not only limited to altering mood or perceptions of service quality. It also extends its impact to a diverse range of behavioural, affective and cognitive outcomes such as purchase behaviour, re-patronage intention and even levels of arousal. This wide range of impacts draws on a broad range of diverse literature as its basis: including environmental psychology, consumer behaviour, retail marketing, and, of course, the services literature. The use of such a wide and rich number of traditions as a foundation for examination means that the relationship between inanimate environment and customer is one that is both well considered and highly developed.

It is perhaps also worth noting that the inanimate service delivery environment not only potentially affects customers, but also employees. The importance of the physical environment on staff is a more recent, and therefore less developed, area of study, and although the two elements are clearly displayed next to each other within the Servuction model, the implications of their interaction – even though both are under the direct control of the provider – is under researched.

Service Personnel

If attention is turned to the service personnel component of the model, a similar pattern of consideration to that of the inanimate environment is displayed. The focus of concern appears to have been the interaction of employees and customers, and the management of this interface. It is clear that the interaction of customers and employees has the potential to greatly influence the customer's perceptions of service quality, and significantly impact their satisfaction (Heskett et al., 1997). This relationship between customer and employee has stimulated much interest; and the nature of this contact and its effect has been well examined (Czepiel et al., 1985; Schlesinger and Heskett, 1991; Zeithaml and Bitner, 1996; Frazer Winsted, 2000).

The scope of the potential implications of employee-customer interaction has been extended beyond its impact on the customer: considering the consequences of contact for the business for example in terms of profit, employee retention and job satisfaction. This element of the Servuction system has perhaps received such attention because of its focus on the 'people' element of the service encounter and the explicit reliance of service delivery on this personal contact. From the perspective of the firm, the management of this contact poses a number of problems. The employees who are primarily involved in this interaction are often relatively junior personnel – such as shop assistants, receptionists and customer service staff (Lovelock et al., 1996). This means that the employees who carry out the majority of customer contact are often young and inexperienced, and have less knowledge of the service than their customers.

This has meant that there has been consideration of the management and *selection* of service personnel in its own right, as a key component of the model. As such an important element, a diverse range of human resource issues is often examined as an aspect of the overall management of the service delivery system.

These include fundamental propositions such as viewing expenditure on service personnel as being an investment that has the potential to reap huge returns, and not simply as a cost that simply needs to be minimized (Lovelock et al., 1996). The issue of emotional labour is perhaps a key concern in supporting such a proposition. When a service is delivered, the customer's perception is not only affected by the meeting of timeframes and technical competence, but by the demeanour and conduct of the service personnel. This often means that, to provide a level of suitable service, companies are reliant on a high level of emotional involvement from the service staff, as well as their ability to project appropriate emotional cues, which may involve a degree of 'role playing'. This highly complex set of managerial concerns is perhaps the reason why this aspect of the Servuction model has received such attention.

The Customer

The second of the person-to-person elements of the model is contact between customers. This area is less thoroughly researched – although potentially no less important in delivering the benefit bundle to the customer (Martin, 1996). Such interactions also have the potential to influence the customer's purchase intentions (Harris et al., 1997) and their re-patronage decisions (Parker and

Ward, 2000). As such, the management of this element also bears careful thought by the service provider.

In some types of service, customer-to-customer interaction is an integral part of the provision; and in some cases, without it, the service experience would be impossible to deliver – e.g. trekking and 'extreme' holidays, karaoke evenings, and bowling competitions. The inclusion of this component within the provider's management responsibilities also gives rise to an area within service delivery where creative techniques need to be employed to facilitate a smooth and successful customer experience. Perhaps one of the simplest management techniques has been the 'segregation' of customers into groups – such as 'business class' and 'standard' – in the hope that, by placing customers of a similar nature together, the opportunities for negative interactions are diminished. However, attention is also turning to the potential of customer interaction management to move beyond this basic approach and begin to utilize the possibility of such contact to add to positive service perceptions.

Such considerations will then perhaps further add to the attention given to the contribution and management of customer participation within the broader service environment. The role of the customer within the Servuction environment has received extensive attention. This is perhaps unsurprising, given the centrality of the customer – and, in the case of many services, the reliance on the customer's participation – in service production.

This element of the model clearly highlights the service characteristic of production and consumption inseparability, and the service provider's potential reliance on the involvement and participation of their customers. In some services, such as self-service retailing and Internet banking, the customer becomes a 'partial employee' – helping the service provider deliver benefits by actually taking on some of the role and responsibilities traditionally fulfilled by staff. This moves the customer beyond the role of co-producer, and embeds them in the heart of the Servuction system.

Extensions to the Servuction Model

The complex set of factors that can be considered using the Servuction model goes beyond its simple appearance and there have been attempts to further develop the model, both to represent such concerns, and also, more recently, to address issues related to developments in service delivery such as the Internet.

The original model shows that the customer is part of the Servuction system. The extended model below indicates that the customer enters the system with some significant contributors to the service experience: mood-state, time availability and other antecedents. Such factors have been shown to be influential in their impact on customer perceptions of service environments (Newman et al., 1995). The other additional element – which links the invisible to the visible, and provides a means of interaction within the Servuction system – is (customer-facing) information technology (Figure 6.2).

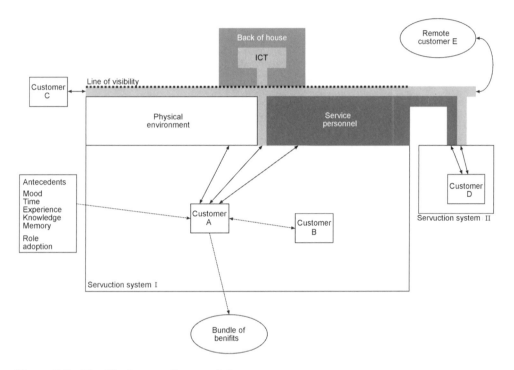

Figure 6.2 Modified servuction model

Source: Baron et al. (2000, p. 2) (adapted from Langeard et al., 1981).

Antecedents

The antecedents depicted can act as an important influence on the bundle of benefits that the customer takes with them, as well as impacting on perceptions of service quality. What a customer may see as good service could well vary with their mood, for example. The already happy customer who enters and experiences a service could be more inclined to feel positively about the experience than if they had entered the service delivery system and were previously disgruntled.

Other antecedent factors such as the customer's experience and knowledge will also affect the way in which they access and even interact with the service system – the experienced customer may well know the service provider's procedures, quirks or processes: and this could enable them to help the service firm deliver the service and enhance its efficiency. Conversely, an experienced or knowledgeable customer could be less tolerant of service failure or inefficiency, because they already have a well-informed expectation of the company's capabilities.

The antecedent elements also include role adoption. The inclusion of this component begins to reflect some of the research on customer-to-customer interaction and the suggestion that customers can play particular roles within a service setting: for example, that of 'help seeker' or 'helper' (McGrath and Otnes, 1995). The adoption of a particular role is itself dependent on various factors such as the customer's prior knowledge – the elements already outlined in their own right impacting the service experience. The inclusion of such antecedent factors in the adapted model also begins to allude to the impact that previous service encounters can have on a customer's interaction and assessment of a service, and therefore on the bundle of benefits received.

Technology

The second major extension to the model revolves around the impact that information communication technology (ICT) can have on the customer's service experience. Technology is seen as affecting service encounters in a number of ways.

Firstly, it can provide an additional point of interaction between the customer and the service provider whilst the customer is within what would conventionally be seen as the service arena. Technology can be used to supplement or supplant the interaction a customer might be involved in through personnel-based mechanisms – for example, the use of multimedia kiosks to help in product selection and specification in the car showroom and hairdresser; or the use of self-scanning and automated payment systems in the supermarket. The use of technology within the service arena provides another point of managerial concern and consideration, and perhaps further adds to the complexity of successful service delivery.

Managerial concern can be further compounded when technology is used to provide a mechanism for remote service delivery. Increasingly, customers are beginning to be given the opportunity to experience services whilst in distant environments that are not primarily in the control of the service provider. The remote ATM located in a petrol station or shopping centre provides one example. Here, the customer's service experience is not only impacted by their direct contact with the ATM itself, but also by factors such as the lighting and security of the remote location – neither of which the provider of the ATM may directly control.

The use of the Internet to purchase books, theatre or train tickets – although quite different in context to the ATM example – has similar properties in terms of the interaction experience. The service provider is again susceptible to a wide range of factors that are not in its direct control: e.g. the nature of the customer's computer, web browser set-up, and the speed and quality of their Internet connection. Here, the potential for the service experience to be impaired by browser and site incompatibility, and other components beyond the service provider's control, is also present. Customer interaction from a distant environment begins to present the service firm with additional issues that need to be planned for, if not directly managed – such concerns adding to what is already a complex task of 'staging'.

Technology can also provide another mechanism through which customer-to-customer interaction can take place. Here, there is the potential for two remote customers to interact through means such as online 'chat rooms', comments forums and (company-moderated) question-and-answer facilities. It would seem therefore, that service companies, as well as developing management techniques aimed at physical and time-bound interaction, must also consider their virtual counterparts, as well as the implications of interactions which can be viewed by many customers at different times. Some of these implications may have legal ramifications – e.g. the passing on of intentionally misleading or incorrect information designed to trick other customers.

Conclusions

These additions to the original Servuction model will perhaps help to ensure that the framework continues to provide a firm foundation for the management and consideration of services. However, this is not to say that any extended model will itself not undergo further development to better meet the needs of service managers or researchers.

One aspect of our daily experiences in service encounters *not* present in the Servuction model is the location of the Servuction system within its context. Dominant in aspects of context is geographical 'place', or *topos*. Retail stores are situated within locations. The nature of that location and its relationship to the specific store may well be an important determinant of consumer reaction to the store. "Location, location, and location" are oft cited as the three most important determinants of a store's success!

Each element of the Servuction model bears close and careful consideration in its own right: in its capacity as a factor in the overall service delivery mechanism, and its potential to deliver an appropriate and valued benefit bundle to the customer.

The following six chapters therefore use the Servuction model as a point of departure. Chapter 7 (*Physical Environment*) – which begins with a consideration of location (or *topos*) – together with Chapter 8 (*Merchandise*), discuss those elements that could be characterized as constituting the inanimate environment. These are then brought together in Chapter 9 (*Atmosphere and Image*) where their impact on the creation, management and effect of store image is considered. The importance of service is also highlighted in Chapter 9. This leads to a more detailed discussion of this important aspect of the Servuction system in Chapter 10 (*The Social Dimension*).

Whilst these chapters consider the main components of the service arena itself, attention is also given to those factors that are likely to influence the *perception* and *reception* of these elements – the temporal dimension (Chapter 11), and the customer's psychological state (Chapter 12).

In summary, the focus of these following chapters is the consideration of the interplay between the elements of the service arena and the retail drama to create and deliver customer satisfaction.

References

Baker, J., Grewal, D. and Parasuraman, A. 1994. The influence of store environment on quality inferences and store image. *Journal of the Academy of Marketing Science*, 22(4), 328–339.

Baron, S., Davies, B.J. and Harris, K. 2000. Editorial. *European Journal of Marketing*, 34(3/4), 256–260.

Baron, S. and Harris, K. 1995. *Services Marketing*. London: Macmillan.

Bateson, J.E.G. 1995. *Managing Services Marketing: Text and Readings (3rd Ed.)*. Fort Worth, TX: The Dryden Press.

Bitner, M.J. 1992. 'Servicescapes: the impact of physical surroundings on customers and employees'. *Journal of Marketing*, 56(2), 57–72.

Booms, B.H. and Bitner, M.J. 1981. Marketing strategies and organization structures for service firms. In Donnelly, J.H. and George, W.R. (Eds.). *Marketing of Services*. American Marketing Association: Chicago, IL, pp. 47–51.

Borden, N.H. 1964. The concept of the marketing mix. *Journal of Advertising Research*, 4, June, 2–7.

Cowell, D. 1984. *The Marketing of Services*. London: Heinemann.

Czepiel, J., Solomon, M. and Suprenant, C. (Eds.). 1985. *The Service Encounter*. Lexington, MA: Heath, DC.

Duddy, E.A. and Revzan, D.A. 1947. *Marketing: An Institutional Approach*. New York: McGraw–Hill.

Fisk, R.P., Brown, S.W. and Bitner, M.J. 1993. The evolution of services marketing literature. *Journal of Retailing*, 69 (Spring), 61–103.

Fisk, G. and Dixon, D.F. 1967. *Theories of Marketing Systems*. New York: Harper and Row.

Frazer Winsted, K. 2000. Service behaviors that lead to satisfied customers. *European Journal of Marketing*, 34(3/4), 399–417.

Frey, A.W. 1961. *Advertising (3rd Ed.)*. New York: The Ronald Press.

Grönroos, C. and Gummesson, E. 1985. The Nordic School of Services Marketing. In Grönroos, C. and Gummesson, E. (Eds.). *Services Marketing –Nordic School Perspective*, Stockholm University: Sweden, pp. 6–11.

Grönroos, C. 1997. Keynote paper from marketing mix to relationship marketing – towards a paradigm shift in marketing. *Management Decision*, 35(4), pp. 322–329.

Gummesson, E. 1994. Service management: an evaluation and the future. *International Journal of Service Industry Management*, 5(1), 77–96.

Harris, K., Davies, B.J. and Baron, S. 1997. Conversations during purchase considerations: sales assistants and customers. *The International Review of Retail, Distribution and Consumer Research*, 7(3), 173–190.

Heskett, J.L., Sasser, W.E. and Schlesinger, L.A. 1997. *The Service Profit Chain*. New York: The Free Press.

Howard, J.A. 1957. *Marketing Management: Analysis and Decision*. Homewood, IL: Richard D. Irwin, Inc.

Langeard, E., Bateson, J., Lovelock, C. and Eiglier, P. 1981. *Marketing of Services: New Insights From Consumers and Managers*. Cambridge, MA: Marketing Science Institute.

Lazer, W. and Kelly, E.J. 1962. *Managerial Marketing: Perspectives and Viewpoints (revised)*. Homewood, IL: Richard D. Irwin, Inc.

Lovelock, C., Vandermerwe, S. and Lewis, B. 1996. *Services Marketing: A European Perspective*. Upper Saddle River, NJ: Prentice Hall Inc.

Martin, C.L. 1996. Consumer-to-consumer: satisfaction with strangers' public behaviour. *Journal of Consumer Affairs*, 32(1), 146–169.

McCarthy, E.J. 1960. *Basic Marketing: A Managerial Approach*. Homewood, IL: Richard D. Irwin, Inc.

McGrath, M.A. and Otnes, C. 1995. Unacquainted influencers: when strangers interact in the retail setting. *Journal of Business Research*, 32, 261–72.

Newman, A., Davies, B.J. and Dixon, G. 1995. A theoretical model approach to terminal shopping syndrome: a future challenge for UK airport operators. *EMAC conference – ESC*, Paris, May.

Normann, R. 1991. *Service management: strategy and leadership in service business (2nd Ed.)*. Chichester: John Wiley and Sons Ltd.

Parker, C. and Ward, P. 2000. An analysis of role adoptions and scripts during customer-to-customer encounters. *European Journal of Marketing*, 34(3/4), 341–358.

Rafiq, M. and Ahmed, P.K. 1995. Using the 7 Ps as a generic marketing mix: an exploratory survey of UK and European marketing academics. *Marketing Intelligence and Planning*, 13, 9, 4–15.

Schlesinger, L.A. and Heskett, J.L. 1991. Breaking the cycle of failure in services. *Sloan Management Review*, Spring, 17–28.

Shostack, G.L. 1977. Breaking free from product marketing'. *Journal of Marketing*, 41, April, 73–80.

van Waterschoot, W. and Van den Bulte, C. 1992. The four Ps classification of the marketing mix revisited (four factors of marketing response). *Journal of Marketing*, 56(4), 83–94.

Vignali, C. and Davies B.J. 1994. The marketing mix redefined and mapped: introducing the mixmap model. *Management Decision*, 34(8), 11–16.

Zeithaml, V. and Bitner, M.J. 1996. *Services Marketing*. New York: McGraw–Hill.

7

THE PHYSICAL ENVIRONMENT

The physical environment for retailing is a multi-layered phenomenon. For the purposes of this book, we concentrate on two particular layers:
- The upper layer, concerned with the centre of shopping (the high street, precinct, mall, and other facilities).
- The lower level, concerned with the specifics of the retail unit itself.
   At both levels, the same broad approach can be employed; although there may be holistic effects at the higher level, which exhibit systemic properties (i.e. the effects in relation to centres of shopping are not simply linear combinations of the effects of individual units). Both levels require managing, in order that an appropriate space for retail consumption is created. Such a managed space provides the stage on which retail performances can be enacted, leading this chapter to consider:
- The twin threads of mass consumption and the privatization of public space – the rise of ever larger private spaces dedicated to activities associated with consumption;
- Environmental cues;
- Sensory modalities;
- Orienting factors; and
- Environmental objects.

Introduction

Within the Servuction model, one of the main elements within the service arena that has an impact on consumers is the physical environment. There is of course, a wider context for the physical environment – that of the location of the site itself – for which a retailer will often have desired qualities. For example, many international up-market retailers are to be found in exclusive shopping streets in cities around the world: e.g. Rodeo Drive, Knightsbridge and the Champs Elysées. A clear pattern emerges, and the environment and the nature of the store seem linked. This, of course, is none too surprising. There is a clear interplay between the nature of the location and that of the retailer's merchandise and its clientele.

In this chapter, the nature of that external physical location is discussed briefly, before the internal store physical environment is given a more thorough examination.

External Physical Location

In the example of the up-market retailer quoted above, the link between the nature of the store and the environment in which the unit is placed is clear. For those retailers who have a particular clientele likely to be found in only a few places, such choices are relatively simple. If the retailer's clientele is made up of an up-market, high income, internationally-oriented group, then the locations for its stores may suggest themselves. Organizations such as Gucci site their stores in appropriate locations around the world: Via Condotti, Fifth Avenue, Shinjuku, Via Montenapoleone. It is not too fanciful to suggest that Gucci's stores will be located near certain other retailers in these various locations. One might speculate that there are other up-market fashion brands, jewellers and similar luxury good retailers who would be found in this type of place.

Where the clientele is more diverse, then the number of possible locations suitable for stores rises considerably. Benetton, for example, is another Italian fashion retailer whose stores are to be found in many locations around the world. Unlike Gucci though, which operates free-standing company-owned stores – or outlets within major department stores – Benetton uses a franchise formula. This approach, coupled with more modest price points, leads to a larger number of units being situated in more mainstream shopping areas.

As the nature of any particular retailer's merchandise offer and prices become more mainstream, then the possibilities for unit location increase enormously. Therefore, middle-market retailers have the greatest capacity for choice in the selection of store locations. However, site choice does need to be guided by the nature of the retail brand, just as is the case with more narrowly-focused retailers.

The Generic Brand Proposition

The choice of initial physical location can therefore be said to rest on an

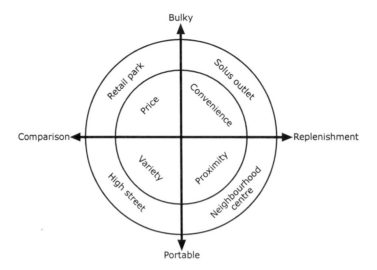

Figure 7.1 Offers at different types of location Source: Davies, 2000

understanding of the generic brand proposition. There are some fundamental drivers of brand proposition related to the clientele and merchandise characteristic:

- Are the goods bulky or portable?
- Are they comparison shopping items or replenishment items?
- Is the merchandise a mass product or highly exclusive?
- Is the offer nationally specific or international?

Figure 7.1 shows how, for mainstream product offers directed at broad markets, the fundamental drivers may interact to create four primary types of shopping location.

With items such as comparison goods, which are relatively portable, then the high street, in British terms (or perhaps the shopping mall in American terms), is the chief type of retail store location. Where bulky comparison goods are concerned and price becomes a particular issue, then retail parks or power centres become a preferred location. For convenience goods that combine a need for replenishment but with considerable bulk, then 'solus' outlets may be suitable. Where the combination of characteristics is between portability and replenishment, then the neighbourhood centre is a major choice. Clearly, these generic brand propositions relate chiefly to mass-market goods. However, as the nature of the market becomes more restricted and more focused, then the choice of a particular location becomes more selective. In other words, even for goods such as those from Gucci, the elements of portability and comparison remain the same. It is just that in the case of such an up-market brand, the choice of 'high street' becomes one that is made at an international level.

In an international context, the precise nature of particular locations suitable for mass-market merchandise will vary with local characteristics. Such characteristics may include the planning regime, controls on store size, prevalence of certain types of operation in the market (such as hypermarkets), or the overall structure of retail space. There is a certain contrast between the continued presence of a wide variety of retail stores in central areas of many European cities: for example, compared to the concentration of non-retail activity in the central business district of many US cities. In high density cities in southern Asia, shopping malls or shopping centres may rise vertically, in a manner that is uncommon in both Europe and North America. These local variations do not, however, overturn the core principle that the nature of merchandise and the nature of intended customers interplay to determine the most appropriate physical location. These same factors – and indeed site location – then, in turn, influence the next layer of environmental concern: that of the store's external look and internal surroundings. Both the store's location and its externalities and internal environment then play a part in influencing consumer perceptions and behaviour. (For a more detailed discussion of location, see Chapter 15).

Where a retailer addresses a mass market, the possibilities for location on an international plane are considerable. Increasingly, the sites of mass consumption, which are growing in size and complexity, fall increasingly under the control of particular organizations. These organizations are frequently private companies, which plan, finance, build and operate complex spaces that have the complexion of 'public space'. In the case of shopping malls, retail parks and similar mass venues, the private nature of the spaces may be well understood. Where the public space remains in public ownership, as in town centres in Europe, then there are efforts to apply some of the 'management' values and characteristics of privatized 'public' space to the remaining public space. Surveillance CCTV schemes, town centre management, 'corporate' branding and advertising, co-operative security measures, local loyalty card schemes... are all examples of this trend. What are seen (or presented) as the demands of the modern shopper, place more elements of the complex upper level of retail environment provision in the hands of corporate organizations. Irrespective of the nature of the retail space, either publicly or privately controlled, the central issue of concern to the retailer, in relation to the physical environment, is understanding its impact on customers' perceptions and behaviour.

Behaviour and the Effects of Environment

The impact of the interplay between physical environment and behaviour is also of interest outside the sphere of retailing. The most general consideration of these types of impact – the relationship between physical setting and behaviour – is to be found in environmental psychology. Within this field, Mehrabian and Russell (1974) developed a theoretical model that they argued is applicable to any built environment. It rests on a stimulus–organism–response (S → O → R) approach. Mehrabian and Russell suggested that the outcome of the impact of various stimuli (present in the environment) was represented by approach or by avoidance behaviour. Intervening between the environment and the behavioural outcomes of approach or avoidance are three emotional states: pleasure, arousal and dominance (PAD). The combination of these three emotional states is seen to determine whether or not a person wishes to remain in a particular environment – i.e. engage in either approach or avoidance behaviour. (See Chapter 12 for a more detailed examination of PAD).

Retailers have to establish mechanisms by which they are able to ensure, or at least increase, the likelihood of approach behaviours being stimulated. This means that retailers must make a careful and conscious use of the stimuli that make up the physical environment. Such management therefore needs to consider both its upper and lower layers. However, the greatest degree of control can be associated with the specifics of the retail unit itself. It is here that retailers can attempt to create approach behaviour that will result in customers being attracted to the particular retail environment. Once in the environment – and in the store – the retailers' next task is to continue to provide an environment (giving appropriate stimulus) that ensures customers' approach behaviour continues.

Figure 7.2 summarizes this proposition and also depicts two clear types of environment – the social and the physical. These two environments are also

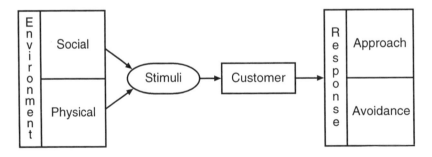

Figure 7.2 Customer responses to the retail environment

depicted within the Servuction model as key constituents of the service arena. The 'physical' is the prime concern of the approach adopted by the environmental psychologists (and is examined in this chapter), but there is also a need within the retail setting to consider the social surroundings (see Chapter 10) that develop within this physical space and the interaction of these two types of environment.

At the first level, the retailer's task is to select locations that are congenial to the intended customers. These locations are determined by core elements of the brand proposition, and the nature of the neighbourhood into which the store is to be inserted. At the second level, the task is to design an internal store environment that elicits the appropriate behavioural responses. Within the general model – using the notion of approach and avoidance – 'approaches', in terms of individual response, are represented in three categories. The first category relates to a person's physical movement towards an environment. The second category of approach behaviour is the degree of attention displayed, or the extent of exploration of the environment that may lead to a favourable attitude, preference or liking. The third category concerns the degree to which a customer feels comfortable with approaching, or being in proximity to, others within the environment. (This last aspect links very clearly to the social dimension within the Servuction model.)

People are obviously affected by their immediate environments, which can 'cue' certain types of behaviour. For example, spectators behave very differently in law courts and in football stadiums (in part due to the situation they are placed in). The spatial layouts and the arrangements of objects and social factors in the Servuction arena limit and define the appropriate type of behaviour. For retail management, it is important to identify the sorts of controllable factors and visual devices that act as the catalyst for certain responses, as well as understanding how to manipulate them to achieve the desired reaction in their customers. Consider, for example, the way in which customers in IKEA are directed through the store. They follow a particular route, which means that they pass most of the room displays and products before they have sight of the checkouts and exit. This means that customers are exposed to a wider range of products, and spend more time in the store environment, than they might otherwise. Much of this time in the store is therefore spent in *looking* at the numerous displays and *experiencing* the IKEA offer.

Therefore with retailing, the images that form the experience mainly stem from visual (and to a lesser degree aural, olfactory and tactile) cues that make statements about a firm's offerings. It is generally accepted in the retail and marketing literature that sight is the most salient of the senses, and therefore the most dominant. It is this visual component that, therefore, forms a major part of a corporation's image. For example, an image is reflected in the physical artefacts of the corporation (corporate name, symbol, logotype, etc.), and in each and every communication the firm distributes to its clients/customers (both internal and external). More often than not, the image will derive in part from the appearance of the corporate headquarters and other major company buildings. This would seem to suggest that when considering the management of the physical environment and the elements of image that develop from it, the visual is of prime importance.

Legibility and the Service Environment

As retailing often has a building- or store-based dimension, then the issue of visual appearance is indeed potentially critical to many retailers. This issue of appearance operates both externally and internally to the store.

Internal layout and presentation are most important for the retailer, as they make a clear statement about the standard and quality of the merchandise and service (total product) offering. At first glance, customers utilize the physical (and social) surroundings to gather the vital clues that inform their expectations prior to service delivery. Throughout these assessments, the effects of physical evidence – such as design features and images presented – are highly important and unquestionably guide consumers' decision-making and evaluative processes (Zeithaml and Bitner, 1996, p. 519).

The overall appearance of a retail setting will therefore tend to pre-determine a customer's attitude towards the organization. Newcomers will certainly base their expectations on this first visual encounter, which then becomes a reference for future visits. This can often be seen again in relation to IKEA – both in terms of the perceptions formed and in the way that customers actually behave. Many regular IKEA customers learn to 'navigate' the store without having to follow the path that retail managers have predetermined.

The Servuction model demonstrates this interactive process between the 'visible inanimate environment' and the client (or customer). In essence, the visible part of the organization itself helps create the service experience or primary benefit of the service encounter. Clearly, the first moments of visual contact are highly likely to shape behaviour, and determine a crucial part of the overall service experience. Once within a Servuction arena, customers continue to 'read' their surroundings. Depending on the emotional response that the reading engenders, customers stay or leave. An environment that helps develop the consumer behaviour desired by retailers is one that can be clearly and appropriately 'read' by target consumers. The predominance of the visual suggests that the first concern of a retailer is to design and deliver a physical environment that is read 'correctly' i.e. an environment that is easily legible and generates appropriate responses.

However, retailers must also consider the social environment that is facilitated and developed within their stores. How does it bolster or detract from the cues provided in the physical environment? The retail environment is a communal one, where the importance of managing the social interaction and space should not be understated. A physical environment that provides appropriate cues that might result in approach behaviour may then, after consideration of the social environment, be avoided. A customer may be attracted to a restaurant on the strength of its exterior and a glimpse of its interior from across a busy street. But, if on closer inspection the establishment is bereft of customers, that fact alone may produce enough of a negative impression to ensure that the potential customer does not enter the restaurant. Equally, an overcrowded environment may for some be highly unappealing. For example, how many customers turn away from a store that has a teaming mass of shoppers elbowing their way to the sales desk? Such potential reactions then raise important questions regarding the impact of 'spatial density' on a customer's approach or avoidance behaviour.

Spatial Factors

The level of 'spatial density' eases or restricts the amount of 'personal space' (see Sommer, 1969; 1974) that can evoke a sense of roominess or compactness within a setting. Surroundings may therefore be characterized by *sociopetal* or *sociofrugal* qualities (cf. centripetal and centrifugal); or the degree to which the layout of the setting impinges on users' 'life space'. (For work on territoriality, see Hediger, 1961; Sommer, 1969; and crowding in retail settings, see Markin et al., 1976; Harrell et al., 1980.) In some situations (such as waiting areas), spatial factors can play a decisive role in signifying behaviour, e.g. interaction with others and task performance, as well as engendering approach and avoidance behaviour.

Too much open space, however, can be impersonal and deny interaction. Conversely, in settings where conditions are cramped, the occupants may be coerced into a stressed and uncomfortable emotional state, due to a lack of required (personal) space. As a result, people may display dominance behaviour (i.e. they can become aggressive), as they have less than the required 'life space' (Hediger, 1961; Sommer, 1969). The actions of shoppers in a supermarket at Christmas can often stem from the feelings generated by such a crowded environment – for instance, the 'aggressive' steering of shopping trolleys and almost predatory behaviour that customers demonstrate, as they compete to secure the last product on the shelf.

Further work on environmental stressors underpins this premise. Epstein et al. (1981) found that individuals who experienced higher levels of density (or crowding) became more physiologically aroused. Persons in low-density environments reported the opposite. Space can restrict the sorts of tasks that people may wish to undertake. In retail settings, for example, crowded communal changing rooms may deter some shoppers from trying on garments, and therefore possibly purchasing them. Or where a store is quiet, those simply wishing to browse in peace may feel overly exposed to unwelcome interaction with store staff. The nature of the spatial density can therefore help to determine, at a relatively specific level, the nature of the behaviour displayed by customers.

Retailers, at times, try to manage this density. This can be seen in the sale period, where certain retailers will control entry to a store to ensure that it does not become overcrowded. Equally, in the restaurant and hospitality sector, to manage the social environment, staff may be asked to play the role of customers when there are no real ones present. However, given that issues of spatial density are created primarily by the number of customers present, active management can be difficult except in extreme circumstances or at specific points: for example, around areas of known congestion, such as the checkouts. What retailers can focus on instead is the creation of an environment that provides customers with a physical space that is easy to navigate.

Orienting Factors

The form or pattern of the physical aspect may aid or impede the efficiency of task-related activities. This suggests that design characteristics – for example, the *clarity* of the layout or signage (*orienting factors*) – can assist with task accomplishment (such as just finding your way to an exit). Lynch's (1960) research emphasized the importance of 'districts' (or neighbourhoods) that people exploit as particular frames of reference. Use of these environmental attributes helps to avoid *lostness* (Newman, 1995) in a variety of situations. Avoiding lostness is one of the main incentives for seeking out familiar features or objects in places (Lynch, 1960). In fact, people seem to display a great sense of emotional attachment to unambiguous settings with recognizable features. To provide constant orientation people use these distinct characteristics. In places where there is no organized or coherent pattern, or with few available features that provide points of reference, users are disorientated and uneasy. Environmental characteristics (or attributes), and in particular those that provide a means of locating ourselves within an environment, help to make sense of complex surroundings.

Lynch's (1960) research provided a convenient and robust conceptualization of these attributes. He argued that surroundings that afford good 'imageability' are more likely to evoke a strong image. A setting that is visually organized with readily 'identifiable features' is more likely to conform to this model. Lynch categorized and termed these identifiable features as: Paths, Landmarks, Edges, Nodes and Districts (PLEND). He also identified that a gridiron format (a matrix-type system of paths, such as those governing modern American city street-planning) also considerably enhanced subjects' orientation. Other elements, such as thematic units (groups of analogous features), provided additional orienting properties. Lynch proposed that the provision of these guiding elements produced a strong image and a frame of reference from which individuals could act. These attributes help people to feel more readily and quickly at home in new surroundings, reducing unfamiliarity.

Such identifiable features can clearly be seen at work within many successful retail settings. For example, within the UK, the national grocery chains employ similar layouts, use similar materials and fixturing for the various categories of merchandise, and provide signage for each aisle. The result is an environment that is familiar to most UK grocery shoppers. Therefore, irrespective of which particular UK grocery retailer's store they find themselves in, customers feel comfortable with the environment and are able, with only slight modification to their behaviour, to shop without difficulty.

Factors That Shape Environments

The issues of spatial density and orienting factors, although unquestionably important in influencing customers' behaviour in retail settings, have not received as much attention as other basic and perhaps more obvious stimuli in the physical environment. Work in consumer research has produced a number of studies that have focused selectively on various physical cues including lighting, décor and texture. Such studies have provided some insight into the impact of selected stimuli. More generally, however, the architectural features and social space that surround the customer have been expressed in an all-inclusive fashion, and termed 'store atmosphere'. (Elements of image and atmosphere are considered in Chapter 9.) The marketing literature however, appears to overlook many issues relating to the physical setting (Newman et al., 1994), and the impact that various surroundings have on people's behaviour.

While research has yet to produce a reliable taxonomy of stimuli that can be used in the context of all physical settings, environmental psychology approaches have been used with some success – music, for example, has been shown to affect people in service environments. (Some thoughts on the effects of such ambient factors are offered by Baker et al., 1994.) 'Warm colours' (such as red and yellow) have been stressed in retail interiors as a means of drawing customers into the setting (Bellizi et al., 1983); although other work has shown colour value to be culturally determined. Such work has usually applied and considered a non-specific and narrow band of environmental factors; and a greater understanding of the various determinants and antecedents of behaviour (frequently based on expectations) is therefore necessary.

The interplay between these stimuli is, of course, complex. There are obvious interactions between spatial density and legibility and orienting factors; and some of these external stimuli may be so strong that they impinge on the senses in a way that those experiencing the stimulus might interpret as immediate. For example, if customers enter an environment that has an unpleasant smell, they may leave immediately, without being conscious of the other internal mechanisms that may be brought into play to process the stimulus. For the most part, where these overwhelming stimuli are lacking, consumers may be unaware, at a conscious level, of the various stimuli and their effects. So a customer may well display certain behaviour as a result of processing information from a number of stimuli, but be quite unaware of the process of interpreting the information itself.

A customer may 'feel' very differently about two branches of the same retailer without actually knowing why. This could stem from the nature of the physical environment itself, but the customer may not even (be able to) articulate that the lower lighting levels and ceilings of the store make it seem more oppressive; they may simply feel that one store is 'better' than the other. This highlights that understanding the potential effect of stimuli, as well as what customers actually express about them, is also important.

The conceptual framework below focuses on the most essential of the potential stimuli that might be present in a retail setting. In doing this, it begins to bring together a number of the areas outlined above. It also adds further determinants and antecedents of behaviour, such as time availability.

A Conceptual Framework

In essence, the framework shows how the consumer's 'image' of a retailer could be altered (perhaps significantly) by the perceived composition of its service setting. If 'image' can be altered by giving effective attention to the elements shown in the framework, this then implies that, for service organizations in particular, positive consumer behaviour could be greatly reinforced by raising the legibility of the service setting. Legibility, as discussed above, refers to the ease with which customers (and staff) can comprehend (work out in their minds) the schema of their surroundings and the service offering that the elements intrinsically represent. The presumption is that when people are faced with unambiguous and stimulating environments, they become psychologically aroused (feel in a good mood) as a result of the properties in the physical setting.

This model (Figure 7.3) of consumer perceptions and behaviour reflects Mehrabian and Russell's (1974) S → O → R (stimulus–organism–response) approach. The upper level concerns stimuli found in a retail context:

- Orienting factors;
- Complexity;
- Spatial factors; and
- Time availability.

The 'organism' is represented through the central area:

- Senses;
- Personal characteristics; and
- Response mediators.

The response mediators concern issues to do with personality characteristics for example, extraversion. These factors stem from the person and are likely to be a consistent component of the person's character and thinking. Therefore, the retailer has little opportunity to directly influence these mediating factors; but an understanding of the importance of such concerns may help to explain the reactions displayed by customers. For example, an extrovert may find a bright, busy, high-density environment that could be described as being highly theatrical, as appealing – whereas an introvert may find the self-same context highly uncomfortable and even threatening.

Where retailers can have more of a direct impact is through those elements and processes that are concerned more directly with the short-term – which includes understanding how sensory information is processed and interpreted, and how personal characteristics affect the customer's information processing.

The final level of the model relates to the 'response' that the customer displays as a result of their processing the information drawn from the retail context. This element of the model draws heavily on the original work of Mehrabian and Russell and subsequent extensions and modifications of their work.

Testing the Environmental Approach

Using Mehrabian and Russell's (1974) model in a services marketing context, Donovan and Rossiter (1982) made an early attempt to evaluate the atmo-

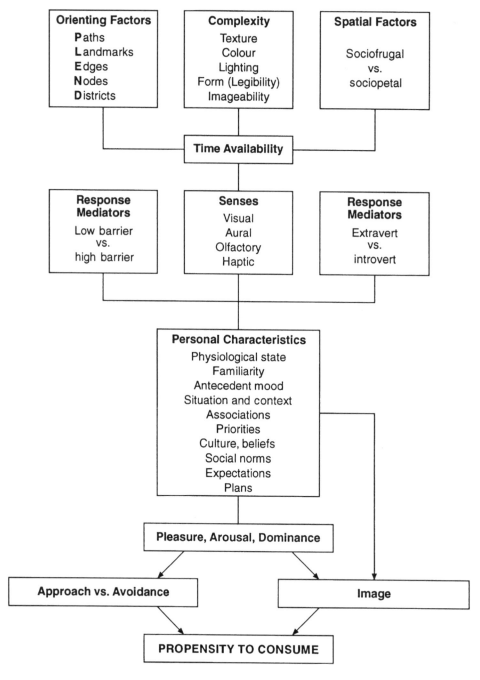

Figure 7.3 Consumers' perceptions and the store environment
Source: adapted from Newman et al. (1994).

sphere of a setting (in this case a department store) by focusing on the image (or atmosphere) of the place. Their results suggested that Mehrabian and Russell's model lacked clarity in the area of its stimulus taxonomy – a short-fall recognized by Mehrabian and Russell themselves. However, the intervening variables of pleasure, arousal, and dominance (PAD), and responses expressed as approach-avoidance, were particularly strong. These elements can be seen in the conceptual framework depicted above, and form a core element of the response level. (Again, see Chapter 12 for a more detailed examination of PAD).

Later research by Donovan and Rossiter (in conjunction with two new collaborators) provided further extensions to the type of model introduced by Mehrabian and Russell (Donovan et al., 1994). To be fully comprehensive however, such models need to incorporate elements that were not present in the initial conceptualization. A contribution by Sherman and Smith (1987), which focused on people's mood states and their image perceptions, verified the theoretical link between the intervening variables (PAD) and outcome variables of approach and avoidance. This later work is also incorporated in the framework displayed above, where PAD is depicted as a progenitor of approach-avoidance behaviour, as well as having a potential impact on the creation of image. It is these twin responses of image and approach-avoidance that are shown as directly influencing the customer's propensity to consume.

The Senses

Given that the elements contained within the stimulus level of the model have been considered earlier in the chapter, the following discussion focuses on the elements contained within the organism layer that are converted by the customer to responses, and, eventually, the propensity to purchase and consume.

Visual

The predominance of the visual sense in the formation of ideas about retail environments has already been stressed, and can be seen clearly to relate to the emphasis on the visual elements of corporate identity evident in the literature. It is also reinforced by the frequent reference to 'image' in relation to retail stores. However, the consideration of the visual sense within the marketing literature is often limited in its focus. There may for example, be consideration of the associations that certain colours may be held to have; there might also be some consideration of concepts such as modernity or contemporaneity being associated with particular elements of visual presentation (style of typeface, period of design).

Although these concerns have an obvious importance within a retail context, it is necessary to move beyond these 'static' elements and begin to contemplate issues such as the perception of movement, complexity and form, which may have an important role to play in influencing customer behaviour. For example, the ability to perceive movement in environments may be more likely to prompt approach behaviour. Taken at its simplest, a retail environment that can be perceived to have no discernible movement within it might be seen as being 'closed', and the customer may never get as far as entering the store.

The perception of form is also important in shaping behaviour, and this is again rooted in the visual. For instance, it may be that buildings dedicated to religious worship present their constituent elements in such a way that even those people who do not know its function can interpret its purpose. This interpretive process giving rise to a perception, rests on the visual, but may be informed by any of the other senses. In the retail context, management therefore need to ask questions such as: can the environment's form be read and its purpose interpreted; or, is the system of service function discernible from the layout of elements in the environment?

The issues of the visual – 'static' cues, movement, complexity and form – all need to be considered and managed in concert, rather than simply focusing on one element, or each in turn. However, whilst such a broader consideration of the visual is to be encouraged, it will not by itself enable retailers to provide an appropriate environment. For this to occur, the impact of other sensory stimuli needs to be addressed.

Aural and Olfactory

The sense of hearing is one that has received insufficient attention in the marketing literature. Again, attention has focused on specific aspects (often the effect of music), rather than considering the overall sound context. This then starts to encompass components of the aural such as acoustic absorption, the level of echo, the sharpness or decay patterns of sound, frequency range and intensity. This can be illustrated by considering a restaurant that has high ceilings, and uses metallic surfaces and hard flooring. In such a situation, the environment takes on a 'clattery' quality, and although not necessarily loud, can act as a stimulus to avoidance behaviour in those that find such noise irritating.

The sense of smell is one that has the power to more forcefully evoke memories and associations than any other. The language with which most people describe their olfactory impressions is relatively 'impoverished'. Smell as a stimulus is more likely to be classified simply as pleasant or unpleasant. If in English, a person says, "That smells", they are unlikely to mean that the smell is pleasant. To describe most smells the language used is purely associative – for example, "it smells of apples" or "that smells eggy". In much of the marketing literature, consideration of the olfactory aspects of service environments focuses on the deliberate introduction of a limited range of smells thought to be pleasant – e.g. baking bread in supermarkets and brewing coffee in a restaurant. The heady perfume of the department store cosmetics and toiletries counters can strike such a discordant note that, for some customers, far from enticing entry, it can act as a repellent. This last example shows the need to distinguish between the ambient scent of an environment and the particular scent, odour, aroma or smell of a constituent element of that environment. (For a discussion of these and other issues relating to "olfaction and aromatizing store environments", see Spangenberg et al. (1996); and for further discussion on olfaction as stimulus, see Scholder Ellen and Fitzgerald Bone (1998).)

Sound and smell, although often considered by retailers, are not managed as 'actively' as visual elements. Given the potential of sound and smell to affect response behaviours, more explicit and detailed thought is required. For example, how can the balance between the visually pleasing appearance of the cosmetics and toiletries counters be managed alongside the potentially problematic issue of the smell that is produced? This complexity is further compounded by considering the issues surrounding the haptic sense – or what is often thought of as 'the sense of touch'.

Haptic Sense

When considering this 'sense of touch', the inclination is to think either of touching – in the sense of physical contact with another person or object – or feeling the surface of an object in terms of its texture, temperature or similar characteristics. In using the word 'haptic' rather than 'touch', there is an attempt to indicate that issues such as the degree of resistance offered by environmental objects to movement and physical feedback are important. Within retail environments, haptic cues are drawn from the feelings of solidity and resistance in objects, ranging from the entrance doors to the feel of a counter that is leant on while waiting in line to pay for goods. Therefore, when entering an up-market clothing retailer, there is an expectation that the door will be heavy to open and solid – perhaps leading to an impression of being well-built. Such cues help develop a sense that things 'feel right': for example, the carpet has an appropriate amount of 'spring'; the push buttons have just enough positive feedback to ensure that there is a sense of confidence that they work well.

In considering a retail environment, the sense impressions generated by flooring, fixturing, customer service equipment, doors, the functions of lifts and escalators and other customer facilities, must be appropriate to the service environment desired, as well as working in conjunction with other sensory cues.

Unless management considers those sensory aspects that may be thought subsidiary to the visual in the design of service environments, there is a risk that some threshold barriers may be crossed, resulting in one set of sense impressions overwhelming all others. There is equally the chance that the 'image' that the retailer is trying to express is 'derailed' by providing inappropriate sensory cues. When constructing the store experience, each must be considered of equal importance – even though the visual is the predominant source of stimuli – simply because, although a customer *uses* this sense most, the information provided by others can actually have a determining effect. The processing and impact of these sensory stimuli is, however, clearly mediated by the personal characteristics of the individual.

Personal Characteristics

'Personal characteristics' label the core elements within the person ('organism' in the $S \rightarrow O \rightarrow R$ model). Research has shown that these factors act as influences on mood state and one's sense of well-being. (See for example: Gardner, 1985.)

The discussion of 'personal characteristics' here focuses on those things that the retailer may be able to control, influence or anticipate directly. In adopting this approach, there is no implicit assumption that the other factors identified as personal characteristics are less important. Culture and belief however, are likely to be deeply embedded and not subject to particular influence by the retailer. Situation and context, on the other hand, are likely to be individually determined by the consumer, and it may be that certain types of service provider or retailer are able to anticipate this.

Physiological State

Many elements impinge on our reaction to environments.

There are those physiological effects that are time dependent: time of day, time of week, and time of year. Each has particular effects within the context of an individual. There are effects due to the experience of a particular temperature, or of a particular humidity, which give rise to physiological states within an individual. Similarly, the state of an individual's emotions may also have a physiological outcome. Additionally, there are physiological effects that relate to sleep, or sleep deprivation, and so on.

There are also physiological effects that are associated with life condition. For example, individuals vary in their degree of mobility or of visual acuity. These variations influence the way in which an individual is able to cope with a particular environment at a given time. For example, as women are generally shorter than men, they are less able to establish sight lines in many retail environments, despite making up the majority of shoppers in many contexts. Retailers therefore need to consider the likely predominant physiological effects being experienced by their consumers in a given location. A retailer whose locations are at transport termini has a different set of physiological factors to consider than one that is located primarily in health spas.

There are times when the 'problems' that arise from the physiological state of the customer can be mitigated by a customer's familiarity with a context or situation. Consider a female shopper who, in a grocery store, may not be able to establish sight-lines. If she is familiar with the store's layout, this may not actually be necessary.

Familiarity

In all likelihood, the extent of place or setting familiarity will assist direction finding and appropriate service-seeking behaviour. This factor can greatly influence people's emotional responses towards and within a setting. Their evaluations of such influences will form the basis for any expectations they have or they develop. These expectations can also arise directly from the 'nature' of the setting. An environment that has cues that indicate considerable expenditure on décor and environmental objects will engender expectations consonant with expensive services. For this type of reaction to occur, consumers require prior exposure to settings that contain these cues, or they must have the ability (based on cultural familiarity) to 'read' these cues in a new setting. Most customers entering Harvey Nichols or Neiman Marcus, even if they were unaware of the name of the store that they had entered, would have a set of expectations generated, given the nature of the environment.

Similarly, where consumers enter a setting with a planned purpose in mind, the act of planning itself requires mental rehearsal. Where there is this planned, rehearsed component, then the setting (if it facilitates the planned purpose) – even if new to the consumer – is likely to be categorized as familiar.

A service setting that offers poor legibility can often lead to consumer delays, frustration, anger, and therefore uncertainty about the service offering (Bitner, 1992). Legibility in this context relates to the consumer's ability to 'read' the purpose, nature, intended audience and service provision from the environmental clues provided. Given the importance of the service encounter (Shostack, 1985), and the relative importance of the 'servicescape' as a measure of service quality, it is reasonable to assume that legibility is a vital component of the offering. However, marketers have carried out little empirical work to evaluate the impact of legibility as a distinct (physically related) dimension of the service setting. Instead, research has generally focused on features like music (already discussed), soft lighting and thick carpeting, which provide 'straightforward' links to image and atmosphere. The potential benefits of creating legibility and familiarity can, though, be heavily dependent on the mood of the customer when entering the store.

Antecedent Mood

There is convincing evidence to show that people evaluate places (and situations) differently according to their moods (or emotional states), which can even affect situations where a customer has had previous experience. Positive moods enhance the chance of various behaviours being performed (Underwood et al., 1973), and people in good moods tend to develop a stronger attitude towards their surroundings – a factor that is reflected in their evaluations (Galizio and Hendrick, 1972).

In the main, mood-state research stems from general psychology, and supports the notion that antecedent moods can influence behavioural outcomes (Belk, 1975). This type of research was confined to creating or identifying negative or positive moods (in very general terms), which have then been linked to types of behaviour. For instance, positive moods increased the likelihood of behaviours with positive outcomes (and therefore associations), and vice versa (Isen and Simmonds, 1978). In addition, mood states and behaviour are apparently linked both directly and indirectly. (An illustration of a direct link may involve associations in memory that tie mood states to certain types of behaviour (or outcomes): e.g. a conditioned response (Bugelski, 1982).)

An extensive study of the mood-state literature by Gardner (1985) demonstrated the relationship between people's evaluations, their mood states, and behavioural outcomes (in this case purchasing). For instance, positive moods in shoppers at the point of purchase can increase the likelihood of positive outcomes that can increase spend. In the marketing of services, the behaviour of contact personnel is believed to contribute significantly to customers' mood states, thereby deciding the outcome of service encounters (Bateson, 1995). Therefore, mood is a critical component that can shape the perceived effectiveness of encounters (Zeithaml and Bitner, 1996). Gardner's (1985) study also endorses this assumption: suggesting that positive moods and outcomes may be induced by a combination of interaction with the service providers and the physical settings of the encounter.

If the capacity to undertake premeditated plans (or tasks) – as well as the complexity of the surroundings – can impact on people's moods, then the general ambience (or atmosphere) of places must additionally influence these moods. If the immediate surroundings – e.g. the design features and choice of fittings in retail settings – are aesthetically pleasing, the sensory stimulation produced is likely to compound the level of effect, thereby enhancing a person's mood.

Other Personal Characteristics

As the brief discussion above indicates, there are considerable interaction effects between the various organism-related elements labelled 'personal characteristics'. Familiarity may link to planning and intent, as may mood. Situation and context are also often relevant in terms of the circumstances encountered by an individual in a particular retail setting at a particular time. The impact of culture and belief should not be ignored, especially where a retailer is seeking to operate outside the territory where the retail proposition was developed.

Conclusions

The services marketing literature clearly establishes the importance of customers' moods (Bateson, 1995, p. 218) arising from the "visible inanimate environment". Indeed, research by Babin and Darden (1995) as well as Gardner (1985), suggests that positive moods (and outcomes) can result from this constant interaction with the physical setting. People continually scan their inanimate (built) environment for evidence, in an attempt to establish an overall impression. Fabricating or creating the right set of cues – or 'production aesthetics' (see Chapter 5) – is therefore key in controlling customers' moods and behaviour.

It is these visual arrangements that direct people's evaluative processes (Zeithaml and Bitner, 1996). Visual evidence creates an instantaneous association or impression that guides behaviour. The literature however, tends to (over)stress the importance of the visual. The other senses each have a role to play. In fact, the other senses may sometimes predominate over the visual; and, in some circumstances, the visual needs to be linked to memory, to plans, or to wider knowledge, in order to make effective sense of a particular servicescape.

Methods for influencing people's moods – which have the potential to enhance (or diminish) the impression of an organization – are therefore of interest to retail management. Various techniques have been attempted, such as fine-tuning the surroundings to produce a stimulating atmosphere, with the intention of enhancing evaluations. Managing moods does require an intimate knowledge of the various components at work in a setting, and a degree of control over these components (Curren and Harich, 1994).

Making strategic changes to settings (e.g. architectural landscape, features, colours, layouts, etc.) is likely to influence behavioural outcomes – frequently through mood. For example, wayfinding is assessed by the consumer in two distinct spheres or forms:

- Pathways, building design, and colours – all of which guide the user/spectator through the structure.
- General signage, features, entrances, and the distinctiveness of setting – which help people to identify the purpose or nature of the setting, and make an overall evaluation of perceived quality.

Needless to say, the building form and colours are also used to formulate this evaluation, and therefore the layouts and configurations of settings are crucial. Past research has indicated that changes to the aspect, or 'gestalt' of the surroundings, can bias people's moods and therefore, in turn, that behaviour (Swinyard, 1993).

The importance of wayfinding suggests that people who are relatively familiar with the layout and construction of their surroundings are apt to experience less difficulty when carrying out tasks (whether premeditated or not). Moreover, it is highly likely that recent knowledge of a place will mediate other factors such as mood. So place familiarity will tend to predetermine people's expectations, and, conceivably, their antecedent moods and behaviour.

Equally, the arrangements of space (both public and personal) in a setting can also impact on expectations, and hint at service quality. Less crowded conditions (although not to the point of denying social interaction) connote a pleasurable atmosphere that can lead to positive mood states leading to a good image. Quite apart from encouraging or denying human interaction, space can generally create difficulties, because of territorial issues. In institutional settings, for example, large open-plan lounge areas are provided for social interaction. Spaces such as these are inherently sociofrugal and tend to force users to the periphery of the room, which then discourages conversation. Ultimately, this can alter the use of the space so that users may 'designate' the place for other than its intended purpose. An overflow of users into other less spacious, areas, may cause crowding and discomfort for occupiers (Sommer, 1969).

The idea that physical environments provide critical data for people's evaluation processes in a retail setting is well established. In many contexts, these physical elements are used by customers as clues to construct (mental) images about places, and the organizations associated with them. Several dimensions have emerged that can be strategically targeted by management. Retailers can clearly work to determine the form and legibility of their service setting; but there remains a critical need to ensure that consideration of the visual does not detract from the attention given to the other senses.

References

Babin, B.J. and Darden, W.R. 1995. Consumer self-regulation in a retail environment. *Journal of Retailing*, 71(1), 47–70.

Baker, J., Parasuraman, D. and Grewal, A. 1994. The influence of store environment on quality inferences and store image. *Journal of the Academy of Marketing Science*, 22(4), 328–339.

Bateson, J.E.G. 1995. *Managing Services Marketing*. Forth Worth, TX: Dryden.

Belk, R.W. 1975. Situational variables and consumer behaviour. *Journal of Consumer Research*, 2 (December), 157–164.

Bellizi, J., Crowley, A. and Hasty, R. 1983. The effect of color in store design. *Journal of Retailing*, 59 (Spring), 21–45.

Bitner, M.J. 1992. Servicescapes: the impact of physical surroundings on customers and employees. *Journal of Marketing*, 56 (April), 57–71.

Bugelski, B.R. 1982, Learning and imagery. *Journal of Mental Imagery*, 6(2), 1–92.

Curren, M.T. and Harich, K.R. 1994. Consumer mood states: The mitigating influence of personal relevance on product evaluation. *Psychology and Marketing*, 11(2) (March/April), 91–107.

Davies, M. 2000. Location network presentation. CIRM Conference, Manchester.

Donovan, R.J. and Rossiter, J.R. 1982. Store atmosphere: An environmental psychology approach. *Journal of Retailing*, 58 (Spring), 34–57.

Donovan, R.J., Rossiter, J.R., Marcoolyn, G. and Nesdale, A. 1994. Store atmosphere and purchasing behaviour. *Journal of Retailing*, 70(3), 283–294.

Epstein, Y.M., Woolfolk, R.L. and Lehrer P.M. 1981. Physiological, cognitive, and nonverbal responses to repeated exposure to crowding. *Journal of Applied Social Psychology*, 11, 1–13.

Galizio, M. and Hendrick, C. 1972. Effect of musical accompaniment on attitude: the guitar as a prop for persuasion. *Journal of Applied Social Psychology*, 2(4), 350–359.

Gardner, M.P. 1985. Mood states and consumer behaviour: a critical review. *Journal of Consumer Research*, 12, 281–300.

Harrell, G., Hutt, M.D. and Anderson, J.C. 1980, Path analysis of buyer behaviour under conditions of crowding. *Journal of Marketing Research*, 17, 45–51.

Hediger, H. 1961. The evolution of territorial behaviour. In Washburn, S.L. (Ed.). *Social Life in Early Man*. New York: Viking Fund Publication in Anthropology, (No. 31).

Isen, A. and Simmonds, S. 1978. The effect of feeling good on a helping task that is incompatible with good mood. *Social Psychology*, 41(4), 346–349.

Lynch, K. 1960. *The Image of a City*. Cambridge, MA: The MIT Press.

Markin, R.J., Lillis, C.M. and Narayana, C.L. 1976. Socio–psychological significance of store space. *Journal of Retailing*, 52(Spring), 43–54.

Mehrabian, A. and Russell, J.A. 1974. *An Approach to Environmental Psychology*. Cambridge, MA: The MIT Press.

Newman, A.J., Davies, B.J. and Dixon, G. 1994. The marketing psychology of store image research, *The Marketing Education Group 1994 Annual Conference Proceedings*, 2(July), p. 729.

Newman, A.J. (1995), Is the way-forward bright? *Professional Marketing*, 3(5).

Scholder Ellen, P. and Fitzgerald Bone, P. 1998. Does it matter if it smells? Olfactory stimuli as advertising executional cues. *Journal of Advertising*, 27(4), 29.

Sherman, E. and Smith, R.B. 1987. Mood states of shoppers and store image; promising interactions and possible behavioural effects. In *Advances in Consumer Research*, 14 (Provo Utah: Association for Consumer Research, 1987), pp. 251–254.

Shostack, G.L. 1985. Planning the service encounter. In Czepiel, J.A., Solomon, M.R., and Suprenant, C.F. (Eds.). *The Service Encounter*. Lexington, MA: Lexington Books, pp. 243–254.

Sommer, R. 1969. *Personal Space: The Behavioural Basis of Design*. Englewood Cliffs, NJ: Prentice–Hall, Inc.

Sommer, R. 1974. *Tight Spaces – Hard Architecture and How to Humanize it*. New York: Prentice–Hall, Inc.

Spangenberg, E.R., Crowley, A.E. and Henderson, P.W. 1996. Improving the store environment: do olfactory cues affect evaluations and behaviors? *Journal of Marketing*, 60(2), 67–80.

Swinyard, W.R. 1993. The effects of mood, involvement, and quality of store experience on shopping intentions. *Journal of Consumer Research*, 20 (September), 271–280.

Underwood, B., Moore, B. and Rosenhan, D.L. 1973. Affect and self-gratification. *Developmental Psychology*, 8(2), 209–214.

Wells, B.W.P. 1965. The psycho–social influence of building environment. *Building Science*, 1, 153–165.

Zeithaml, V.A. and Bitner, M.J. 1996. *Services Marketing*. New York: McGraw–Hill Companies, Inc.

Merchandise

In a retail setting, merchandise obviously has a central place. Its role is essential in many retail exchanges and as such, it has an importance greater than that which might be attached to the props in a stage play. However, there is a sense in which any type or item of merchandise may have a symbolic value or meaning attached to it by the purchaser. Thus, a major task in this area is for the retailer to ensure that the selection and display of merchandise reinforces the messages sent by the physical environment in such a way as to ensure that the intended customers are able to easily read the script.

Given these concerns, and those that stem from the organization – such as the creation of profit – this chapter examines:
- Retail buying and merchandise selection;
- Merchandise management and display;
- Space-planning; and
- Locating merchandise within the benefit bundle.

Introduction

To a retailer, the sale of merchandise provides the foundation of their business. It is central to the nature of a store and the retail experience itself – from both the retailer's and customer's viewpoints. The shop provides a fixed point of exchange where a visitor to the store is hopefully converted to a customer – where if well executed, the experience provides mutual benefit. However, to see the retail store as purely an environment for the sale of merchandise is overly simplistic. In fact, it is difficult to conceive of retail provision ever being completely 'functional' in this sense.

Retail exchange, although bound up with the purchase of goods, is in essence a human process. Here, social interaction and exchange – be it with the retailer or with other customers – is an integral component of the process. This is clearly depicted in the original Servuction model (discussed in Chapter 6), where those elements of the service arena that the retailer provides – the inanimate environment and service personnel – can be seen to generate interactions that make up part of the total experience. This is also true of the customer-to-customer contact depicted within the model, which provides an additional source of potential benefit, but is much more difficult for the service provider to control. The Servuction model therefore strongly emphasizes the social elements of the service experience.

Locating Merchandise Within The Servuction Model

It is perhaps unsurprising that, whilst the Servuction model highlights the importance of human interactions, it does not detail the potential role of merchandise. This may be because the model was developed with a broader context of service provision in mind rather than retailing specifically. It could also perhaps be assumed that the inanimate environment element of the model subsumes merchandise as a component of the wider physicality of the store. However, this does not appear to be the case. In the literature on the Servuction model, and the inanimate environment in particular, the inclusion of merchandise as a factor contributing to the system or environment is lacking. The concern is rather with the physicality of the store itself – created, for example, by colour, lighting and fixturing. This omission is perhaps made even more surprising given the degree of empirical work concerning the inanimate environment that has been conducted in a retail setting. (See for example: Mazursky and Jacoby, 1986; Zimmer and Golden, 1988; Baker et al., 1994.)

One explanation for this may be the varied viewpoints often applied to the examination of merchandise. It is necessary to note that within this chapter the focus is more on those merchandise issues that are readily visible to the customer, and therefore topics such as inventory control and logistics, are not addressed. However, if back-of-house concerns are considered, this widens the range of merchandise-related topics still further – adding even more complexity.

Store Image and Merchandise

Merchandise has been considered at the broadest level in relation to the development of store image and retailer brand. The emphasis in this context has been to develop a coherent and consistent image by using the interplay between dimensions such as merchandise, the physical environment and price. (See Chapter 9 for a more detailed discussion of store image.) This literature guides the retailer to think in terms of merchandise management as a means of helping to create the overall character and personality of a store or retail brand. Whilst it is clear the merchandise mix of a retailer has a large part to play in this context, the store image literature does not provide a detailed 'route map' or lay down a process that the retail manager could apply to facilitate the creation of a consistent image.

Retail Buying and Merchandise

The store image literature does not perhaps tackle the provision of such a 'route map' because other subject areas devote considerable attention to guiding merchandise selection. The retail buying (and merchandise management, in particular within the fashion context of the US) literature provides more specific guidelines in relation to merchandise-related issues (Donnellan, 1996; Kunz, 1998). These range from the development of a merchandising strategy (Diamond and Pintel, 1985; Omar, 1999), to the consideration of the depth of the merchandise mix (Samli, 1989).

Within this literature, attention is also paid to other operational issues related to merchandise management – for example: supplier selection, developing own-label products, calculating price and stock order quantities (Diamond and Pintel, 1985; McGoldrick, 1990; Omar, 1999). Within the American fashion context, texts are also available that consider the specifics of buying and merchandise mathematics (Tepper, 2000; Kotsiopulos, 1994). The focus here is often to provide a framework that outlines potential processes and best practice for retail management. This body of literature has a highly practical focus – which is not to suggest that it lacks theory, but more that it is less conceptual than other areas related to retailing, for example consumption, dramaturgy and environmental psychology. Much of the literature in this field stems from the observation of retail practice, which is then used to develop process-based models, as well as often emphasizing the importance of the creativity of those involved.

There is a clear link between consideration of merchandise strategy and the consideration of assortment within the store image literature. Merchandise strategy seeks "to select the right mix of products or services to sell at the store" (Omar, 1999, p. 175); and merchandise within the store image literature is treated in much the same way – the provision of a merchandise mix that complements and reinforces the personality of the store. Although there is a degree of consistency on this point, this is one area of the retail buying literature where less 'practical' advice is offered on how to construct such a merchandise strategy or to develop the personality of a retail brand through its merchandise. The crux of the problem is perhaps that, beyond providing a framework of guidelines and general principles, the task becomes one that relies on creativity and therefore cannot be blueprinted. The responsibility appears to rest with those charged with buying merchandise; and as with any creative task, no set pattern of approach can be ascribed as each retail context potentially necessitates a different approach.

Merchandise Selection

Merchandise selection is therefore, in large part, a means of operationalizing a particular retail strategy. It relies on the creativity of the buyer to construct a 'story' that fits with the overall trajectory of the store's message, and provides potential customers with their desired shopping experience and benefits. However, meeting customer demands provides only one set of objectives for the retail buyer who is, at the same time, balancing these concerns with the cost of carrying inventory (Stassen et al., 1999). This is further complicated by the need to consider the assortment ranges of competitors and how one retailer's merchandise mix relates to another's.

Early work in marketing suggests that potentially such tensions exert diametrically opposed forces on the merchandise assortment decisions of the retail buyer. Alderson (1965) notes that "There are two competing tendencies among competitors at any level. One is to meet competition directly by offering an identical product. The other is to try to get some advantage over competitors by offering something different" (p. 80).

This highlights the issue of assortment overlap between competing stores. At one level it is desirable to offer the same products as a competitor, perhaps especially those that are brand leaders, or that the customers expect to see. However if ranges are too similar, then the potential for differentiation resides in issues such as service levels, store environment and convenience that give rise to the intangible benefits a customer derives from a shopping experience – or of course, the much more tangible benefits related to price-based competition. The wholehearted pursuit of both types of benefits is highly improbable in the retail environment. If a store that is unable to differentiate itself through its merchandise selects to provide intangible benefits as a means of generating competitive advantage, then it is likely that this focus will be offset by charging customers higher prices to not only cover the costs of carrying inventory, but the costs of delivering higher service levels. This gives rise to the development of offers such as full delivery services in the grocery market; but the potential of this, on its own, to provide the basis for long-term success appears limited. If the alternate position is adopted – low price, low service – the possibility of providing a more stable base for differentiation appears much greater. The success of limited-line deep discounters in the grocery sector provides one example. In this situation the role of the buyer changes in its emphasis to one of price negotiation and the maintaining of supply, rather than creativity.

This is not to say however, that the potential for service-based differentiation is impossible; although it does necessarily tend to be coupled with the provision of 'uniqueness' within the merchandise assortment itself. In such a context buyers again seek balance – but this time between conformity with competitors' assortments and the provision of points of differentiation within the merchandise mix. This combined approach of points of merchandise uniqueness and higher service levels is common, for example, within the UK grocery market. Such patterns can be seen in a number of players, including the two largest, Tesco and Sainsbury. In the clothing market, department stores such as US-based Nordstrom also follow such a pattern. Where however merchandise uniqueness is possible, this can be combined successfully with either a service- or price-based approach. The potential for a retailer to create a completely unique merchandise assortment that has no overlap with competitors is reliant upon the retailer having a mechanism for ensuring the products it stocks cannot be sold to other retailers. This can be achieved through a number of means: for example, backward integration, or the development of own-label lines.

Functional Decisions

These broad-level concerns can be subdivided into several functional decisions that have to be made:

> …breadth of assortment across the store (narrow or wide) and the depth of the assortment within each category (deep or shallow). In addition, retailers have to decide the quality of the items stocked within the assortment – high or low, national brands or store brands. Related to this, retailers need to decide on their pricing policies, across categories and within. Finally, retailers have to decide whether assortments generally should be stable over time or whether there should be surprise, specials, or customization in their assortments.
>
> Kahn, 1999, p. 289

Juggling all these concerns, as well as those of a higher order, must take place without losing sight of the story – no simple task.

This process of creating a retail story through merchandise selection is made even more difficult as a result of the mismatch that can occur between the product lines offered by manufacturers and the required assortments of

---

retailers (Cadeaux, 1997). Part of the reason for this mismatch lies in the 'volatility' of the product category. Where manufacturers introduce and delete products to their lines relatively quickly, retailers may be unable to establish a strong feel for consumer response to individual items. This in turn, may lead the retailer to stock more of the manufacturer's products than they might otherwise, in order to provide customer choice. In such a situation, the retail buyer is somewhat disadvantaged – not only in terms of cost and power concerns – but also in relation to the creation of a cohesive 'story'. For example, in an attempt to second-guess the market in relation to new products, they may dilute or over-elaborate the story that they are trying to establish. However, where manufacturers' ranges are more stable, the buyer may have the upper hand and be able to give greater consideration to developing their range in relation to both operational and strategic concerns (Cadeaux, 1997).

The task of merchandise selection and planning becomes yet more involved when a retailer operates a number of stores over a wide geographical area. Such a situation often necessitates the tailoring of the merchandise mix to the specific needs and tastes of local customer groups. The delivery of such customized assortments can provide the retailer with distinctive competitive advantage (Grewal et al., 1999); but it relies even more heavily on the creativity of buyers and, potentially, store managers. This type of approach does however mean that the product selection and planning process is problematical – again placing additional emphasis on the buyers and store managers; they must deal with greater range complexity and flexibility than in stores with a standard range across all branches.

The use of ranges across stores that accommodate regional variances also gives rise to a further problem related to measuring retail productivity – the comparison of stores not only with regional differences, but those potentially stocking quite distinct product assortments. This issue has led Grewal et al. (1999) to develop a productivity measure that facilitates both regional and assortment differences, and, in so doing, helps to examine and propagate 'best practice'.

Display and Merchandising

The display of merchandise can also have significant implications for the story that a retail buyer is trying to represent to support the store image (Lea-Greenwood, 1998). One such example of this support is given by Smith and Burns (1996), who examine the 'power aisle' – a massed display of a limited number of lines, used predominately by deep discount chains. They find that the fewer number of lines that are displayed, the greater the likelihood that customers perceive the products as being heavily discounted.

The potential of display to reinforce store image perceptions, as well as promote individual lines, is also highlighted by Ward et al. (1992).

Buttle (1988) implies that this visual merchandising, this "promotion of individual lines, is the 'silent salesman' of the retail context". However, visual merchandising, particularly in relation to window displays, is a somewhat neglected area within the traditional retail literature (Lea-Greenwood, 1998). One notable exception is in the American fashion context, where a few texts have been devoted to the subject – for example, Pegler (1998). The approach here is practitioner-based, rather than stemming from academic examination and as such, it adds further weight to the notion that visual merchandising is a somewhat neglected topic for retail academics. It has perhaps been a functional area that has not been given the prominence that it deserves.

This is despite the early efforts of writers such as L. Frank Baum (the author of the *Wizard of Oz* books), who, as far back as 1900, produced a seminal text on window display entitled *The Art of Decorating Dry Goods Windows and Interiors*. He could in fact, be considered a founding father of visual merchandising, as his text was a composite of many of his articles previously published in *The Show Window* – a trade publication which he started in 1897. He also wrote on merchandising issues for the *Chicago Dry Goods Reporter*, as well as earning part of his living as a window-dresser. Baum also founded the National Association of Window Trimmers, the first trade organization related to visual merchandise, whose goal was "the uplifting of mercantile decorating to the level of a profession".

Lea-Greenwood (1998) suggests that within the UK fashion industry, visual merchandising has only recently been elevated to a position of professionalism, as well as becoming an issue of board-level concern. (Only a century after Baum began his quest for very much the same thing in the US.) The potential for visual merchandising to support, and itself *develop*, store image – and thereby support and develop retailer differentiation – has only lately been paid any attention by the retail literature. As Lea-Greenwood (1998) notes, this an area that warrants much further exploration. Such consideration would help to draw together concerns as wide ranging as the integration of visual merchandising with promotional effort across the retail brand and the development of best practice.

Display also has the potential to influence the customer's perception of the goods on show. This potential can lead to tension in the buyer-supplier relationship (Buchanan et al., 1999). In their research, Buchanan et al. (1999) considered the importance of display structure (whether the products are displayed individually or with others) and display precedence (looking at the superiority given to products in the display). They found that, in displays where more than one product line is used, customers are more prone to re-evaluate the brand propositions of the products on offer – particularly those brands with which they are familiar. Equally, if superiority in the display was given to products that were unfamiliar to customers, there was a tendency for customers to again re-evaluate the relative merits of the products on offer. Buchanan et al. therefore conclude that not only do retailers have the power to influence customer perceptions of individual brands through their displays, they also have the potential to alter the ways in which customers understand the relationships between product brands themselves.

Product Attractiveness and Visibility

The overall purpose of in-store merchandising is obviously to make products both more attractive and more visible, thereby leading, hopefully, to their purchase (Hart and Davies, 1996). Traditionally, it has been suggested that the scope for developing attractive displays and merchandising has been greatest in sectors where shoppers are more inclined to browse and see shopping as a leisure activity, e.g. ladies fashion. In such contexts, merchandisers have been urged to be creative in their displays. Conversely, in sectors such as grocery retailing, where the assumption is that shoppers are seeking convenience and speed, it has been advised that merchandising should focus on the familiar and avoid the experimental, based presumably on the assumption that shoppers in this context will have little time (or sympathy) for change or the unusual (Cook and Walters, 1991). However, as Hart and Davies (1996) note, there is much greater scope for merchandising in the modern grocery store, where customers are much happier with forms such as 'store-in-store', as well as the intermingling of non-food and food categories.

A further issue closely related to product attractiveness through merchandising is the potential effect of product display. Here, one focus has again been on the interplay between single and multiple product displays. Understanding the intricacies of the possible inter-relationships necessitates an awareness of how customers make decisions in two basic situations, where only one product is displayed and the situation where choice is available. Tversky and Shafir (1992) found that the degree of conflict generated by a display of goods was of particular importance. Where only a single 'attractive' product was displayed, this produced minimal conflict during the decision-making process, and purchase therefore was much more likely. Conversely, the availability of a selection of products with similar attractiveness, raised conflict levels and decreased the likelihood of purchase. However, where one product was seen as clearly *more* attractive than others offered in a comparative display, this increased the prospect of the more attractive product's purchase. This is consistent with the findings of Huber et al. (1982) and Simonson and Tversky (1992). Simonson (1999) goes further by proposing that such product relationships can be used to the retailer's advantage. A retailer can carefully manage the sub-set of products that customers draw from its particular merchandise mix to maximize the likelihood of customers purchasing the *retailer*'s preferred product (for example, that which has the highest margin).

Hsee and Leclerc (1998) extend such work by considering the importance of the mental product reference group that is used in such contexts. They found that when a product is perceived to be better than the reference, it is more likely to be purchased, as it will be perceived to be more attractive. Customers will also in fact, be more likely to buy the product when it is displayed individually than when presented jointly. However, if the product is perceived to be less attractive than the mental reference, it is more likely to be purchased when displayed with other products than simply on its own. Hsee and Leclerc suggest that this is because, where it is possible to compare products directly, a customer is less likely to have recourse to their mental reference.

This is an important point for helping retailers decide on whether or not to provide joint product displays. Where a retailer is trying to sell a product that is likely to be perceived as more attractive than the 'average' product, there is more scope for display. Where a retailer is selling goods that are perceived to be less attractive than the average product, then it is better to utilize a *comparative* display. By using such displays, the customer is less likely to have recourse to their mental reference and instead rely on making a decision by simply comparing what is on offer.

As Hsee and Leclerc (1998) note however, there are number of factors that may moderate the way in which products are evaluated. For example, if a customer is familiar with a particular product category, then they are less likely to limit their considerations to the set of products displayed. Equally, if the products displayed are not easy to evaluate against one another, this may mean that a customer resorts to using their mental reference. This potential for individual variation of course, makes the retailer's decisions regarding display much more difficult.

Merchandise Range and Consumer Response

Customers' responses to merchandise are also affected by other retailer determined factors. Here, there are a number of issues to be considered. One such factor is the response to assortment width – the number of different classes of product carried by a particular retailer (Omar, 1999).

Assortment Width

Bawa et al. (1989) investigated the impact – on customer selection and brand switching behaviour in a grocery store context – of the width of product assortment, in conjunction with both display and other in-store promotional activity. The basic premise for their research was that customers, when faced with too much information or too many choices, seek to simplify their buying task (Lussier and Olshavsky, 1979).

One means of such simplification is by focusing on just one factor of in-store promotion – be that the displayed product, some special feature, or price-related offers. Consumers may use such cues to generate a consideration set that only includes those products that are being specially promoted, thereby simplifying the range of products that they consider for purchase. Customers who act in this manner are 'deal prone' and also tend to display lower brand loyalty, making them more likely to switch between products and try unfamiliar brands (Bawa and Shoemaker, 1987).

Where customers do not simplify their decision-making in stores with wide assortments, but actually increase their consideration set, the end result is the same. In this situation, brand switching is also increased, but here it is as a result of a wide assortment provoking variety-seeking behaviour, rather then simplification (Bawa et al., 1989).

In fact, Bawa et al. (1989) conclude that stores with larger assortments prompted the following response in customers:

- A lower degree of loyalty to any one brand of product.
- A higher sensitivity to in-store promotion (it potentially acting as a useful heuristic for screening a large number of product options).
- A greater degree of price sensitivity (possibly as a result of the ability to compare one price against a wider selection of goods).
- A higher propensity for new product trials.

These findings suggest a number of practical implications. Where retailers utilize wide assortments as part of their overall offer, there is the opportunity to influence buying behaviour through targeted promotional activity. This can obviously help a retailer either clear certain stock; promote products that provide a higher level of margin, or introduce new products. This final element is further supported by customers' willingness to trial products in this type of merchandise environment, which would also enable retailers to charge suppliers either wanting to launch new products or wanting to promote existing products.

Conversely by implication, retailers that utilize smaller assortments can expect a higher degree of product brand loyalty. This too can provide a potentially powerful tool in bargaining with suppliers. It also places a higher degree of emphasis on managing stock levels. If customers are highly brand-loyal, then the impact of stock unavailability might be considerably greater than in stores where customers are much more prone to switch brands. Brand-loyal customers are likely to be less price sensitive, and this may provide the retailer with additional scope to develop higher margins.

Importantly, Bawa et al. (1989) also determined that assortment width had a greater effect than in-store promotion in determining the level of product-level brand loyalty displayed. This suggests that it is indeed *assortment* that plays the key part in purchase behaviour. Although, as Bawa et al. themselves note, part of the effects observed stem from the nature and attitudes of the customers themselves. However, these did not have the strength of impact on behaviour that was displayed by assortment width.

Assortment Depth

The effects of assortment depth – the number of lines within a particular product class (Omar, 1999) – have also been examined to determine its potential influence on customer behaviour. The impetus here has come from retail management's desire to minimize costs. This need became particularly acute in the early 1990s when retailers in general, and grocers in particular, were urged to reduce the number of lines that they sold. These concerns were raised by industry commentators, although retailers themselves were reluctant to follow the advice offered (Broniarczyk et al., 1998). This unwillingness stemmed from evidence that customers developed a positive assessment of the store based in part on its assortment mix (Arnold et al., 1983) – a strong component of the store image literature. Retailers therefore worried that, by decreasing the items offered in their merchandise range, customers' perceptions would be negatively influenced; and this would then decrease customers' propensity to shop at an individual store. This meant that two opposing concerns were at work: the need for cost reduction, and the maintenance of a deep assortment.

However, the mid 1990s onwards witnessed an increase in the number of studies which reported that a reduction in the number of lines held by a retailer could in fact increase sales (Dreze et al., 1994). This provided retailers not only with such increased sales, but also reduced costs (as predicted); although the impact on customer perception was unclear. In 1998, Broniarczyk et al. attempted to consider the impact of item reduction on the customer perception of assortment depth, and also examined the influence of favourite product availability, as well as the shelf space devoted to a particular category.

This study, in common with that of Bawa et al. (1989), rests on the premise that customers are unlikely to actively process all the information available when making purchase decisions – especially those that can be classified as being low in involvement (Dickson and Sawyer, 1990). Therefore, it is unlikely that customers will actively make assessments of the merchandise mix on each visit – unless drastic change has taken place.

This proposition – as Broniarczyk et al. (1998) importantly suggest – implies that customer and retailer views of assortment are not formed in the same manner. Retailers must obviously consider merchandise from a detailed perspective, which means that they take into account each product line and the operational issues attached to providing their selected mix. Customers conversely in the main, do not develop such a detailed consideration of the assortment provided: rather than seek to simplify their decision-making and not complicate it. Additionally:

> ...individuals are able to detect a change in the environment only when it surpasses a certain threshold or 'just noticeable difference'. Therefore, consumers who use the total number of SKUs [stock keeping units or lines]... cue might not be able to detect small or moderate changes in the number of items offered.
>
> Broniarczyk et al., 1998

Their study demonstrated that the reduction of lines in their test categories by twenty-five per cent made no impact on customers' perceptions of the product assortment. This was however, to a large extent, moderated by the availability of the customer's favourite product. If this was unavailable, then customers began to notice the reduction. Customers' perceptions were also moderated by the space given to a category. If category space was held constant, the assortment reduction went unnoticed. Interestingly, where both category space was held constant and the favourite item was available, customers actually thought that assortment levels had increased. Broniarczyk et al. (1998) went on to establish the 'just noticeable difference' for the reduction of stock lies somewhere between twenty-five and fifty per cent. Their research – although initially conducted under experimental conditions – then went on to test this in a real store, and the patterns established earlier continued to be seen.

Implications

This research would seem to suggest that it may be possible for retailers to reduce the number of lines within categories, and, rather than this negatively impacting assortment perception, it can in fact be perceived as an assortment increase. As assortment perception has been positively linked to store choice, this provides retailers with the potential to cut costs in tandem with increasing the positive perceptions of customers. However as Stassen et al. (1999) note, the pursuit of such a goal may have dramatic – and perhaps unwanted – results. They suggest "that a retailer choosing to make consistent reductions in depth across categories would face a different competitor or set of competitors". This would obviously alter the position of the retailer within the market, and could place them in competition with limited-line retailers – dramatically changing the nature of the competitive environment that they face. Therefore, although removing lines creates a large number of benefits, it can result in the retailer's market position being significantly altered. The implications of such shifts can be equally dramatic, and therefore item reduction needs careful consideration.

Additionally, to fully understand the implications of removing (or in fact adding) items to assortment depth on customer purchase patterns, there needs to be an understanding of these implications coupled with issues of product substitution, price, store environment effects and the presence of competing offers, as well as the customer's purchase goal. Koelemeijer and Oppewal (1999), in their study of the fresh-flower category, found that store environment (either that of the selected store for purchase, or indeed that of competitors) made no significant impact on purchase decisions. However, if the store has a poor environment and a competitor is located close by, then, unsurprisingly, they found that it was likely that the customer would go to the competitor. Perhaps more interestingly, they reported that assortment size had a strong effect on purchase intention.

This suggests, as does the work of Broniarczyk et al. (1998), that there is a point at which too limited an assortment acts as a detractor. What Koelemeijer and Oppewal (1999) also found is that customers' perceptions of what products substituted for which, were not as straightforward as might at first be presumed. For example, red and white roses are not substitutes, but tulips of different colours are. Asymmetrical dominance effects were also observed.

Here, the addition of a white flower to the assortment mix had little effect on the sales of red flowers of the same variety; but the converse was not seen – adding a red flower decreased the sale of the white variant. Such complex interactions between merchandise items make the management of assortment depth even more difficult. Koelemeijer and Oppewal (1999) however, developed a mathematical model to enable retail managers to model the impact of changes in assortment depth, whilst considering the impact of competitive and customer factors; and although this is still in an early stage of development, it does provide the possibility of practical help for managers in carrying out this complex task.

The Current State of Merchandise Management and Customer Response

One of the most comprehensive theoretical articles – that also provides a range of practical propositions related to merchandise management (based on previous empirical work) – is that of Simonson (1999). He develops eleven propositions (some of which are further subdivided) that encompass a wide range of merchandise management issues – including a number that have been discussed above:

The Effects of Considered Assortment on Consumer Purchase Decisions

- Proposition 1a: The probability that a consumer will make a purchase is enhanced if the considered assortment is designed such that one option is clearly superior to another.
- Proposition 1b: The choice probability of a particular target option can be enhanced by adding an option that is clearly inferior relative to the target option, but not to other options in the considered product assortment.

The Effects of Preferences for and Against Compromise Options on Purchase Probability

- Proposition 2: Consumers tend to favour compromise (middle) options for some product categories and attributes, and tend to avoid compromise options for other categories and attributes. A consistent preference for compromise options is expected when the differentiating dimensions are characterized by diminishing marginal values; whereas preferences for non-compromise options are expected when the instrumental attribute is characterized by increasing marginal value.

The Effect of the Number of Quality Levels in a Product Assortment on Purchase Decisions

- Proposition 3a: The purchase likelihood of a higher price, higher quality item can be enhanced by introducing an even higher price, higher quality item to the subset of options that the customer considers.
- Proposition 3b: If the considered product assortment includes two options that vary in price and quality, the addition of either an intermediate or a

high price, high quality alternative takes more share from the low price, low quality option, than from the other existing option.

The Effect of Offering Multiple Attractive Products on Purchase Timing

- Proposition 4: Presenting consumers with two equally attractive options can lead to a purchase delay and a loss of sales.

Assortment Choice Set Effects Across Related (Complementary) Categories

- Proposition 5: For items that are purchased on the same occasion, the attribute levels of one item can affect the attribute levels of another item, even when the two are not functional complements or substitutes. Specifically, in trade-offs between a goal and a resource, consumers make consistent choices within an episode, whereas in trade-offs between two goals they prefer balancing the two goals within each consumption episode.

Side-By-Side Versus Separate Brand Displays

- Proposition 6: Consumers are relatively more likely to purchase high (perceived) quality, high price brands when they are displayed separately rather than next to competing options; and vice versa for low quality, low price brands.

Assortment Display By Brand Versus By Model

- Proposition 7: The choice share of the cheapest considered brand is lower when products are displayed by model tier; whereas the share of the least expensive model is lower when product display is organized by brand.

Using Incomplete Option Descriptions to Influence Consumer Choices

- Proposition 8: Retailers can increase the share of a target option by making it easy for buyers to compare products on attributes on which the target option is superior, while making comparisons on other attributes more difficult.

The Effect of Considered Assortment on Asymmetric Promotional Response

- Proposition 9: Asymmetric promotional response – whereby regular buyers of low-tier products are more likely to switch to a promoted high-tier product than high-tier buyers are to switch to a promoted low-tier product – is eliminated when buyers consider products at three quality tiers.

Product Enhancements and Promotional Premiums

- Proposition 10: The effects of premiums and added features on sales depend on the share of buyers who perceive them as offering value, with premiums/features that are perceived by many as offering little or no value potentially decreasing sales.

Purchase Quantity and Variety Seeking

- Proposition 11: Retailers can increase the quantity of purchase (in relevant categories) by offering bundles of different preferred items. Retailers can increase the variety of options that buyers select using promotions and other means that encourage the purchase of multiple items in a category.

These propositions begin to provide a culmination of the different merchandise-related issues. They do not however, address in an overt way, a further merchandise issue – that of space planning.

Merchandise and Space Planning

The issue of the space devoted to categories of merchandise, as well as the space devoted to a particular line, are examined from a different perspective within the literature on space planning or space allocation. This area has received attention in part as a result of the importance it is given by retailers themselves, as:

> ...the product-display area available constitutes a strictly binding constraint. Moreover, evaluating the consequences of shelf rearrangements is not a trivial exercise because these influence both distribution costs and items' sales in various ways.
>
> Bultez et al., 1989

For example, increasing the facings given to one line may increase its sales, but this may in turn decrease the sale of similar products on offer. Such a move not only has implications for sales and profit, but also for inventory management and logistics.

The operational topic of space allocation is one where retailers have spent much time and investment – both financial and human – developing mechanisms for maximizing sales-floor usage and returns. One of the chief difficulties in this pursuit has stemmed from the ability to consider sales-floor space at many levels (Davies and Ward, 2000).

Store Level

- The first level is that of the store. Decisions need to be made regarding the overall components of the sales-floor. In a grocery store for example, how much floor space should be devoted to fruit and vegetables, dairy, and frozen food? Where would these 'departments' be best located; and which should be placed next to each other? This level of decision-making concerns merchandise in its broadest groupings – that of the section or department.

Category Level

- The second level involves the categories within a department. Continuing the grocery store example: dairy could be subdivided into various categories including yellow fats, milk, cheese and dairy-based desserts. Again, how much space should be given to each; what order should they follow; and where within a department's space should they be located?

Product Level

- The final level concerns the individual product lines within a category. For instance skimmed, semi-skimmed and full fat milk in all its various sizes, containers and variants. Here, too, the same issues can raised.

Of these three levels, it is that of the category and the product that have received most attention in the literature, and this has mainly been from either an operational or marketing perspective. This approach was established by Corstjens and Doyle (1981) who building on work that extended over thirty years, sought to develop rules for the space allocation of narrow categories such as chocolate and ice-cream. The rules that were developed used inventory and handling costs as well as space elasticities as a foundation. In 1983, they incorporated growth factors, with the aim of building a dynamic model and foresaw that data generated by electronic point-of-sale (EPOS) technology would increase the possibility of more 'scientific decision-making'.

A Scientific Approach

The search for a more scientific process for space allocation subsequently flourished – with various commentators developing different rule-sets and later, decision support systems. (See for example: Thurik and Kooiman, 1986; Zufryden, 1986; Borin et al., 1994; Urban, 1998). The approaches used were varied, as were the factors taken into consideration – ranging from corporate constraints to category importance, and from display to product contribution. The general pattern was the use of more complicated rule-sets facilitated by the increasing speed of processing technology.

As a result of this, the approaches developed in the literature are technique-driven and not managerially-orientated. There has also been a tendency to 'isolate' one level of space from the others and this – both in the literature and in practice – means that the treatment of space and merchandise allocation within it has not been holistic. There is often a 'gap' between those that develop merchandise allocations at the store level and those that deal with the category and product level (Davies and Ward, 2000). This obviously has serious implications for retailers and their efficient and effective management of space.

It is necessary to note that almost all of the space allocation literature has been developed with a grocery context in mind – perhaps due to the large number of lines sold and the relatively straightforward nature of the fixturing employed. However, despite this narrow focus, many of the concerns raised are as appropriate in any retail context as they are in the grocery sector.

To a certain degree, there has been a dissociation of formal space allocation mechanisms in the literature from other merchandise-related concerns – for example, store image and display. This leads space planners to see part of their role as being the management of the aesthetic concerns that impact the development of the store's 'look' (Davies and Ward, 2000). This is also the area that is perhaps least well-served by the technical procedures in place for space allocation. It is here that the space planners are able to modify the solution developed by their computer systems to take into consideration the requirements and expectations of customers. Therefore, formal space planning mechanisms, although by their very nature related to merchandise, appear to lack an easy means of considering the nature and implications of space from the customer's perspective – they in essence lack creativity.

The Problem of Merchandise-Related Research

It is worth noting that much of the literature developed from empirical work, which considers merchandise-related issues, is derived from experimental approaches that do not, in the main, utilize real situations (unlike

Broniarczyk et al. (1998), above). Rather, much of the research draws on the use of visual stimuli; written descriptions of merchandise; or perhaps at best, physical mock-ups of categories. The lack of empirical research conducted utilizing the manipulation of assortments in actual retail settings is perhaps understandable (Baker et al., 1992). Given the central importance of merchandise in creating income, it is unlikely that a retailer will allow the manipulation of assortments simply to find what will be the result. This does mean that it is difficult to ascertain customers' actual response to merchandise alterations – especially when all the other elements of the service arena are also acting upon the customer and potentially influencing their decision-making processes (Areni and Kim, 1994; Smith and Burns, 1996).

The retail environment, although focused on providing a location for the sale of goods, also facilitates a number of more abstract and personal exchanges. This is especially true in contemporary western environments – where as Chapters 2 and 4 suggest, the role of the store has developed to provide a space for theatre, fantasy and self-expression. In such contexts, the nature and role of the store takes on a much broader perspective, but the provision of merchandise continues to provide a central element of retailing.

Locating Merchandise Within The Benefit Bundle

This proposition can be expressed by adapting the 'flower of service model' developed by Lovelock (1996), which displays the potentially multifaceted nature of any service-based offer.

In the retail context, merchandise is depicted as central – the very 'eye' of the flower. Around it is a disc of ancillary services that could include:

Credit;
Wedding lists;
Gift wrapping;
Personal shoppers;
Café and customer toilets;
Home delivery; and
Parent-and-child parking spaces.

The first two elements of the flower are under the retailer's control and might be seen as the basis of the specific retail offer (Figure 8.1). Arranged around these are the 'petals', which can also form part of the retail offer, but are not directly under the retailer's control. The petals depict the 'human' elements of retail provision – those things that a customer could derive from the retail experience.

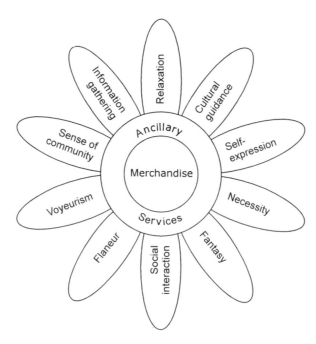

Figure 8.1 The retail offer

Merchandise acts as the central element for the retail offer, because it is the locus of exchange. Whilst a customer may be happy to pay in part for a pleasurable experience – the opportunity to relax, the space to engage in fantasy, or for the provision of ancillary services – the most tangible and obvious component of the retail exchange process is the merchandise.

However, it need not necessarily be the most enduring component that a customer receives from the retail exchange process. This can for example be the memory of a particular social exchange or the recollection of a 'good day out', where the memory of the specifics of what was purchased is at best vague or even forgotten.

What merchandise does provide is, at the very least, an immediate and concrete marker of the retail offer and exchange process. Consider how often consumers say "I bought *this* today" – displaying the items purchased – and then possibly go on to recall and recount other elements of the exchange process: for example, "They were really helpful" or "This guy in front of me was really rude". In this sense, within the short-term, merchandise provides an anchor for the complete retail exchange process, although in the longer term its importance in the customer's mind may decline.

Conclusions

The role of merchandise is a lynchpin in terms of both the retail offer and the exchange process. Given this proposition, merchandise management is an area that needs particular attention – not only in terms of creating consistency with components of the total offer (Samli, 1989) – but as a foundation for the whole offer itself and in creating an anchor for other elements that the consumer may take away with them from the retail experience. Of primary concern, from the retailer's perspective, is the key role of merchandise as a sales and profit generator.

The lack of concerted and consistent attention given to the management of merchandise and its display is perhaps a result of the highly varied and potentially context-specific nature of the issues raised. For example, item reduction in a grocery context may provide one outcome in terms of customer perceptions; but a similar reduction within a merchandise category in a fashion context may have very different results. Part of the reason for such discrepancies in outcome stems again from the interconnected nature of the retail offer. Merchandise works with other factors, such as store environment and service level, and therefore to simply consider merchandise in isolation leads to a situation where it is difficult to generate 'rules' that can be applied across all retail offers uniformly.

This perhaps helps to explain why issues related to merchandise management can be found in so many different contexts. There is, however, a need to try and unite these different approaches and perspectives, whilst maintaining an understanding of the interconnectivities of merchandise and other elements of the retail mix, to provide a deeper understanding of this central area of retail concern.

References

Alderson, W. 1965. *Dynamic Marketing Behavior: a Functionalist Theory of Marketing*. Homewood, IL: Irwin.

Areni, C.S. and Kim, D. 1994. The influence of in-store lighting on consumers' examination of merchandise in a wine store. *International Journal of Research in Marketing*, 11 (March), 117–125.

Arnold, S.J., Oum, T.H, and Tigert, D.J. 1983. Determinants attributes in retail patronage; seasonal, temporal, regional and international comparisons. *Journal of Marketing Research*, 20, 149–157.

Baker, J., Levy, M. and Grewal, D. 1992. An experimental approach to marking retail store environmental decisions. *Journal of Retailing*, 68(4), 445–460.

Baker, J., Grewal, D. and Parasuraman, A. 1994. The influence of store environment on quality inferences and store image. *Journal of the Academy of Marketing Science*, 22(4), 328–339.

Baum, L. Frank. 1900. *The Art of Decorating Dry Goods Windows and Interiors*. Chicago, IL: Show Window.

Bawa, K., Landwehr, J. and Krishna, A. 1989. Consumer response to retailers' marketing environments. *Journal of Retailing*, 65(4), 471–496.

Bawa, K. and Shoemaker, R.W. 1987. The coupon-prone consumer: some findings based on purchase behaviour across product classes. *Journal of Marketing*, 51 (October), 99–110.

Borin, N., Farris, P.W. and Freeland, J.R. 1994. A model for determining retail product category assortment and shelf space allocation. *Decision Science*, 25(3), 339–384.

Broniarczyk, S.D., Hoyer, W.D. and McAlister, L. 1998. Consumers; perceptions of the assortment offered in a grocery category: the impact of item reduction. *Journal of Marketing Research*, 35(2), 166–177.

Buchanan, C., Simmons, C.J. and Bickart, B.A. 1999. Brand equity dilution: retailer display and context brand effects. *Journal of Marketing Research*, 36(3), 345.

Bultez, A., Naert, P., Gijsbrechts, E. and Vanden Abeele, P. 1989. Asymmetric cannibalism in retail assortments. *Journal of Retailing*, 65(2), 153–193.

Buttle, F. 1988. Merchandising. *European Journal of Marketing*, 18(5), 4–25.

Cadeaux, J.M. 1997. A closer look at the interface between the product lines of manufactures and the assortments of retailers. *International Journal of Retail and Distribution Management*, 25(6/7), 197–204.

Cook, D. and Walters, D. 1991. *Retail Marketing: Theory and Practice*. Hemel Hempstead: Prentice–Hall.

Corstjens, M. and Doyle, P. 1981. A dynamic model for strategically allocating retail space. *Journal of the Operational Research Society*, 34(10), 943–951.

Davies, B.J. and Ward, P.J. 2000. Space allocation in the UK grocery sector. *British Food Journal*, 102(5), 406–419.

Diamond, J. and Pintel, G. 1985. *Retail Buying*. Englewood Cliffs, NJ: Prentice Hall.

Dickson, P. R and Sawyer, A. G. 1990. The price knowledge search of supermarket shoppers. Journal of Marketing, 54(July), 42–53.

Donnellan, J. 1996. *Merchandise Buying and Management*. New York: Fairchild Publications.

Dreze, X., Hoch, S.J. and Purk, M.E. 1994. Shelf management and space elasticity. *Journal of Retailing*, 70(4), 301–326.

Grewal, D., Levy, M., Mehrotra, A. and Sharma, A. 1999. Planning merchandising decisions to account for regional and product assortment differences. *Journal of Retailing*, 75(3), 405.

Hart, C. and Davies, M. 1996. The location and merchandising of non-food in supermarkets. *International Journal of Retail and Distribution Management*, 24(3), 17–25.

Hsee, C.K. and Leclerc, F. 1998. Will products look more attractive when presented separately or together? *Journal of Consumer Research*, 25(2), 175–186.

Huber, J., Payne, J.W. and Puto, C. 1982. Adding asymmetrically dominated alternatives; violations of regularity and similarity hypothesis. *Journal of Consumer Research*, 9 (June), 90–98.

Kahn, B.E. 1999. Introduction to the special issue: assortment planning. *Journal of Retailing*, 75(3), 289.

Koelemeijer, K. and Oppewal, H. 1999. Assessing the effects of assortment and ambience: a choice experimental approach. *Journal of Retailing*, 75(3), 319.

Kotsiopulos, A. 1994. *Merchandising Mathematics*. New York: Fairchild Publications.

Kunz, G.I. 1998. *Merchandising Theory, Principle and Practice*. New York: Fairchild Publications.

Lea-Greenwood, G. 1998. Visual merchandising; a neglected area in UK fashion marketing? *International Journal of Retail and Distribution Management*, 26(8), 324–329.

Lovelock, C. 1996. *Service Marketing (3rd Ed.)*. Upper Saddle River, NJ: Prentice Hall.

Lussier, D.A. and Olshavsky, R.W. 1979. Task complexity and contingent processing in brand choice. *Journal of Consumer Research*, 6(September), 154–165.

Mazursky, D. and Jacoby, J. 1986. Exploring the development of store image. *Journal of Retailing*, 62(2), 145–165.

McGoldrick. P.J. 1990. *Retail Marketing*. Maidenhead: McGraw–Hill.

Omar, O. 1999. *Retail Marketing*. London: Pearson Education Limited.

Pegler, M.M. 1998. *Visual Merchandising and Display (4th Ed.)*. New York: Fairchild Publications.

Samli, A.C. 1989. *Retail Marketing Strategy: Planning, Implementation and Control*. New York: Quorum Books.

Simonson I. and Tversky A. 1992. Choice in context: tradeoff contrast and extremeness aversion. *Journal of Marketing Research*, 19 (August), 281–295.

Simonson I. 1999. The effect of product assortment on buyer preferences. *Journal of Retailing*, 75(3), 347.

Smith, P. and Burns, D.J. 1996. Atmospherics and retail environments: the case of the "power aisle". *International Journal of Retail and Distribution Management*, 24(1), 7–15.

Stassen, R.E., Mittelstaedt, J.D. and Mittelstaedt. R.A. 1999. Assortment overlap: its effects on shopping patterns in a retail market when distributions of prices and goods are known. *Journal of Retailing*, 75(3), 371.

Tepper, B.K. 2000. *Mathematics For Retail Buying (5th Ed.)*. New York: Fairchild Publications.

Thurik, R. and Kooiman, P. 1986. Modelling retail floorspace productivity. *Journal of Retailing*, 62(4), 431–445.

Tversky, A. and Shafir, E. 1992. Choice under conflict: the dynamics of deferred decision. *Psychological Science*, 3 (November), 358–361.

Urban, T.L. 1998. An inventory-theoretic approach to product assortments and shelf–space allocation. *Journal of Retailing*, 74(1), 15–35.

Ward, J.C., Bitner, M.J. and Barnes, J. 1992. Measuring the prototypicality and meaning of retail environments. *Journal of Retailing*, 68(2), 194–220.

Zimmer, M.R. and Golden, L.L. 1988. Impressions of retail stores: a content analysis of consumer images. *Journal of Retailing*, 64(3), 265–294.

Zufryden, F.S. 1986. A dynamic programming approach for product selection and supermarket space allocation. *Journal of the Operational Research Society*, 37(4), 413–422.

Atmosphere and Image

Whilst the notion of retail image has had currency since the late 1950s, the image attributes that have been identified often relate to functional aspects of the store. The cognitive and affective ways in which a more generalized notion of retail image influences consumer actions is therefore presented.

The importance of store image may lie in the need to expand on merely economic or geographic predictors of store attractiveness, as image has been shown to be related to store loyalty and patronage. In such circumstances, the manipulation of controllable elements to create positive image, and thus 'liking', is a major component in a retailer's ability to differentiate its offer from that of its competitors. This leads to an examination of:

- Atmosphere and ambience;
- Branding and differentiation;
- Liking and image; and
- Patronage motives.

Introduction

The 'staging' of the retail drama through the physical environment – both internal and external – the approach of the actors, the nature of the merchandise on display and the fundamental qualities that the retailer embodies – coalesce to create a specific retail offer. This offer has an important role to play in influencing how a retailer is perceived. The expectations and perceptions created by the offer, and perhaps ultimately the experiences that a shopper has when interacting with the retailer, all help to generate a particular 'view' of the store in the shopper's mind. The view that a consumer holds of the Danish food discount store Netto is likely to be very different from their perception of the up-market UK grocery retailer Waitrose. It is not simply the differences between the two companies' pricing policies that creates such divergent views, but a number of cues taken from a wide range of sources – including the 'look' of the stores, the breadth, depth and composition of their respective merchandise ranges, and the levels of service provided. The view created of a retailer is therefore a complex construct, which develops in the consumer's mind as the result of various stimuli and their interactions.

This notion of the creation of a 'view' led Martineau (1958), one of the first writers to express the potential importance of such concerns, to suggest that "...the way in which the store is defined in the shopper's mind..." could be described as its 'store image'. He went on to propose that the shopper's 'definition' of the store strongly affected their patronage intentions, thereby clearly expressing the potential of store image to act as an important contributor to a retailer's 'attraction'. The level of attraction that the consumer feels towards Netto and Waitrose, if they are the only potential sources of groceries, will influence where the consumer decides to do their shopping. In suggesting such a relationship, Martineau's work began to introduce another strand of thought that could assist in understanding retail patronage decisions. At the time, it also served as an alternative to the various models based on central place theory that provided relatively poor results in their attempts to predict patronage decisions (Engstrøm and Hartvig Larsen, 1987).

In beginning to consider the potential of store image as a predictor of patronage, Martineau provided the foundation for a rich area of study that would subsequently became a major issue for academics and practitioners. The idea encompasses not only the *impression* created by a retailer, but its impact on shopper patronage, purchasing and loyalty.

A Focus on Store Image

In his work, Martineau (1958) identified store image as being created by two components derived from the totality of the retail offer: "...functional qualities and ...psychological attributes". He outlined a number of potentially interconnected elements – including location, price ranges and merchandise – as being functional; and more ephemeral concerns such as a store's personality as being related to the psychological components of store image. In doing this, Martineau also helped to create two distinct concerns in the work on store image that followed.

Defining Store Image

Firstly, Martineau's influence is felt in the nature of the definitions of store image that were later developed. There is a clear trend to consider not only issues related to the concrete physicality of the store and its offer, but also to concerns that extend to the emotional responses that develop in the shopper. As Bloemer et al. (1998) note, store image, since Martineau's seminal work, has been invariably treated and defined as a 'gestalt', reflecting a shopper's overall impression of a retailer. This is clearly depicted in the definitions developed by Arons (1961) and Dichter (1988), who both describe store image as a 'global' impression created by a complex bundle of meanings. Such sentiments are also echoed in Keaveney and Hunt's (1992) definition of store image, and can equally be seen in that generated by Baker et al. (1994).

They suggest that store image is a combination of an individual's cognitive and emotional responses, which are generated from their perceptions or memories of a particular store, and which also represent what the store signifies to the individual. It is clear that what is central to the notion of store image is the customer's *perceptions* of the retail offer – not necessarily simply on the basis of an individual interaction, but as the result of ongoing experiences. A Netto shopper who returns weekly might perceive the store to offer good quality products at very low prices, including occasional special non-food bargains, in a simple and clean environment, without providing 'superfluous' augmenting services (such as a café or gift vouchers) that they do not value. In this example, it is the customer's interaction with the physical retail environment that appears to be critical.

This is reflected in many of the definitions of store image, where there is an implicit focus on physical interaction between the customer and the retailer's Servuction arena (see Chapter 6). However, this is perhaps an overly narrow focus, and the perceptions that a customer develops towards a specific retail offer may also be affected by that retailer's promotion and by the impressions that others – either personal contacts such as friends and family, or impersonal sources including the media – express in relation to a store. A grocery shopper who has never visited a Netto store might develop an image of the store based purely on its promotion and the attitudes expressed by others. This could be that the store is 'primitive' and sells brands that are unfamiliar and are therefore inferior. Or perhaps that it provides a valuable means for those on limited incomes to make the most of their money. Or even that it sells goods at realistic prices and exposes the inflated prices charged by other grocery retailers. It seems likely that, no matter how a customer perceives a store's personality, their perception is influenced by how that image is depicted by the store's promotion and by others through their comments and views – as well as, of course, the customer's own memories and interpretations of previous experiences. It would therefore seem appropriate to suggest that store image is indeed the customer's overall impression of a retail offer, which is formed by the totality of interactions that relate to the retailer – be they physical or inferred.

Defining the Dimensions of Store Image

Secondly, Martineau's (1958) work created a strong interest in developing dimensions related to the functional qualities and psychological attributes of store image. This later work has primarily related to those dimensions that are under the direct control of the retailer. Over the years, researchers have developed various conceptualizations of which dimensions act as reference points in the construction and interpretation of store personality. Peterson and Kerin (1983) noted that attempts to identify the dimensions of store image had been so numerous that in the twenty years since the early 1960s, approximately one academic article per month had been published on the subject. This volume then presents a major difficulty in developing a full review of the literature on store image. However, what it is possible to provide is an overview of the common themes that emerge from the copious literature that in some way concerns store image dimensions.

Porter and Claycomb (1997) – drawing on the work of Lindquist (1974), Martineau (1958) and Zimmer and Golden (1988) – list fashion, selection, quality of merchandise, customer service, sales personnel, physical condition and atmosphere of the store as commonly cited store image dimensions. To this list they add the nature of overall brand mix carried by the shop.

Similar breakdowns of store image are given by Grewal et al. (1998) using, as a basis, the work of Baker et al. (1994) and Zimmer and Golden (1988). Grewal et al. (1998) in their work also propose that store name and the merchandise brand names carried by the retailer have a role to play in the creation of store image. Bloemer and de Ruyter (1998) use previous work on store image by Doyle and Fenwick (1974–1975), Lindquist (1974) and Bearden (1977) plus the retail marketing mix outlined by Ghosh (1990), to additionally highlight price, store location and promotion as dimensions of store image. Given the attempts of these various authors to provide an outline of the dimensions of store image, the following list can be synthesized:

- Merchandise

  - Assortment
  - Quality
  - Brand mix
  - Price

- Store

  - Location
  - Environment (internal and external)
  - Atmosphere
  - Name/fascia

- Service

  - Personnel
  - Levels and quality

- Promotion

  - Advertising/public relations
  - In-store

However, as Erdem et al. (1999) report, there is considerable variation in the number of dimensions that researchers have used in store image studies. It is also worth noting that the derivation of store image dimensions in the retail literature has been predominantly achieved through the application of two main approaches. The first is demonstrated above, where potentially appropriate dimensions are identified using previous studies. This approach relies heavily on the efficacy of the previous work. Therefore, it can be difficult to develop a 'true' sense of what is indeed important to customers when they develop a particular store image, as customers' responses have obviously been 'filtered' by those who conducted the original research.

The second method for determining store image dimensions is also prone to potential bias and distortion. Researchers identify what *they* believe to be the most relevant attributes (potentially using previous literature), and then ask customers to score the importance of these dimensions. Such 'forced choice' techniques necessarily constrain customers to use these pre-selected dimensions – which could have implications for the overall validity of the research.

However, there *were* early attempts to apply more open-ended techniques by Cardozo (1974), and by Kunkel and Berry (1968). Although both proved to be successful approaches, such patterns of enquiry have not been the norm. So, whilst the store image dimensions outlined above offer an intuitively logical analysis, it must be remembered that their derivation is potentially subject to bias.

It must also be noted that the dimensions are not to be viewed in isolation, but are rather to be seen as interacting with each other to influence the customer's overall gestalt of store image (Shrimp, 1990). There is therefore a need for the retailer to consider how the dimensions of store image coalesce to produce the larger 'personality' of the store. This in turn means that thought has to be directed at the interaction of the dimensions, and the potential to use them to develop the desired tone for a store. To achieve this goal there needs to be consideration of the 'principle of totality'.

> This states that all features of a design must share a common purpose. The design process should not consider features of the design in isolation, but within the context of their relationship to all other features and the purpose for which they exist. Within a design, each aspect is equally important and its eventual fulfilment is essential for the design to be considered total. The principle of totality is concerned with ensuring that there is a logical relationship among the components of the retail mix, the retailer's self-perception, the perception of the customer and the customer's requirements.
>
> Doyle and Broadbridge, 1999

Within the general framework of identified dimensions, store atmosphere is perhaps the one that is itself most highly dependent on the interaction of the other elements.

Store Atmospherics

Of all the store image dimensions, atmosphere (or ambience) is the most ephemeral: it relates to the "mental or moral environment; a pervading tone or mood" (*The New Shorter Oxford English Dictionary*, 1993, p. 139). It is the mood exuded by the complete retail offer, which is then interpreted by the customer. As such, store atmosphere is very much 'in the mind of the customer' – it is the individual's perception of the cues provided both separately and collectively by the store, and perhaps also primarily by its location, environment and personnel. To return to the language of the theatre metaphor introduced in Chapter 5, store atmosphere is heavily influenced by store staff/actors (the characters that they portray, and perhaps more importantly, the fundamental qualities that are manifested in these characters); the store's aesthetic, and the staging of the retail drama. These serve to present the customer with a particular tone – be it the nostalgic familiarity and hushed calm of the traditional bookstore, or the almost ecclesiastical grandeur of that modern cathedral of consumption, the regional shopping centre.

This presentation of atmosphere is broader than is traditional within the retail literature, where the work of Kotler (1973) has provided a focus. He defined atmospherics as:

...the conscious designing of space to create certain effects in buyers. More specifically, atmospherics is an effort to design buying environments to produce specific emotional effects in the buyer that enhance his purchase probability.

Given this definition, it would appear that the physical environment is the key medium through which store atmosphere can be created and manipulated. This is, to some degree, supported by Lambert (1989), who suggests that organizations consciously or unconsciously exude messages about themselves through the physical environments that they create. These include both the externalities and the internalities of corporate spaces, and Lambert chose to focus on the *visual* perception of these physical environments.

Such views do not take into consideration the impact of service cues and the context of the broader location of the store in providing the tone of the retail offer, or indeed of the interaction between atmosphere and other store image dimensions. In the Tokyo department store Mitsukoshi, the atmosphere of the store is as much created by its staff, including the 'greeters' who bow and offer words of welcome to all the store's visitors, as it is by the decor and fixturing.

This focus on the physical environment also leads Kotler to describe a store's atmosphere in terms of the sensory channels that are used to gather information about it, and in particular the visual, aural, olfactory and tactile. Whilst these sensory channels can provide rich information, perception takes place within the brain and it is here that interpretation occurs. This interpretation is affected by the perceiver's cultural background, associations, mood and other intervening factors.

Therefore, the representations provided by Hayne (1981, cited in McGoldrick, 1990) of the effects of colours in retail stores are more to do with the psychological interpretation and associations of colour in a western context than they are concerned with 'simple' colour perception. Such perceptions can be highly subjective; and, whilst there is the possibility of some consensus, it is just as likely that there will be a divergence of opinion. The white high gloss finish, silver and light wood used by the clothing retailer Kookai in its retail stores may for some consumers create a modern, clean, crisp atmosphere; but for others, could evoke a feeling of clinical sterility. Atmosphere therefore, is indeed affected by the physical environment, and perhaps more specifically by the customer's reading of the cues that are provided by their senses; but it also goes beyond this to encompass a wider range of stimuli. These include the tone projected by staff and the perception and interpretation of this by the customer. What might to one customer be staff attentiveness – helping to create an overall store atmosphere of friendliness and helpfulness – may to another be cloying and provide an atmosphere that is claustrophobic.

Store atmosphere, as with store image, is a gestalt concept. It is composed of all the elements that provide the 'mental environment' (cognitive response) or the 'pervading tone' (emotional response) that the customer perceives. These elements are not simply drawn from the physical environment, but can come from a much wider range of concerns. The 'weight' of each element is determined primarily by the perceiver: which again suggests that there is the potential for different interpretations of a store's atmosphere by different viewers (or in fact by the same viewer at different times). However, as many viewers might have a common cultural background, there is scope for their interpretations of store atmosphere to be similar. If this were not the case, it would be almost impossible for the retailer to 'design' and implement elements to generate the desired tone for their stores.

The specifics of the physical store environment in helping to create both atmosphere and therefore store image, were explored in greater detail in Chapter 7. Here, the focus is to highlight the fact that retail atmospherics have been perhaps regarded too narrowly – and that for a retailer to fully 'stage' a retail drama it must use all the cues at its disposal to provide customers with a 'text' from which they are likely to read the intended or desired atmospheric qualities. These will themselves also play an important role in creating the customers' perception of store image. If Kookai customers perceived the store atmosphere to be modern and crisp, this could be reflected in the overall store image that they develop, which could be of a contemporary, youthful and minimalist high fashion retailer.

The way in which store atmosphere and store image are both perceived is obviously therefore affected by the individual, their expectations and preferences. This means that a store cannot be all things to all people, as different groups of customers place different importance on various store image dimensions (Steenkamp and Wedel, 1991). A retailer must therefore select which store image dimensions it wishes to emphasize, and this decision should ideally be guided by the importance attached to the various dimensions by its target customers. The significance of developing a store image that conforms to the expectations of a retailer's target customers has been repeatedly stressed (Doyle and Fenwick, 1974-75; Hansen and Deutscher, 1977–78; Rosenbloom, 1983).

Variation in Perceived Store Image Dimensions

An individual customer's perception of the disparate dimensions of store image is only one factor that can lead to the creation of a variation in perception. There are a number of other situational factors that can also affect what dimensions are used to develop store image, and equally the extent to which single dimensions contribute to the creation of overall store image.

Geographic Influences

One such factor is the geographic nature of the market in which the retailer is located. Hirschman et al. (1978) suggested that the dimensions underlying store image were not consistent in the seven domestic markets that they investigated. However, what was similar was the relative ranking of each store attribute. This therefore suggests that those attributes that are 'highly salient' in one market will also be relevant in another.

On a wider geographic basis, there are differences in the importance customers place on dimensions dependent on their nationality. Arnold et al. (1983), in their longitudinal study of grocery store image dimensions and patronage behaviour in America, Canada, the Netherlands and the UK, found that Europeans placed more emphasis on locational convenience than their North American counterparts. However, there was a degree of agreement on which two store image dimensions were the most important across all four countries – locational convenience and price – even though their order differed. This begins to suggest that within the grocery market these dimensions are of major significance. Arnold et al. (1983) also noted that to a smaller degree there was a level of disagreement regarding the relative importance of different dimensions within each country. This conclusion stemmed from a comparison of consumers' perceptions when grouped into smaller geographic markets.

Temporal Influences

Arnold et al. also found that customers' perceptions of the importance of store image dimensions changes over time. This notion is also supported by Tigert (1983), who examined a number of studies regarding store image and also found variation in the importance placed on store image dimensions due to time. The change of store image perceptions and the passage of time can also be linked to the potential effects of ageing. Joyce and Lambert (1996) found that perceptions of store image were shaped by the relative age of the customer. The 'older' consumers (aged 30–60) were consistently less pleased with various aspects of store image than 'younger' consumers (under 30 years of age). It would appear that as we age there is a tendency for us to become either more critical or discriminating of our retail experiences, leading to retail image assessments that are less positive.

Store image perceptions are therefore prone to change based on personal, geographic and temporal influences. What does however emerge is that there are a number of dimensions that would appear to be particularly important, and that these remain relatively constant over both time and geographic markets, but are subject to some slight variation.

Sector and Store Type Influences

Sector and store type add further complexity to the issue of store image and its constituent dimensions. Hansen and Deutscher (1977–1978) considered the relative importance of store image dimensions between department and grocery stores. They demonstrated that the relative importance of a limited number of dimensions did indeed differ, for example that of cleanliness was perceived as being slightly more important for a grocery store (an understandable conclusion). Such variation was also observed by Tigert (1983) in his work across grocery, fast-food, DIY and fashion sectors, and by also by Arnold et al. (1978) between food and fashion. Such variation is obviously closely linked to the nature of the product category in many instances.

The relative importance of particular dimensions in creating store image is clearly affected by a wide range of issues. However, what is constant throughout all the research outlined is that store image, once formed, then effects a customer's liking and patronage behaviour.

The Relationship Between Store Image, Store Choice and Patronage

There has been extensive work conducted on the relationship between image and actual patronage behaviour (for example, Erdem et al., 1999; Lumpkin et al., 1985; Hansen, 1969). The thrust of such work has been that the more favourable the image formed of a retail outlet from its salient dimensions, the more likely it is that the customer will use and purchase from the store.

However, there has been some suggestion that there may be inconsistencies between what consumers perceive to be salient features of store image and their subsequent behaviour. For example, Hortman et al. (1990) noted in their study of supermarket patronage that those respondents who perceived price to be the most important store image attribute did not shop in discount outlets. This indicates that, to a certain degree, there is a potential mismatch between stated and actual behaviour. Nevertheless, there has been a much larger body of work (including Malhotra, 1986, and Verhallen and de Nooij, 1982) that points to a positive relationship between store image dimensions and store choice and patronage. Stanley and Sewall (1976) even suggest that positive store image can mitigate locational inconvenience, and draw customers from a wider geographic area.

Given that a favourable store image increases the likelihood of selecting a particular store as a shopping destination, it then becomes critical for a retailer to understand what will enhance store image in the customer's eyes. Therefore, understanding how the manipulation of store image dimensions impacts customer perceptions and patronage intentions becomes a primary concern. Porter and Claycomb (1997), in their study of the effect of merchandise brand on store image in the fashion sector, concluded that the presence of a merchandise mix that contains a relatively high number of recognizable brands (and in particular the inclusion of 'anchor brands') that themselves generate positive perceptions, provides a viable tactic for creating favourable store image. This is achieved through the direct and specific effect of merchandise brand on the fashion dimension of store image. The more positively a customer perceives these brands, the more assured they are about the store's overall 'fashionability'; and where this is an important consideration, it is more likely that the store will be selected as a potential shopping destination. So, in order to manipulate the appropriate dimension, it would appear that a retailer must first establish which ones are critical to the target customers.

The Congruency Proposition

When trying to establish which store dimension factors are most important to a particular group of customers, a common approach has been to look for elements of congruency between store image and the customer's self-image (Thompson and Chen, 1998). This has led Doyle and Fenwick (1974–1975), Hirschman and Stampfl (1980), and Weale (1961) to try to establish whether a 'matching mechanism' exists that drives customers to match their own self-image to that of a store based on dimensions that are perceived as important, e.g. innovativeness. So, do customers who perceive themselves as being one step ahead of the fashion commentators seek out stores that set clothing trends with their merchandise rather than follow them? What seems important for making store choice and patronage decisions is a customer's preferences for particular store image dimensions that can be aligned with important elements of their self-concept. Erdem et al. (1999) state that if this is indeed the case, then it is important to understand how such preferences are formed. They suggest that the origin of such store image dimension preferences may stem from personal values, as "consumers upholding certain values as important goals to achieve or as important modes of conduct may also prefer certain attributes to be present in the stores they choose to shop in" (Erdem et al. 1999, p. 139).

Thompson and Chen (1998) also go beyond the link between self-concept and store image. They consider the underlying personal values that consumers have and the potential effect such values may have on store image differentiation. To facilitate this they employ a means-end chain model, which:

> ...seeks to explain how product or service attributes facilitate consumers' achievements of desired end-states of being such as happiness, security or enjoyment (Gutman, 1982). A means-end chain is a cognitive representation of the connection between a person's knowledge about a product or service and their self-knowledge (Mulvey et al. 1994). There are three levels of abstraction or categories of meaning that are typically associated with a concept such as store image:

1. attributes (the means);
2. consequences of store patronage; and
3. important psychological and social consequences and values (the ends).

> Thompson and Chen, 1998, p. 162

They further illustrate the potential connection between store knowledge and self-knowledge through Figure 9.1.

This diagram brings together Martineau's functional qualities and psychological attributes of store image, and provides a diagrammatic representation of the way in which these can be transferred beyond the customer's self-concept (instrumental values) to terminal values such as self-respect and friendship. Thompson and Chen's (1998) research, which was conducted with women and concerned fashion outlets, concluded that the dominant chain comprised: reputation – quality – durability – not waste money – spend money wisely – nice feeling – enjoyment and happiness/quality of life: the implication being that functional qualities of store image such as reputation and quality can eventually be traced through the chain to dominant hedonistic values that the customer wishes to achieve.

This suggestion goes beyond simple congruency propositions and begins to imply that customers can make store choice decisions to help achieve deep-seated personal goals – even if not perhaps explicitly. Their work also, interestingly, indicated that the store image dimensions of atmosphere and environment did not act as a starting point for a clear means-end chain, but rather

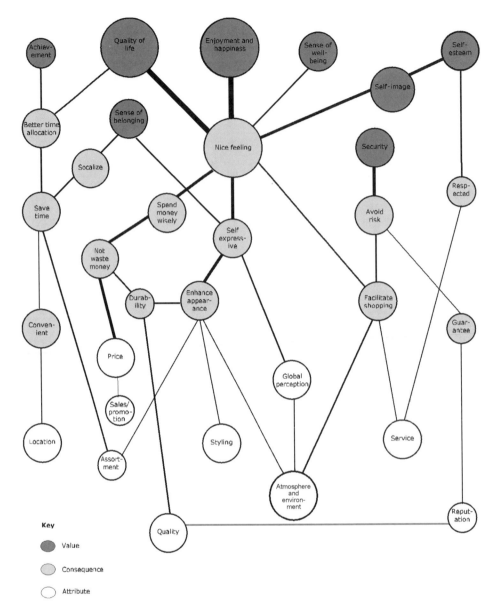

Figure 9.1 Connecting store- and self-knowledge
Source: Thompson and Chen, 1998, p. 168.

connected to several paths leading to various end values. It would seem that atmosphere and environment are highly interactive dimensions of store image, and that their management must be conceived as an integral element of the overall offer that has significant impact on various customer values.

By establishing which store image dimensions lead to desired end-values there is also the opportunity for the retailer to focus its main efforts on managing these specific concerns. It can also help to isolate those store image dimensions that have the most significant impact on store choice and patronage decisions. Erdem et al. (1999) also contend that it is highly likely that customers will only use a limited number of store image dimensions, as they will have difficulty in evaluating too many dimensions due to information overload. So, trying to make their lives easier, customers in their quest to make a store patronage decision, will only employ a limited number of dimensions, customers will base this on their assessment of the importance of the dimensions in helping them reach their desired goal. This has an additional benefit for retailers, who can identify these key store image dimensions, as not only can they project an appropriate and enticing image, they can also begin to develop predictions of patronage behaviour that can be vital to retail planning. This proposition is supported by Hansen (1969), who found that predictions of retail patronage based on three key dimensions were as good as those made using a more comprehensive list of twenty-four elements.

Store Image and Purchase Intention

Perhaps an even more critical concern for the retailer is the potential impact of store image on purchase intention. Grewal et al. (1998), in their research on bicycle purchasing intentions, note that a favourable store image positively influences a customer's purchase intentions. They go on to propose that a store that is perceived as having a good image provides 'added value' to the consumer – that such a retailer imbues a product bought from it with more value than an identical product purchased from a retailer that is perceived as having a less positive image. This not only provides the retailer with higher potential to convert store 'visitors' into customers, but also gives them a palpable advantage in negotiations with suppliers. Given the pivotal position of the retailer within many distribution channels, developing a positive store image provides advantages that radiate in both directions – enabling the development of a strong position with both consumers and suppliers.

Although the presence of a positive store image has been shown to significantly impact store choice, patronage and even purchasing behaviour, it must be remembered that it is not the only factor affecting these decisions (Steenkamp and Wedel, 1991). Stanley and Sewall (1976) for example, in addition to store image, also used drive time and size of store in predicting grocery store patronage.

Store Image and Loyalty

Positive evaluations of image have additionally been linked to the development of store loyalty (Lessig, 1973; Sirgy and Samli, 1985), and to share of household budget (Hildebrandt, 1988). Conversely, the nature of a customer's loyalty has also been shown to affect which store image dimensions they value, and, in particular, the relative weight given to various elements of store image (Mitchell and Kiral, 1998).

However, before going further, there has to be careful consideration of what is meant by the term loyalty. Loyalty has been frequently defined as observed behaviour, and this has led to its operationalization being through measures that focus on repeat purchase or visiting sequence (Bloemer et al. 1998). This has been criticized as lacking a conceptual basis and for having an 'outcome focused' view of what is in fact a complex and dynamic process (Day, 1969). Therefore, the simple application of behavioural measures may fail to capture the richness of the situation. For example, is a customer that visits their local neighbourhood grocery store on a regular basis for single items loyal, or are they simply the sort of consumer that needs, for whatever reason, to engage in frequent top-up shopping? Without trying to understand the reasons for this shopper's actions and their attitude to their local grocery store, it is difficult to label them 'a loyal customer'. If convenience is what motivates their behaviour, then the opening of a grocery store that is nearer or quicker to get to may be all that is needed for this customer to switch stores. Loyalty must therefore not only encompass behavioural concerns but also a customer's psychological disposition to a store (Bloemer et al. 1998); and it is a combination of these that ultimately may lead to store commitment.

Consumer commitment to stores can obviously vary considerably. This again suggests that there is perhaps a store loyalty continuum.

> At one end of the continuum, one finds true store loyalty; the repeat visiting behaviour based on a maximum amount of commitment. At the other end of the continuum, one finds spurious store loyalty; the repeat visiting of the store not based on any commitment at all.
>
> Bloemer and de Ruyter, 1998, p. 500

The notion that behavioural outcomes can be located on a single continuum, which presumably runs from 100% to zero, may be questioned. Purchase behaviour on any particular occasion is contingent on a number of factors, of which commitment is only one. A customer may perceive themselves as loyal to a single store, but in fact be unable to visit it and therefore have to purchase elsewhere. It is therefore clearly difficult to operationalize loyalty in a way that does not examine proportion of purchases, regularity of visit or similar behavioural measures. If loyalty is in some ways adequately interpreted as a particular affective state or set of attitudes, then a psychologically oriented instrument would be needed to measure this. The ability of such an instrument to be efficiently implemented is limited. It is therefore perhaps enough that retailers consider loyalty in terms of behavioural outcome, but remember that choice, change and other contingent factors influence the behavioural measure in ways that might overstate the level of true loyalty.

Bloemer and de Ruyter (1998), in their empirical work, investigated the connection between store image, store satisfaction and loyalty. They concluded that a positive relationship exists between store image, the level of customer satisfaction, and also between the level of satisfaction and store loyalty. This last relationship was, however, negatively mediated by customer involvement and customer deliberation. A customer who is well-informed and more involved in a certain type of shopping is likely to be less loyal to any specific store. A woman who has bought fashion items from a range of outlets is both involved in fashion and knowledgeable about stores, and is therefore less likely to be loyal to any given store. However in combination, satisfaction, motivation and ability to discriminate are positively linked to loyalty. So if the female fashion shopper derives satisfaction from a store, as she is already both motivated and able to discriminate, it is likely that she will display higher levels of psychological loyalty to that store.

Store Image, Brand and Differentiation

Store image – given its potential to affect store choice and patronage decisions, as well as retail store loyalty – also has implications for developing differentiation. In fact, Rosenbloom (1983) comments that if a retailer possesses a unique store image, the image provides a valuable tool to create competitive advantage that cannot easily be duplicated by its competitors. Such a proposition can be supported by the success of American-based high-street clothing chain Gap. Its retail proposition is distinguished by the clear image that has been developed around the store. This image adds more to the success of Gap than its merchandise, pricing policy or location strategy – none of which are unique. This retailer has created a distinctive personality, not only for its stores but also at a broader level, for its brand. This has been achieved through careful management of the store, and through creative advertising that sets the tone for its offer.

However, in the final quarter of 2000, Gap experienced a downturn in its profits that has been ascribed to uninspiring merchandise, poor management, and the move to a dispiriting advertising campaign that focuses on in-store promotion rather than the brand-building television adverts, which had been an integral component of establishing its image (Martinson, 2000). This shows that without constant and careful management, that the successful image developed can be quickly eroded. Once image has been damaged, concerted and sustained effort needs to be applied to regain what has been lost. This may well be more difficult than simply reinstating those store image dimensions and branding mechanisms that had proved successful in the past. The potential difficulty of regaining a positive store image and strong brand is highlighted by Cuneco (1997), who suggests that a lack of both these critical elements was responsible for the demise of the once great American retail giants Montgomery Ward & Co. and Woolworth Corp. These difficulties are also brought into sharp relief by the turbulent performance of Marks & Spencer in the late 1990s and its efforts at reinventing both its store image and brand in 2000.

Conclusions

The literature on store image and the varied benefits that are claimed for it, or that common sense would suggest would flow from store image, is conceptually ill-defined. For example, Martineau described 'psychological attributes' that later authors fastened on to, and then extended the term 'attribute' to cover functional qualities such as price and even physical dimensions of the store image. Therefore at times, the language used in the literature is potentially confusing.

Of the psychological attributes identified, 'store atmosphere' is the most prevalent within the store image literature. However, the important question of whether store atmosphere is in fact a consumer construct or an attribute of the store is not adequately addressed. Nor is atmosphere itself adequately defined. This thicket of confusion does not assist retail management in designing and delivering a store image that produces the desired consumer responses.

Korgaonkar et al. (1985) suggest that a favourable image is a key means for a retailer to maintain its market position and therefore be able to maintain customer patronage. This proposition, while intuitively appealing, is difficult to support with clear guidance for management. There is a greater possibility of giving more guidance to retail management when considering the physical and social aspects of the setting. This may in fact provide some insight for the focus on physical environment in particular within the literature on store atmosphere.

The ability to provide guidance to store management is hampered not only by difficulties in defining and measuring store image. The interplay between image, loyalty, satisfaction and patronage also seems, on the basis of some research, to be quite intricate. Coupling this intricacy with the lack of adequate operationalization makes successful management of these issues difficult for retailers. For example, a retailer may benefit from its customers perceiving it as having a favourable image, but the retailer may only be aware of the importance of *some* of the dimensions that create this effect. Even if research is conducted, the complex nature of the issues being explored may preclude the development of simple and definitive answers that can easily be applied back into the business.

To illustrate this, if the relationship between the merchandise dimension and store image is considered, much of the literature would suggest that having an appropriate merchandise mix adds to the development of positive store image. There is however an equally compelling view that positive store image adds to the perceived value of the merchandise mix.

> If the chain has a poor image, for example its stores are perceived as low quality with disinterested staff, low levels of customer service and failing to deliver a pleasant shopping experience, these 'values' will be transferred to the [merchandise].
>
> Burt, 2000, p. 884

This clearly depicts the complex and perhaps non-unidirectional relationships between store image and the individual dimensions that collectively are used to create that very image.

For retail managers this creates a further difficulty in actually managing store image. Given the potential of an action to work in a number of directions, it is difficult to determine before implementation the potential nature of its impact – let alone its strength. Understanding the interwoven mesh of individual dimensions, store image, patronage and loyalty is far from a simple task. Pinpointing why a retailer has a successful image, and the effects of that image is difficult enough; but trying to revitalize an ailing image becomes far more thorny.

It is tempting to suggest that explicit consideration of atmosphere or image is not a useful jumping-off point for retail management. Consideration of corporate identity may therefore be a more fruitful point of departure. As Chapter 7 demonstrates, the ability of consumers to 'read' settings designed to be 'legible' is undoubtedly present. Within the context of retail store space, the key features that contribute to legibility have been identified and can provide the foundation for the development of store design, which, when appropriately supported through for example appropriate corresponding merchandise and pricing decisions, should lead to the creation of a retail identity that is appropriately read and in turn leads customers to create the appropriate image.

References

Arnold, S.J., Ma, S., and Tigert, D.J. 1978. A comparative analysis of determinant attributes in retail store selection. *Advances in Consumer Research*, 5, 663–667.

Arnold, S.J., Oum, T.H., Douglas, J. and Tigert, D.J. 1983 Determinants attributes in retail patronage; seasonal, temporal, regional and international comparisons. *Journal of Marketing Research*, 20, 149–157.

Arons, L. 1961. Does television viewing influence store image and shopping frequency. *Journal of Retailing*, 37(Fall), 1–13.

Baker, J., Grewal, D. and Parasuraman, A. 1994. The influence of store environment on quality inferences and store image. *Journal of the Academy of Marketing Science*, 22(4), 328–339.

Bearden, W.O. 1977. Determinant attributes of store patronage: downtown verses outlying shopping areas. *Journal of Retailing*, 53, 15–22.

Bloemer, J., de Ruyter, K. 1998. On the relationship between store image, store satisfaction and store loyalty. *European Journal of Marketing*, 32(5/6), 499–513.

Bloemer, J., de Ruyter, K. and Peeters, P. 1998. Investigating drivers of bank loyalty: the complex relationship between image, service quality and satisfaction. *International Journal of Bank Marketing*, 16(7), 276–286.

Burt, S. 2000. The strategic role of retail brands in British grocery retailing. *European Journal of Marketing*, 34(8), 875–890.

Cardozo, N.R. 1974–1975. How images vary by product class. *Journal of Retailing*, 50(4), 85–98.

Cuneco, A.Z. 1997. Shakeout sends stores scurrying for a niche. *Advertising Age* (September 29), 26.

Day, G.S. 1969. A two-dimensional concept of brand loyalty. *Journal of Advertising Research*, 9, 29–36.

Dichter, E. 1988. What's in an image? *Journal of Consumer Marketing*, 2 (Winter), 75–81.

Doyle, P. and Fenwick, I. 1974–75. Shopping habits in grocery chains. *Journal of Retailing*, 50(4), 39–52.

Doyle, S.A. and Broadbridge, A. 1999. Differentiation by design: the importance of retailer repositioning and differentiation. *International Journal of Retail and Distribution Management*, 27(2), 72–83.

Engstrøm, H. and Hartvig Larsen, H. 1987. *Husholdningernes butiksvalg*. Erhvervsøkonomisk Forlag.

Erdem, O., Oumlil, A.B. and Tuncalp, S. 1999. Consumer values and the importance of store attributes. *International Journal of Retail and Distribution Management*, 27(4), 137–144.

Ghosh, A. 1990. *Retail Management (2nd Ed.)*. Chicago, IL: The Dryden Press.

Grewal, D., Krishnan, R., Baker, J. and Borin, N. 1998. The effects of store name, brand name and price discounts on customers' evaluations and purchase intentions. *Journal of Retailing*, 74(3), 331.

Gutman, J. 1982. A means-end chain model based on customer categorization process. *Journal of Marketing*, 46(2), 60–72.

Hansen, F. 1969. Consumer choice behaviour: experimental approach. *Journal of Marketing Research*, 6(November), 436–443.

Hansen, R.A. and Deutscher, T. 1977–1978. An empirical investigation of attribute importance in retail store selection. *Journal of Retailing*, 53(4), 59–72.

Hayne, C. 1981. Light and colour. *Occupational Health*, 33(4), 198–205.

Hildebrandt, L. 1988. Store image and the prediction of preference in retailing. *Journal of Business Research*, 17, 91–100.

Hirschman, E.C., Greenberg, B. and Robertson, D.H. 1978. The intermarket of retail image research: an empirical examination. *Journal of Retailing*, 54(1), 3–12.

Hirschman, E.C. and Stampfl, R.W. 1980. Roles of retailing in the diffusion of popular culture: microperspectives. *Journal of Retailing*, 56(1), 16–36.

Hortman, S.M., Allaway, A.W., Mason, J.B. and Rasp, J. 1990. Multisegment analysis of supermarket patronage. *Journal of Business Research*, 21, 209–233.

Joyce, M.L. and Lambert, D.R. 1996. Memories of the way stores were and retail store image. *International Journal of Retail and Distribution Management*, 24(1), 24–33.

Keaveney, S.M. and Hunt, K.A. 1992. Conceptualization and operationalization of retail store image: a case of rival middle-level theories. *Journal of the Academy of Marketing Science*, 20(2), 165–175.

Korgaonkar, P.K., Lund, D. and Price, B. 1985. A structural equations approach toward examination of store attribute and store patronage behaviour. *Journal of Retailing*, 61 (Summer), 39–60.

Kotler, P. 1973. Atmospherics as a marketing tool. *Journal of Retailing*, 49(4), 48–64.

Kunkel, J.H. and Berry, L.L. 1968. A behavioural conception of retail image. *Journal of Marketing*, 32, 21–27.

Lambert, A. 1989. Corporate identity and facilities management. *Facilities*, December, 7–12.

Lessig, V.P. 1973. Consumer store images and store loyalties. *Journal of Marketing*, 37 (October), 72–74.

Lindquist, J.D. 1974. Meaning of image – a survey of empirical and hypothetical evidence. *Journal of Retailing*, 50(4), 29–38.

Lumpkin, J.R., Greenberg, B.A. and Goldstucker, J.L. 1985. Marketplace needs of the elderly: determinant attributes and store choice. *Journal of Retailing*, 61 (Summer), 75–105.

Malhotra, N.K. 1986. Modeling store choice based on censored preference data. *Journal of Retailing*, 62(2), 128–144.

Martineau, P. 1958. The personality of the retail store. *Harvard Business Review*. 36 (January/February), 47–55.

Martinson, J. 2000. Jean pool dries up for chino champion. *The Guardian*, Saturday November 18, p. 30.

McGoldrick, P.J. 1990. *Retail Marketing*. Maidenhead: McGraw–Hill.

Mitchell, V.-W. and Kiral, R.H. 1998. Primary and secondary store-loyal customer perceptions of grocery retailers. *British Food Journal*, 100(7), 312–319.

Mulvey, M.S., Olson, J.C., Celsi, R.L. and Walker, B.A. 1994. Exploring the relationships between means-end knowledge and involvement. *Advances in Consumer Research*, 21, 51–57.

Peterson, R.A. and Kerin, R.A. 1983. Store image measurement in patronage research. In Darden, W. and Lusch, R. F. (Eds.), *Patronage Behaviour in Retail Management*. New York: Elsevier, pp. 720–751.

Porter, S.S. and Claycomb, C. 1997. The influence of brand recognition on retail store image. *Journal of Product and Brand Management*, 6(6), 373–387.

Rosenbloom, B. 1983. Store image development and the question of congruency. In Darden, W. and Lusch, R. F. (Eds.), *Patronage Behaviour and Retail Management*. North-Holland: Elsevier.

Shrimp, T.A. 1990. *Promotion Management and Marketing Communications, (2nd Ed.)*. Orlando, FL: Dryden Press.

Sirgy, J.M. and Samli, C.A. 1985. A path-analytic model of store loyalty involving self-concept, store image, geographic loyalty, and socioeconomic status. *Academy of Marketing Science*, 13, 265–291.

Stanley, T.J. and Sewall, 1976. Image inputs to a probabilistic model: predicting retail patronage. *Journal of Marketing*, 40 (July), 48–53.

Steenkamp, J-B.E.M. and Wedel, M. 1991. Segmenting retail markets on store image using a consumer-based methodology. *Journal of Retailing*, 67(3), 300–321.

The New Shorter Oxford English Dictionary (4th Ed.). 1993. Oxford: Clarendon Press.

Thompson, K.E. and Chen, Y.L. 1998. Retail store image: a means-end approach. *Journal of Marketing Practice: Applied Marketing Science*, 4(6), 161–173.

Tigert, D.J. 1983. Pushing the hot buttons for a successful retailing strategy. In Darden, W. and Lusch, R.F. (Eds.), *Patronage Behaviour and Retail Management*. North-Holland: Elsevier, pp. 89–113.

Verhallen, T.M. and de Nooij, G.J. 1982. Retail attribute sensitivity and shopping patronage. *Journal of Economic Psychology*, 2, 39–55.

Weale, B. 1961. Measuring the customer's image of a department store. *Journal of Retailing*, 37(2), 40–48.

Zimmer, M.R. and Golden, L.L. 1988. Impressions of retail stores: a content analysis of consumer images. *Journal of Retailing*, 54(3), 265–291.

10

THE SOCIAL DIMENSION

In the social context of the larger setting for retailing e.g. the mall, there are two principal groups:
- People present for the same purpose – users; and
- Those visiting for other reasons – visitors.

Within this larger setting there are also two staff groups:
- Those who are attached to the general venue; and
- Those associated with a particular retailer.

In a particular retail setting, there are users and service personnel who may be involved in a directing or facilitating role. As these actors are placed within a setting that has a particular socio–cultural character, this must also be considered in any detailed analysis of the overall social *milieu* – aspects of which give rise to feelings of liking, belonging, understanding and safety. These feelings may be strengthened through the particular content of any interaction that the individuals may have, as well as the extent to which they perceive themselves as having behavioural control. The elements of the social nature of retailing must be understood and explored:
- Other users;
- Visitors; and
- Venue staff; and
- Directing and facilitating retail staff.

Introduction

The final two elements that provide the basis for the retail Servuction arena are the social surroundings that are encountered within the service system and the less physical issue of time. These elements provide a basis for the broader context within which the interaction between customer and the other elements of the retail offer take place. (There is additionally, the joint issue of the customer's feelings and psychological state, which also affects the way in which the customer will interact with the retail offer. The issue of the customer's psychological state is covered in Chapter 12.)

Compared with the elements covered previously, the social and temporal dimensions are more difficult for the retailer to manage as completely. Where these issues are concerned, particularly with certain aspects, the retailer is less a 'director' than perhaps a 'facilitator': for example, the retailer is less able to have a direct input in the conduct and content of customer-to-customer interaction. Retailers are also, of course, limited in their ability to influence the time availability of customers.

Given these difficulties, it would perhaps appear easiest if retailers simply did nothing – allowing these interactions and influences to develop as a result of (and contained within) those components of the Servuction arena that they *can* manage fully. However, in both the social and temporal contexts, there *is* scope for the retailer to provide certain cues and to use techniques that are aimed at developing a particular reaction from the customer. There is however, less certainty when these mechanisms are employed, especially given the nature of the issues that they concern. From the perspective of the retailer, if the dramatic metaphor is applied, it is probably best to view these techniques as a means of facilitating and marshalling improvisation.

In a play that uses improvisation as the mainstay of its performance, a director hopes that the framework of character, plot and staging will interact to provide a boundary for creativity. This framework will therefore serve to produce appropriate, and – perhaps, most importantly – *desired* interactions: both in terms of their content, duration and repetition.

In a retail context, improvisation is therefore in a large part, concerned with issues of both time and social interaction. This chapter considers the impact of the social dimension from both the perspectives of retailer as framework provider, and of customer as (co)improviser. The temporal aspects are dealt with in the next chapter.

Social Surroundings

The social surroundings encountered in the retail setting, from the customer's perspective, play an important role in developing a sense of satisfaction or, at the very least, either adding to or detracting from it. This can be seen in the emphasis placed on the people-to-people components of the service arena within the Servuction model. These person-based interactions provide a significant element of the benefits that are derived from the experi-ence (Adelman et al., 1994; Beatty et al., 1996; Bitner, 1995; Gwinner et al., 1998). This is not surprising, as people are predominantly social animals whose sense of contentment often revolves around the interactions that they have with others (McAdams, 1988).

For many, shopping is a good opportunity for such interaction – as has been highlighted throughout previous chapters. This is not to suggest that every customer always seeks a high-level of social interaction. For example, selecting to use an ATM outside the bank rather than going inside can be seen as a mechanism for avoiding human contact. However, even when using an ATM, there is likely to be some social interaction – whilst waiting in line, or in negotiating space on the pavement with other pedestrians. This example indicates two of the potential points for social interaction:

- With other customers; and
- With others 'sharing' the physical space.

These two groups can be identified in all physical retail settings. For instance, if a customer visits a shopping mall to make a number of purchases, there are usually other people present for the same purpose (in this instance, to buy products) – who could be termed 'users'. There are also those present (who are not employed by the mall or the retailers within it) who are simply there because it is a place to meet, 'hang-out' and/or interact with others. These people, who could range from the ubiquitous 'mall-rat' to the business traveller wanting to kill a few hours, can then be classed as 'visitors'. They exploit the physicality of the retail space as a place to *be* or be *seen*, rather than as a place to purchase.

Components of Interaction

The social interactions that occur with and between these two groups ('users' and 'visitors') can be examined at two distinct levels – that of *verbal* commu-nication and that of the *non-verbal*. In fact, from the wider perspective of social interaction, these two elements provide a framework for analysis: both in situations where the interaction is at the face-to-face level, and when it is mediated by technology. (In circumstances where technology is used, the degree of non-verbal communication can, of course, be more limited, if not totally absent.)

Non-Verbal Communication

The combination of these verbal and non-verbal elements provides a powerful means of communication but, as linguist David Abercrombie comments, "we speak with our vocal organs, but we converse with our entire bodies" (Abercrombie, 1968). This helps to highlight the potentially vital role of the non-verbal element. Hudson (1983) states that this component of communication can help reflect:

- Relationship markers – for example, 'power-solidarity' relationships established through the distance one person stands from another when talking;
- Structure markers – which guide the *pattern* of interactions, and can be reflected in entries and exits into conversation and in turn-taking during speech;
- Content markers – that directly reinforce the verbal elements of speech: for instance, at its most simple, the nodding of the head whilst uttering 'yes' (at least in Western Europe and America).

Non-verbal markers can be of particular significance in a retail context, where issues such as the nature of the relationships that are developed with others can be an important factor. For example, if whilst in a store, a customer seeks directions from another person and that person comes too close, or perhaps touches them, this can induce strong feelings of discomfort. These feelings can then pervade the total experience and even become the over-riding memory of the shopping event. Equally, if the person with whom the customer is interacting displays inappropriate turn-taking signals and behaviour, this can be interpreted as 'rudeness' that can lead to negative emotions that again colour the total experience.

There are also instances where such non-verbal behaviour can have a positive influence – and even be critical. Consider the importance of the affirmative nod, smile and positive verbal cue for a customer that emerges from a changing room having tried on an item that they like, but are unconvinced will suit them. The coupling of the verbal and non-verbal can provide sufficient positive affirmation to support the item's purchase. If the same situation is envisaged, but this time the positive content markers are *not* present, the customer may treat the verbal affirmation as having less credence and decide not to make a purchase. From this last example, it is clear that these 'little' non-verbal components can have a significant impact on both the interpretation of social interaction and responses to it. In doing this, the non-verbal markers act as 'accents' to the words actually spoken.

Verbal Communication

In fact, the verbal component of communication provides the central core of any discourse, but it does not simply encompass "the words actually spoken". Crystal (1997) illustrates this point by using the familiar comment – immortalized in song – that "'tain't what you say (it's the way that cha say it)". This statement provides an easily understood indication of the content of what, in linguistic terms, is called 'suprasegmental analysis'. This considers how the segments of speech (syllables, words and sentences) are pronounced. There are, in broad terms, two aspects of suprasegmental analysis: one focusing on the *prosodic* features of sound, the other on *paralinguistic* features (Crystal, 1997).

The *prosodic* features relate to the basic psycho–acoustic properties of sound that are commonly used to create linguistic effects, such as pitch and loudness, and to the distinctive use of speed and rhythm. These devices not only enable a person to discern a question from a statement, they also facilitate the expression of additional meaning and emotion in speech. In the changing room example, if the person who is providing comment says "That really suits you", but places the stress on different words, the meaning that is interpreted can itself be quite different. If the stress is placed on the word "really", then the phrase sounds quite emphatic. If the stress in the sentence is quite even, the phrase becomes relatively 'flat' in the emotion that is expressed. The meaning 'behind' the word "really" is also affected by the other element of suprasegmental analysis – the paralinguistic features.

Paralinguistic features concern the 'tone of voice' adopted. For example, if speech is whispered, this can add a 'conspiratorial' tone. The interpretation of these tones is, however, not universal. A 'breathy' or 'husky' tone in many cultures is associated with deep emotion or sexual desire – but in Japan, is used to indicate respect or submission (Crystal, 1997). If the changing room example is again considered, there is a distinct difference between what is likely to be interpreted from the phrase "That really suits you" with the stress placed on "really", if the tone of voice is disparaging and sarcastic, or if it is (sincerely) enthusiastic.

The interaction that takes place within the retail setting is therefore as much a mix of these elements as it is anywhere else. The interpretation of the signals sent by combining words, intonation, tone of voice and body language is something that is developed as part of the natural socialization process, but it is culturally determined. These signals can have a profound effect on behaviour and the development of satisfaction with the overall experience. Therefore, not only do the different groups of people – other users, visitors, staff – make a potentially significant impact on a customer's shopping experience, but so do the different components of the social interaction that takes place. As such, it is not only worth considering the relationships between these groups more fully, but it is also appropriate to explore the elements of their interaction.

Other Users

As depicted in the Servuction model in Chapter 6, there is the potential for interaction between 'users' whilst within the shopping arena. The issue of customer-to-customer interaction has received some attention within the literature (for example: Anderson and Zemke, 1990; McGrath and Otnes, 1995; Harris et al., 1999), although this attention has been relatively limited, both in terms of its duration and its volume (Parker and Ward, 2000). However, the nature of customer-to-customer interaction that *has* been studied has been relatively broad. It ranges from the interaction between friends or 'purchase pals' (McGrath and Otnes, 1995) to the conversations held by strangers in retail settings (Harris et al., 1999). It also covers a wide spectrum of topics (identified below).

The impact of such interaction on service quality perceptions and customer satisfaction has received considerable attention (Grove and Fisk, 1992; Grove and Fisk, 1997; Harris et al., 1995, 1997; Martin, 1997; Parker and Ward, 2000). Martin (1996) suggests that customer-to-customer interaction can be both positive and negative: leading to either satisfaction or dissatisfaction with a service experience. In a traditional retail context, some of the elements that stimulate behaviours that often cause dissatisfaction are usually not present – for instance, consumption of alcoholic drinks and the ability to smoke. Harris et al. (1997) found that, in the majority of cases, customer-to-customer interaction in a retail situation leads to increased satisfaction. This in part stems from the perception that such interactions are 'honest', especially in the context of offering opinion on products. For the retailer, finding ways to stimulate such interactions, and with increasing frequency, is therefore beneficial.

The issue of interaction frequency has been considered as a topic in its own right (Grove and Fisk, 1997; Harris et al., 1994; Parker and Ward, 2000). Here, Parker and Ward (2000) found that over half the respondents questioned stated that they occasionally spoke to other customers. But, when asked about the shopping trip that they had just been on, less than ten percent stated that they had engaged in customer-to-customer interaction as such. This demonstrates that, whilst for many customers such behaviour is common, it is not an activity that occurs on each and every shopping trip. There would therefore, seem to be 'untapped' potential here; and one of the first stages in facilitating such interaction might be for retailers to identify and focus on those customers who are most likely to engage in such behaviour.

The creation of typologies of interaction type and role may provide a mechanism for the identification of such an 'interactive' customer (Adelman et al., 1994; Anderson and Zemke, 1990; Harris et al., 1999; Hoffman and Bateson, 1997; McGrath and Otnes, 1995; Parker and Ward, 2000). For example, Feick and Price (1987) identify 'market mavens' who "have information about many kinds of products, places to shop, and other facets of markets, and initiate discussions with consumers and respond to requests from consumers for market information" (p. 85). Market mavens are therefore more likely to engage in customer-to-customer interactions. This capacity for information transfer is reflected in the typology developed by McGrath and Otnes (1995) – consisting of: help seekers, reactive helpers, proactive helpers, admirers, competitors and complainers.

The first category (help seekers) is the only one that relates to a customer seeking support from other customers. Parker and Ward (2000) extend this by subdividing this category into those customers that *prompt* interaction – termed 'proactive help seekers' – and those that seek help, either as a result of interaction with others or provide subtle non-verbal cues to attract help – 'reactive help seekers'. This diversity of roles suggests that customer-to-customer interaction is complex, and that in order to manage the process as effectively as possible, retailers need to assess the nature of customers and if possible, 'match' roles – for instance, matching reactive help seekers with proactive helpers, and proactive help seekers with reactive helpers.

If retailers were to develop programmes to facilitate such 'appropriate' customer-to-customer interaction, as has already been suggested, this should lead to increased satisfaction with the overall retail experience. Whilst from the retailer's perspective, this is beneficial in itself; understanding the effects of such interaction is also essential. Harris et al. (1997) found that in the main, where customers discussed products, interactions stressed positive qualities, and were often based on direct knowledge (as, for example, with Amazon.com and its book reviews). However, the impact of these positive exchanges often depended on the product being purchased – for instance they are more likely to influence the purchase of books, plants and DIY goods than the purchase of, say, a car. The outcome was also affected by the attitude and perception of the customer receiving the advice, in particular the level of credibility ascribed to the other customer. However, where negative opinions *were* given, in many situations these were particularly powerful in dissuading purchase. Customer-to-customer interaction therefore provides a potentially underdeveloped area, that can generate *indirect* benefit to the retailer in the form of increased satisfaction, and, to a lesser extent, *direct* benefit in relation to purchase intention.

The research conducted on customer-to-customer interaction has also focused on verbal interaction. These examinations have tended to treat this as a single entity, rather than explicitly considering both "the words spoken" and the prosodic and paralinguistic elements of speech. However, there has been an implicit consideration of these different elements in relation to issues such as service quality perceptions and purchase intention. Whilst such studies provide a useful indication of the power of customer-to-customer interaction, they do not identify the specific effect of the various elements that compose the interaction. So at present, it is difficult to identify what is in fact the most 'important' element of verbal customer-to-customer interaction. This research does not even begin to consider the importance of the *non-verbal* components. However, such non-verbal elements, as highlighted earlier, can play a conclusive role in the perception of the meaning of interaction.

The examination of customer-to-customer interaction is still, therefore, at an early stage of development. However, even as the consideration of such issues becomes more detailed, the potential for variation is huge – especially given the impact of personal, situational and cultural factors on interpersonal interaction. This potential for variance does not indicate that examination is unwarranted; it rather suggests that any examination should consider these factors to provide as rich as possible understanding of customer-to-customer interaction. It is only with such a well-developed awareness that retailers will be able to generate appropriate managerial techniques to direct and stimulate favourable customer-to-customer interaction wherever possible. There is likely to be a limit, though, to the way in which retailers can affect such interaction. Such boundaries also exist when customer-to-*visitor* interaction is considered.

Visitors

In spaces where there is a concentration of retail provision – for example, the town centre, the neighbourhood parade of shops, or the mall – there are often people who use the location simply as a place to 'be' or a point for social interaction. This phenomenon has raised particular interest in the context of the shopping mall, as such locations have become important meeting places, particularly for the young and the old (Bloch et al., 1994). This has led in part, to the managers of such centres providing 'special events' such as art exhibitions, live music, children's entertainment and demonstrations. Such activities then provide a focus for those that are not using the space as a place to shop. They also further augment the experiences of those that are primarily there because it is a place to purchase products. In both instances, such events are intended to add positively to the experience.

In fact, it has been argued that the goal of consumption is to have satisfying experiences rather than just buying satisfying goods (Belk, 1982; Holbrook and Hirschman, 1982). In this context, simply being in the location may be a source of pleasurable experience, which is itself 'consumed' by visitors; and that these…

> visitors… engage in activities indicative of consuming the experience of the locale itself such as socializing with friends…. Similarly, recreational browsing in luxurious, 'Galleria-class' malls also may reflect experiential consumption of the physical habitat itself apart from merchandise-focused activity. In a more practical vein, some consumers use climate-controlled shopping malls as locations for exercise during bad weather.
>
> Bloch et al., 1994

In their study of visitors to shopping malls, Bloch et al. (1994) examined the perceived benefits that motivated visits to such locations. Six underlying factors were uncovered:

- Aesthetics – enjoyment and appreciation derived from the design or appearance of the mall;
- Escape – the provision of a means of relieving boredom and loneliness or escaping from routine;
- Exploration – enjoyment gained from the novelty facilitated by exploring new products and stores;
- Flow – a pleasurable state of absorption with which time simply seems to flow by;
- Epistemic – the gaining of new information, or learning about new trends; and
- Social – enjoyment associated with talking to and socializing with others.

Three of these motives (escape, flow, social) are associated with social interaction. Interestingly, interaction could be with *any* other person present in the shopping mall, not just with another 'customer'.

Those people seeking to reduce the loneliness that they feel may simply wish to be in a mall, or other retail space, because the likelihood that other people will be present is high. By being there, they may feel part of a 'community', or, at least, in touch with other members of society. This can be the case, irrespective of their engaging in verbal interaction; simply negotiating the space with others will entail non-verbal communication and as discussed above, this can provide a 'high' level of interaction. For such visitors, the opportunity to make a purchase could be of peripheral importance or even not at all relevant. Those motivated by such concerns provide a 'human backdrop' to retail activity: helping reinforce shopping's social role, for both themselves and for those actually shopping.

Visitors may also wish to 'pass time', or may be 'passing time' simply as a by-product of being absorbed in the shopping experience itself. They therefore could, as well as 'throwing' themselves into the purchase process, use the potential of social interaction as a means of achieving this goal. This could be done in two broad ways: again by engaging in social interaction itself, or by watching social interaction. The latter utilizes the 'watching the world go by' voyeuristic approach, placing the viewer outside the specific social interaction being observed, but nevertheless losing themselves in the act of social interaction.

The final motive, termed 'social', for visiting a retail space is most obviously based on human interaction. However, the focus of that interaction is verbal – seeking to talk to and socialize with others. The labelling of this motive as social perhaps reflects a predisposition to describe spoken communication as 'social interaction' – possibly as it necessitates 'conscious' involvement. It is possible to send non-verbal cues without such consideration as they are needed to facilitate human group living. For example, a quick micro-expression or shift of body position can be used to indicate that a seat is not taken, or signal that one person will occupy one side of the aisle and the other will walk on the opposite side.

However, what this motive indicates is the potential importance of verbal communication to shopping mall visitors. The shopping mall provides a large number of points for such communication to take place; for instance, through the provision of seating around certain spaces, or near lifts and doors where interaction is often necessary, as well as cafés and other 'attractions' that many other public places provide. Such points create a focus for verbal social interaction not only for those using the retail facilities, but also those seeking a social space and encounter.

Whatever the motives of those visiting the retail space as a place to 'be', they are as much an element of the overall social milieu, and part of the social interaction that is facilitated, as are other customers (users). Equally, so too are the final group of people that are likely to be present in retail spaces – service employees.

Service Employees

There is a third possible broad-level of social interaction likely to concern the perceptions and behaviour of retail space users – that of a customer with a service employee (Bowen and Lawler, 1992). In fact, within their typology of service quality, Zeithaml et al. (1990) identify three components that clearly relate to customer-to-service employee interaction: empathy, assurance and responsiveness. The potential importance of customer-to-service employee interaction (sometimes termed the service encounter) has generated extensive interest in the subject and along with it, a wealth of literature. This literature has used a broad range of service settings to investigate the importance of such interaction: including the examination of retail encounters. However the overall perspective taken is itself much broader – based in a services paradigm rather then a specifically retail-based one. These studies therefore provide a rich foundation for the evaluation of employee-to-customer interaction.

Just as with customer-to-customer and customer-to-visitor interaction, customer-to-service employee encounters can involve both verbal and nonverbal components. The relative importance of these elements is again difficult to judge. But, as with the other forms of interaction, there has been a general emphasis on the words spoken and actions taken. Frazer Winsted (2000) provides a useful investigation of the performances of specific behaviours by service employees and their relationship to customer satisfaction. She develops a range of behavioural factors based on previous literature that examines service encounters and service quality, and which have been identified as having a significant impact. These are:

- Authenticity – which relates to the 'naturalness' of the encounter (or the extent to which it is not forced), as well as the sincerity and trust displayed and engendered by the service employee;
- Caring – equating to the level of empathy displayed towards the customer and the degree of attention and interest shown;
- Perceived control – which has three elements: behavioural control (the ability to control a threatening situation, and be flexible), cognitive control (the ability to reduce stress), and decisional control;
- Courtesy – which (although mostly self-explanatory) has been linked to other elements of service quality, or which has itself been used as a determinant of service quality;
- Formality – concerning issues of social distance, role deference, forms of address and ritual behaviour;
- Friendliness – again, self evident;
- Personalization – which has also been termed 'customization' – relating to the extent to which the customer is treated as an individual with a concomitant degree of variation; this factor therefore also hinges on interactivity; and
- Promptness – concerning the timeliness, speed and efficiency of an encounter.

These factors were then used alongside empirical research to develop a list of behavioural measures, which helped identify the underlying factors of satisfaction arising from customer-to-sales staff interaction in two distinct service settings. The results obtained show a high degree of consistency across both situations, and can be reduced to three behavioural classifications, which strongly indicate the elements that customers need in order to be satisfied with their interactions. The behavioural classifications are:

- Concern – which combines empathy, assurance, responsiveness, authenticity, perceived competence, listening and dedication. It involves behaviours such as: appearing intelligent and knowledgeable; enquiring whether everything was satisfactory and checking that the customer's needs were met; being helpful, attentive and available; appearing honest, genuine and natural; and engaging in conversation.
- Civility – primarily the issues here relate to the service employee's attitude. It concerns behaviours that stimulate a *negative* response from the customer – passing beyond their 'tolerance' threshold. The behaviours that stimulate such concerns in the customer include perceiving that the employee acted arrogantly; was rude or abrupt; or showed no positive cues (such as smiling).
- Congeniality – this factor is in some ways the obverse of civility. It focuses on the *positive* attitude displayed by the salesperson and the personality that they display. Customers appear to use behavioural markers such as being cheerful, displaying a sincere expression and appearing to have a 'warm' demeanour.

These three behavioural factors are clearly interrelated, and emphasize the scope for 'small' aspects of the service encounter to impinge on customers' perceptions. Whilst in many ways, the manner in which service personnel interact with customers can be managed – by providing training on procedures and process and customer handling, or even by providing a script for staff to follow (see Chapter 5) – there are inevitably behavioural triggers that cannot be trained. The significance of going beyond training is displayed by Bitner et al. (1990, p.71):

> …exemplary firms understand that managing the service encounter involves more than training employees to say "have a nice day" or to answer the phone on or before the third ring. Effective management of the service encounter involves understanding the often complex behaviours of employees that can distinguish a highly satisfactory service encounter from a dissatisfactory one, and then training, motivating, and rewarding employees to exhibit those behaviors.

This importance of behavioural triggers that cannot be trained is perhaps most obvious in relation to the final factor of congeniality. The behavioural markers are as much about the cues that service personnel might display as a result of their 'nature' or 'emotional intelligence'. Such actions are difficult to instil, as they not only rely on 'personal' elements of the service employee, but are also often transmitted by subtle non-verbal aspects of behaviour. This aspect of customer-to-service employee interaction has been less well-examined than many other aspects of the service encounter.

The Non-Verbal Aspect

Two notable exceptions to the focus on the spoken word are the work of Gabbott and Hogg (2000) and Sundaram and Webster (2000). The latter pair develop a conceptual model that considers the potential for a service provider's non-verbal behaviour to influence a customer's perception of the provider's friendliness, courtesy, empathy, competence and credibility. In their examination of non-verbal behaviour they include paralanguage, kinetics, proxemics and physical appearance; and for each of these elements – based on previous literature from various fields – they develop a number of hypotheses.

The use of various elements of paralanguage, (which they take as being pitch, vocal loudness or amplitude, pauses and fluency) it is suggested will have the following effects:

- The service provider's usage of a slower speech rate, lower pitch, moderate pauses, and less inflection, will enhance customers' perceptions of friendliness and credibility. (Compare Margaret Thatcher's style of delivery at the beginning of her political career with that at the end of the her reign as Prime Minister.)
- The service provider's usage of a faster speech rate, higher pitch, high vocal intensity, and higher inflection will enhance customers' perceptions of competence, but will reduce the perception of friendliness.

The second element – kinetics – concerns body movement. It includes body orientation, eye contact, nodding, hand-shaking and facial expressions such as smiling. Here the suggestion is that:

- Smiling, light laughter and frequent eye contact by service providers will enhance customers' perceptions of friendliness and courtesy.
- Head nodding by service providers will enhance customers' perceptions of empathy, courtesy and trust.

When considering proxemics – the distance and relative postures of those interacting – the emphasis is on the role of touch:

- Service providers' usage of touch will enhance customers' perceptions of friendliness and empathy (but not perhaps in all cultures – see below).

The final element – physical attractiveness – also considers the use of appropriate dress-codes to enhance a service provider's attractiveness. The suggestions being that:

- The physical attractiveness of the service provider will be significantly related to the customers' perceptions of friendliness, credibility, competence, empathy and courtesy.
- The colour and the shade intensity of clothes worn by service providers will affect customers' perceptions of friendliness, competence and credibility.

These hypotheses provide a useful range of testable propositions. However, apart from perhaps the two final propositions related to physical attractiveness, they are highly likely to have an element of unintentional but inbuilt 'bias'.

As Gabbott and Hogg (2000) indicate, non-verbal communication is affected by a wide range of factors. Firstly, gender provides a source of variation in both its use and interpretation. This can mean that what would be appropriate when a male member of sales staff interacts with a male customer, may not be so when the customer is female. For example, men often avoid physical contact with other men, whereas a woman interacting with a man might not be as 'touch averse'. Gabbott and Hogg (2000) also suggest that women respond more positively to appropriate touching than do men.

Such gender-based implications for non-verbal communication are themselves set in the wider sphere of cultural differences. The use of non-verbal cues and their interpretation is vastly different between cultural groups – even those with a considerable degree of similarity – for instance, those sharing the same language or geographic proximity. This then has implications for the hypotheses developed by Sundaram and Webster (2000). Given that the authors are both based in the United States, and that much of the literature that they use is also drawn from American authors, the hypotheses provided are likely to 'work' best in that cultural context. For example, the use – and most importantly – acceptability of touch in non-intimate interactions is different in America, the UK, France and Germany. What these propositions emphatically reinforce is the potential importance of non-verbal interaction in customer-to-service provider exchanges.

Gabbott and Hogg (2000) actually provide an empirical investigation into the effect of non-verbal communication between customer and service provider. Their manipulation of non-verbal cues – sent by an actress playing the role of a hotel receptionist – provides support for the importance of these factors in service exchanges. Where 'positive' cues were displayed, this had a significant positive impact on service satisfaction and the overall impression of the hotel, as well as the responsiveness, empathy and assurance that respondents perceived that the receptionist had displayed. These results clearly show that the issue of non-verbal communication can have an impact far beyond developing a perception of just the other person involved in the interaction. Where that person is employed as a service employee, there are also implications for the perception of experience quality and ultimately, the way in which the firm itself is seen.

If this is indeed the case then, as Sundaram and Webster (2000) suggest, although it is more difficult to provide service staff with exact guidelines for non-verbal interaction, making them aware of its importance and providing indications of its possible effects is useful. It also reinforces two significant points when customer-to-employee interactions are considered within a retail setting. Firstly, that the role of retail manager can be that of director; and secondly that without guidance in relation to the characteristics that they are supposed to be conveying, staff can be at a disadvantage in creating an appropriate performance.

The role of customer-to-employee interaction can however also be considered beyond the direct retail setting. In many retail spaces there are staff employed by the retailers themselves (e.g. a department store within a regional shopping centre), but there are often also staff employed by the managers of the enclosing retail space (i.e. the retail centre itself) – including security staff, cleaning staff, those providing information or entertainment – who can collectively be termed 'venue staff'. The interactions between customers and venue staff have just as much potential to affect customers' perceptions of the overall shopping experience as do interactions with retail staff.

Venue Staff

There has been no specific work conducted regarding the impact of venue staff on customers' perceptions of the shopping experience, or its quality. However, the work conducted in relation to service employee and customer interaction provides a useful guide on its possible impact. The problem remains that there is no indication of the specific responses that customers display to such encounters; and perhaps, even more critically, the level of effect that these interactions have on the customer in relation to those with retail staff. Developing an understanding of this may be of importance not only for retailers, but also for those managing the retail space.

The interactions that customers have with venue staff will no doubt help them form an image of the retail space – just as in a shopping centre so would the provision of themed eating areas and the décor. For those managing retail spaces, understanding venue staff-to-customer interaction, and providing appropriate direction for it, are as important as they are to a retailer. In addition, these interactions could be equally important to the retailers who inhabit the retail space. Locating a store within a particular environment often sends messages to customers, and this message is heavily dependent on the image developed by the retail space, which will itself be influenced by the venue staff. So, from the retailers' perspective, venue staff-to-customer interaction can have a significant impact on customers that visit their stores. The level of control that retailers have in developing management arrangements for such staff may, however, be limited. Retailers are therefore somewhat at a disadvantage. This also emphasizes the importance of considering the fit between – and impact of – the image developed by retail spaces and retailers own retail image at the preliminary stages of search for a suitable location.

Retail Staff

It is here that the retailer has the greatest potential for directly guiding the aforementioned 'improvisation'. The issues raised in relation to the interaction between service employees and customers are of specific importance here. Retailers must consider the wide range of factors highlighted to ensure that the interaction between their staff and customers is managed appropriately. However, what also needs additional thought is the nature of the interaction that is desired by both the retailer and by the customer, given the context of the retail offer itself. The nature of the interaction required may vary considerably between a grocery store and a store providing bridal wear. In this example, the different requirements for the level and intensity of interaction can in part be ascribed to the type of products on offer. This is, however, perhaps an over-simplification.

The determinants governing the level and intensity of interaction stem from the customer's familiarity and certainty in relation to the product (see Chapters 8 and 12). Where a customer is unfamiliar and uncertain, the likelihood that they will seek reassurance from staff is increased. These factors are strongly aligned to frequency of purchase – with items bought regularly being less likely to need high-level and high-intensity interaction to support the process. The issue is further complicated by the notiom of customization. In those retail contexts where there is a high degree of customization – irrespective of the customer's familiarity, certainty or frequency of purchase – interaction is likely to be at a high level and of a high intensity. These issues, coupled with interaction frequency and intensity, can be conceptualized in the manner shown in Table 10.1.

The nature of interaction is therefore determined by a combination of the customer, the goods and the situation. Once a retailer has gauged the specifics of their context, they can develop general guidelines for the nature of

Table 10.1 Understanding interaction frequency and intensity

	Low interaction *frequency*	High interaction *frequency*
Low interaction *intensity*	Infrequent 'commodity' purchase e.g. electrical superstore	Frequent 'commodity' replenishment e.g. grocerysuperstore
High interaction *intensity*	Infrequent 'speciality' purchase e.g. bridal-wear store	Frequent 'speciality' replenishment e.g. boutique

the likely interaction and the consequences of managing it. For instance, whilst the basic elements identified in relation to customer-to-service employee interaction will remain constant, the relative importance of various factors will change. In retail contexts where high levels and intensities of interaction are probable, the importance of staff displaying 'concern' and appropriate non-verbal cues is increased – with civility being almost taken for granted. In the grocery store with frequent interaction but low intensity, civility may be elevated in its importance, with less stress on issues of reassurance and listening. These different concerns may then translate themselves into recruiting, training and retaining different types of staff that are best suited to the interaction needs of the particular situation. In the grocery store, given the potentially more limited intensity of interaction, finding staff with high levels of emotional intelligence will not be as critical as in the bridal-wear store.

The issue of interaction frequency also raises another area of concern, whose effect is potentially difficult to predict – what is the impact of interaction frequency and intensity on the perception of inappropriate interaction or interaction failure? In each of the cells presented in Table 10.1 the same questions can be asked. Would this combination of intensity and frequency either promote tolerance to failure or make failure more evident? In the low frequency, low intensity quadrant, does this combination lead customers experiencing interaction failure to be tolerant, given that they do not perhaps have as well-formed expectations, or have lower expectations? Conversely, it could be suggested that this combination will perhaps throw interaction failure into stark relief, and provide less opportunity for addressing the problem.

These basic questions apply in each situation. What is different, however, is the rationale behind them. This makes prediction difficult, but also serves to highlight that the individual customer's response will be the determining factor. It also begins to suggest that issues related to the customer are predominant in understanding interaction. Even in the grocery store there may be those customers that seek both frequent and intense levels of interaction with staff. So, whilst the table developed provides general guidelines, it does not constitute an absolute.

Conclusions

The social interactions that customers have while shopping play a significant part in creating the overall experience, and inform their reactions to it. These interactions can take place between a number of 'actors' – customer (user), visitor, venue staff and retail staff – and can take place in various combinations and frequency within a single shopping visit. The content of these interactions is also likely to vary, both in terms of the verbal and non-verbal communication that takes place as well as the subject of communication, from for example, the exchange of simple pleasantries, to asking for directions or even product advice.

The importance of various aspects of non-verbal communication in relation to the subject discussed and those 'actors' involved in it, has, as yet, received less attention than it deserves. The significance of 'getting right' the cues sent non-verbally has been clearly demonstrated. So also has its impact been demonstrated in situations where the interaction takes place between customer and employee where potential effects go beyond that of the immediate interaction and reflect onto perceptions of the company.

Therefore for retailers, it is imperative to understand that managing the social interactions that take place between staff and customers involves more that providing a script – however loose. Whilst the company cannot hope to 'prescribe' non-verbal behaviour, it can provide guidelines and training to support the use of appropriate cues and as importantly also help staff 'read' such communication.

It is with their own staff that retailers' can exercise the most 'direction', but this does not mean that they should not consider the other points of interaction that influence the shopping experience. Of particular importance is customer-to-customer interaction that takes place within the retailer's Servuction arena. Direction can be provided here, but not obviously in the form of training. Here, subtler management techniques need to be developed that make use of the different roles that customers play in such interaction. This could be the provision of areas where the likelihood of such activity increases – for instance seating areas, displays and demonstrations. In this latter example staff can also play a part in creating appropriate opportunities for such interaction e.g. asking questions to prompt interaction and comments. This again underlines the importance of staff in managing social interaction within the retail context – this time however not as actors, but as 'directors' of improvisation themselves.

Retail staff also have a final and critical role to play in social interaction within the retail store. They provide the potential for the development of relationships over time with customers. The 'permanence' of a member of staff as part of the retail context means that they can act as a focus for relationship development. This issue and others related to time are considered in the next chapter.

References

Abercrombie, D. 1968. Paralanguage. *British Journal of Disorders of Communication*, 3, 55–59.

Adelman, M.B., Ahuvia, A. and Goodwin, C. 1994. Beyond smiling: social support and service quality. In Rust, R.T. and Oliver, R.L. (Eds)., *Service Quality: New Directions in Theory and Practice*. Thousand Oaks, CA: Sage.

Anderson, K and Zemke, R. 1990. Customers from hell. *Training*, 26(February), 25–31.

Beatty, S.E., Mayer, M.L., Coleman, J.E., Reynolds, K.E. and Lee, J. 1996. Customer-sales associate retail relationships. *Journal of Retailing*, 72(3), 223–347.

Belk, R.W. 1982. Acquiring, possessing and collecting: fundamental processes in consumer behavior. In Bush, R. and Hunt, S. (Eds)., *Marketing Theory: Philosophy of Science Perspectives*. Chicago, IL: American Marketing Association.

Bitner, M.J. 1995. Building service relationships: it's all about promises. *Journal of the Academy of Marketing Science*, 23 (Fall), 246–251.

Bitner, M.J., Booms, B.H. and Tetreault, M.S. 1990 The service encounter: diagnosing favorable and unfavorable incidents. *Journal of Marketing*, 54(1), 71–84.

Bloch, P.H., Ridgway, N.M and Dawson, A. 1994. The shopping mall as consumer habitat. *Journal of Retailing*, 70(1), 23–42.

Bowen, D.E. and Lawler, E.E. III 1992. The empowerment of service workers: what, why, how and when. *Sloan Management Review*, 33(3), 31–39.

Crystal, D. 1997. *The Cambridge Encyclopaedia of Language (2nd Ed.)*. Cambridge: Cambridge University Press.

Feick, L.F. and Price, L.L. 1987. The market maven: a diffuser of marketplace information. *Journal of Marketing*, 51 (January), 83–97.

Frazer Winsted, K. 2000. Service behaviors that lead to satisfied customers. *European Journal of Marketing*, 34(3/4), 399–417.

Gabbott, M. and Hogg, G. 2000. An empirical investigation of the impact of non-verbal communication on service evaluation. *European Journal of Marketing*, 34(3/4), 384–398.

Grove, S.J. and Fisk, R.P. 1997. The impact of other customers on service exchanges: a critical incident examination of 'getting along'. *Journal of Retailing*, 73(1), 63–85.

Grove, S.J. and Fisk, R.P. 1992. The service experience as theater. In *Advances in Consumer Research*. Provo UT: Association for Consumer Research, pp. 455–461.

Gwinner, K.P., Gremler, D.D. and Bitner, M-J. 1998. Relational benefits in service industries: the customer's perspective. *Journal of the Academy of Marketing Science*, 26 (Spring), 101–114.

Harris, K., Baron, S. and Davies, B.J. 1999. What sort of soil do rhododendrons like? Comparing customer and employee responses to requests for product-related information. *Journal of Services Marketing*, 13(1), 21–37.

Harris, K., Davies, B.J. and Baron, S. 1997. Conversations during purchase consideration: sales assistants and customers. *The International Review of Retail, Distribution and Consumer Research*, 7(3), 173–190.

Harris, K., Baron, S. and Ratcliffe, J. 1995. Customers as oral participants in a service setting. *Journal of Services Marketing*, 9(4), 64–76.

Harris, K., Baron, S. and Ratcliffe, J. 1994. Oral participation of customers in a retail setting: an empirical study. *Proceedings of the 3rd International Research Seminar in Service Management, La-Londe-les-Maures, France*, pp. 24–27.

Hoffman, K.D. and Bateson, J.E.G. 1997. *Essentials of Services Marketing*. Orlando, FL: The Dryden Press.

Holbrook, M.B. and Hirschman, E.C. 1982. The experiential aspects of consumption: consumer fantasies, feelings and fun. *Journal of Consumer Research* 9(3), 132–140.

Hudson, R.A. 1983. *Sociolinguistics*. Oxford: Cambridge University Press.

Martin, C.L. 1997. *Bowling's Team Concept*. Merriville, IN: ICS Books Inc.

Martin, C.L. 1996. Customer-to-customer relationships: satisfaction with other customers' public behaviour. *Journal of Consumer Affairs*, 30(1), 146–169.

McAdams, D.P. 1988. Personal needs and personal relationships. In Duck, S.W. (Ed)., *Handbook of Personal Relationships*. New York: John Wiley and Sons.

McGrath, M.A. and Otnes, C. 1995. Unacquainted influencers: when strangers interact in the retail setting. *Journal of Business Research*, 32(1), 146–169.

Parker, C. and Ward, P. 2000. An analysis of role adoptions and scripts during customer-to-customer encounters. *European Journal of Marketing*, 34(3/4), 341–358.

Sundaram, D.S. and Webster, C. 2000. The role of non-verbal communication in service encounters. *Journal of Services Marketing*, 14(5), 378–391.

Zeithaml, V.A., Parasuraman, A. and Berry, L.L. 1990. *Delivering Quality Service: Balancing Customer Perceptions and Expectations*. New York: The Free Press.

11

THE TEMPORAL DIMENSION

Within the context of retail interactions, there are also a number of aspects related to time that can have a particular impact on the way in which an individual engages with a retailer. The pattern of engagement may itself vary over time.

It is within this complex web of time-based factors that relationships may develop; that usage may produce liking; that demands made by a given user may vary over time and from occasion to occasion. This issue of time is one that retailers have increasingly considered as an element of the retail management task. It can be explored in relation to a number of factors:

- Extended interchanges versus brief exchanges;
- The temporal dimension and the development of relationships;
- Time-rich versus time-poor;
- Time availability; and
- Orientation – past or future.

Introduction

The preceding chapter focused on the importance of social interaction on customers' perceptions and behaviour. The importance of such interaction stems from human nature and the fact that in a large part, we are a social animal that seeks contact and is partially defined by it. One of the other defining elements of our existence is time. We measure its duration in relation to particular events, celebrate its passing and beginning, seek to 'balance' the activities in our lives by using time and also often mark our memories and hopes in relation to it. Time therefore provides a strong contextual element in our lives. It is used to help make sense of events and relationships. In this way, not only do we live within time, but it is also an important factor in giving meaning to our lives.

This pervading nature of time means that it is commonly considered in relation to any human activity. This is equally true within the study of consumer behaviour – for example, consider research into the importance of early socialization on the long-term shopping behaviour and product preferences. In this example the issue of time is readily evident in two separate contexts: the period of time constituting 'early socialization' and the concept of 'long-term'. It is therefore not surprising that in much of this book, the issue of time plays an significant role in helping provide context and definition. However, its *explicit* importance has not yet been considered. This chapter therefore aims to provide a discussion of the effects of time on customers within retail contexts.

Given the significance of both time and the social dimension, examining the interconnectedness of the two provides an appropriate starting point, as it highlights the part played by time in the development of social relationships. In a retail context, such relationships – as highlighted in the previous chapter – are defined by the Servuction model (see Chapter 6), although there is no inherently obvious depiction of time within it. Rather time is something which is implied by the connecting arrows of the model – as at the very least, duration of interaction provides an important element in understanding the nature of the social relationships developed. From the perspective of the retailer, the most important social relationship is that of customer and retail employee, given that this is where the retailer can exert greatest 'control'.

The Temporal Dimension and the Development of Relationships

Czepiel (1990) suggests that a relationship can be formed between customer and salesperson when there is repeated and on-going interaction between the two. As a result of this sequence of contacts, the two parties then begin to 'know each other'. Beatty et al. (1996) and Gwinner et al. (1998), also contend that this relationship yields specific benefits to the customer in two categories: the functional and the social. Reynolds and Beatty (1999) suggest that functional benefits include time savings, convenience and better purchase decisions, and that the social benefits encompass concerns such as enjoying the salesperson's company and spending time with them. Such social benefits are likely to influence the degree to which customer-to-service employee interaction serves the 'emotional' needs of the customer – where the encounter is a positive one helping to create a positive emotional response (Hoffman and Kelly, 2000). This 'personal' connection between customer and salesperson also has the potential to act as a platform for the development of a relationship between customer and company (Bitner, 1995; Gwinner et al., 1998; Reynolds and Beatty, 1999).

The study conducted by Reynolds and Beatty (1999) focuses specifically on the causal relationship between customer and salesperson interaction and the functional and social benefits that impact the customer's satisfaction, loyalty, the making of positive recommendations and share of spend (sometimes collectively known as 'engagement'). These 'dependent' issues all provide the company with potential advantage. Their study of clothing store customers found that when a customer perceived that they were receiving both functional and social benefits from the interaction, they were more likely to be satisfied with the salesperson themselves. Perhaps even more importantly from the retailer's perspective, Reynolds and Beatty (1999) noted that:

> ...salesperson satisfaction appears to translate to vital bottom line consequences for the firm – company satisfaction, company word of mouth, and possibly most importantly, share of total purchases of clothing.

This suggests that the development of a relationship over time between customer and salesperson provides a vital element in creating a satisfied customer and one that is loyal – both in terms of the individual salesperson and the company. Such propositions are also echoed by Hoffman and Kelly (2000). For the retailer, facilitating the development of this connection is imperative – as it is through an ongoing sequence of interactions that such positive benefits are accrued. This presents a number of challenges for retail management.

The first challenge, as Reynolds and Beatty (1999) imply, is to create the perception in customers that establishing and maintaining a relationship with a member of sales staff is beneficial to them. This is perhaps central, as a customer who sees that no benefit would be derived from such a relationship will not have the necessary motivation to either establish one themselves or respond positively to the attempts of sales personnel to create one (Beatty et al., 1996). Retail management therefore needs to convey a clear message that maintaining a relationship with a member of staff is in the customer's best interests. How this is best achieved is dependent on the type of image that the retailer is trying to establish and the nature of its customers. For example, in the context of an up-market clothing store, word-of-mouth and the ability to directly observe benefits that accrue to a customer with an established salesperson relationship may provide appropriately subtle cues. However, for a mid-market department store, the provision of customer testimonials or a more obvious play on the benefit of customer-sales staff relationships in its promotion, alongside word-of-mouth, may be more appropriate. Irrespective of the retail context and the methods selected to inform customers of the potential benefits, it will always be necessary to ensure that staff are available on the sales floor on a day-to-day basis, as well as in the longer-term, to develop such relationships.

Therefore, the second issue for retail management relates to continuity within the staffing base as without this, there is limited potential for the creation of a positive relationship between salesperson and customer – and by implication, customer and retailer. This means that the retailer must consider the issue of staff turnover, and try to ensure that levels are as low as realistically possible. This is perhaps of greatest importance in those retail sectors where such relationships are likely to be established, and perhaps most importantly where they are valued by the customer e.g. clothing, furniture and computing. Here, consideration of employee satisfaction, motivation and reward (employee 'engagement') is central to minimizing staff turnover. However, in those areas where customers do not seek relationships, the issue of employee retention may be important for other operational reasons (e.g. the cost of hiring, etc.).

The third challenge is perhaps more difficult to tackle as it relates to the hiring of staff who have the necessary skills or qualities to develop such relationships. It additionally requires the provision of appropriate training and also the facilitation of staff's attempts to generate customer relationships. These issues are also related to the 'direction' provided by retail management.

The customer–salesperson relationship is based on a series of retail interactions or improvisations, which are themselves bounded by the framework of qualities that the retailer wishes staff to express, alongside other elements that comprise the staging of the event – such as the physical environment. Therefore, to propagate these potentially beneficial relationships, retailers not only need to hire the appropriate people, but also provide appropriate direction and freedom to improvise – in an appropriate setting.

In doing this, the retailer will help to facilitate the development, and maintenance, of relationships. These relationships are however, subject to change – in particular in relation to duration and its impact on customer perceptions. Reynolds and Beatty (1999) found that those customers who had been in longer-term relationships with a member of sales staff perceived that they received higher social benefits, more actively provided recommendations for both the salesperson and the retailer, and were more loyal to the salesperson than customers who had been engaged in shorter relationships. As they went on to note, these longer-term customers appear to have formed 'closer' relationships and acted as important advocates for the company to others.

As Bolton and Lemon (1999) note, customers inevitably decide future patronage on the basis of their evaluations of their experiences, and that these patronage decisions have a substantial impact on the long-term profitability of the company. Whilst they acknowledge the importance of the provider–customer relationship, they also emphasize that customer's patronage decisions are made in relation to how resources are exchanged within the relationship. This helps to highlight that whilst extending the overall duration of customer–staff interaction provides benefit to both customer and company, issues such as price can affect the best of relationships. If the price of the product exceeds what customers perceive they will derive in benefit – be that either direct or indirect – then it is unlikely that they will continue their relationship with the company, irrespective of previous duration. So, the benefits gained by increasing the length of relationship between staff and customer may be mitigated by changes in the retail offer that are perceived negatively.

Kandampully and Duddy (1999, p. 51) stress this in a slightly different manner, stating that companies must:

> ...think for the customer, and... conceive and implement new ways to serve them better... [and that] in order to develop and maintain customer relationships, an organisation needs the assistance and partnership of their respective stakeholders; for example, employees, suppliers and distributors.

As with many other issues, it is the whole offer, as well as the elements that support that offer, that will ultimately dictate the length of time that the customer is involved with the company.

Time is not only important in terms of the duration of a relationship, it is also a significant factor in customer decision-making and purchase behaviour. The amount of time available to customers for shopping not only colours the approach that they select, but also their expectations and levels of tolerance. Therefore, developing an appreciation of time availability and its implications is crucial.

Time-Rich Versus Time-Poor

> The old adage "Time is money" is meant to remind us that time is a scarce resource. Most of us hardly need the reminder. As society becomes more affluent, we are able to buy more material objects, but even the wealthy are limited to 24 hours per day. For many, time is not just a scarce resource; it is *the* [emphasis added] scarce resource.
>
> Leclerc et al., 1995

Time Loss

Leclerc et al. (1995) explore the way that people approach the potential loss of time in purchase situations. They attempt to provide a more detailed understanding of how choices are made under a variety of conditions, and to ascertain whether time and money are treated similarly. In each of the conditions they explore, the addition of time to the purchase experience is a negative factor – rather than providing the customer with additional benefit, it is clearly a detractor.

Firstly, Leclerc et al. (1995) consider the impact of situation and context on a customer's approach to the value of time. Here, there appears to be a relationship between approach to time loss and the overall time of the 'experience'. Where customers are faced with an experience that they know is going to take a considerable time, adding a short amount of additional time does little to help. The attitude is rather a stoical one – "it's going to take over four hours, so what difference does an extra 15 minutes make?". However, the *addition* of time to an experience that is supposed to be short *does* have an impact, e.g. travel – customers actually preferring to pay extra to maximize the potential for the experience being shortened. It seems, therefore, that when customers have 'blocked out' a large period of time for an event, the addition of a small amount of time is acceptable and it is not worth paying extra money to shorten the time taken. But, where the event is only due to take a short period of time, paying to decrease that time is preferable. It is perhaps because this may positively affect what else can be undertaken in a day that customers are willing to pay to maximize their time availability (which partly explains the rapid uptake of Internet grocery shopping, with its additional delivery charges).

However, the cost of the product being purchased also has an impact. The value of time is generally perceived as being higher when waiting is associated with a product of a high price rather than low price. There appears to be a trade-off between cost and time. If a product is perceived as being 'cheap' in terms of its monetary cost, then the additional time taken to secure the product is not problematic. Only when a product is seen as having a high price does there seem to be a propensity to offset this by reducing the time component of the purchase. So, whilst there is evidence to suggest that customers are stoical when the event is scheduled to take a long time, or when the financial cost is seen as offsetting time loss, for those products that are perceived as being monetarily expensive, such flexibility in attitude is absent. This, in part, helps to explain the potentially different responses to waiting in line whilst shopping for groceries at an up-market store and a discount store. In the discount store, the prospect of making financial savings is set against issues such as service levels, which in turn impact the time it takes to process customers at the checkout. Fewer checkout staff may mean longer waiting times – but customers may say "Well, at these prices you can't expect the same level of service"; or, "I'm saving so much money that I don't mind if it takes a little longer at the checkout". In an up-market grocery store, the converse may be true. Customers could feel that they do not mind paying the higher prices, as they are going to receive better service levels that will help them minimize the time spent on shopping and waiting in line.

Secondly, Leclerc et al. (1995) found that consumers prefer to integrate, rather than separate, time losses. If time is to be lost during a purchase situation, the preference is that all the time losses occur together, rather than being split into smaller discrete time losses. The value of time is such that, rather than experience losses over an extended period, there is a preference that they are amalgamated: which provides maximum time without loss and not periods punctuated by separated losses.

Thirdly, they noted that in purchase decisions where consumers faced a situation where there was the potential to 'gamble' with time, consumers were risk averse, or at best risk neutral. This, they suggest, stems from the nature of time, primarily the inability to transfer time losses or savings to new situations. For instance, if you achieve a time saving at one point in the day it is not always possible to transfer it to another point when it might be useful. Time, in essence, cannot be stored. This means that planning becomes an important issue and in order to plan, it is easiest to operate under conditions that are certain. Therefore, in situations where there is a potential time-related risk, consumers opt – in the main – for choices that provide a clear indication of the time implications associated with them.

Consumers are clearly sensitive to loss of time – just as they are to loss of money. However, the way that time loss is approached and managed is distinct from the way that loss of money is considered. The intangible nature of time means that customers treat it in a very different manner – irrespective of their level of time availability, i.e. whether they are time 'rich' or time 'poor'.

Time Availability

However, there is a need to consider the time actually available for shopping, as it does appear to relate to a range of consumer behaviours. Time availability can be defined by "consumers' perceptions of the time required to perform the intended shopping tasks relative to the actual time available to perform such tasks" (Park et al., 1989). Given this definition, time pressure exerts itself when customers are faced with situations in which the time available for shopping is less than that which they perceive is necessary. The stimulus for such an interpretation can stem from a number of sources.

For example, a customer may have to 'fit' the shopping activity into a particular time-frame based on other commitments: they may need to shop in their lunch break; car-parking time, or the perceived need to get home and cook. The time pressure here may be either 'real' or perceived. In fact, even those customers who are not looking to fit their purchasing activity with other tasks, may feel that shopping should take them a specific amount of time and no longer. This can provide the same perceived 'constraints', and it is also this feeling of time constraint that best describes time pressure that stems from the shopper themselves.

There is little that retailers can do to prevent such notions developing. However, time constraint perceptions can be influenced and, to an extent, managed, once the customer is in the store. Such notions can also be either accentuated or stimulated by what a customer encounters within the retail environment.

Time availability influences both customers' cognitive and affective responses whilst they are within the retail environment. If there is limited time, then the degree of information processing that a customer can engage in whilst in the store is itself limited (Park et al., 1989). Therefore, those customers who are time poor are better served by environments that carry a 'low load', have clear and simple displays and provide 'limited' choice. Limited time availability can also have an emotional effect, as it raises the level of stress that a customer might experience. This itself also has implications for other mental functions such as the retrieval of memories that are not often recalled. For example, remembering product inventory levels at home, which are then in turn used to inform the customer's decision-making process (Park et al., 1989).

Decisions made in situations that are significantly affected by time-induced stress can also lead customers to make trade-offs between speed and accuracy in their decision-making. Firstly, customers tend to examine information much more quickly when they feel they are under time pressure (Ben Zur and Breznitz, 1981). Secondly in doing this, there is an accompanying tendency for customers to place greater emphasis on meaningful features and negative information (Ben Zur and Breznitz, 1981). Where time pressure is encountered, customers tend to fail in making their intended purchases, and a decision to defer purchase is made. This can lead in some instances, to frustration on the part of the customer, which then can have a direct impact on the retailer.

The connection between increasing time pressure and the choice to defer a decision is not however a simple linear relationship. Other factors also work with time pressure; and it is the combination that signals either product purchase or purchase deferral. Dhar and Nowliss (1999) identify the importance of having a clear 'best' option. Where a product can easily be identified as 'superior' (see the next chapter), time pressure does not lead to purchase deferral. However, if there is no clear choice, or a wide-range of options, this can lead to purchase deferral. As Herrington and Capella (1995) also note, there are two other by-products of time pressure – customers tend to spend less time making each product selection decision, and they spend more money in the time available to them. This suggests that time-pressured shoppers may provide retailers with potential benefits as well as difficulties.

However, as highlighted above, the issue of time pressure should not be examined as a singular concern; and consideration of other personal and situational variables needs to be undertaken alongside it. Park et al. (1989) note that the effects of limited time availability are often combined with other stress-inducing factors such as lack of familiarity with the store. When such combinations are found, customers have a tendency to brand/product switch. This is a result of difficulty in locating their desired choice, or the unavailability of the preferred selection. Here, whilst retailers may wish to encourage brand/product switching, there may be implications for the overall level of satisfaction that the customer derives from the experience. (The impact of such issues are on store image are highlighted in Chapter 9 and are also considered in relation to merchandise in Chapter 8 and the individual in Chapter 12.)

As Aylott and Mitchell (1999) note, lack of time – although previously identified as the single largest cause of pressure – can be coupled with a range of factors to induce stress in shoppers. These include crowding, staff attitude, store layout/relocation (raising issues of store knowledge highlighted by Park et al., 1989), impulse purchasing pressure, product assortment, music and lighting. Each of these factors in itself can also create stress. This facility to stimulate an unpleasant reaction, i.e. stress, would seem to fit with issues related to the discussion of the physical environment (Chapter 7) and the customer's psychological state (Chapter 12). In both these chapters the potential for the retail environment to cause 'avoidance' behaviour is highlighted. Such behaviour can be seen as a direct result of the stress induced in a customer by the experience of shopping. Time availability works with other situational elements to induce negative responses in customers that then, in turn, influence negatively the experience and perceptions of it. Given the potential development of such negative responses, it would seem likely that customers would act to reduce them wherever possible.

However, as East et al. (1994) note in their study of grocery shopping behaviour, customers are creatures of habit. They appear to be 'loyal' to a particular shopping time – both in terms of day and hour – even when they know that this will bring with it factors that are likely to increase stress. This loyalty is not developed, in large part, as a result of constraints in when shopping activity can take place. It does, however, highlight that even though customers are aware of the time-related issues, and the associated situational factors such as crowding, this is not enough to precipitate a change in visit timing behaviour: although, it can have a significant impact on the individual's affective and cognitive responses, as well as specific behaviour whilst in the store. This poses a number of interesting questions that retail managers must consider carefully.

Given East et al.'s (1994) findings that, in a grocery shopping context, visit timing behaviour is unaffected by the stressors – coupled with customers' other 'habits' in relation to store visited and products purchased – should retailers be overly concerned in managing the sources of such stress? Once such patterns of behaviour have been established, if all other things remained equal, then perhaps retailers could indeed find themselves in a situation where habit militates against customer defection. The problem is of course, that things very rarely remain equal; and whilst habit might provide retailers with a cushioning effect, disaffected customers that are presented with an alternative are more likely to take it. Customer's perceptions of limited time availability coupled with other factors, are likely to increase stress; and this in turn, will affect attitudes and behaviour at various levels. Whilst this appears both intuitive and has been empirically supported, what it does not consider is the importance of the underlying attitudes customers hold in relation to time and its effect on their perception of time availability.

Orientation: Past, Present or Future

Whilst time is itself, in the everyday sense, a 'constant' – a year, a week, a day, which is itself composed of twenty-four hours, an hour of sixty minutes, something that the clock measures – its perception is a subjective experience (McDonald, 1994). As Gibbs (1998) notes, this has led to a dissatisfaction in the consumer research literature with simply treating time as 'clock time' and has given rise to the consideration of time as experience. The notion of time as experience mirrors movements in other areas that study human behaviour and refocuses the approach taken (Gibbs, 1998). The suggestion is that, in order to develop an understanding of an individual's time perceptions, there needs to be an awareness of how past, present and future are considered – both in the short and long term (Guy et al., 1994). The notion of an individual's time orientation, although clearly centred on the person, must however be seen as located within a wider social context. It is highly dependent on the socialization process that has helped shape the individual

(Davies, 1994); therefore this perspective on time also presents a link between the temporal and social dimensions – even if at the broadest level.

The view of time as experience is used by Bergadaa (1990) to develop an understanding of predominant orientation in individuals and its link to their attitudes towards consumption and their purchasing behaviour. Those who are future-orientated do not believe in fate, and see themselves as being responsible for their own future (Bergadaa, 1990). In addition, Bergadaa found that future-oriented individuals purport to display a particular attitude to consumption – they seek to 'enrich' themselves intellectually, and want to keep a high degree of control over the consumer process. In contrast, people that are present-oriented consider that they are subject to fate, and seek to simplify their lives, often looking to entrust the consumer process to other people, and reacting to external stimuli (Bergadaa, 1990). Those that are past-oriented display traditional views and have a tendency to be nostalgic both in their attitudes and behaviour to purchasing. These differences clearly play a significant role in what is bought – but as Chetthamrongchai and Davies (2000) suggest, time orientations could also be antecedents to shopping attitudes more generally.

In their study of food shoppers, Chetthamrongchai and Davies (2000) found that time orientation could be used alongside other time attitude measures (such as time pressure) and shopping attitudes (including convenience seeking and enjoyment derived) to model shopping behaviour. They developed a typology of food shoppers that contained four distinct groups:

- The time-pressured convenience seekers – often young, employed, educated and living in larger homes. This group displayed high time pressure coupled with future-orientation and convenience shopping behaviour. They disliked food shopping and tended to operate as 'random' shoppers – shopping at irregular intervals.
- Hedonists – older and employed. They enjoy shopping, and see it as an event. They also have a tendency to be present-oriented.
- Apathetic but regular – as the name suggests, this group are regular shoppers, who on the whole dislike the activity (although not as much as the first group). They are highly past- and present-orientated – so, although they see shopping as part of their routine, they also focus on the here and now.
- Convenience seekers – predominantly males. But, unlike the first group, their orientation does not stem from any perceived time pressure. They have the lowest shopping frequency of all four groups.

These groups not only had different attitudes towards and timings for shopping activity, they also patronized different stores and spent different amounts of time on the activity. The importance of time perceptions as a factor in explaining the variations found in shopping patterns is also supported by McDonald (1994). Time perception provides an alternative lens through which to examine shopping behaviour – one which has the potential to generate new insights.

Conclusions

Whilst time is a factor that has been mentioned in relation to an extraordinarily large number of issues, it is often given a limited degree of consideration. This is perhaps surprising considering its pervasive nature. However, this very nature may be the issue that has generated this broad, but shallow examination. Time is something that has been treated as context and backdrop, rather than being given the prominence it deserves.

Time is also not a single or necessarily linear concept. Understanding this, and approaching the examination of time and shopping from different perspectives, provides a diverse range of conceptualizations that add significantly to understanding relationships, choice, attitude and actions.

Therefore, examining time in all its various conceptualizations helps to create deeper appreciation of customers' shopping behaviour. For retailers, it can help to generate new methods of segmenting their markets; and, when combined with the other elements of the Servuction arena, can aid the development of appropriate and effective retail environments.

References

Aylott, R. and Mitchell, V.-W. 1999. An exploratory study of grocery shopping stressors. *British Food Journal*, 101(9), 683–700.

Ben Zur, H. and Breznitz, S.J. 1981. The effect of time pressure on risky choice behavior. *Acta Psychologica*, 47 (February), 89–104.

Beatty, S.E., Mayer, M.L., Coleman, J.E., Reynolds, K.E. and Lee, J. 1996. Customer-sales associate retail relationships. *Journal of Retailing*, 72(3), 223–347.

Bergadaa, M.M. 1990. The role of time in the action of the consumer. *Journal of Consumer Research*, 17(3), 289–302.

Bitner, M.J. 1995. Building service relationships: it's all about promises. *Journal of the Academy of Marketing Science*, 23 (Fall), 246–251.

Bolton, R.N. and Lemon, K.N. 1999. A dynamic model of customers' usage of services: usage as an antecedent and consequence of satisfaction. *Journal of Marketing Research*, 36(2), 171.

Chetthamrongchai, P. and Davies, G. 2000. Segmenting the market for food shoppers using attitudes to shopping and time. *British Food Journal*, 102(2), 81–101.

Czepiel, J.A. 1990. Service encounters and service relationships: implications for research. *Journal of Business Research*, 20, 13–21.

Davies, G. 1994. What should time be? *European Journal of Marketing*, 28(8/9), 100–113.

Dhar, R. and Nowliss, S.M. 1999. The effect of time pressure on consumer choice deferral. *Journal of Consumer Research*, 25(4), 369.

East, R., Lomax, W. Willson, G. and Harris, P. 1994. Decision making and habit in shopping times. *European Journal of Marketing*, 28(4), 56–71.

Gibbs, P.T. 1998. Time, temporality and consumer behaviour. *European Journal of Marketing*, 32(11/12), 993–1007.

Guy, B.S., Rittenburg, T.L. and Hawes, D.K. 1994. Dimensions characteristics of time perceptions and perceptions among older consumers. *Psychology and Marketing*, 11 (January/February), 35–56.

Gwinner, K.P., Gremler, D.D. and Bitner, M-J. 1998. Relational benefits in service industries: the customer's perspective. *Journal of the Academy of Marketing Science*, 26 (Spring), 101–114.

Herrington, J.D. and Capella, L.M. 1995. Shopper reactions to perceived time pressure. *International Journal of Retail and Distribution Management*, 23(12), 13–20.

Hoffman K.D. and Kelly, S.W. 2000. Perceived justice needs and recovery evaluation: a contingency approach. *European Journal of Marketing*, 34(3/4), 418–432.

Kandampully, J. and Duddy, R. 1999. Competitive advantage through anticipation, innovation and relationships. *Management Decision*, 37(1), 51–56.

Leclerc, F., Schmitt, B.H., Dube, L. 1995. Waiting time and decision making: is time like money? *Journal of Consumer Research*, 22(1), 110–119.

McDonald, W.J. 1994. Time use in shopping: the role of personal characteristics. *Journal of Retailing*, 70(4), 345–365.

Park, C.W., Iyer, E.S. and Smith, D.C. 1989. The effects of situational factors on in-store grocery shopping behavior: the role of store environment and time available for shopping. *Journal of Consumer Research*, 15(4), 422.

Reynolds, K.E. and Beatty, S.E. 1999. Customer benefits and company consequences of customer-salesperson relationships in retailing. *Journal of Retailing*, 75(1), 11.

12

CUSTOMERS' PSYCHOLOGICAL STATE

Each of the various factors introduced in the arena for retail drama can be seen as having an impact on the consumer's psychological state. Each consumer of course, enters the retail drama in a particular psychological situation, or antecedent mood state, that can impinge on his or her reaction to any interaction. Understanding the importance of the following can provide the retailer with rich insights for the creation of an 'appropriate' retail drama:

- Pleasure, arousal and dominance;
- Planned intention;
- Previous experience;
- Risk; and
- Decision-making.

Introduction

The way a customer 'feels' before embarking on a shopping experience, and the feelings induced whilst on that trip, mediate their behaviour and their subsequent perceptions. A customer who sets off with a friend to spend the day browsing – and then whilst out shopping, makes a number of unplanned purchases; engages in light-hearted banter with an enthusiastic shop assistant, and feels that the purchases that they have made have received the approval of their companion – may well end the day with a sense of satisfaction, in relation to their own decision-making, the experience of shopping, and the retailer where they made the purchases. However, if the very same customer leaves to go shopping with a specific item in mind and decides to return to the same retailer, but is pressed for time and then meets with an apathetic or ill-informed reception from very same member of sales staff that previously served them enthusiastically, the customer may at the end of the experience, feel that they have been pressured into making a purchase, and that both the retailer and the total experience were significantly less than satisfactory.

In this example, the customer, the retailer and the member of staff are constant. All that has been altered is the 'finer elements' of the situation: the mood state of the customer; the pressure that they feel; the reception that they receive from the sales assistant, and the presence of a 'shopping pal'. With the exception of the last element, the changes are relatively 'ephemeral' in their nature. They relate to customer's psychological state and perhaps in part, to its 'reading', and the subsequent reaction of the member of sales staff (as well of course, as the employee's own psychological state at the time).

The impact of these factors should not be underestimated. A retailer needs to understand the potentially moderating effect of a customer's psychological state and perhaps even more importantly, understand how the retail environment affects it. The 'happy and relaxed' customer described in the first half of the example above could quite easily have turned into an 'unhappy' one if the retail environment experienced was, for example badly stocked, poorly organized or uncomfortably hot; or if the service received fell short of expectations or requirements. The customer in the second half could have been positively influenced by many factors – for instance, swift and helpful service – to leave them feeling satisfied. In this instance though, it is the service that the customer encounters that is the largest factor in influencing their perception and mood.

Customers' psychological state can therefore, be moderated by a wide range of elements once they are in the retail environment. Their psychological state can also impact their behaviour whilst in the store and their interpretation of their experience after having left the retail environment. The following discussion therefore focuses on a number of pertinent factors that can affect a customer's psychological state. The factors selected relate to the example provided earlier in the introduction. Their inclusion does not mean that they are necessarily the most important factors; nor does the exclusion of other concerns suggest that they are unimportant. Rather the discussion aims to illustrate a range of concerns which, if understood by a retail manager, can provide a foundation for understanding how the psychological state of the customer can impact their perception and behaviour. Perhaps of most interest from the perspective of retail management is the impact of elements that they directly control and that are easy to change, e.g. the 'physicality' of the retail environment.

Pleasure, Arousal and Dominance (PAD)

Mehrabian and Russell (1974), in their study of built environments, found that people respond to the cues provided in the physical setting with feelings that can be described in terms of three dimensions – pleasure, arousal and dominance. These feelings then influence the behavioural responses of the individuals within the environment, precipitating either approach or avoidance behaviour. (A more detailed discussion of the retail physical environment can be found in Chapter 7.)

The pleasure dimension relates to the degree of 'happiness' that a customer experiences as a result of their interaction with the retailer's physical environment. There are many different things that can lead to a customer perceiving an environment as pleasant. For example: a delicatessen that displays its products in an 'attractive' manner, is decorated in a style that resembles a somewhat nostalgic ideal of an independent shop in a provincial Northern European town and has high standards of cleanliness could, for some, provide such cues. For others 'reading' these cues, the store could be perceived as 'unpleasant', given their preferences; or could generate no distinct feeling. The degree of 'pleasure' that is perceived in an environment is a matter of personal taste, expectation and norms.

Arousal concerns the degree of stimulation that is generated in the customer. Here again, cues are subject to personal interpretation and preference. Loud music in a retail environment is likely to increase the stimulation felt by a customer. However, what is perceived as being 'loud' may vary to quite an extent between customers (and to a degree, is probably related to the customers liking for the music being played).

Dominance is associated with the level of control over (or the extent to which you are controlled by) the environment. Again, to a degree, an element of variety in what is preferred by individuals is likely. However, it is unlikely that many people feel comfortable on occasions where they perceive that they have little control over (or knowledge of) the situation. There is a strong difference between the feelings generated by placing control of the situation in the hands of an amusement ride operator and the feeling of 'being adrift' that customers face when they feel that they do not understand what is expected of then in a retail environment. In the first case, a lack of dominance can add to the enjoyment of the experience – it can give a sense of surprise and enhance the 'thrill'. In the latter, not feeling in control can mean that customers are uncomfortable – potentially to the extent that they seek to leave the retail environment as quickly as possible. To watch this in operation all you need to do is see the reactions of a first-time IKEA customer on entering the store. Or simply watch in a restaurant where it is unclear if you should pay the bill at the table or move to a separate pay-point.

The interplay of pleasure, arousal and dominance can therefore significantly impact a customer. However, in their analysis, Mehrabian and Russell (1974) added a further dimension that relates in more general terms to the 'information' component of an environment. This dimension was termed 'load', and can be defined as the degree of novelty, complexity and spaciousness of particular settings. Mehrabian and Russell suggested that it directly relates to the level of arousal that an environment generates. For example, a high load environment leads to a high level of arousal.

However, what this does not consider is that different individuals have different levels of arousal-seeking behaviour (Newman et al., 1994), which acts as a moderating influence. For an individual with low levels of arousal-seeking, a high load environment will not produce heightened stimulation leading to a positive response, but will rather (over-) stimulate leading to a negative response or avoidance behaviour. For those customers that prefer a simple and fairly standard environment, entering a store that provides a less than mainstream approach can result in their feeling uncomfortable and leaving. A store that might produce very different reactions, dependent on the levels of arousal-seeking behaviour, is NikeTown. Given the 'extreme' format of the store, the range of reactions provoked could be incredibly varied, but it is also likely that the response will be either highly positive or negative rather than simply neutral. Providing such a distinctive offer is one way that retailers are likely to generate a behavioural response in customers. However, this approach is potentially dangerous, as it will induce avoidance as well as approach behaviour. A retailer must therefore consider what the characteristics are of its target market, and develop an environment with an appropriate 'loading'. This necessitates a more specific understanding of the retail context.

PAD in Retail Environments

The work of Mehrabian and Russell has acted as the foundation for a number of influential examinations of retail environments. One such study was that conducted by Donovan and Rossiter (1982) and later, that of Sherman and Smith (1987). Both these studies focused specifically on retail environments and considered the links between pleasure, arousal and dominance and in-store behaviour. Donovan and Rossiter (1982) provided a range of more specific hypotheses for the nature of the relationship between pleasure, arousal and dominance and a customer's propensity to engage in either approach or avoidance behaviour in the retail context. The first hypothesis being that in environments that are neither pleasing nor displeasing, moderate arousal enhances approach behaviour. However, very high or very low arousal typically leads to avoidance behaviour. Whereas, if the environment is deemed pleasant, greater levels of arousal lead to greater levels of approach behaviour. Conversely, in unpleasant environments, the greater the level of arousal, the greater the level of avoidance behaviour.

Extremes of approach and avoidance behaviour appear to occur – as might be imagined – when the retail environment creates a strong impression, be it either positive or negative, on the customer, as is the case with NikeTown. This suggests that if a retailer plans to create a 'definite statement' through the inanimate environment of its stores, there is a higher likelihood of generating approach behaviour in those customers that display arousal-seeking characteristics and that find the appeal 'pleasant'. It is just as probable though, that the environment will elicit negative responses in other customers. A safer option it would seem, is to adopt a middle-of-the-road approach. However, in doing this, the potential for using the physical environment to support the creation of differentiation becomes limited. For some retailers, taking the more extreme approach to 'environmental load' appears to be a more logical action, as long as there is a realization that in so doing, negative responses are inevitable.

Sherman and Smith (1987) found that the development of favourable mood-states was positively related to the amount of time spent in store, the number of items purchased, and the amount of money spent. The creation of an appropriate loading therefore not only helps to create store image, but also generates responses in customers that retailers will find beneficial – both in terms of profit potential and in opportunities to produce loyalty. Using the physical environment to develop favourable moods and approach behaviour should therefore be of central interest and benefit to retailers.

The relationship between the effects of the physical environment and customer's psychological state was also observed by Becker (1977) and by Bitner (1992). Bitner went on to suggest that customers additionally use environmental cues to make inferences regarding the nature of the retail offer and to provide indications of expected behaviour. This further emphasizes the importance of the physical retail environment and its potential impact on customers' perceptions and feelings. It appears that the physical environment, perhaps alongside other external cues (such as the social environment) creates an image that is 'perceived' by customers which is in turn, often mirrored by the feelings that they then experience. One of the factors that can perhaps moderate the way in which the physical environment is perceived and interpreted by the customer is whether the customer is engaged in a highly-focused shopping trip with specific planned intent, or is simply browsing.

Planned Intention

Shopping behaviour that is guided by planned intent necessitates that the customer has engaged in some degree of consideration before entering the store. Kollat and Willett (1967) proposed a typology of such planned behaviour:

- Product and brand decided
- Product category decided
- Product class decided
- General need recognized
- General need not recognized

The first four categories involve varying degrees of planned intent from a very specific idea of what is required: e.g. a 475g can of Heinz baked beans; to a much looser notion that a particular problem exists, which can be resolved by making a purchase: for instance, the need to purchase a birthday present for a friend.

The behaviour that a customer is likely to display if acting under the influence of the various categories is markedly different. The customer requiring the 475g can of Heinz baked beans may, on reaching the appropriate category in the store, simply seek out their planned product. They may not consider other goods on display or note promotional offers. What is perhaps more interesting is the likely behaviour when the desired product is not available. If the customer perceives that *only* the pre-planned product will meet their needs, then they may not make a substitute purchase from that store and prefer to look elsewhere (perhaps unlikely in the case of a can of beans!); or postpone purchase to a time when the product is available. If however, they are willing to consider a substitute product, the customer is likely to evaluate the goods on display in relation to their pre-defined 'reference' product. When a pre-planned product is not available there can be important implications for the satisfaction that a customer feels – especially for those customers that are product-loyal. If the retailer fails to make enough of these preferred products available, customers can judge that 'quality' has been diminished, and even choose to shop elsewhere.

In the second to fourth categories of the planned intent typology, the degree of specificity decreases. It is therefore increasingly likely that the customer will use the product range on offer to provide a choice set. From the retailer's perspective, each category progressively provides a 'better' opportunity to influence the customer's decision-making. The less defined the decision before the outset of the shopping trip, the more flexibility there is in what goods will satisfy the planned intent. In the case of the customer that wishes to purchase a birthday present for a friend, there are many more potential opportunities for the retailer to influence what is purchased: through display, promotional techniques and the assistance provided by sales staff. Customers who are acting under the fourth category of planned intent – general need recognized – are much more likely to spend time in the store browsing, than those that are acting under category one – product and brand decided.

This means that each category of planned intent brings with it various challenges and potential benefits for retail management. For example, where customers tend to act under category one, a retailer must first identify and then offer those goods that are specifically desired. There is also a need to focus on stock control and availability. However, less time needs to be spent on considering promotional offers, and the issue of price can be treated with less sensitivity, as does offering a wide range of products. Customers are less likely to spend time in the store, and providing an environment that is efficient is also potentially a key concern. If the customer is acting under category four, then a retailer needs to provide appropriately wide ranges that facilitate and prompt product comparison and choice. (Although there is likely to be a fine balance between too narrow a range and an 'appropriate' range, the concern from the retailer's perspective is to provide a 'feeling' of choice whilst steering product selection in the desired direction.) Issues relating to the in-store environment and promotion are also likely to be more important. In this instance, there is more need for the environment to facilitate browsing rather than speed.

The level of planning adopted provides very different customer mindsets and requirements that retailers must respond to appropriately. This is perhaps made more difficult by the fact that in most retail contexts it is likely that different customers will be acting under different categories of planned intent within the one environment. This means that retailers must provide a degree of 'flexibility' in their approaches, but perhaps be guided by the predominant approach that customers apply (in their type of store). In addition, some customers could be acting under the final category, which does not involve any degree of planned intent and could perhaps be considered to equate to an impulse purchase. Such behaviour raises further questions that are explored later in the chapter.

Retail Brand Intent

What the Kollat and Willett (1967) typology does not consider however, is the place of planned intent in relation to the *retail* brand. There is no mention of the possibility that a customer may have as wide a range of planned intentions in relation to retail provision as they do to merchandise. For example:

- Retail brand (and store) decided
- Store type decided
- Store class decided.

These retail brand categories, when combined with those related to product brand, provide a more detailed – powerful? – typology of planned intent (Table 12.1).

Table 12.1 Retail and product brand intent

	Retail brand (and store) decided	Store type decided	Store class decided
product and brand decided	totally focused		product focused
product category decided			
product class decided			
a general need recognized			
general need not recognized	store-specific browsing		browsing

Although it is difficult to provide 'neat' names for each potential combination, the grid does begin to encompass all potential behaviours. For example, returning to the case of the customer that wishes to buy a present for a friend: they may not know the nature of the required product, but feel that a particular store type (or even a specific retail brand) is more likely to provide an appropriate solution. This perhaps begins to explain why some customers, when faced with such situations, resort to buying a Marks and Spencer gift voucher (or, in fact, any retail store-specific voucher).

There are clear implications for retailers – primarily, how do they ensure where possible, that the retail brand that is called to mind is theirs. The case of Marks and Spencer perhaps provides a degree of insight – its voucher offers a distinctive set of benefits that for many customers, means that it provides an acceptable solution. Understanding what is therefore 'acceptable' provides a solid starting point.

The interplay of product and retail intent is a rich mechanism through which retailers can understand the requirements of their customers. It is however, not the only element of planned intent that is important, or that leads to variation in consumer behaviour and purchase patterns. For example, consumers may vary in the frequency and in the regularity of their visits to a store. Kim and Park (1997), in their study of the grocery market, found that shoppers who tended to visit a store at regular intervals (routine shoppers) spent more money on a given trip, were loyal, but the time between their visits was longer than those customers who displayed a more random pattern of store visits. They go on to suggest that these different patterns of planned visits might stem from different underlying approaches to shopping that customers adopt. Routine shoppers are driven by constraints, such as time, that mean that their behaviour is bounded and therefore more predictable. For example, what could be termed their 'loyalty' to a particular store is probably as much a result of constraints that prevent their switching between stores, as it is a liking of the store at which they shop. However, the random shopper (who shops at irregular intervals) is perhaps more likely to be price sensitive. This in turn, drives their shopping patterns which are not only more varied in their timing and duration, but also more varied in the choice of store (see the previous chapter for a more detailed discussion of the effect of time on shopping).

Customers' shopping behaviour is therefore not simply driven by purely bipolar extremes of planned and unplanned intent. When planned intent is considered there are issues relating to the level of intent towards goods and retail brand as well as frequency and regularity of visit. These need to be recognized and the potential implications for retail management explored. It would be equally over simplistic to assume that those purchase that are unplanned are easily understood. There is as much variety in unplanned intent as is to be found in that which is planned. It is also important that retail managers develop an appreciation of these variances.

Impulse Purchases

Impulse purchases have often been classified in the literature as 'unplanned' (Cobb and Hoyer, 1986). However, as Beatty and Ferrell (1998) suggest, this is a somewhat limited perspective that does not fully consider the full nature of impulse buying. They provide the following definition:

> Impulse buying is a sudden and immediate purchase with no pre-shopping intentions either to buy the specific product category or to fulfil a specific buying task.
>
> Beatty and Ferrell, 1998, p. 170

As such, it does not include the purchase of a planned gift, or of an item remembered as currently 'out-of-stock' at home. It also suggests spontaneity, impulsiveness and lack of full consideration or reflection (Rook, 1987) – thereby going some way beyond the issue of being simply 'unplanned'. As Bayley and Nancarrow (1998) point out, there has also been a tendency to see impulse buying as irrational. However, as they then discuss, this is difficult to assess given that it is common for customers to post-rationalize their decisions; and as Thompson et al. (1990) suggest, simply because an action is emotional rather than rational, it does not by implication mean that it is in fact 'irrational'.

The issue of impulse buying has generated considerable interest and this has in the main, focused on the personal *or* situational elements – for example, normative elements (see, for example, Rook and Fisher, 1995) – that influence such behaviour. In this context, customers attempt to control their impulsive tendencies, because they do not wish to appear immature or irrational (Hausman, 2000). These investigations have tended to consider personal variables, or a particular situational factor, rather than attempt to model the antecedents of impulse buying. Beatty and Ferrell (1998) try in their research to provide such a model, which includes two personal elements (shopping enjoyment and impulse buying tendencies) and two situational factors (time and money availability).

Shopping enjoyment is potentially developed through a number of inputs – one of these being the nature of the individual's attitude to shopping. Westbrook and Black (1985) found that there are those individuals who see shopping as a recreational activity and therefore, unsurprisingly, tend to spend more time shopping: they find the activity itself more gratifying than benefits derived from the goods purchased. Such shoppers are also likely to enter into the shopping experience in a positive mood and develop positive emotions as a result of interaction with the retail environment. Given these factors, recreational shoppers are more inclined to spend time 'browsing', which itself can add to shopping enjoyment – although a clear empirical link has yet to be established (Beatty and Ferrell, 1998).

Babin et al. (1994) and Sherry (1990) suggest that browsing is part of the hedonistic value of shopping: helping to provide entertainment and pleasure. This means that browsing can be associated with the development of enjoyment, which, as Beatty and Ferrell (1998) suggest, can be considered to be a 'positive affect' that is likely to be reflected in the enthusiasm and alertness of the individual. This also means, by implication, that those customers that develop a positive emotion through browsing are more likely to make an impulse purchase. The more they browse the more likely it is that they will come across a product that stimulates an impulse purchase urge; and, if in a positive frame of mind, the chances of actual purchase are increased as the customer is in close proximity to the stimulus (Rook, 1987), and equally more likely to engage in approach behaviour (Donovan and Rossiter, 1982). This presents the beginning of a somewhat 'virtuous circle': as there is also likely to be a positive impact on mood as a result of the impulse purchase (Dittmar et al., 1996) – even to the extent that some impulse purchases are made to lift mood. This again, in turn, is likely to itself enhance approach and browsing behaviour.

Approach behaviour and browsing are also affected by the amount of time available for a particular shopping trip. Generally the more time is available, the more time will be spent browsing, and the more likely it is that impulse purchasing will take place (Beatty and Ferrell, 1998). The propensity to impulse buy has also been linked to the availability of money (Beatty and Ferrell, 1998) – either actual or 'virtual'. As Beatty and Ferrell (1998) conclude, there is still much that needs to be understood about what drives impulse purchasing and how the urge to buy is either translated into actual behaviour or equally importantly, how it is suppressed.

The work of Bayley and Nancarrow (1998) goes some way to meeting these aims – and considers both personal and situational factors. They identify four 'styles' of impulse buying:

- Accelerator impulse – centres on purchases made (often on special offer) to fulfil future needs and to confirm the self-image of 'good shopper'.
- Compensatory impulse – involves purchases as a self-gift to either reward or compensate for issues experienced elsewhere, often in an attempt to lift mood ('retail therapy' or compensatory consumption (Woodruffe, 1997)).
- Breakthrough impulse – concerns the stimulation to resolve a potentially unconscious conflict through purchase and can have life-changing implications.
- Blind impulse – revolves around a sense of being overwhelmed by the product, simply having to have it.

It is clear that the motivation in each style is potentially quite different and needs to be better understood. However, there is nothing to suggest that at times, styles may or may not be used in combination, with perhaps one being dominant. This would suggest that the motivation for impulse buying is multi-layered.

Hausman (2000) supports this proposition, proposing that impulse buying offers a number of non-economic benefits – such as enjoyment, fantasy, and social or emotional gratification – and potentially represents a 'rational' alternative to more time-consuming search behaviours. She goes on to state that retailers should provide environments that can relieve customers of their negative perceptions of impulse buying, perhaps stressing the 'rationality' of the approach and its non-economic rewards. Creating an environment where impulse buying is more likely to occur can perhaps be achieved by increasing the levels of information processing that customers need to engage in. It is more likely that customers will use a simplifying device such as impulse purchasing to facilitate decision-making. It must be remembered though, that creating 'high load' conditions that are too 'stimulating' through the use of the store's physical environment and merchandise has the potential to generate avoidance behaviour. (See Chapter 7 for a discussion of the physical environment and Chapter 8 for merchandise-related issues.)

Additionally, further investigation of what occurs to the customer and their level of satisfaction with their impulse buys after purchase needs to take place. This will further enable retailers to either facilitate impulse purchases or if appropriate, provide mechanisms to support the development of satisfaction in the post-purchase evaluation phase. If customers develop a pattern of satisfaction with their impulse purchases, this past experience can positively affect subsequent behaviour. This helps to highlight the fact that when customers enter any retail environment they bring with them a set of memories that can help determine their actions on that specific occasion.

Previous Experience

The issue of previous experience is often considered in relation to many aspects of consumer behaviour, e.g. the development of approach or avoidance behaviour, and the nature of purchases either planned or impulsive. In all of these contexts the customer's previous experience can impact both how a customer feels and how they behave. Given this, Hoch and Deighton (1989) state that it is perhaps surprising that the issues of previous experience, the learning derived from it, and the potential for retailers to influence this process, have received relatively little attention. They go on to suggest that this limited consideration may be a direct result of the assumptions that have been made in relation to the knowledge gained from product consumption. The primary assumption has been that once a product is experienced, a customer will simply learn the *objective* truth about it. However, Hoch and Deighton (1989) suggest that what actually occurs is *subjective* and is open to influence. To this end they develop a four-stage model of the 'belief updating' process – hypothesizing, exposure, encoding and integration – which provides focal points for intervention at each stage (although there is a realization that the stages are potentially iterative and are not necessarily fixed in a linear sequence).

Hoch and Deighton (1989) also suggest that there are three key environmental influences on learning from experience – familiarity, motivation and ambiguity. Where a customer is unfamiliar with a product category, learning is much more open to influence as novices gain only a holistic understanding of the experience rather than developing a detailed analytic appreciation (Alba and Hutchinson, 1987). The novice is therefore more susceptible to direction after experience. Equally, if the experience is open to interpretation, there is also a higher chance to influence learning – ambiguity provides a means of presenting the customer with an interpretation that favours the desired outcome. Of course, in such situations this means that rival messages compete for acceptance, just as they do *before* experience.

The final element is the customer's motivation to learn. The customer that is highly motivated to learn is much more likely to spend time considering and evaluating product experience. Given that the majority of consumption decisions are relatively routine, and the outcome of limited importance, motivation to learn is likely to be low. In such cases retailers have the potential to influence both purchase and post-experience learning. When a customer is not motivated to develop a clear set of ideas before setting off on their shopping trip, they may be more inclined to use the information presented by the retailer to make their choice. There may well be links here to planned and impulse purchases and the approaches employed when making decisions under these conditions.

The issues of familiarity, motivation and ambiguity can also be aligned with another issue that potentially has significant impact on a consumer's decision-making approach – that of perceived risk and the associated concern of dealing with this risk.

Perceived Risk

The perceived risk a consumer attributes to a purchase – and the related level of uncertainty that this generates – has been identified as one of the formative factors in the consumer buying process (Bauer, 1960; Mitchell, 1992). There have been a variety of propositions regarding the nature of perceived risk in relation to the consumer buying process. Risk has most often been used in consumer research to mean "the consumer's perceptions of the uncertainty and adverse consequences of buying a product (or service)" (Dowling and Staelin, 1994, p. 119). This suggests that the outcome of a 'purchase event' is far from certain. There are numerous situations where the customer might feel uncertain, e.g. the purchase of a suit, car or even personal-grooming products. The retailer therefore has the opportunity to allay such concerns, and, in so doing, provide the customer with additional benefit and satisfaction.

The nature of the uncertainty and the potential adverse consequences that a customer might experience have been classified into a number of perceived risk dimensions (Cox, 1967; Roselius, 1971; Jacoby and Kaplan, 1972; Gemünden, 1985). These risk dimensions include:

- Financial – relates to the potential of monetary loss associated with a purchase. For example is it too expensive, or will it cost too much to maintain?
- Performance – this concerns the potential for the product not to perform the required task, or what has been promised. Will it do exactly what is says on the tin?
- Physical – here the issue is one of physical safety, either personal or of others that might come into contact with the selected product. For instance, will the child car seat protect the infant in the event of an accident?
- Social – the focus here is on the potentially negative opinions of others that the product might generate. What will people say and think of me for buying this?
- Psychological – here uncertainty relates to potential negative self-perception as a result of purchase. Do I look like a fool in this?
- Time – relates to the loss of time due to either searching for the product or once purchased time lost due to product failure. How much time will I waste in relation to this purchase and product?
- Opportunity – this concerns the uncertainty that capital (monetary, personal and temporal) invested in a particular product would have been better spent elsewhere. If I buy this I won't be able to purchase that – is this my best option?

There has been an overwhelming focus on empirical studies that consider tangible goods (Bauer, 1960; Cox, 1967; Jacoby and Kaplan, 1972; Mitchell and McGoldrick, 1996), and much less consideration of services (Guseman, 1981; George et al., 1985; Mitchell and Greatorex, 1993). Given the nature of the retail experience, and the mix of elements that constitute the 'final offering' that the consumer takes with them when purchasing an item, both tangible and intangible components of the retail offer must be considered. Therefore, when considering a customer's retail experience, attention must be paid to the service elements of the consumer's benefit bundle.

Grönroos (1993) and Flynn and Goldsmith (1993) assert that the unique characteristics of services increase the uncertainty associated with purchase. In retail contexts this suggests that there is a continuum of uncertainty – with those offers that have a high service-based component (e.g. the design service provided by a furniture, kitchen or bathroom retailer) at one end; and the retailers of branded packaged goods (such as many grocery products) at the other. The position of a retailer on such a continuum may be as much determined by the customer and their prior knowledge, expectations and preconceptions, as it is by the nature of the retail offer itself. A holistic view of risk and uncertainty in relation to goods and services, although broadly useful, does not provide an in-depth understanding of the *nature* of the risk experienced by the customer, and therefore does not establish a highly developed basis for the formulation of retail responses.

Understanding Risk Associated with Goods and Services

Both the studies conducted by George et al. (1985) and by Mitchell and Greatorex (1993) go some way to developing a more detailed understanding of the nature of the risk associated with goods and services: suggesting also that it is an oversimplification to presume that the levels of perceived risk for services are consistently higher than those associated with goods. The George et al. (1985) study used a tangible-intangible paired approach, considering case pairs such as the purchase of a quartz watch against watch repair, rather than using unrelated service and product offerings. It concluded that the social and psychological risks were higher for goods than services, and that performance risk was higher in services. These results were repeated to a large extent by the Mitchell and Greatorex (1993) study, which compared goods and services that generated similar 'seriousness' ratings. Here it was found that, on average, financial and psycho–social risks were significantly less important for services than goods.

These results begin to generate a useful backbone for considering risk in a retail context – where both goods and service are encompassed by the retail offer. For example, when a customer purchases a new fitted kitchen, the styling of an individual range is often one of the first things that is considered. Does it suit the 'look' that is being created; and what does that style choice say about those selecting it – both to themselves and to others? These clearly are psychological and social uncertainties, which may be so strong that they override other concerns. How many customers would purchase a kitchen purely on its practicality or build quality? It is more likely that such concerns will only be given specific consideration once a range has been deemed appropriate in its styling. Equally, a more detailed understanding of risk helps to explain why many customers are happy to pay for design services – but only if they are convinced that the result will be pleasing – in other words that such a service will 'perform'. However, what the results do not provide is an understanding of the order in which risk dimensions occur and at which point in the decision-making process do they occur.

The development of answers to such questions is difficult for a number of reasons. Firstly, as Lovelock (1981) suggests, "many commonly heard generalizations about services marketing do not hold true across a wide-range of service industries or situations". Therefore, there may be different patterns of risk in relation to the goods and service components in varied retail contexts. In addition, the work of Wright (1995) and George et al. (1985) asserts that the boundary between goods and services is becoming more fluid and blurred, as is the level of risk associated with given sectors.

It is also the case that the level and pattern of risk dimension development is also varied between situations. What a customer feels in one retail situation may be very different to what they experience in another. A further difficulty relates to the individual. Customers will obviously vary in the degree of risk that they are comfortable with or even seek. There is no guarantee that this is itself constant, the level of risk that is acceptable will change possibly day-by-day, and in different purchase situations. These three factors: the nature of the offer – its mix of goods and service, the situation and the individual – provide considerable scope for variation when perceived risk is considered.

This again means that the development of definitive and universally applicable risk constructs is difficult. Rather, what is perhaps needed is that retailers become sensitive to the issue of risk and its links to and impact on the different components of the offer. Such an understanding will not remain static, but would provide a platform for the development of considered and appropriate responses.

It would appear that irrespective of the retail sector, perceived risk can have a significant impact on a customer's psychological state and therefore, as a result, their behaviour. For retailers, understanding the broad-based make-up of their offer and its impact on various types of risk provides the starting point for the development of mechanisms to help reduce such risk and thereby influence behaviour.

Risk-Reduction Strategies

There has been more recent consideration of the importance of risk-reduction strategies (RRSs) on the purchase process, and, to a lesser degree, the potential for the delivery of such mechanisms to reassure customers (Mitchell and Boustani, 1992; Van den Poel and Leunis, 1996). The work of Mitchell and McGoldrick (1996) provides a review and synthesis of the somewhat 'neglected' topic of risk-reduction. They identify thirty-seven RRSs that have had varying degrees of attention in the literature. They also go on to classify these strategies into three groups: simplifiers, clarifiers, and ones that could act in either manner depending on the particular set of circumstances in which they are applied.

Table 12.2 The number of studies using various risk reducers[a]

Number of studies	Risk-reduction strategy	Clarifying/simplifying
30	Ask family and friends	Either
17	Buy a well-known brand	Simplifier
17	Information from TV commercials	Clarifier
16	Information from printed commercials	Clarifier
15	Private testing/consumer reports	Clarifier
14	Brand loyalty	Simplifier
13	Price information	Either
12	Information from packaging and merchandising	Clarifier
10	Free sample/trial size	Clarifier
10	Ask the salesperson	Either
8	Past experience	Either
7	Visit or call the retailer	Clarifier
6	Well-known or reputable manufacturing company	Simplifier
6	Store reputation/image	Simplifier
5	Money-back guarantee	Simplifier
5	Warranty quality	Either
4	Number of brands examined	Either
4	Shopping around	Clarifier
3	Government tested and approved	Simplifier
3	Endorsements/testimonials	Simplifier
3	Spend more time gathering information	Clarifier
3	Country of origin	Either
3	Pre-purchasing deliberation	Simplifier
3	Referrals from other professionals	Simplifier
2	Using someone in a convenient location	Simplifier
2	Yellow Pages	Simplifier
2	Product newness	Simplifier
1	Service contact	Either
1	Postpone decision	Simplifier
1	A free gift	Simplifier
1	Using someone known socially or through business	Simplifier
1	Information from direct mail	Clarifier
1	Information from journal papers and articles	Clarifier
1	Coupons	Simplifier
1	Joint decisions	Either
1	Goal avoidance	Simplifier
1	Delegation of buying responsibility to others who are more competent	Simplifier

[a] Source: Mitchell and McGoldrick (1996, p. 7).

The emphasis in this area has, however, been firmly placed on the use of RRSs relating to search qualities e.g. pre-purchase information gathering that relates to the nature of the goods and the associated levels of performance. The gathering of such data has been identified as a potent RRS, particularly in the purchase of high involvement products (Mitchell and McGoldrick, 1996) (see Table 12.2). However, relatively little attention has been paid to the use of experience qualities e.g. staff encounters, financial services provided and the nature of the retail environment itself. Notable exceptions are George et al. (1985) and Mitchell and Greatorex (1993). Given the composition of retail offers, these are potentially as important – if not, perhaps at times, even more critical. For example, a customer may be happy with a piece of furniture and wish to buy it. But, if the price is more than they can afford at that time, without the ability to allay the financial risk that they are experiencing – through perhaps an interest-free credit service – they are unlikely to buy the goods. Here, a retailer also needs to ensure that the service elements of its offer are provided with similar levels of support and credibility as the goods that they sell. A customer is only likely to enter into a credit agreement with a company if they are satisfied that the risk in doing so is acceptable. An augmenting service in a retail environment can therefore – as well as acting as a RRS in relation to the goods on offer – develop its own level of associated risk that also needs management and consideration.

There is some suggestion that the use of RRSs commonly associated with goods – such as satisfied customer testimonials; service standardization; the development of clear brand image, and the use of service guarantees or warranties – would provide a potential means of addressing service-related risk as well (George et al., 1985). Many retailers apply some of these to the service components of their offer. For example, customer testimonials for design, planning and fitting services, or the development of a clear retail brand that is partly anchored on service provision, as is the case with Nordstrom, the US department store.

Additionally, Choi and Kim (1996) propose that (particularly in services) where quality remains uncertain, and the use of search related RRS is difficult, consumers can use surrogate measures to generate quality assessment. They suggest that potential customers can engage in 'herding' behaviour – where the conduct of other customers acts as a partial determinant of their own response. The development of such behaviour is dependent on the ability of one customer to observe the actions of others. Therefore, Choi and Kim (1996) propose that the size of the customer base and its longevity can have a significant impact as a means of accessing the quality of service components prior to purchase. The 'trust' that is placed in many national multiple retailers such as Tesco or Gap is a possible illustration of such behaviour – "all those other people shop there and are happy with the benefits that they receive, so it must be a retailer that provides a certain quality in both the goods and service components of its offer". Here, therefore, the use of these surrogate quality indicators could be classified as additional risk-reducing strategies that may predispose customers to view a particular retailer as low in risk.

Bitner et al. (1997) suggest that companies can adopt an alternative approach to managing the problems faced by customers in assessing service quality in particular. Companies can explicitly consider customer contribution and role management. Bitner et al. (1997) say that this can be achieved in a number of ways: through customer education – where the company takes on the position of 'teacher' (Lovelock, 1981), by effective and realistic expectation setting, and by staff facilitating the customer's role in the delivery process. The deployment of such corporate management approaches also has the potential to provide a range of additional RRSs.

For instance, even in retail contexts where the service component of the offer is very much a minor feature – such as limited-line deep discounters – the development of realistic expectations means that customers who enter such stores do not find their perceived risk levels rising due to the lack of expensive shelving, café or customer services desk. In short, the majority of customers entering Aldi, Lidl or Netto know what to expect, and, as a result, are not made more insecure when presented with a retail experience that, for many, is very different to that associated with middle-market grocery stores that they might be used to. Equally, in contexts where customers may feel less knowledgeable – such as the purchase of furniture – providing staff who are clearly proficient and capable of offering 'expert' advice may enable customers to feel more comfortable with both their role in the purchase situation and with the level of risk that they face.

Where retailers pay attention to the issues raised by Bitner et al. (1997) and provide appropriate responses, customers could use these in assessing purchase risk at either the pre-purchase stage or during the experience element of the process. This would potentially enable customers to continue the application of RRSs beyond pre-purchase search elements and also apply them to the experience qualities of retail.

However, the focus of much research in the field appears to be clearly related to RRSs that centre on the *tangible* aspects of the benefit bundle and not those associated with service elements. Developing a clearer understanding of both provides retailers with a much richer palette of options – that if aligned with the dimensions of risk customers experience and applied at appropriate points in the decision-making process, can significantly lower risk perception and increase the likelihood of purchase. Understanding consumer decision-making (whether in relation to a particular purchase or in locating a 'comfortable' environment in which to shop) has been a central feature of all the topics presented so far in this chapter. Additionally, each issue raised has an important role to play in determining the *approach* taken to decision-making. However, what has not been explicitly addressed is the format of the decision-making process itself.

The Decision-Making Process

The most commonly presented model of the consumer decision-making process is split into five stages as follows:

- Need recognition;
- Search for information;
- Evaluation of alternatives;
- Purchase; and
- Post-purchase evaluation.

Whilst this is a widely-used analysis of decision-making and provides a simple, clear and logical path to follow, it must be recognized that it is also a mechanistic and rigid framework. This is, in part, because such frameworks are based on assumptions such as that there is a *universal* and also *rational* decision-making process, which can lead to potential problems. For example, the framework presented above works well where a decision is classified as relating to a product that 'matters' to the customer and therefore carries with it high risk. In such cases, the *pattern* of decision-making outlined is often clearly evident.

Consider a person whose television begins to lose its picture quality and where this fault becomes progressively more noticeable. At some point there is recognition that a new television is required (perhaps after other avenues such as repair have been exhausted) and a purchase-related problem has been identified. The person then begins the process of gathering information to guide their purchasing – perhaps through reading specialist magazines, visiting shops, talking to others and recalling their past experiences. In marshalling this information, the application of certain criteria enable the information to be sorted and certain products to be excluded from the decision set. These criteria could range from size of screen or digital capabilities, to sound quality and price. These criteria provide a means of evaluating the alternatives and thereby aid the decision-making process. Once a 'preference' for a particular product has been established, the person may then turn their attention to deciding from which retailer they would prefer to make the purchase, or in finding a retailer that can provide the product that they require – both in terms of the product and the service elements of the offer. If a suitable location of supply can be found, the choice to buy or to postpone purchase needs is then addressed. If the choice to buy is made, once the selected television is installed a period of evaluation occurs – both in terms of the actual set and also perhaps in relation to the choice of retailer. Post-purchase rationalization occurs and the seeking of affirmative comment from others. If the customer's internal evaluation and/or external comment are positive, it is more likely that the customer will feel satisfied with their purchase.

This example is however, underpinned by a number of assumptions – that the customer has well-defined preferences; that each product option in the choice-set has utility, or subjective value that depends only on the product itself; and that the customer has the skills or ability to calculate which option will maximize the utility that they receive and act accordingly (Bettman et al., 1998). These assumptions underlie rational choice theory. However, alternative approaches have been proposed that move away from such assumptions and begin to take a more 'human' perspective.

One such notion is that of 'bounded-rationality', which states that decision makers have information processing limitations; perception is attuned to change rather than absolute magnitudes and diminishing sensitivity to stimuli changes; and, that behaviour is shaped by the interaction of the human information processing system and the properties of the task environment (Bettman et al., 1998). The bounded-rationality approach enables the consideration of the development of preferences from a very different viewpoint. Rather than having well-defined preferences, customers may *construct* them on the spot when they are needed, i.e. when a choice has to be made and there is little familiarity or experience with the product. Therefore, rather than having one approach to decision making, customers can have a wide variety of decision strategies. Such an approach is highly context-specific and also facilitates the consideration of changes in decision-making behaviour as a result. This is not to say that there are times when a rational choice model is applicable, but rather to highlight that it cannot fully explain behaviour at all times. (For a detailed discussion of the differences between the approaches and the implications of adopting a bounded-rationality approach, see Bettman et al., 1998).

The efficacy of the five-stage decision-making process is also brought into question if the nature of the purchase is not one where extensive problem-solving is required. For example, if a routine purchase is considered, it is more difficult to clearly demarcate the stages of the process. The argument here is that the decision-making process becomes truncated and the customer passes from need recognition to purchase without explicit consideration of the intervening stages. These have rather been internalized from the *original* consideration of the purchase and are simply recalled (even if not consciously) to facilitate the purchase. Whilst this is itself a plausible idea, what is perhaps more difficult to fit within the confines of the model is impulse purchasing – or a purchase where the risk is seen as being so great that a 'distress' purchase is made – with no consideration of information search and the evaluation of alternatives. This model of decision-making provides a simple and widely applicable framework, but is not universal. It is important that retail managers remember this, and ensure that they do not assume that the decision-making of all their customers can be understood by using this framework – especially when linked to rational choice theory. However, it is perhaps fair to suggest that the five-stage breakdown of decision-making does help to highlight potential areas where a retailer might hope to influence decision-making.

Information Search

The area of the decision-making process that has perhaps received the most attention in the literature is that of information search. This element has been investigated from various viewpoints including: economics, marketing, consumer behaviour, and geography. This is perhaps because "information and preference are inextricably linked" (Pipkin, 1981, p. 315), and therefore it is an inherent element in explaining purchase behaviour (Miller, 1993). Miller (1993) provides a detailed review of three different approaches to consumer information search: optimal search theory based on an economic perspective; empirical evidence based on research by marketers and consumer research; behavioural search models that reconcile some of the tensions between the previous two perspectives.

Optimal search theory provides a theoretical notion of how customers will manage information search given that they are perfectly rational, risk neutral, have access to limited information and seek to maximize their welfare whilst minimizing search costs. In most part, it also assumes that the relevant selection criteria for goods can be reduced to price. These assumptions mean that optimal search theory hinges on a standard 'neoclassical economic' framework of cost-benefit and leads to comparison shopping (Miller, 1993). These propositions are clearly not tenable in the 'real-world', and optimal search theory does not attempt to describe what occurs, but is rather concerned with how consumers *ought* to conduct their search. By doing this, it is possible to 'predict' how the search phase will take place under a given set of conditions.

However, as Miller (1993) goes on to highlight, there are a number of inconsistencies between the empirical evidence related to search and the predictions made by optimal search theory. These include:

- Searchers using 'satisficing' rather than optimizing decision objectives ("I know it's probably not the best, but it's satisfactory in this instance");
- Risk attitudes and their effects are unclear;
- Searchers use heuristics to simplify the search process;
- Search extent can vary in relation to the type of goods sought; and
- Prior knowledge has a complex effect on the extent of search.

These differences suggest that unsurprisingly, optimal search theory and its assumptions do not provide a comprehensive basis for predicting and understanding the actual search behaviour of customers. This has, in part, led to the development of behavioural models of search behaviour that seek to combine elements of the optimal models and evidence gained by empirical research to provide a basis for predicting consumer search behaviour that is more realistic. Miller (1993) holds that such model can provide the potential for generating detailed hypotheses and predictions about consumer search behaviour, which can then be used to help retailers develop appropriate strategies, concerning diverse issues including market strategy, information provision, store choice and product choice.

The issue of information search, and in fact the wider issue of decision-making, is complicated further when there is more than one individual involved in the process. Here, it is not only the issue of managing the purchase itself that is of interest, but also the issue of 'managing' the process, and perhaps most importantly, of managing the others involved within that process (Ward and Sturrock, 1998).

Joint Decision-Making

One situation where the impact of other individuals and their preferences, beliefs and convictions is often observed is joint decision-making. A central concern in the literature on joint decision-making has been conflict and its resolution. This is because where combining individual preferences to form shared ideas is needed, it is likely that conflict will occur (Lee and Collins, 1999), and is in fact the norm (Kim and Lee, 1996).

Lee and Collins (1999) provide summary categories of conflict resolution strategies based on previous research. These categories are:

- Experience – focusing on information search and joint discussion (Belch et al., 1980);

- Legitimate – where power or expert status associated with a 'recognized' role is exerted to direct decision-making (Corfman and Lehmann, 1987);
- Coalition – the combining of two or more members who collude to influence the outcome;
- Emotion – the use of either persuasion or dominance with an emotion-based appeal to sway the decision (Davis, 1976);
- Bargaining – which entails the use of a trade-off approach between members of the decision-making 'unit' (Davis, 1976).

These forms of conflict resolution have been seen in the 'simplest' form of joint decision-making, which is dyadic, e.g. between partners or customer and shopping pal.

Spousal Joint Decision-Making

There have been several attempts in the literature to assess the spousal influences and the nature of the roles played at various point in the decision-making process (Davis and Rigaux, 1974; Putman and Davidson, 1987). Kim and Lee (1996) provide a taxonomy of couples based on the conflict resolution strategies that they employ as well as the sex-role attitudes displayed:

- Compromising – where there is a greater reliance on bargaining and reasoning;
- Wife-driven – here wives seek a reasonable compromise that is satisfactory to both partners;
- Dogmatic – here not only are rational approaches adopted but there is also a much greater reliance on authority and emotional tactics; and
- Light-influencing – where there is little attempt by either partner to exert any influence at all.

Developing an appreciation that when both partners are involved in decision-making this does not simply mean that each one will be equally involved in the process provides additional opportunities for retailers to target their offer. However, operationalizing this is perhaps more difficult, as deciding which category a couple fall into is not a simple matter. When couples are actually in the retail environment it becomes the role of service staff to try and categorize couples and react accordingly. This relies heavily on the staff member's tacit skills, as well as providing adequate training. Further complexity both in the nature of the relationships and in terms of retail management is added when the number of individuals increases – for example when a whole family is involved.

Family Decision-Making

Lee and Collins (1999), in the observational research that they conducted of decision-making in families with two adolescent children, found that the use of conflict resolution strategies was also evident in this situation. Of particular interest was the importance of children in families where the predominant conflict resolution strategy was emotion – here the children had much more influence. Lee and Collins (1999) also found considerable use of coalition strategies involving children. However, the gender of those involved and gender sequence of the children in particular appears important, e.g. fathers and daughters (in particular, *eldest* daughters) forming alliances. Where there are two daughters, this pattern is not as evident – in such situations a female coalition of *mother* and daughters is more likely. Coalitions between mother and sons are also common, interestingly especially where there are two male children. This then suggests a complex picture, where not only should attention be paid to the conflict resolution strategies adopted, but also to the demographic make-up of the family unit and the resulting influence coalitions that are likely to develop. This presents the retailer with an increased range of concerns.

Conclusions

The customer's psychological state is affected by a wide-range of elements – including everything from their past experiences, their perceptions of the retail environment, their attitude to risk and its management, to their approach to planning the purchase and who accompanies them on their shopping trip. Not only is a customer's psychological state affected by a large number of elements, but the individual's response to these factors is also likely to be varied. This means that the development of universally applicable 'rules' is problematic.

However, gaining an understanding of these issues is important. Without such knowledge it is perhaps impossible for retailers to develop an offer that is likely to suit the majority of their customers for the majority of their visits.

References

Alba J.W. and Hutchinson J.W. 1987. Dimensions of consumer expertise. *Journal of Consumer Research*, 13 (March), 411–454.

Babin, B., Darden, W.R. and Griffin, M. 1994. Work and/or fun: measuring hedonic and utilitarian shopping value. *Journal of Consumer Research*, 20 (March), 644–656.

Bauer, R. 1960. Consumer Behaviour as Risk Taking. In R. Hancock (Ed)., *Dynamic Marketing for a Changing World*. Chicago IL: American Marketing Association, pp. 389–398.

Bayley, G. and Nancarrow, C. 1998. Impulse purchasing a qualitative exploration of the phenomenon. *Qualitative Market Research: An International Journal*, 1(2), 99–114.

Beatty, S.E. and Ferrell, M.E. 1998. Impulse buying modeling its precursors. *Journal of Retailing*, 74(2), 169–191.

Becker, F.D. 1977. *Housing Messages*. Stroudsburg, PA: Hutchinson and Ross Inc.

Belch, M.A., Belch, G.E. and Sciglimpaglia, D. 1980. Conflict in family decision making: an exploratory investigation. *Advances in Consumer Research, Vol. 7* (Ann Arbor, MI: Association for Consumer Research), pp. 475–479.

Bettman, J.R., Luce, M.F. and Payne, J.W. 1998. Constructive consumer choice processes. *Journal of Consumer Research*, 25(3), 187.

Bitner, M.J. 1992. Servicescapes: the impact of physical surroundings on customers and employees. *Journal of Marketing*, 56 (April), 57–71.

Bitner, M.J., Faranda, W.T, Hubbert, A.R. and Zeithaml, V.A. 1997. Customer contributions and roles in service delivery. *International Journal of Service Industry Management*, 8(3), 193–205.

Choi, C.J. and Kim, J-B. 1996. Reputation, learning and quality uncertainty. *Journal of Consumer Marketing*, 13(5), 47–55

Cobb, C.J. and Hoyer, W.D. 1986. Planned versus impulse purchase behavior. *Journal of Retailing*, 62(4), 384–409.

Corfman, K.P. and Lehmann, D.R. 1987. Models of cooperative group decision making and reflective influence. *Journal of Consumer Research*, 14, 1–13.

Cox, D. 1967. Introduction. In D. Cox (Ed)., *Risk Taking and Information Handling in Consumer Behaviour*. Cambridge MA: Harvard University Press, pp. 1–20.

Davis, H. 1976. Decision-making within the household. *Journal of Consumer Research*, 2 (March), 241–260.

Davis, H. L. and Rigaux, B. 1974. Perception of marital roles in decision process. *Journal of Consumer Research*, 1 (June), 51–62.

Dittmar, H., Beattie, J. and Friese, S. 1996. Objects, decision considerations and self-image in men's and women's impulse purchases. *Acta Psychologica*, 93.

Donovan, R.J. and Rossiter, J.R. 1982. Store atmosphere: An environmental psychology approach. *Journal of Retailing*, 58 (Spring), 34–57.

Dowling, G., and Staelin, R. 1994. A model of perceived risk and intended risk handling activity. *Journal of Consumer Research*, 12, 119–134.

Flynn, L.R. and Goldsmith, R.E. 1993. Identifying innovators in consumer service markets. *The Service Industries Journal*, 13(3), 97–109.

Gemünden, H. 1985. Perceived risk and information search: a systematic meta-analysis of the empirical evidence. *International Journal of Research in Marketing*, 2(2), 79–100.

George, W.R., Weinberger, M.C. and Kelly, J.P., 1985. Consumer risk perceptions: managerial tool for the service encounter. In Czepiel, J.A., Solomon, M.R. and Suprenant, C.F. (Eds)., *The Service Encounter*. Massachusetts: Lexington Books.

Grönroos, C. 1983. *Strategic Management and Marketing in the Service Sector*. Cambridge, MA: Marketing Science Institute.

Guseman, D.S. 1981. Risk perception and risk-reduction in consumer services. In Donnelly, J.M. and George, W.R. (Eds)., *Marketing of Services*. Chicago: AMA.

Hausman, A. 2000. A multi-method investigation of consumer motivations in impulse buying behaviour. *Journal of Consumer Marketing*, 17(5), 403–419.

Hoch, S.J. and Deighton, J. 1989. Managing what consumers learn from experience. *Journal of Marketing*, 53(2), 1–20.

Jacoby, J., and Kaplan, L. 1972. The components of perceived risk. *Proceedings of the 3rd Annual Conference of the Association for Consumer Research*, pp. 382–393.

Kim, C and Lee, H. 1996. A taxonomy of couples based on influence strategies: the case of home purchase. *Journal of Business Research*, 36, 157–168.

Kim, B. and Park, K. 1997. Studying patterns of consumer's grocery shopping trip. *Journal of Retailing*. 73(4), 501–518.

Kollat, D. and Willett, R. 1967. Consumer impulse purchasing behaviour. *Journal of Marketing Research*, 4 (February), 21–30.

Lee, C.K.-C. and Collins, B.A. 1999. Family decision making and coalition patterns. *European Journal of Marketing*, 34(9/10), 1181–1198.

Lovelock, C.H. (1981). Why marketing, management needs to be different for services. In Donnelly, J.M. and George, W.R. (Eds). *Marketing of Services*. Chicago, IL: AMA.

Mehrabian, A. and Russell, J.A. 1974. *An Approach to Environmental Psychology*. The MIT Press.

Miller, H.J. 1993. Consumer search and retail analysis. *Journal of Retailing*, 69(2), 160–193.

Mitchell, V.-W. 1992. Understanding consumers' behaviour: can perceived risk theory help? *Management Decision*, 30(3), 26–31.

Mitchell, V.-W. and Boustani, P. 1992. Consumer risk perceptions in the breakfast cereal market. *British Food Journal*, 94(4), 17–26.

Mitchell, V.-W. and Greatorex, M. 1993. Risk Perception and Reduction in the Purchase Consumer Services. *The Service Industries Journal*, 13(4), 179–200.

Mitchell, V.-W. and McGoldrick, P. 1996. Consumers' risk-reduction strategies: a review and synthesis. *The International Review of Retail Distribution and Consumer Research*, 6(1), 1–33.

Newman, A.J., Dixon, G. and Davies, B.J. 1994. *Towards a Study of Airport Retailing: The Physical Setting and Purchasing Behaviour*. Manchester: Manchester Metropolitan University, Institute of Advanced Studies Research Paper.

Pipkin, J.S. 1981. The concept of choice and cognitive explanations of spatial behaviour. *Economic Geography*, 57, 315–331.

Putman, M. and Davidson, W. 1987. *Family Purchasing Behavior II: Family Roles by Product Category*. Columbus, OH: Management Horizons, Inc.

Rook, D.W. 1987. The buying impulse. *Journal of Consumer Research*, 14 (September), 189–199.

Rook D.W. and Fisher, R.J. 1995. Normative influences on impulsive buying behavior. *Journal of Consumer Research*, 22 (December), 305–313.

Roselius, T. 1971. Consumer rankings of risk-reduction methods. *Journal of Marketing*, 35, 56–61.

Sherman, E. and Smith, R.B. 1987. Mood states of shoppers and store image; promising interactions and possible behavioural effects. *Advances in Consumer Research, Vol. 14* (Provo, UT: Association for Consumer Research), pp. 251–254.

Sherry, J.F.Jr. 1990. A sociocultural analysis of a midwestern flea market. *Journal of Consumer Research*, 17 (June), 13–30.

Thompson, C.J., Locander, W.B. and Pollio, H.R. 1990. The lived meaning of free choice: an existentialist-phenomenological description of everyday consumer experiences of contemporary married women. *Journal of Consumer Research*, 17(3), 346–361.

Van den Poel, D. and Leunis, J. 1996. Perceived risk and risk-reduction strategies in mail-order versus retail store buying. *The International Review of Retail Distribution and Consumer Research*, 6(4), 351–371.

Ward, P. and Sturrock, F. 1998. She knows what she wants: towards a female consumption risk-reducing strategy framework. *Marketing, Intelligence and Planning*, 16(5), 327–336.

Westbrook, R.A. and Black, W.C. 1985. A motivation-based shopper typology. *Journal of Retailing*, 61 (Spring), 78–103.

Woodruffe, H.R. 1997. Compensatory consumption: why women go shopping when they're fed up and other stories. *Marketing Intelligence and Planning*, 15(7), 325–334.

Wright, K. 1995. Avoiding services marketing myopia. In Glynn, W. and Barnes, J. (Eds)., *Understanding Services Management*. Chichester: Wiley.

Part 3

The Retail Enterprise in Context

13

THE STRATEGIC CONTEXT

Retail strategy is the process of creating the desired broad retail climate and appropriate consumer expectations. The retail strategy process is therefore a balancing and blending of running stores for efficiency and effectiveness.

As the book focuses on consumer-related aspects of retailing, there is less attention paid to those aspects that occur behind the line of visibility. However, this chapter emphasizes the retailer's opportunity to manage for efficiency in these areas.

This chapter therefore considers a mix of the relevant 'customer-visible' and 'customer-invisible' areas:

- Logistics;
- Sites and location;
- Design and merchandising;
- Personnel;
- Organization; and
- Image.

Introduction

There is a view of strategy within retailing that stems from the development of strategy writing within the more general management and marketing literatures. This defines retail strategy as the key mechanism through which retail management seeks to obtain relative competitive advantage. Retailers therefore seek to innovate, create and sustain significant added value for their customers through the control of the various resources at their disposal.

Strategy and Policy – the General Perspective

Strategy is a word that has been, to a certain extent, devalued (and denuded of meaning) in the business and marketing worlds through constant over-use. In its original form, it relates to the "art of the military general" (derived from the Greek), and is concerned with the achievement of objectives through the application of resources – and, if possible, without conflict. (Schelling (1980) actually suggests the use of conflict is a particular strategy in itself.)

In business, 'strategy' is used often as a 'comfort' word, and often takes an adjectival form, to make either the actions or the speaker seem important. There are 'strategic' sales promotions, 'strategic' marketing managers, and 'strategic' initiatives of this or that sort; to set alongside promotional 'strategy', relationship 'strategy', and customer service 'strategy'. There may be some sense in which each of the items or activities are of a 'strategic' kind, but that sense is often one that is over-extended.

The tendency to use the word in this loose and unhelpful way has a long history, with Boyd and Larréché commenting critically on this type of usage in a paper in 1978. They observed that even then, the most common use of the word strategy in marketing was in relation to the various elements in the marketing mix – product strategy, distribution strategy and so on. However, they did accept this type of hierarchical usage, and sought to position the various 'strategies' in relation to each other: corporate, marketing, mix elements. They also went on to use the position developed by Ansoff (1965) in his key work.

This views *corporate strategy* as the set of rules that govern the deployment of resources to determine the relationship between a firm and its environments. Therefore, the process that selects and fixes these rules is *strategic planning*. The strategic planning process is then used to determine the nature of the interrelationships between the various products within the corporate 'product portfolio'. Core to this process is the requirement of identifying product/market relationships (and their 'growth vectors'), which Ansoff identified in his well-known product/market matrix as being:

- Market penetration;
- Market development;
- Product development; and
- Diversification.

At the same time as the strategic planning/product/market combination approach was being developed, a focus on what was labelled 'business policy' was also appearing (Christensen et al., 1965). In this view, the key distinctive feature was the adoption of the perspective of the chief executive or general manager – a 'corporate' or business-level view. This business policy approach used another key feature incorporated into many marketing strategy approaches today – the 'SWOT' analysis (strengths and weaknesses, opportunities and threats). Knee and Walters (1985) maintain this distinction: suggesting that policy gives overall direction, which is determined at board level; and strategy is the 'working-out' of the resource deployment, which determines how policy is actually implemented.

Strategy and Policy – Retail Applications

This distinction between what they termed policy, and what they saw as strategy, was an important one to Knee and Walters (1985). In their book, *Strategy in Retailing– theory and application*, they initially focused on corporate policy issues and the nature of business definition. This, they suggested, rests on perceived opportunities (external to the firm) and existing expertise (within the firm). Corporate and functional policies are then derived from this business definition. Knee and Walters argued that too much emphasis was placed on objective setting and the terminology used to describe organizational goals. They use Hofer and Schendel's definitions from their key work of 1978 as examples of over-complexity in this area.

Within their work, Knee and Walters placed a modified version of Ansoff's matrix at the core of product/market definition. They illustrated the dangers of an inappropriate business definition by citing the experience at that time, of the UK Woolworth chain. By retaining an attachment to an outmoded concept – that of the variety chain store – they believed that Woolworth had trouble in the marketplace with its target consumers. Marks & Spencer, though, replaced Woolworth as Britain's most profitable retailer. (Given the current difficulties of Marks & Spencer, and its retrenchment to focus on the 'core' UK business, there is a sense in which the strictures concerning appropriate and relevant business definition may continue to apply over a decade and a half later.)

For Knee and Walters, a workable business definition required:

- Description of the key elements in a firm's activities;
- A direction for business development; and
- Precision and use of functional rather than physical descriptors.

Knee and Walters also identified the following as areas for which successful retailers have corporate policies:

- Segmentation and positioning;
- Geographical coverage;
- Outlet size and location;

- Operational level controls;
- Financing; and
- Growth rate and method.

More recently Walters and Hanrahan (2000) identified five elements in the development of retail strategy (p. 41 emphases in the original):

- Determining a *mission*, or the scope of the business;
- Deciding upon strategic positioning;
- Developing a *strategic direction* and its themes, attributes and activities;
- Deciding performance criteria for *strategic management effectiveness*; and
- Planning the operational implementation.

Their work continues in the established tradition: bringing in some of the later work of the planning/competitive advantage type. In relation to a value-based approach to strategy, these later contributions also include the work of Porter. Walters and Hanrahan, in referring to strategic positioning, use a concept that differs from the consumer-centred approach used by other authors.

The Consumer-Centred Approach

Davies and Brooks (1989) presented an argument of considerable importance: arguing that the main strategic challenge to the retailer was the successful relative positioning of its retail image. This concept of 'image' or of 'identity' has become a core one in many areas of business and consumption (see Chapter 9). Davies and Brooks summarized their perspective as one within which corporate strategy defines the direction a business should take. They suggested that the concepts introduced in the 1960s (such as synergy, integration, life cycle and diversification) were improved through the advent of superior planning techniques in the 1970s (planning gap analysis, experience curves, and portfolio analysis). Also – using an explicit consideration of environmental effects in the 1980s (Porter's 1979 competitive strategy and the five forces model of competition) – they go on to provide a perspective that relates well to the retail context.

In addition to the need to acknowledge the concepts derived from the policy and strategy literature, Davies and Brooks pointed to the use, by leading retail practitioners, of concepts usually associated with marketing approaches. Principal amongst these concepts is image, coupled with an extension of the 'systems retailer' approach to the adoption of a retail formula. Here, image is identified as the creation by a retailer of a clear perspective of what the retailer 'stands for' in the minds of potential customers. If a retailer stands for something in the minds of customers, then image and position have been developed (again, see Chapter 9).

To move beyond 'systems retailing' to having a *formula*, is to move from consistency in offering standard merchandise assortment, pricing, display, personnel policies and so on store by store, to a situation where the selections made in these areas have an internal consistency that enables the store and the merchandise to 'tell a story' to its customers.

By blending the results of their empirical work with those of others in the field, Davies and Brooks (1989) concluded that effective differentiation; avoidance of price as a primary differentiator, and control of design, service and merchandise (in that order of importance), were the keys to successful positioning in retailing – based on image. The three issues identified as paramount in implementing a positioning strategy in retailing were:

- An organization able to react to long-term trends;
- The clarity of, and coherence between, levels of image-generating elements (department, store and chain, for example); and
- Using promotion, especially advertising, as a support, but no more, in the development of image.

Retail Competitive Advantage

In their initial consideration of the sources of retail competitive advantage, Bradley and Taylor (1992) – examining the same area as Davies and Brooks (1989) – suggested that in the 1970s, such advantage rested on pricing, technology and sites. In the 1990s, the main source of advantage was seen as coming from human resources – the company's employees. They later refined the overall list of factors to consist of:

- Technology and systems;
- Warehousing and distribution;
- Sites and location;
- Design and merchandising; and
- Personnel and human resources.

There is a clear overlap between the factors chosen by Bradley and Taylor, and those proposed by Davies and Brooks. In the matter of service – which arises from the actions of staff – and in design, they are at one. The area of greatest potential difference between them is what Bradley and Taylor classify as 'technology and systems', and what Davies and Brooks call 'organization', which only reflects the focus of Bradley and Taylor on one specific form of organization. In using the term 'technology and systems', Bradley and

Taylor focus on the operational deployment of systems such as EPOS; while Davies and Brooks' notion of 'organization' represents a much higher-level concept.

In addition, Stern and El-Ansary (1992), in the fourth edition of their influential book, *Marketing Channels*, suggest that the nature of a retail business is determined by management choices relating to:

- Margin and inventory goals;
- Assortments of merchandise to be carried;
- Location of outlets; and
- Customer services to be offered.

In Summary

The lists of key areas of concern identified above relate to the notion of business policy – as distinct from strategy. The distinction that exists between the lists of 'planning' questions and the 'factors' that determine the nature of a retail business, exemplify the distinction that writers drawing on these traditions would see in terms of 'strategy' and of 'policy'.

At the same time, in the more general marketing strategy literature, the traditions established in the 1960s continue to be evident. In a work initially published at the same time as Bradley and Taylor, Wilson et al. (1992) present a staged process relating to 'strategy development', consisting of five steps:

- Where are we now?
- Where do we want to be?
- How might we get there?
- Which way is best?
- How can we ensure we arrive?

There is little discernible difference between the import of these questions and actions identified by Knee and Walters (1985):

- Ascertaining the current business position;
- Identifying and establishing future directions;
- Evaluating and selecting strategies to achieve objectives; and
- Monitoring performance levels of selected strategies.

Irrespective of whichever set of questions or areas is used, all the approaches outlined above are based on the same core premise – that of an ordered and *rational* basis to the development of strategy. These approaches are intuitively appealing, as they provide a 'blueprint' for the development of a corporate strategy. There have been instances however, where such approaches have failed.

The failure of such 'rationality' in decision-making informs the work of Collins (1992). In his text for practitioners, he identifies many moments in his senior management career when he asked himself if "we were so crazy as to do this or that, or take this or that decision" (p. 15). However, his response is to return to the type of insight offered initially by Ansoff, and to provide checklists of questions for managers. There is a perception that by sticking more closely to the rules, a better class of decision can be made. Therefore, the rational approach is not seen as being at fault: it is rather the failure of management to *adhere properly* to the approach.

However, there have been those who see that the problem is really a reflection of the inadequacies of the rational approach and that rather than try to stick more rigidly to it (come what may), there is a need to consider alternative perspectives.

Other Perspectives – in General and in Retailing

The consequences of the approach identified in the corporate policy and business strategy literature outlined briefly above, reveal themselves in an extended treatment of management as a careful, analytical, rational, considered and disciplined series of steps. Such a description of management actions is often at variance from what is observed at both the strategic and the operational levels of a business (for an extended critique of the strategic planning approach in the business domain, see Mintzberg (1994)). In areas of management outside marketing and business strategy, this super-rational view has been more contested.

The Super-Rational Approach

Lindblom (1959) – writing in the context of public administration rather than business – observed that it was curious that the literatures of decision-making, policy formulation and planning tended to emphasize this super-rational approach (which he labelled the *'rational-comprehensive'* perspective or *root* method), rather than the *successive limited comparison* approach (or *branch* method), as the basis of decision-making in management. It was his view that the second approach accorded much more closely with what he observed was the "science of muddling through". However, he noted that the successive limited comparison approach was not free of fault, but often looked superior. What is striking is that the rational comprehensive perspective *still* dominates much of the marketing literature today. However, Quinn (1980) found evidence for the type of approach proposed by Lindblom; and in *his* study, he found that this 'incrementalism' was in fact a dominant mode of strategic decision-making in business.

The Garbage Can Model

Others have also provided alternative approaches to the decision-making necessary in formulating business strategy For example, Cohen et al. proposed the 'garbage can model' of organizational decision-making (1972). In their view, the super-rational model is unrealistic, as well as being useless to mangers. In the garbage can model, decisions are made by groups or individuals trying to 'get their own way' – seeking to implement their preferred solutions to decision-making problems. The garbage can contains a series of unconnected solutions, contributed by anyone within the organization, which are essentially independent and without a logical thread joining them together. When a decision need arises, the solution is 'pulled' from the can. Therefore, Cohen et al. describe organizations as a collection of choices looking for problems.

Stepping Stones and Pathways

However, this particular perspective is an extreme one, in that it denies the probability of a real thread of strategic thinking. Others have found a more linear approach is taken in organizational decision making: e.g. Mintzberg et al. (1976), who observed decision-makers attempting to move through various stages, in a manner suggested by the super-rational models. This linearity, though, was disturbed by interruptions, repeats, and discontinuities.

The paths and stages of decision-making were more explicitly examined by Hickson et al. (1986), who categorized the decision processes they observed in a large sample of firms as *constricted, fluid* or *sporadic*.

Constricted decisions were narrowly channelled – characterized by the application of expertise and existing information, but few meetings – with the decision being taken below the highest level. Fluid decisions were paced, channelled and fast, with few delays, little impediment and limited negotiation; but with the decision finally being taken at the highest level. Sporadic decisions were informal, spasmodic and protracted – characterized by delays, impediments, personal contact, information variability and negotiation, with decisions being taken again, at the highest level. (see Hickson, 1990).

These decision pathways have the qualities of both the rational and the incremental approaches, which suggests that there is a need to consider the *reality* of decision-making in order to develop an appropriate view of effective strategy development and implementation.

Mintzberg argued for just such a consideration. Effective strategies in his view, mix 'deliberate strategy' with 'emergent strategy' in ways that reflect environmental and other conditions. In his conceptualization, effective strategy development needs to couple analysis with intuition. Therefore, there is a requirement to consider process as a key element in the development of strategy within organizations in a 'rich', rather than simply formalistic way. This combination of the formal and the intuitive/creative is also reflected in the work that draws on a postmodern perspective.

The Postmodern Marketing Perspective

In the marketing arena, Brown (1997, p. 105) – within what he identifies as a paradoxical milieu – says that where…

> …organizations are exhorted to be both global and local, centralized and decentralized, large and small, planned yet flexible, and are expected to serve mass and niche markets with standardized and customized products, at premium and penetration prices, through extensive and restricted distribution networks and supported by national yet targeted promotional campaigns, it is perhaps not surprising that the traditional, linear step-by-step marketing model of analysis, planning, implementation and control no longer seems applicable or appropriate.

Firat and Shultz (1997) concluded – from their review of the literature on postmodernism and marketing – that there was little evidence of explicit consideration of the strategic implications for *marketers*. This reinforces the five characteristics of postmodernism originally offered by Firat and Venkatesh (1993):

- Hyperreality;
- Fragmentation;
- Reversal of consumption and production;
- Decentring of the subject; and
- Paradoxical juxtaposition of opposites (this being the core of the contradictions posed by Brown).

Van Raaij (1993) added the notion of 'pluralism', to this list; and Firat and Shultz suggested that Brown (1993a,b) extended it again with notions of:

- The perpetual present;
- The emphasis on form/style; and
- The acceptance of, or resignation to, states of disorder and chaos.

Brown (1995) later went on to identify (using what he described as inappropriate 'modern' criteria to simplify the complex and incoherent) seven key features of postmodernism:

- Fragmentation;
- De-differentiation;
- Hyperreality;
- Chronology;
- Pastiche;
- Anti-foundationalism; and
- Pluralism.

In their own work, Firat and Schultz (p. 202) amalgamate many of the previous listings, and provide a table (see Table 4.1) showing their synthesized ten elements of the postmodern condition arrayed against the market implications and consequences for marketing strategies. However, they caution that by presenting the 'pigeonholes' of table cells, readers should understand that the interactions and consequences cannot be confined to a particular cell, but that all elements, in fact, interact. In particular, Firat and Shultz emphasize that the consequences of postmodernism are revealed in fragmentation; the image becoming the product, and in the consumer becoming co-producer with the marketing organization (see Chapter 4).

The stages in the planning or marketing management canon seen by Brown as no longer applicable – goal setting, situation review, strategy formulation and resource allocation and monitoring – are less than relevant in current circumstances if it is assumed that the postmodern characteristics outlined above are actually present in society. This is particularly marked in a number of areas widely accepted as the cornerstones of 'modern' marketing:

- Traditionally, the 'segmentation, targeting and positioning' process has been seen as a core element in marketing management, but this is weakened by fragmentation.
- Rather than the importance of brand, it is the notion of image that becomes central to marketing endeavours.
- The rise of the active consuming co-producer negates the traditional view of the passive consumer (see Chapter 3).

If the 'traditional' approach to strategy formulation (and marketing management) is thus outmoded, then a consideration of the insights from a 'business policy' perspective may be useful. This is because this approach places the consideration of board-level perspectives on the business definition, at the commencement of the process, which does not *require* the complete enumeration and consideration of all the factors often implied in the 'strategy' approach. This perspective also reflects an explicit choice from within an array of options, not merely the notion that there is one best (or indeed, only one possible) view. Such an approach is likely to be better able to cope with the contradictions and tensions identified by Brown (1997, p. 105) in the "current paradoxical milieu".

In a postmodern era denied the comforting certainty of earlier periods, it is no any longer tenable to imagine management teams heroic enough to undertake rational-comprehensive, root-type reviews of retail strategy. The tasks are:

- Firstly, to define the retail store format in a manner that is meaningful to participants.
- Secondly, to consider the areas shown to be key.
- Thirdly, to ensure that decisions can be enacted in appropriate ways by staff members.
- Fourthly, to provide for evaluation and review over time.

In selecting the areas known to be key, the chief difference in the recommended approach (from the rational-comprehensive literature) is the focus on image. To make image a core part of strategic review and development is therefore consistent (inasmuch as anything can be) with postmodern approaches.

Strategy Review and Development

By linking the categories developed by Davies and Brooks and those of Bradley and Taylor (see above), six principal areas of concern in retail strategy are identified. These six areas may then be cross-referenced to the features of the postmodern in marketing identified by Brown (1995). Table 13.1 shows some possible manifestations and potential consequences of these factors (or trends or currents) for retail strategy. This is similar to the approach adopted by Firat and Shultz (1997), commented on above. (As Brown notes: to attempt such a modernist treatment of the postmodern is doomed to failure. But, hey, what the heck?! ...as an ironic postmodernist might observe).

The process that is suggested for retail strategy development works through the chief areas of concern iteratively. In order to cope with current complexities and uncertainties, the process begins with a consideration of business definition. It then moves to image, design and merchandising, and sites and location (the three areas most visible to customers). These three areas have a particular degree of overlap and interaction. The two internal (less visible to customers) areas of organization and logistics are then considered. Finally, services (or personnel) are then considered.

Table 13.1 The six principal areas of concern in retail strategy

	Logistics	Sites and location	Design and merchandising	Personnel (Service)	Organization	Image
Fragmentation	Multiple channels Product assortment complexity	Locational option Format variety	Merchandise assortment growth Scrambled merchandising	Situational responsiveness Local control Empowerment	Local marketing	Multiple publics Long-lived brands
De-differentiation	Joint facilities Vertical marketing	Alternative concentrations of trade space	Erosion of trade boundaries Museum styling	Participation in consumption Consumers co-produce	Virtual organizations	Blurring of forms
Hyperreality		Simulated stores in e-tailing	Fantasy Simulated milieus	Role by rote Character playing	Organizational 'character'	Theme and package
Chronology	On-line tracking	Return to the past	Backwards looking Authenticity	Earlier values	Longevity and contemporary existence	Imagined pasts
Pastiche		Architectural play	'Egypt in Las Vegas'	Historical forms	Capacity for play with purpose	Ironic iconic
Anti-foundationalism	Carrier choice		Revise and revamp	Individualism	Heterodoxy	
Pluralism	All the above	All the above	All the above	All the above	All the above	All the above

Business Definition in Retailing

Within the business definition element of strategy development, there is a need to state the core operation of any retail firm under scrutiny. Knee and Walters (1985) label the type of definition required as 'functional'. They work through an example that moves from broad 'retailing' to supermarket operations selling defined types of goods from particular locations. To be considered adequate in contemporary retailing, the business definition would require explicit treatment of all of the six key headings depicted in the top row of Table 13.1.

The treatment of a supermarket operation in this way throws up some divergences from the earlier example. The definition might become:

- A supermarket retailer operating a variety of store formats each having particular customer appeal (this reflects issues listed under 'sites and location');
- Merchandised within a store environment that reflects commitment to core concepts of relevance to customers, such as 'good for fresh food' or 'good for specialist food' ('design and merchandising');
- Using staff that are noted for being helpful ('personnel');
- With an identity that capitalizes on associations between our operational style and the customer ideal – through careful positioning ('image');
- Supported by centralized distribution and control of stores ('logistics');
- Modified by local market issues ('organization').

There is scope, though, for business definition to be compounded with the notion of 'corporate mission'. This can be achieved by adding suitable modifying adjectives – 'best', 'preferred', 'leading', etc. – to the business definition.

Walters and Hanrahan (2000) suggest that the approach of Abell (1980) represents the one that will have the most impact in the area of business definition. Abell proposed that there were four core sets of issues that needed to be addressed in defining a business:

- Strategic issues;
- Organizational issues;
- Conceptual issues; and
- Planning process issues.

To these, Walters and Hanrahan added the notion of core competencies (taken from Prahalad and Hamel, 1990).

This type of definition carries with it the risk that management thinking can become locked in to a particular perspective. To avoid the perils associated with such risks, the definition needs to be checked against the environmental trends considered significant. Once a business definition has been formulated, the process of considering each of the six key areas in more detail can be started.

The Strategy Process in the Arena of Retail Consumption

From the perspective of managing the retail strategy process – and to a greater extent of course, the 'management of the arena of retail consumption' (see Part 2 of this book, encompassing Chapters 5 to 12) – what is now required is detailed consideration of the chief elements of the domains discussed above, along with their implementation.

Of particular importance, however, is the need to ensure that whatever approach is taken it is grounded in a secure understanding of the customer and *their* perspective.

Customer-Visible Factors

The three elements of image, design and merchandising, sites and location, identified above are clearly central, in that they provide those elements that are visible to the customer (and the dominance of the visual sense in the manner in which we form impressions has been well documented – see Chapter 7). In the arena of the 'visible' (or of the senses), the focus of management must therefore be on the *effective* deployment of the resources at their command.

This distinction between the customer-visible world – where effectiveness is paramount – and the world of the organization *invisible* to the customer – where *efficiency* may drive concerns – is central to the Servuction model (see Chapter 6). To determine what is most effective in that part of operations visible to customers, though, requires an explicit understanding of their preferences. It is not enough that management's own preferences – or management's *belief* about customer preferences (as evidenced by customers' current retail purchase behaviour) – determine the core strategic propositions. The view requires substantiation through research. The difficulty that then ensues is that the very nature of the topics does not lend itself to precision in customer response. In such circumstances, the controlled use of testing and trialling have much to recommend them. However, there remains no particular basis for believing that ideas or concepts that trial well represent anything approaching some sort of optimum.

Image has been held to be of critical importance. As has been pointed out, image is created in the customer's mind. What the corporation can seek to control though, is its identity (see Chapters 7 and 9). This identity is composed of those design elements over which the firm exercises control – extending from fascias and store design (expressed through visual merchandising, fixturization and so on), through vehicles and corporate livery, advertising and promotional items, packaging and bags, to choices in location and proximity to other retailers.

Retailers should therefore concern themselves with managing these elements, along with any other sensory devices (in terms of these stimuli's impact on customers). The effective manipulation of these sensory cues should be central to the creation of an appropriate (customer-appealing) image through design and merchandising.

Behind the Line of Visibility

Out of the sight of the consumer, retailers have greater freedom to focus on those aspects of operations that give rise to efficiency. Logistics and organization (including systems and technology) are elements that appear chiefly in the 'back of house' area of the Servuction model (see Chapter 6).

Managing for efficiency is the traditional focus of management. The theory of the firm in its neo-classical form emphasizes the axiom of optimization (leading to allocative efficiency across the market), which is a direct expression of the drive for efficiency in input–output relationships. Where management is divorced from ownership, the theory has developed into managerial capitalism. Again, however, the core driver remains efficiency, even though the managerial firm is held to be less efficient than the simplest of neo-classical owner-managed firms. This would suggest that the theory relating to logistics (warehousing and distribution), systems and technology, and of organization itself, would tend to emphasize efficiency as the primary goal.

By contrast, personnel, in their capacity to deliver service, would normally be located within the *visible* area of the Servuction arena. The reason for their treatment in this sub-section, though (rather than with the visible design elements above), is that the focus here is on how they are supported and equipped by the organization to deliver services efficiently (such treatment is of course, arbitrary). Where staff *do* make a major contribution to the designed 'image,' then it may however, be more productive to consider their contribution in the context of the visible arena.

Logistics

The notion of retailing success as flowing from 'the right goods in the right place at the right time and at the right price' puts physical distribution at the heart of a retail system and this means that implementing a logistics system that supports the 'delivery' of the business definition developed is paramount.

Physical distribution – or supply chain management, or warehousing and distribution, or logistics – are all terms that are applied to the task of controlling the process of consolidating, carrying and delivering merchandise stock to the point of acquisition by customers. (Logistics though, is a term defined by many in a more strategic or all-encompassing sense than the others, and is therefore the one used here. It encompasses the contribution of packaging, stockholding and service levels to outcomes; the location of facilities, such as warehouses or regional distribution centres; and materials management – all within a system that also manages information flows.)

Store-based retailing is the predominant form of logistics system supplying consumer goods. Other forms such as mail order, vending or Internet-based retailing, utilize different logistics systems. Each system has its particular costs and benefits to the consumer. The choice of which retail means is used to acquire goods (and other benefits) is one that consumers are able to determine in relation to each purchase occasion. The store-based form, though, drives the discussion presented here.

Multiple Retailing and Logistics

Logistics has been defined as:

> the systematic management and study of the planning, allocation and control of the financial, physical and human resources committed to physical distribution, stockholding and service levels. It deals with all aspects of movement and storage facilities in the system from the point of acquisition to the point of customer consumption, for the purpose of providing adequate customer service at reasonable cost to the firm.
>
> Baron et al., 1991, p. 111

A key element in the logistics approach is to view the costs involved in the processes at a system level. This approach gives rise to the 'total logistics cost concept'. As such a term indicates, this provides a clear basis for considering the input–output efficiencies of the logistic system. Within the system, there are the usual systemic interdependencies, giving rise to interplay between cost and benefit in related areas. In such a context, the approaches associated with operational research (or management science) have a particular role to play. These approaches are often coupled to concepts from related fields such as economics (especially cost–benefit analysis) or management accounting (activity based costing, for example). Examples of the type of application that are particularly common include stockholding costs, economic order quantities, trade-off analyses. (Brassington and Pettitt, 2000, provide a good introduction to these issues.)

Approaches to Logistics

A number of approaches to logistic systems have found particular application in retailing. Efficient consumer response (ECR) is one such. ECR relies on EDI (electronic data interchange) as a core component, in the search for distribution channel level efficiencies that meet the requirements of consumers for service level (in-stock availability) in store. (In a trial held between May 1995 and April 1996, Somerfield (a major British supermarket operator) collaborated with 12 suppliers of FMCG products and GE Information Services as the EDI supplier. The trial reduced stocks by 25%, and service levels rose (Bicknell, 1996.) This example highlights the potential for approaches to logistics to have a significant impact on the nature of the business and its definition.)

One difficulty that ECR (and other techniques such as category management) face is the control orientation of many multiple retailers. The emphasis (in the postmodern context) placed by many retailers on *exercising* channel captaincy reflects a potentially outmoded form of organizational response. This has led to a slower spread of these techniques than might be supposed. A further difficulty is the absence of a broadly applicable theoretical basis for supply chain improvement (New, 1996). The traditional approaches of retailers *are* being replaced by a more collaborative and relationship oriented stance. The traditional type of control-oriented response to issues that, for most effective resolution, require collaboration is still strong.

This response remains prevalent also in a period when the consideration of *relationships* elsewhere within marketing heralds what some identify as a radical reappraisal of the discipline of marketing. Establishing effective supplier relationships is a key task for retail management, in a period that requires a shift in attitudes and organization to accommodate postmodern consumers. The evidence in some instances suggests that multiple retailers have not risen well to this particular challenge, because the policies that have historically led to market success rest on assumptions relating to the efficiencies that accrue to direct control. A postmodern retail world may, as we have seen, require a move to effectiveness as the main criterion for measuring capability and success.

Organization

Structure

To oversimplify (but perhaps not by much), the pattern of organization that has dominated the structure of multiple retail firms is one of a major central function, exercising tight control over the operational activities of a set of relatively homogeneous stores. In this model, the central function provides buying, merchandising, design, marketing, logistics, some human resource management (payroll, training), store layout, category management, and accounting and information technology functions. The stores follow a pattern of operation and apply rules developed (for them) in the head office. This type of operation is the one that led to the description 'chain store,' where each outlet is but one identical link. It is described as 'system retailing' by Davies and Brooks (1989).

In differing retail areas, these control features may be relaxed to varying degrees. Departmental stores for example, may exercise significantly more store level control of operational features, than say, variety chain stores. In retail organizations that control a portfolio of varied stores, the 'head office' functions may migrate to a divisional head office.

In developing retail strategy, management must question the style and pattern of control that is applied to the outlets. There is a need to ensure that the balance of 'loose and tight' elements of control reflects the needs of the market place. Consideration of the contemporary approach to business policy suggests the need to more finely balance central control against effective local delivery. As the requirements for playfulness and engagement for (and from) the customer rise in the store environment, the issues of structuring delivery mechanisms for this assume significance. These types of concerns (for local marketing and merchandising, or for playfulness) do not fit easily into a framework based on efficiency. The test of success in these sorts of areas is more likely to be found again in effectiveness, i.e. in customer-related measures, rather than in cost ratios.

Technology and Systems

At the level below that of the organization (though increasingly interacting with it) sits information technology systems. The rise in the capability and decrease in relative cost of IT systems opens up possibilities not previously present. In the classic model, task, technology, structure and people were identifiable elements that interacted. Technology, in the form of information systems, has reached levels where it can provide the glue that binds together a virtual organization. For retailers, this creates the possibility of using virtual groups to undertake specific tasks, or tackle specific projects. A tension is also created between the store-based, and IT-based forms of retail service delivery. One might supplant the other in a particular transaction, or they may function in complementary ways.

The evidence for the use of customer-facing IT systems such as EPOS and EFTPOS is strong in many developed economies. The evidence relating to internal systems development is also characteristically strong. Such internal usage would include data mining and modelling, planning, payroll, stock control and similar systems. However, when the evidence concerning inter-organizational usage is considered, a different pattern emerges. Vijayasarathy and Tyler (1997) comment in their empirical findings that it was surprising that in the retail industry, EDI is primarily used for order and invoicing transactions. They point out that EDI has been in use for nearly thirty years, but that their findings are consistent with Bamfield's (1994) UK data. They regard the use that retailers make of EDI as effectively impoverished. In a related arena, a study of the adoption of interactive IT at the customer interface, Ward et al. (1999) found that retail perception of the rate of adoption lagged the views of both academics in the fields and IT suppliers when timescales were concerned.

These findings suggest that retailers, despite evident sophistication in some areas, do not fully engage with the potential that information technology presents in their industry.

Personnel

As noted, the treatment of personnel as an 'invisible' element in the retailers' Servuction systems is inappropriate in many respects (see Chapter 6). The focus here, however, is on the way the organization supports them – in terms of role, scope for personal action and similar issues – rather than their individual contribution to service delivery.

In their US-based study, Cappelli and Crocker-Hefter (1996) considered pairs of companies in the same industry that were both regarded as successful but very different from one another. Their comparator firms for retailing were Sears and Nordstrom, two successful department store firms.

Sears uses a calculating type of approach in its recruitment. It relies on sophisticated testing for employee selection, and hired employees are trained extensively. Employee attitudes are subject to regular survey. Sales assistants are paid on a salaried basis, with little commission component. They receive particular training in merchandise, operating systems and selling methods.

Nordstrom by contrast, makes little use of formal practices (see Chapter 5). Recruitment is decentralized and tests are not used. Recruitment focuses on discerning 'innate' characteristics – pleasant personality and motivation. Little training is offered, instead the focus is on motivational programmes. Sales assistants are paid largely on commission, promoted to management on the basis of sales performance, and work with a company handbook with one rule: "Use your best judgement at all times".

In these two examples, there are elements that illustrate Cappelli and Crocker-Hefter's overall findings:

- On the one hand, where organizations operate opportunistically, there is little incentive or need to provide extensive training. A retailer that uses the ability of employees to empathize with customers, to be 'inside' some market (such as fashion), provides motivational programmes and pays by commission can afford a high turnover of labour.
- Conversely, where organizations operate in established markets, then there is a direct pay-off in trained staff using defined procedures. This is so if turnover in employees is low. A retailer that is in an established market position or niche could follow such policies. Marks and Spencer use this type of approach in the UK, with average staff age increasing as a result. Some see this as distancing the company from the female fashion market, which was identified as 'young'. (This difficulty remains unresolved in 2001.)

Cappelli and Crocker-Hefter observe that there may be considerable difficulties in moving between these two strategies in relation to personnel.

The 'strategic' choice, in broad terms, is between these two contrasting styles. Retailers may also need to consider how, in relation to more thematic approaches in structuring store environments, they can provide support for staff. Recruiting 'enthusiasts' for a market sector, and picking those with 'warm' personalities may be workable if the other elements of the operation do not become highly systematized. When this position is abandoned in the search for the incorporation of particular customer ideals to reflect 'positioning', then control issues need to be addressed.

Conclusions

The key features that relate to decisions in the field of strategy (or business policy) are that such decisions are difficult to undo; are longer lasting; commit a greater proportion of resources, and have organizational-level consequences. Because strategy is 'important', over-use has devalued the word.

Strategy reflects the expression of corporate intent for the longer term, using a consistent deployment of resources. More simply, it is a statement of what the organization wishes to achieve, and how.

The process of strategy development in business falls into two broad areas – the choice of objectives (or aims, or goals, whichever word is chosen is probably of little relevance); and the selection of the means to achieve these aims. Within retailing, the key strategic decision areas have been identified as:

- Logistics;
- Sites and location;
- Design and merchandising;
- Personnel;
- Organization; and
- Image.

The last of these, and its relationship to effective differentiation, using a clear business definition, is paramount.

References

Abell, D. 1980. *Defining the Business: the Starting Point of Strategic Planning*. Englewood Cliffs, NJ: Prentice Hall.

Ansoff, H.I. 1965. *Corporate Strategy*. New York: McGraw–Hill.

Bamfield, J. 1994. Technological management learning: the adoption of electronic data interchange by retailer. *International Journal of Retail and Distribution Management*, 22/2, 3–11.

Baron, J.S., Davies, B. and Swindley, D. 1991. *Macmillan Dictionary of Retailing*. London: Macmillan

Bicknell, D. 1996. *Brothers in Arms*. Computer Weekly, September 26, 42.

Boyd, H.W. and Larréché, J.-C. 1978. The foundations of marketing strategy. In Zaltman, G. and Bonoma, T. (Eds)., *Review of Marketing*. Chicago, IL: American Marketing Association, pp. 41–72.

Bradley, K. and Taylor, S. 1992. *Business Performance in the Retail Sector – the Experience of the John Lewis Partnership*. Oxon: Oxford University Press.

Brassington, F. and Pettitt, S. 2000. *Principles of Marketing (2nd Ed).*, Harlow: Pearson Education.

Brown, S. 1997. Six sixty-six and all that (or, what the hell is marketing eschatology?). *European Journal of Marketing*, 31(9/10), 639–653.

Brown, S. 1995. *Postmodern Marketing*. London: Routledge.

Brown, S. 1993a. Postmodern marketing: principles, practice and panaceas. *Irish Marketing Review*, 6, 91–100.

Brown, S. 1993b. Postmodern marketing? *European Journal of Marketing*, 27(4), 19–34.

Cappelli, P. and Crocker-Hefter, A. 1996. Distinctive human resources are firms' core competencies. *Organizational Dynamics*, 24(3), 6–22.

Christensen, C., Andrews, K. and Bower, J. 1965. *Business Policy – Text and Case*. Homewood, IL: Richard D. Irwin.

Cohen, M., March, J. and Olsen, J. 1972. A garbage can model of organizational choice. *Administrative Science Quarterly*, 17, 1–25.

Collins, A. 1992. *Competitive Retail Marketing – Dynamic Strategies for Winning and Keeping Customers*. Maidenhead: McGraw–Hill.

Davies, G. and Brooks, J. 1989. *Positioning Strategy in Retailing*. London: Paul Chapman Publishing.

Firat, A.F. and Shultz, C. 1997. From segmentation to fragmentation: markets and marketing strategy in the postmodern era. *European Journal of Marketing*, 31(3/4), 183–207.

Firat, A.F. and Venkatesh, A. 1993. Postmodernity: the age of marketing. *International Journal of Research in Marketing*, 10(3), 227–249.

Hickson, D. 1990. Reading 6 'Politics Permeate'. In Wilson, D. and Rosenfeld, R. (Eds). *Managing Organizations – Text, Readings and Cases*. Maidenhead: McGraw–Hill.

Hickson, D., Butler, R., Cray, D., Mallory, G. and Wilson, D. 1986. *Top Decisions: Strategic Decision-Making in Organizations*. Oxon: Blackwell.

Hofer, C. and Schendel, D. 1978. *Strategy Formulation: Analytical Concepts. (The West Series in Business Policy and Planning, Hofer and Schendel, Consulting Eds)*. St. Paul, MN: West Publishing Company.

Knee, D. and Walters, D. 1985. *Strategy in Retailing*. Deddington: Philip Allen Publishers.

Lindblom, C. 1959. The science of 'muddling through'. *Public Administration Review*, 19 (Spring), 79–88.

Mintzberg, H. 1994. *The Rise and Fall of Strategic Planning*. Hemel Hempstead: Prentice Hall International.

Mintzberg, H., Raisinghani, D. and Theuret, A. 1976. The structure of 'unstructured' decision processes. *Administrative Science Quarterly*, 21, 246–275.

New, S. 1996. A framework for analysing supply chain improvement. *International Journal of Operations and Production Management*, 16(4), 19–34.

Porter, M. 1979. How competitive forces shape strategy. *Harvard Business Review*, March–April, 137–145.

Prahalad, C. and Hamel, G. 1990. The core competence of the corporation. *Harvard Business Review*, May–June, 79–91.

Quinn, J. 1980. *Strategies for Change: Logical Incrementalism*. Homewood, IL: Richard D. Irwin.

Schelling, T. 1980. (Reprint Ed). *The Strategy of Conflict*. Cambridge, MA: Harvard University Press.

Stern, L. and El-Ansary, A. 1992. *Marketing Channels (4th Ed).*, Englewood Cliffs, NJ: Prentice Hall.

van Raaij, W. 1993. Postmodern consumption. *Journal of Economic Psychology*. 14, 541–563.

Vijayasarathy, L. and Tyler, M. 1997. Adoption factors and electronic data interchange use: a survey of retail companies. *International Journal of Retail and Distribution Management*, 25(8/9), 286–292.

Walters, D. and Hanrahan, J. 2000. *Retail Strategy: Planning and Control*. Basingstoke: Macmillan Press.

Ward, P.J., Davies, B.J. and Wright, H. 1999. The diffusion of interactive technology at the customer interface. *International Journal of Technology Management*, 17(1–2), 109–128.

Wilson, R., Gilligan, C. and Pearson, D. 1992. *Strategic Marketing Management – Planning, Implementation and Control*. Jordan Hill: Butterworth–Heinemann.

14

SERVICE CHARACTERISTICS AND CONTEXT

This chapter introduces the role and extent of services in the developed economy; and the four characteristics of services:

- Intangibility;
- Inseparability;
- Heterogeneity; and
- Perishability.

The use of typologies and classification systems as aids to management are discussed. Quality measurement and management propositions from a range of sources are compared and contrasted. These propositions form the basis for the use of particular techniques designed to measure quality. The approach to measurement of quality in a retail setting is shown to be contingent on a number of factors. In particular there are component effects due to factors arising from the:

- Purchase situation;
- Merchandise type;
- Market position; and

Introducton

In the traditional three-fold model of economic activity, the primary (or extractive) industries are mining, fishing, agriculture and forestry. The secondary (or goods-producing) sector comprises manufacturing and processing. The tertiary sector (or service sector) takes in the rest. This third category accounts for more than two-thirds of activity in many developed economies. However, despite services now being so predominant, they still remain in an undifferentiated bundle in a single sector. This serves as an indication of some of the definitional and classificatory problems that permeate the area of services in the economy and in management.

The particular difficulties related to the classification and identification of the value added by service occupations are as old as the formal study of economics itself. Although today there is general agreement on the value created by service, the historical difficulties associated with services sometimes still reveal themselves. Some people hold to the view that the service economy must rest on some manufacturing base. They speak as if manufacturing (which is concerned with adding value through changing the 'form' of pre-existing constituents) is somehow more real (or worthwhile, or deeply contributive to welfare) than the ephemeral values (time, place and possession utilities, for example) added by services.

Fitzsimmons and Sullivan (1982) present a classification of economic activity first proposed by Foote and Hatt in 1953 – comprising *five* sectors. The first two sectors – extractive and manufacturing – remain as usual. Services, however are further sub-divided. In this classification, the third sector is termed 'domestic services', which comprises activities such as hospitality, personal care, maintenance and repair. Their fourth sector is trade and commerce – retailing, transportation, communications, finance and insurance, property services and government. The fifth sector contains those services that refine and extend human capacities: health, education, research, recreation and the arts. This schema, though never widely applied, places retailing as an industry in a particular service (the 'quarternary' sector area of the economy). For retailing, when considered as a service industry or producer of service *product*, questions arise regarding the nature of such products, and the consequences of such production for both producers (retailers) and consumers alike.

Service Characteristics

Although there may be some disagreement as to how the sphere of economic activity is split (especially regarding services), there is wide agreement on the four characteristics of services themselves. These are usually identified as:

- Intangibility;
- Inseparability;
- Heterogeneity; and
- Perishability.

Intangibility

Many writers in the field of services marketing hold intangibility to be the key distinguishing feature of a service. Services are often defined by such writers as performances, deeds, actions or activities (see for example, Fitzsimmons and Sullivan, 1982; Kotler, 1991; Zeithaml and Bitner, 1996). Others state that the three remaining features of services actually flow from their intangibility (see Kasper et al., 1999).

The suggestion is: goods are tangible; services are intangible. The niceness of this distinction, however, is somewhat spoilt by the observation of many – including those authors who use this type of framework – that the products that consumers purchase do not fall neatly into either the goods *or* services category. Services often *require* facilitating goods; and additional services often *support* goods.

Intangibility, therefore, *may* describe one difference in properties between an idealized 'pure' good and an equally 'pure' service. (Although this characteristic has the advantage of seeming 'obvious', the fact that it is *not* can be illustrated by presenting two items characterized by various authors as almost a pure good: salt (most famously used by Shostack, 1977), and a painting or sculpture.)

Definitions

This distinction between intangibility and tangibility in the marketing literature may have its genesis in the definitions developed by the American Marketing Association in 1960 (*Marketing Definitions: A Glossary of Marketing Terms*, AMA, Chicago). These contained three categories of products: durable goods, non-durable goods and services. The time over which the goods 'survived usage' distinguished the two categories of goods. The AMA also defined, in part, services as "activities, benefits or satisfactions" (p. 21).

However from a *linguistic* perspective, examination of the word 'tangible' reveals that there are two principal, though related, definitions. Table 14.1 shows these, alongside some possible synonyms and antonyms:

As the table indicates, the seemingly simple notion of 'tangible' – and therefore *in*tangible – is fraught with complication. The use of one term in one source – intelligible – to provide a definition, which is then identified as an antonym in another source, demonstrates these difficulties.

The recipient of a service may well see, hear or feel the performances, deeds or actions (when delivered within the framework of a marketing exchange) integral to the provision of that service. Therefore, it is not appropriate to extend the quality of 'intangibility' (not susceptible to haptic sense) to the property of being inaccessible to *all* the senses, as some have suggested. If definitions such as those involving the use of deeds, actions or performances as descriptors are useful, then those deeds, acts or performances

Table 14.1 Definitions of 'tangible'[a]

Tangible	Synonyms	Antonyms
Perceptible by touch	Touchable Tactile Palpable (haptic)	Untouchable
Clearly *intelligible*; not elusive or visionary	Definite Material Real Physical Corporeal Solid Concrete Manifest Sensible Evident Substantial Ostensive	Indefinite Immaterial Unreal Invisible *Intelligible* Inevident In/Unsubstantial

[a] Sources: New Shorter Oxford Dictionary; Reader's Digest/Oxford Complete Wordfinder; Webster's New World Thesaurus (Laird/Meridian).

can be detected through the senses – most likely by observation. The fact that deeds, actions and performances *are* susceptible to sensory perception, illustrates that one sense (touch) does not itself provide a clear conceptual basis for categorization. Other senses (smell, taste, etc.) are not used to classify outputs or distinguish categories in the same way.

Other authors have pointed to the passing of legal title (ownership) as a test of tangibility, and hence of the status of a product as a good. Some consider the issue of the lack of possibility of ownership as indicative of the existence of a service product – such 'service products' do not give rise to ownership. Services by this definition, are those purchases where title (to a good) does *not* pass from provider to client. There is seldom any discussion by these writers of the legal distinction in some jurisdictions between goods and chattels. (A chattel can be an immaterial possession in which title passes e.g. a lease.) The use of the criterion of the passing of title is therefore also not a satisfactory method of distinguishing goods from services.

What is at the heart of the difficulty is the breakdown that occurs between forms of description:

- Firstly, there is the problem caused by combining the various senses almost to represent a single sense – 'intangible' coming to stand for 'inaccessible to *all* the senses'.

- Secondly, utilizing 'tangible' in a narrow sensory meaning, but contrasting it to the wider conceptual sense, as a counterpoint to 'imaginary'.
- Finally, the melding of categories of entities, so that ownership pertains to only two possible classes – those of goods and services.

Extended consideration of this particular aspect of service is both necessary and useful. Necessary, because it is possible to accept the observation of 'intangibility' at face value and ignore its complexities. Useful, because the property of intangibility (if, indeed, it is in any way a singular property) gives rise to the other characteristics said to be integral to the definition of services – inseparability, heterogeneity, perishability (and, possibly, ownership).

Inseparability

This term identifies the quality or characteristic of service products that are usually produced and consumed at the same time. The audience visits the theatre to see a performance. A customer sits in the barber's chair for a haircut. Inseparability therefore gives rise to the 'service encounter'. It also results in the need to consider the Servuction arena, as this is the location where customer and service-provider interact (see Chapter 6).

Heterogeneity

This is the variation in service encounters derived from the active participation of service personnel and customers in co-production. As an interactive human process, the service encounter is therefore not entirely predictable, controllable or uniform.

Perishability

As a process, activity, performance or deed, a service ceases to 'exist' when these actions stop. As the capacity to deliver these actions is also (usually) limited, then a process which is not operating at its full capacity, is 'losing' service potential. The 'unprovided' service proportion perishes as the remainder of the capacity is used. This characteristic is described also as the inability to inventory (stock) a service.

Consequences for Service Firms

These last three 'characteristics of a service' concern more the *process* of service delivery itself (which can be defined by the elements in the Servuction model), rather than the service 'benefit bundle' received by the customers or their experience of service delivery. These three characteristics therefore form the core consideration for the *management of service delivery systems*, whereas the first (intangibility) provides a prime focus for *marketing in service industries*. The close relationship between these four facets of service delivery means that the interplay between operations and marketing (as functions within the organization) is closer in service industries than in manufacturing.

This interplay also gives rise to a situation – frequently found in retailing – where the activities of marketing as a function are limited, in effect, to promotional elements of the traditional marketing mix. As many have observed, in a service organization, all those engaged in service delivery are marketers.

Retail firms – particularly those operating store formats – clearly provide a bundle of benefits that includes a key tangible element: the merchandise. This connects, to differing degrees, with various intangible elements that relate to the store, its environment, the sales and other contact staff, and the corporate identity and values (image) of the organization.

Classification of Service and Retail Contexts

Retail operations cover a considerable spectrum (see Chapter 2). Various writers in the domain of services and of retailing have addressed the classification of these different contexts.

In goods marketing, many texts differentiate between industrial and consumer markets. The basis for this distinction rests on a number of factors, which includes the nature of the buying process, the nature of the buyers themselves, and the types of products.

The dimensions used to delineate differing contexts in marketing are many. Copeland (1923) provided one classification, which – elaborated by Holton (1958) and Bucklin (1963) – is still used today. This places consumer goods into three categories: those of convenience, shopping and speciality goods. The characteristics that underpin the classification initially were related to the processes used by consumers in seeking out the types of goods, rather than explicitly residing in the goods themselves. This distinction (between the customer activity and the characteristics of the goods) has tended to disappear in use, so that it is the goods themselves that are categorized (industrial goods, and the three types of consumer good).

Lovelock (1983) commented that there was a greater likelihood of marketing executives moving between the sectors selling these different categories, within the consumer goods market, and between industrial goods industries; than between industries in the *service* sector. Lovelock argued that this lack of wider experience in the service sector (in general) was likely to impede the development of an all-round marketing perspective, in service industries, to the detriment of management capacity and capability.

He suggested that there was a need to classify services on a basis other than their industry (e.g. hospitality, railroads, retailing). He provided a review of previously proposed schemes for services classification. He examined nine prior suggestions, dating back to 1964; and then presented five basic questions, each designed to highlight strategic insights for management. The questions related to operational characteristics of the service delivery systems in three cases:

- The nature of the service act;
- The customization and judgement – or discretion for service personnel; and
- The service delivery mechanism.

In the other two questions, the focus is on market demand and on relationships.

Lovelock then combines these questions with other factors to produce a series of matrices. These matrices, he claims, contribute to management practice in two ways: firstly, by requiring mangers to ask questions in order to develop understanding; and secondly, by stimulating mangers to consider which other service providers contend with similar issues. Each cell of the various matrices presented contains identified products and industries. Retailing (merchandise-based, store format) however, does not appear in the examples given by Lovelock. Using his categorizations, retailing is:

- A tangible action, directed at people's bodies.
- A set of discrete transactions, but with no formal relationship.
- Low in the extent to which personnel have discretion; combined with low customization of service characteristics.
- Not constrained by peak demand exceeding supply, with wide fluctuation in demand over time.
- A multiple site operation, serving customers who visit the facilities.

Each of these categorizations could of course, be incorrect for a particular retailer. What such categorizations apply to are those system, formula or chain retailers who account for the greater proportion of retail sales in many economies.

In 1988, Lovelock extended these ideas. From each of the various selected matrices, he developed a series of challenges for management. There is no reason why retail management could not use this method to develop strategic insights.

Other Classificatory Systems

Other dimensions and aspects of a generic service offer have been used to develop either indexes or matrices of service types. From an operations rather than marketing perspective, Chase (1978) identified the extent of provider–customer contact as a major determinant of potential service system efficiency. His index of operations ranged from:

- The low-contact chemical plant;
- Through 'quasi-manufacturing': which included wholesalers and bank head offices; then
- Through 'mixed services', including bank branches and post offices; to
- Pure services, such as hotels and restaurants.

Again, merchandise retailers were not included in the examples given. Retailers however, would probably feature as 'mixed services', especially at the branch level.

Chase extends the argument to the consequences of the level of contact in particular operations. Firstly, high-contact systems have greater uncertainty in daily operations, as customers may make varying demands. Secondly, the volume of demand will not be well-matched to available capacity (Chase cites supermarket waiting lines as an example). Thirdly, the workforce requires significant public relations (sic.) components in its skill-base. Chase then poses four points for service mangers to consider:

- Identification of the type of system for which they are responsible.
- Matching the compensation system for employees to service system needs (operating procedures geared to structure).
- Possibilities for realignment of operations systems to reduce unnecessary customer service.
- Potential benefits realizable from efficiencies of low contact operations.

These areas remain germane for retailers who as mixed service providers, should ask if their policies follow from the consequences and questions posed by Chase.

Maister and Lovelock (1982) combined the contact dimension used by Chase (1978) with the degree of customization provided to service users. In his discussion of their matrix, Bateson (1995) uses the restaurant sector and travel agency as examples. His central point is that as the service (or retail provision) migrates to the high-contact/high-customization quadrant, the possibility for efficiency declines (as does its relevance). The adapted version of the matrix shown in Figure 14.1 gives one possible set of retail examples:

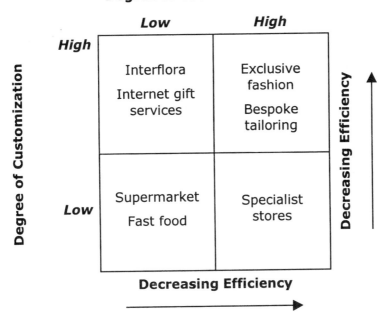

Degree of Customer Contact

	Low	High
High	Interflora Internet gift services	Exclusive fashion Bespoke tailoring
Low	Supermarket Fast food	Specialist stores

(left axis: **Degree of Customization**, right axis: **Decreasing Efficiency**, bottom axis: **Decreasing Efficiency**)

Figure 14.1 Retail classification 'technology' matrix
Source: adapted from Bateson (1995).

Bateson refers to this as the 'technology' matrix. There are clear links between the use of technology and the search for delivery efficiencies in appropriate parts of the service production system. Chase's observation concerning the appropriateness of efficiency (as contrasted with effectiveness) as the measure of managerial success in service systems needs to be remembered here.

Schmenner (1986) presented a matrix that used labour intensity and interaction and customization as axes. Using a two-by-two arrangement, he proposed that service factories (low intensity/low customization); professional services (high/high); service shop (low/high), and mass services (high/low) could be distinguished. Efficiency is a characteristic that provides a good basis for management action in the service factory and mass service quadrants of his classification.

Bateson (1995) reinforces the possibility for inappropriate service delivery, in relation to the firm's provision and the customer's requirement. He provides a table (p. 87) indicating the matched and mismatched possible combinations, and their potential for poor or positive outcomes. The basis for categorizing outputs as poor or positive rests partly on the perspective of the service user. However, the inclusion of the service user's perspective shifts the emphasis from an internal 'production' perspective, importantly, to a more externally focused, market-linked one.

Classifying Service Types

Dotchin and Oakland (1994) build on the work of Chase, Maister, Lovelock, Schmenner and of Hayward-Farmer (1988). They present a five-fold classification of service types:

- Personal services;
- Service shops;
- Professional services;
- Mass services; and
- Service factories.

Personal Services

Personal service organizations are engaged in the provision of service to people on an individual basis. Such services include hairdresser, dentist or driving school. Such service provision is high in labour intensity, in customer contact and in interaction. It offers adaptive customization, providing a high degree of specificity to customer requirement. The actions or processes are applied to people. Within merchandise retailing, there are few types that meet these criteria. Examples include bespoke tailoring, and craft-based manufacture to fit the customer: saddlery, sporting goods.

Service Shops

The service shop provides an equipment-based environment, with high levels of contact and interaction, and customization that is adaptive, or customization that is based on a pre-determined range of choices. Retail examples of 'service shops' might include store-based photo processing, service stations or personalized printing services for cards and stationery.

Professional Services

Professional services generally fall outside merchandise retailing. The category includes that provision where the service provider is able to work independently of client and work on things rather than the client's person. Medical services would not fall into this category, but legal and accounting services would.

Mass Services

High levels of labour intensity, high degrees of contact but low levels of interaction characterize mass services. Customization is usually choice from a pre-determined range, but the direct subject of the service may be either people or things. Retailers who might be regarded as mass service providers include supermarkets and department stores.

Service Factories

This final category consists of those services that aim to process customers in a production-line manner. This approach is based on both low levels of interaction and low levels of customization and intensity. These characteristics enable the application of a standardized and routinized approach that seeks to move customers along the service delivery process in a pre-defined and tightly managed environment. Here, there is little scope for improvisation, and customers can feel that the service rendered is mechanistic and process driven. Such services include airlines, hotels and recreation facilities.

Each of these service types gives rise to a particular set of management concerns and focus. There is the question of a focus on internal efficiencies, or on customer effectiveness, or on an operational view, or a marketing perspective.

There is a considerable contrast between the internal and external perspectives. The internal production perspective has almost a natural focus on 'production efficiency' and on the application of production (output) standards. The external perspective requires consideration of the degree to which the service outputs match the requirements of service customers during a particular service encounter. The introduction of the customer's viewpoint moves the focus from behind the line of visibility in the Servuction system, to the Servuction arena itself. Within that arena, the suggested criterion for judging system outputs is *effectiveness*, not efficiency (see Chapter 6). The effectiveness of a system (or retailer's) outputs at the conclusion of a service experience rests, in this model, with the customer. The consideration of the service user's judgement of service outputs plays a major part in the determination of judgements of service quality.

Sources of Quality Measurement

The definition and measurement of quality in the context of services (in general) presents a picture of considerable contention, diversity and confusion. There are a number of elements to dictionary definitions of quality. The major notions pertaining to objects and to people are of 'distinguishing characteristics' (e.g. has the quality of being innovative, or of having a bluish quality); of 'degree of excellence' (the product is available in three qualities); or of absolute excellence (a quality product), or of a general standard (the product has a quality).

The 'intangible' nature of much service provision makes it difficult to apply certain types of quality measure, especially those that rely on directly accessible and determinable aspects of an entity: i.e. require the presence of certain 'tangible' or measurable dimensions or characteristics.

For example, gold and other precious metals are subject to assay to test their standard, and are then often hallmarked. The hallmark gives a particular indication of quality: 14 carat, 22 carat, and so on. Another related form of quality indication or certification associated with tangible goods relates to the ingredients used and the method of their manufacture: the Reinheitsgebot for German beer purity, or of Champagne for both methods of making and of geographical origin. There are similar longstanding examples for some staple foodstuffs, particularly bread. Such standards are in wide use, and often cover ingredient composition, weight and method of making, for example.

Many of these measures and designations have long historical antecedents: hallmarking was in use in the 7th century in Byzantium, the beer purity laws in Germany in the sixteenth century. These forms of quality designation relate to 'standards' and the prior definition of a 'level' against which the product is judged. Some authors (e.g. DeSarbo et al., 1994) have seen standards that relate to conformity to measurable parameters as coming from the engineering paradigm. To view such standards in this way is unnecessarily restrictive. To do so ignores those earlier antecedents that relate very clearly to consumer protection, through the regulation of both products and markets. There is a need to include those standards that provide consumer protection in food and drink (and other products that are literally consumed), 'purity' standards of whatever kind, as well as those that are 'engineered'. Today, some standards related to 'purity' or types of origin are in widespread consumer use – organic foodstuffs and hypoallergenic toiletries, for example. The use of an 'engineering' tag to describe the standards behind such products seems misplaced.

The establishment of a standards or conformance approach to quality relates well to those goods where wholesomeness or purity are major criteria in purchase and use. The conformity to specification approach lends itself well to manufactured (engineered) goods. In both of these areas though, the emphasis is on goods. Where this type of conformity notion carries over into services, then the criteria (or standards) applied relate to the characteristics of particular elements within the service production process. This could be, for example, in 'standards' that concern the maximum length of queue permissible at a checkout, or the number of minutes waiting time. The service provider or retailer determines these 'standards'. The standards are not necessarily based on customer requirements or perceptions. They may be unrelated to the determinants of quality as far as the customer is concerned.

As the rise of mass consumption has gathered pace, there has been a growing engagement with the notion of the most appropriate standard being that set by the customer. This idea of 'conformity to customer requirement' as the test of quality is strongly associated with the approach advocated by Crosby (1980). According to Crosby, a product that meets customer requirements is a quality product. This approach is applied in circumstances both where the 'product' being purchased is simple – a pound of apples – and in more complex products such as motorcars. Where a customer is looking for a vehicle as a city runabout, then a small hatchback may represent 'higher quality' than a large luxury saloon. This type of approach is of greater relevance where the consumer is able to exercise a degree of choice, in terms of both available merchandise and capacity to purchase.

When the individual customer sets the benchmark, then there is greater scope for variation. With goods, this variation occurs between boundaries that pertain to product categories (small hatchback or large saloon), and between dimensions that relate to product characteristics (luxury or basic). The limit of such variation relates to the extent to which markets are segmented and product variety offered. For example, advertising for Mercedes-Benz cars suggests that with 76 model offerings, not all Mercedes drivers can be the same. These vehicles are produced within a system of production that ensures the minimum of unintended variation between like models. The system is able to manufacture according to a high degree of varying specification, within a single model category, however. The system is a long way from that characterized by the remark attributed to Henry Ford that the customer could have it in any colour he or she wished, as long as it was black.

The extent of variation (or lack of homogeneity) in the service arena is even more marked than that offered by contemporary manufacturing systems for cars. As each service encounter is in some way unique, the number of possible variations is infinite. The containment of this variation to within manageable limits has been at the heart of the service operations management approach. In service operations management, there has been a useful and constant reference to the lessons learned from production management. For example, Bolton and Drew (1994) comment "Organizations have traditionally managed service delivery processes by manipulating 'objective' features … such as answer time… … (or) minutes of system down time" (p. 173). They point out that such measures have a distinguishing feature in that they are internally generated. This internal generation of measures contrasts sharply to the external, customer determined requirements that underpin the Crosby model.

With measures external to the organization, then customers become the major source of measures (there remains the possibility of inter-firm comparison, using externally available data). Placing the emphasis on external customer evaluation of service quality fits well with the notions of 'conformity to requirement' and of consumer choice.

Measuring Service Quality

The measurement of service quality from an external, customer perspective has a long informal history and a briefer formal one. Owners, managers and staff have traditionally asked for feedback as to service after many encounters. The question 'Was everything alright with your meal?' has become a cliché. The posters that say 'If you've enjoyed shopping with us, tell your friends, if not – tell us' are also familiar. This type of request for unstructured feedback has its limitations. First, it may be ignored – try telling a server that no, everything was not all right with the meal. Second, systematic gathering of the data is unlikely. Third, linking of the data to other vital aspects, such as customer type, will not occur. Fourth, the development of measures over time, other than counts or volume indication, is unlikely. Fifth, the information as to the major elements in what constitutes quality will not be gathered.

The measurement of service quality requires a different basis if it is to address these issues. The starting point remains customer feedback. There is a requirement for feedback to be structured. There is a need to determine what the dominant aspects of the service are in deciding consumer reactions to questions of quality. The core of the dominant approach to these concerns has been the development of the 'expected' service vs. 'perceived' service premise.

Grönroos (1983) provided an early statement of this approach. In his view, this premise rested on the observation of earlier writers that expectations for performance had an impact on post-consumption evaluations. The "perceived quality of a given service will be the outcome of an evaluation process where consumers compare their expectations with the service they perceive they have got" (p. 38). Central to his conjecture was his distinction between two aspects of service quality: what the customer receives, or technical quality, and how the customer receives it, or functional quality. He suggested that technical quality (room and bed for the hotel guest, or transport of goods from warehouses for the customer of a logistics firm) can often "be measured in a rather objective manner" (p. 39). His argument is that, because services rely on provider–client interaction, technical quality does not account fully for the total quality received. The appearance and behaviour of the service providers while providing the service, and the manner of how they perform and what they say influence the customer's view of the service. Grönroos also explicitly recognizes the influence of 'production-related' routines and the behaviour of other customers as influences on 'functional quality'. An additional major element in the model proposed by Grönroos was the inclusion of corporate image as a mediating factor between the twin aspects of service quality and customer perception. His emphasis on the centrality of image in customer perception of quality concurs with the position advocated by Davies and Brooks (1989, q.v.). Lehtinen and Lehtinen (1982, in Parasuraman, 1995) also argued for the inclusion of an image element in the assessment of service quality. Their premise was that assessment of service quality by customers rests on the physical quality of the facilitating goods and structures; corporate quality, which depends on a firm's image and reputation; and interactive quality, determined by the process of service delivery between personnel and customers.

Other authors who agreed with Grönroos that the core of the definition of service quality rests on a comparison of expectations with experience included Sasser et al., (1978), Lewis and Booms (1983) and Parasuraman et al., (1985). These authors applied a similar conceptual base to Crosby in the more general quality literature. The definition of service quality (or perceived service quality – the distinction is unclear) offered by Parasuraman et al. was 'the degree and direction of discrepancy between customers' service perceptions and expectations'.

Service Quality Measurement Instruments

The most widely used (in an academic context) approach to the measurement of service quality, having a basis in structured feedback from customers is the 'SERVQUAL' approach of Parasuraman et al. (1988, 1991, 1993, 1994). The authors of the approach have presented a number of papers discussing their technique, its application, its revision and replies to criticism. The SERVQUAL approach has received a great deal of attention, and a number of review papers on the instrument and its use have appeared (e.g. Buttle, 1996; Paulin and Perrien 1996). The current status of SERVQUAL seems to be in doubt, in terms of its conceptual basis, reliability and validity, but it is still widely encountered (Lam and Woo, 1997; Philip and Hazlett, 1997; Davies et al., 1999).

The dimensions that (finally) arose from the SERVQUAL approach were reliability, assurance, tangibles, empathy and responsiveness ('RATER'). To these dimensions, Grönroos (1988) added 'recovery'. Sasser et al. (1978) had earlier posited that the dimensions of service quality were: security (i.e. confidence and safety), availability (accessibility), consistency (reliability, or lack of variation), attitude (of service personnel), condition (of facilitating goods and structures), completeness (of total service bundle), and the training of staff. These 'lists' of dimensions have served as a basis for customer research in many settings since, with SERVQUAL dimensions being used in a number of service contexts.

Service Quality in Retailing

A number of studies have used the SERVQUAL approach (or variations from it, including SERVPERF, a performance-only version) in retailing – Carman (1990); Finn and Lamb (1991); Koelemeijer (1992); Dabholkar et al. (1996); Mehta et al. (2000). These last three papers provide an extension and/or comparison of method in retail settings. Mehta et al. (who used the Dabholkar et al. and SERVPERF instruments in their study) concluded that a combination of factors from the two instruments (identified as 'service personnel', 'physical aspects', 'merchandise', 'confidence' and 'parking') were the determinants of service quality in the settings studied – supermarket and electrical goods retailers.

Zeithaml et al. (1993) provide a categorization for factors that form customers' expectations of service. There is a strong time-line in their model, which Bateson (1995) relates to overlapping phases in the consumption experience. Bateson uses three stages – pre-purchase, consumption and post-purchase – to examine consumer behaviour. He suggests that the three phases might relate differently to particular perspectives on behaviour. In the pre-purchase phase, risk-reduction stratagems may be applied. In the purchase phase, customers may seek behavioural control, use either roles or scripts, or become partial employees, which each in their way gives a particular perspective on appropriate managerial response. As his concern is with services, Bateson identifies the post-purchase phase as an evaluation phase, linking it to satisfaction and to the use of particular models by consumers to conduct the evaluation. Bateson points out that no model is wholly correct, but that the models can provide frameworks for marketing research, and that striving to understand consumers' implicit models is a major challenge for marketing management.

For retail service providers, the issue is to identify the variables of particular significance in their market sector. This needs support from an understanding of the decision-making processes used by customers for their type of merchandise, especially in relation to price positioning. In moving from pre-purchase phase to service experience phase, the emphasis shifts to the mechanisms which management uses to structure the service encounter. In the post-purchase phase, the emphasis is on consideration of customer satisfaction, arising from the service encounter.

Service Quality and Customer Satisfaction

Alongside the (continuing) strand in the literature that relates to measuring the underlying dimensions that determine perceived service quality, researchers have also considered customer satisfaction and customer attitude. The debates concern the extent to which (if at all), judgements about 'service quality' correspond to feelings and attitude towards the service provider, or relate more to expressed satisfaction arising from a service encounter. As with the definition of service quality, the debate remains unresolved. What does seem to be managerially useful though, is the understanding that a number of factors affect service quality perceptions. Which factors are most significant will in part depend on the nature of the service provision, and in part on the extent to which any particular feature is satisfactory. It is this last link that contributes to difficulty in measuring service quality.

The picture presented by the evidence suggests that service quality is not a unitary concept – it comprises a number of facets or dimensions. The salience of the facets varies in relation to the type of service. The various elements identified – e.g. the 'RATER' dimensions from SERVQUAL – are not present in the same way in all service settings. The relative importance of each of the dimensions – its 'weight' – may vary. The effects of the presence (or absence) of a particular amount, or degree, of any of the attributes represented by the dimensions are not monotonic, linear and increasing (decreasing). There is some evidence to suggest that the absence of the requisite degree of a particular element may lead to a poor customer response (possibly dissatisfaction). On the other hand, increasing levels beyond the required amount does not lead to an increase in satisfaction. There is a similarity in relation to Herzberg's well-known observation regarding the elements that contribute to motivation. There are some elements whose absence leads to demotivation (hygiene factors), and some whose presence may contribute to motivation (motivators). Similarly, there may be service attributes whose absence leads to poor perceived quality (customer dissatisfaction), and other factors that contribute directly to high perceived quality (satisfaction). The relationship between satisfaction and service quality remains imprecisely understood, however.

'Satisfaction' is often defined as a customer 'state' arising from a particular service encounter. This approach is conceptual only in the definitional sense, and lacks much in the way of a reasoned conceptual basis, despite the frequency with which the position is stated. Liljander and Strandvik (1995) provide a useful review. A number of the reviewed studies relate to satisfaction with the performance of goods. Liljander and Strandvik conclude that performance was a better predictor of satisfaction than inferred or direct measures of disconfirmation (in the SERVQUAL manner). They also question the absence of price as an indicator of value, in most studies, as quality, they suggest, relates to the provider's costs.

Conclusions

The difficulties encountered in the development of a single, reliable, valid questionnaire instrument for measuring retail service quality arise from a number of factors. First, there is the diversity of environments and types of setting in which merchandise retailing takes place. The physical elements of the setting are an element in the findings of many studies. Second, there is the variation in the merchandise itself, spanning the whole range of product categories. The risks consumers perceive in the various categories change (both with the category, the consumer and the purchase occasion). Third, the interaction effects arising from the interaction and 'performance' components of retail service encounters. The salience of such encounters within the retail setting varies widely, depending on the setting and purchase occasion. Fourth, the extent of prior experience with the retail setting differs between customers to a large degree. This divergence in experience has an impact on the customer's readiness and ability to provide evaluations of service quality.

Other difficulties relate to the desire to 'contain' within a relatively simple instrument a number of the different facets of 'quality', as if it were a unitary concept. There may be merit in separating out both different aspects of 'quality' and disentangling the features of retailing that consumers use as a reference in judging service quality. This could provide a series of separate quality (or customer satisfaction) instruments. Separation could be based on either notions of search, experience or credence qualities (Zeithaml and Bitner, 1996; Davies et al. 1999), or on the phases in the purchase cycle (Bateson, 1995), or on the elements that combine to produce the product (Philip and Hazlett 1997). These last authors suggest that their Pivotal–Core–Peripheral attributes model applies in any service setting. The use of a single market research instrument remains a desirable but elusive goal in assessing service quality in retail settings.

References

Bateson, J. 1995. *Managing Services Marketing (3rd. Ed.)*. Fort Worth, TX: The Dryden Press.
Bolton, R. and Drew, J. 1994. Linking customer satisfaction to service operations and outcomes.

In Rust, R. and Oliver, R. (Eds.). *Service Quality: New Directions in Theory and Practice.* Thousand Oaks, CA: Sage.

Bucklin, L. 1963. Retail strategy and the classification of consumer goods. *Journal of Marketing,* 27 (January), 50–55.

Buttle, F. 1996. SERVQUAL: review, critique, research agenda. *European Journal of Marketing,* 30(1), 8–32.

Carman, J. 1990. Consumer perceptions of service quality: an assessment of the SERVQUAL dimensions. *Journal of Retailing,* 66(1), 33–35.

Chase, R. 1978, Where does the customer fit in a service operation? *Harvard Business Review,* November–December, 137–142.

Copeland, M. 1923. The relation of consumers' buying habits to marketing methods. *Harvard Business Review,* 1(April), 282–289.

Cowell, D. 1984. *The Marketing of Services.* London: Heinemann.

Crosby, P. 1980. *Quality Is Free.* New York: Mentor.

Dabholkar, P., Thorpe, D. and Rentz, J. 1996. A measure of service quality for retail stores: scale development and validation. *Journal of the Academy of Marketing Science,* 24 (Winter), 3–16.

Davies, B., Baron, S., Gear, A.R.E. and Read, M. 1999. Measuring and managing service quality. *Marketing Intelligence and Planning,* 17(1), 21–32.

DeSarbo, W., Huff, L., Rolandelli, M. and Choi, J. 1994. On the measurement of perceived service quality. In Rust, R. and Oliver, R. (Eds.). *Service Quality: New Directions in Theory and Practice.* Thousand Oaks, CA: Sage Publications.

Fitzsimmons, J. and Sullivan, R. 1982. *Service Operations Management.* New York: McGraw–Hill.

Dotchin, J. and Oakland, J. 1994. Total quality management in services, part 1:understanding and classifying services. *International Journal of Quality and Reliability Management,* 11(3), 9–26.

Finn, D. and Lamb, C. Jr. 1991. An evaluation of the SERVQUAL scales in a retailing setting. In Holman, R. and Solomon M. (Eds.). *Advances in Consumer Research, Vol. 18,* pp. 483–490.

Foote, N. and Hatt, P. 1953. Social mobility and economic advancement. *American Economic Review,* May, 364–378.

Grönroos, C. 1983. *Strategic Management and Marketing in the Service Sector.* Lund, Sweden: Studentlitteratur, and Bromley, Kent: Chartwell–Bratt.

Grönroos, C. 1988. Service quality: the six criteria of good perceived service quality. *Review of Business,* 9(3), 10–13.

Haywood-Farmer, J. 1988. A conceptual model of service quality. *International Journal of Operations and Production Management,* 8(6), 19–29.

Holton, H. 1958. The distinctions between convenience goods, shopping goods and specialty goods. *Journal of Marketing,* 22 (July), 53–56.

Koelemeijer, K. 1992. Measuring perceived service quality in retailing; a comparison of methods. *Proceedings of the 21st European Marketing Academy Conference (EMAC), Aarhus, Denmark,* (pp. 729–744).

Kotler, P. 1991. *Marketing Management: Analysis, Planning, Implementation and Control (7th. Ed.).* Englewood Cliffs, NJ: Prentice–Hall.

Lam, S. and Woo, K. 1997. Measuring service quality: a test-retest reliability investigation of SERVQUAL. *Journal of the Market Research Society,* April, 39(2), 381–391.

Lehtinen, U. and Lehtinen, J. 1982. *Service Quality: a Study of Quality Dimensions.* Unpublished research report, Service Management Group Oy, Helsinki, Finland. Cited in Parasuraman, 1995.

Lewis, R. and Booms, B. 1983. The marketing aspects of service quality. In Berry, L. and Upah, G. (Eds.). *Emerging Perspectives in Services Marketing.* Chicago, IL: AMA.

Liljander, V. and Srandvik, T. 1995. The Relation Between Service Quality, Satisfaction and Intentions. In Kunst, P. and Lemmink, J., Jaques G. and Hendrikx M. (Eds.). *Managing Service Quality, Vol. 1*. The Netherlands/London: Innovation Trading/Paul Chapman Publishing, Vught.

Lovelock, C. 1983. Classifying services to gain strategic marketing insight. *Journal of Marketing*, 47 (Summer), 9–20.

Lovelock, C. 1988. *Managing Services: Marketing, Operations and Human Resources*. Englewood Cliffs, NJ: Prentice–Hall.

Maister, D. and Lovelock, C. 1982. Managing facilitator services. *Sloan Management Review*, Summer, 19–31.

Mehta, S., Lalwani, A. and Han, S. 2000. Service quality in retailing: relative efficiency of alternative measurement scales for different product-service environments. *International Journal of Retail and Distribution Management*, 28(2), 62–72.

Paulin, M. and Perrien, J. 1996. Measurement of service quality: the effect of contextuality. In Kunst, P. and Lemmink, J. (Eds.). *Managing Service Quality, Vol. 2*. London: Paul Chapman Publishing.

Parasuraman, A. 1995. Measuring and monitoring service quality. In Glynn, W. and Barnes, J. (Eds.). *Understanding Services Management*. Chichester: Wiley.

Parasuraman, A., Berry, L. and Zeithaml, V. 1993. More on improving service quality measurement. *Journal of Retailing*, 69(1), 140–147.

Parasuraman, A., Berry, L. and Zeithaml, V. 1991. Refinement and reassessment of the SERVQUAL scale. *Journal of Retailing*, 67(4), 420–450.

Parasuraman, A., Zeithaml, V. and Berry, L. 1988. SERVQUAL: a multiple-item scale for measuring consumer perceptions of service quality. *Journal of Retailing*, 64 (Spring), 12–37.

Parasuraman, A., Zeithaml, V. and Berry, L. 1985. A conceptual model of service quality and its implications for future research. *Journal of Marketing*, 49 (Fall), 41–50.

Parasuraman, A., Zeithaml, V. and Berry, L. 1994. Reassessment of expectations as a comparison standard in measuring service quality: implications for future research. *Journal of Marketing*, 58 (January), 111–124.

Philip, G. and Hazlett, S.-A. 1997. The measurement of service quality: a new P–C–P attributes model. *International Journal of Quality and Reliability Management*, 14(2–3), 260–286.

Sasser, W., Olsen, P. and Wyckoff, D. 1978. *Management of Service Operations: Text and Cases*. Boston, MA: Allyn and Bacon.

Shostack, G.L. 1977. Breaking free from product marketing. *Journal of Marketing*, 41(April), 73–80.

Zeithaml, V., Berry, L. and Parasuraman, A. 1996. The nature and determinants of customer expectations of service. *Journal of the Academy of Marketing Science*, 21(1), 1–12.

Zeithaml, V. and Bitner, M. 1993. *Services Marketing*. New York: McGraw–Hill.

15

THE LOCATIONAL CONTEXT

In a treatment consistent with the other areas of the book, concern here is with the two selected levels of locational context:
- The store itself (pico level); and
- The upper layer, concerned with shopping (micro-level).
  Brief consideration is given to two further aspects:
- The network and area question (meso-level); and
- The region and the particular development of international retailing (macro-level).
  Based on this selected approach, the following elements of the locational context are touched upon:
- Managing the urban retail drama:
  - retailers;
  - developers;
  - the audience;
  - planning authorities;
  - ancillary service providers; and
  - other provision.
- Research strands from geography, marketing and consumption studies.
- Shopping malls and town centre management.
- Location studies and trade area assessment.
- Retail internationalization.

Introduction

A number of particular perspectives and traditions have considered the issues related to location in retailing. Chief among them are geography and marketing (management), with a perspective beginning to emerge from consumption studies (Clarke et al., 1997; Clarke, 2000). The focus of these traditions has differed. The geography tradition has emphasized the spatial distribution of provision (an emphasis which has informed much of the planning legislation and public policy related to retailing) and more recently the development of managerial approaches to locational choice. However, the marketing approach has adopted a managerial perspective from the outset. Within marketing, the location decision is under the rubric of 'place' within the standard formulation of the marketing mix. The marketing treatment (for the most part) is less spatially oriented than the geographical. The emerging treatment in the consumption literature has its roots in the postmodern project. The origin is often the 'commodification' of consumer goods (Lee, 1993) on the one hand, or the sites and architecture of places of retail consumption on the other (Shields, 1992). (The commodification of the sociologist is vastly different from that of the marketer, however.) These strands in the consumption literature were a re-statement of the treatment of consumption in sociology that had become important in the 1980s (Bocock, 1993).

All these various strands (though having a spatial component), do not provide a multi-level treatment of retail location, for the most part. Although the approaches applied to the issue of retail location start from different perspectives, each either implicitly or explicitly acknowledges that the concept of location can be examined at a number of levels.

The Layers and Dimensions of Retail Location

There has been a long-standing recognition of the possibility of distinguishing the layered nature of locational concerns in retailing. Brown (1992) pointed out that the micro ("pertaining to the siting of outlets *within* planned shopping centres and unplanned shopping districts" (p. xiii) – emphasis in the original) was the relatively less researched area. Brown argues that the interaction processes in retailing (the intertwining of demand and supply) prevent a unitary representation of the spatial pattern of retail provision as an *outcome* of processes of demand and supply. The consequence of this interplay is that our ability to distinguish between various effects is restricted, rather than there being an ability to provide unique distinct outcomes from particular process interactions. A compounding factor is the presence of three spatial levels of consideration. These different levels of consideration inform the nature of the process to be observed at each level.

These three 'structural dimensions' in Brown's (p. 230) summary of retail location characteristics are: geographical, hierarchical and compositional.

'Geographical' refers to the core arrangement present in different retail sectors: dispersion and agglomeration. The processes of agglomeration give rise to 'hierarchy', (albeit of a less clear-cut order than classically suggested), and such agglomerations in turn, differ significantly as to their 'composition'. Each dimension gives rise to a subordinate 'pattern', which itself exhibits both demand and supply side influences.

Levels or Tiers of Analysis

In this chapter, the concern ranges from the pico-level (pertaining to the internal spatial arrangements of stores) through the micro-level, to questions at the network or macro-level and to mega-level concerns in the international sphere. With such a wide range, it is not possible to give a full or extended treatment to each particular level. The concern is rather the desire to link considerations of the supply and demand (consumption) influences that may be apparent. The focus is broadly on the lower levels (pico and micro), with less detailed consideration of the higher order effects. The terminology of pico (item and category level), micro (store within centre), meso (centre within agglomeration) and macro (agglomeration within market and inter-market relationships) and mega (over-arching concerns, such as internatio-nalization) offers a potential shorthand, but is not one that has been used. Hernandez et al. (1998) use the terminology of macro/meso/micro, and provide a relation to the strategic, monadic and tactical levels of retail deci-sion-making.

Pico-Level Considerations

The internal spatial arrangements of retail stores are not generally considered as elements in 'retail location'. Many would view them as elements in design considerations. Within a store, the precise form and layout of merchandise items within departments and of departments (or categories) themselves, forms part of the consideration of 'space planning' (see Chapter 8). The emphasis in space planning has long been one of 'optimization', in those trades where there are high numbers of lines (particularly grocery). The aesthetic considerations have assumed greater significance in retailers such as department and apparel stores. The core concern of most space planners and space planning remains the economic.

Space planning in stores may be seen to involve the generation of appro-priate adjacencies between categories of product, the determination of the allocation of space to individual stock keeping units, the layout of the aisles and fixtures and a myriad of other concerns. What is striking is that it is not uncommon for these concerns to be divided between differing management groups within retail organizations. Such groups may be category managers, store development and planning, buying and merchandising. The focus of the groups and the scale of their analysis may also differ considerably (Davies and Ward, 2000). The issue of the level of spatial scale that is being examined is one that reappears at many points in the consideration of retail location.

Hernandez and Bennison (2000) suggest that the three levels of decision might be the strategic, the monadic and the tactical. The strategic level focuses on firstly, the nature of the sites required to support the marketing strategy, in terms of sizes of outlet and type of site. The choice of territorial coverage and the specifics of market relation and penetration form the second component. The monadic decision concerns the elements that relate to a single store. These they identify as:

> Roll-out/extension: namely the opening of a new store, or the extension of floorspace in existing ones;
>
> Relocation; the movement of a store from one location to another within the particular town or area where a better site is available;
>
> Rationalisation: the closure of individual stores, or the disposal of a division;
>
> Refascia: altering the image of outlets by changing the name or appearance ...;
>
> Refurbishment: improving/updating the physical fabric of an existing store;
>
> Remerchandising: altering the product range and merchandise to tailor the offer more closely to local consumers.
>
> Hernandez and Bennison, 2000, p. 359

Their use of the term monadic is they argue, justified by the unique feature of store based retailing: the relationship between immediate environment and individual store. Their inclusion of activities such as 'refascia', refurbishment, and remerchandising, supports the contention that the interplay between marketing (and possibly aesthetic) issues and physical location is so intertwined that an integrated perspective is necessary.

Another aspect of consideration at the level of the unit *is* the aesthetic. Consideration of the likely 'appeal' of a particular design is often uppermost in the minds of retail management. This is considered alongside the requirements for operational efficiency (see Chapter 6). What is not articulated is the incorporation within the aesthetic of considerable elements of the locational and spatial.

Micro-Level Considerations

The micro-level, for present purposes, is seen as being the level of the mall or the street or shopping district at small scale. Brown (1992) provides insight on the use of general principles (often developed at higher levels of analysis, such as the regional) to examine lower-scale effects. He identifies the presence of a small number of high order stores within agglomerations, and the sequence of adjacent stores that appear in shopping malls as *micro*-spatial effects.

The Mall and Customer Movement

For the mall, the marketing concern has often been to present a pattern of distribution of tenants such as to encourage movement over the greater part of the complex by consumers. Jones and Simmons (1990, pp. 125–126) suggested that:

> The large anchor (generative) tenants are placed at the ends of the malls, so that customers will visit both ends and pass by the smaller suscipient stores in the process;

> Access is strictly controlled, to minimize the number of mall exits at intermediate locations, so that customers cannot escape. Downtown malls try to create an internal street parallel to the real one;

> This 'street' is often curved or zigzagged, in order to extend the street length and increase the number of shop fronts;

> Clusters of closely related or competitive activities may provide sub-foci in their own right. Food stores are grouped near the supermarket. Fast-food outlets form a 'gourmet-court' (sic). with communal tables and seating facilities. Retailers serving different age or income groups are kept separate; stores catering to teenagers, for example, are segregated from upscale retailers. In the largest centers the fashion stores and the mass market retailers may be located on different floors or in different wings.

The general principles that can be seen at work here (of agglomeration, dispersion, composition, etc.) relate well to the principles articulated by Brown. Jones and Simmons demonstrate also that a process of mimicry may be involved, as the design of the mall replicates some of the features of the unplanned street. The marketing management approach is, in Jones and Simmons' formulation, informed by the geographical. Their overt usage, of some of the features of the higher-order locational context, provides a example for the argument that any attempt to examine retail location *should* involve consideration of all possible levels of analysis, within some coherent frame.

The Shopping Cluster or District

Brown (1992) comments that studies in the twin traditions of the empirical-behavioural and the cognitive behavioural have delivered consistent results.

"[these studies show] firstly, the critically important customer attracting role of magnet or anchor stores; secondly, shoppers…reluctance to exert themselves…and the strong distance decay effect [this causes]…; thirdly, the dominant influence of entry and exit points…; fourthly, the high level of customer interchange that occurs between complementary retail outlets" (p. 161). These types of observations would sit as well within a marketing perspective on these issues as within a geographical one.

From a more overtly retail marketing standpoint, Clarke (2000) argues that, at the local level of supply to a consumer market, there is a need to consider the availability of choice (competition from a retailer perspective). There are five elements that, in his view, require further work. First, there is a need empirically to test work on consumption. This would help ground conceptual frameworks. Secondly, the effects of structural change in local retail systems and its effect on behaviour in shopping requires elucidation. Thirdly, there is need to model dynamically changing patterns of expenditure within local retail systems (what and how much consumers buy, as well as where). Fourthly, changes need to be seen not only from the store-based perspective of a retailer, but also in relation to the social embeddedness of consumption in families and communities. Fifthly, research must adopt a pluralistic approach to methodology, if it is to explore the questions from a managerial as well as consumer perspective.

The Aesthetic and Psychological Components

To the 'rational' principles (whether from marketing or geography) concerning the allocation of space inside the mall that inform the usual management perspective, Guy (1994) adds the notion that the external appearance is designed (aesthetically) "to impose a presence and authority for the centre" (p. 166). The use of terminology such as 'authority' might be contested by other commentators, but there is a view that the aesthetic and the "narrow economic calculation" (Ferguson, 1992, p. 34) are in some sort of dynamic balance. Ferguson argues that shopping centres embody (though each imperfectly), the dream psychology of the modern relations of consumption. This psychology contains elements of infinity, incompleteness, arbitrariness, fragmentation, indifference, novelty and nostalgia.

The department store (seen as a precursor to the shopping mall) offered a perspective on *total* inclusivity – 'from an ashtray to an elephant' for Harrods, with its telegraphic address of Everything, London. The mall in contrast, offers a series of *limited* excursions, through each retail unit, into the *infinite* commodity world beyond it. It presents a series of selected highlights, which have a dynamic quality, as tenants and their merchandise portfolios change over time. The endless variety of goods available as commodities means that there is a necessary *incompleteness* in the offer in a shopping centre. As malls enable (through unconstrained and effortless consumption) consumers to respond to wishes, rather than wants, *arbitrariness* is introduced as rational choice is abandoned. The patterns of consumption established led to a *fragmentation* of self, as we are able to do no more than sample the commodities set before us. The commodities, which carry an arbitrary distributed value, tend to become identical, leading to *indifference* on the part of the consumer.

These general trends are counteracted, Ferguson argues, by the two remaining characteristics: novelty and nostalgia. Novelty is associated with a particular kind of glamour, to which some may feel attachment. Keeping up with fashion is thus a sensible course of action. By linking to the past, 'shameless nostalgia' becomes an appropriate style for architecture. These two elements in contrast to the effects of the infinite, serve to provide anchors or rootedness for consumers, even though the legitimacy of their basis may (in this perspective) be questioned.

The type of reasoning exhibited in Ferguson's approach touches on the locational and spatial, but does not foreground them. He applies more attention to consideration of aesthetic issues, and this distinction characterizes much of the consumption literature. Jackson and Thrift (1995) suggested that work in the consumption literature had from a geographical perspective, been focused on *sites* of consumption, *chains* that link multiple locations of consumption and *spaces and places* of contemporary consumption. They included in their review work by geographers and those whose work had a spatial dimension, including those from consumption studies. Ferguson, in common with many cultural commentators, bases his view on consideration of the *shopping mall* as a particular *site* or perhaps *space and place* of consumption.

The mall, which is frequently a focus in contemporary writings, is the counterpart to the focus on the department store in historical considerations. In this stream of work on the mall (and urban centre also) in contemporary culture, there is an examination of the *dis-location* of the sites of consumption. "Consumption has become so fundamental to the character of urban environments that cities could in fact be construed to be 'unreal' in the sense that they could be anywhere; they have, in effect, lost a sense of place" (Miles, 1998 p. 68). Miles goes on to argue that there is a strong connection with the processes and effects of globalization and the erosion of the sense of place in specific locations.

Brown (1992), in his gloss on the behavioural perspective, also commented on this effect. "From the retailing perspective, the sense of place that inheres in some locations and the 'placelessness' that characterises others would seem particularly important" (p. 161). The contrast between the rooted and the placeless is between the city centre and the mall, but as malls develop in scale and sophistication there is a possibility for them to develop a sense of place. In contrast, the rise in city centre management may bring about greater uniformity in the differentiated place.

Links Between Scale and Perspectives

The geographical stream focuses particularly on spatial inter-relations, the marketing on the control of channel relations and the management of in-store space, while the consumption study literature focuses on the relation of self to environmental stimuli. Pine and Gilmore (1999) provide a link (albeit a managerial one) between some aspects of these traditions. They provide a description (which accords well with Ferguson's nostalgia) of the use of historical pastiche to create a unified 'sense of place' firstly, in the conversion of one unplanned district converted into a planned shopping centre, and secondly the creation of one of the largest malls in the USA. The relation between this activity and the more commonly understood notions of retail location planning arises because, within the focus on the aesthetic, there is a necessary consideration of agglomeration, nucleation, clustering and dispersion. These locational elements have an aesthetic component, giving rise as they do to pleasing concentrations, discernible massing (of similar architectural elements), and the physical embodiment of choice.

They may also give rise, more problematically, to a retail hyperspace (Clarke, 1996). Hyperspace requires the deployment of a greater sophistication of understanding than has generally been present in the approaches arising in geography. To deal with hyperspace may form part of the task in developing a new geography. Lowe and Wrigley (1996) indicate that the development of 'new landscapes of consumption', that integrate the economic and the cultural, is a significant task for the sub-discipline of retail geography.

Part of Lowe and Wrigley's consideration for the development of the new retail geography is the notion of the *captured market*. A captured market (in this terminology) arises when large numbers of potential consumers are gathered in a specific location with time on their hands. The airport is the prime (archetypal) form of the captured market in contemporary studies. Further examples might include other transport termini, large hospitals, and major office developments. Each of these has the aspect of being sufficiently large to have some characteristics of urban, public space, but to be (largely) private managed space, often of unitary architectural type. The blurring of the boundaries between previously distinct types of space (or possibly also levels of analysis) takes a further turn.

The issues of the blurring of distinctions between the various scale-determined levels of analysis and the inter-relatedness of effects brought about by the processes of globalization is a key one for many critical commentators in these debates. These concerns form part of the desire to develop an economic and cultural geography of retailing. From the perspective of this book, such a project is to be welcomed, if it can include a consideration of the marketing element and eschew the sometimes strident (and essentially naïve) dismissal as all of the retail effort as manipulative. (See Storey 1999, for a discussion of the issue that 'consumption-as-manipulation' raises.) The scale at which the level of the sometimes critical commentaries focuses tends to be either at the global (and the 'deleterious effects' of the erosion of a presupposed difference), or at the level of the site of consumption, and the substitution of the synthetic or pastiche for the 'real'. These distanced but specific levels are selected because they reflect the two levels over which corporations are seen to exercise greatest control – the choice of regional markets and the selection and operation of specific sites.

Meso-Level Considerations

Within our schema, meso-level refers to the pattern of location of retail facilities discernible within the city, or comparable unit of analysis in less urbanized areas. This type of consideration of location has often been termed 'area analysis'. Brown (1992) suggests that (typically) retailing textbooks show this level to be the link that connects the regional decision to specific site selection. Such an unproblematic treatment is not appropriate, if the unfolding of the levels is to be successfully accomplished. Omar (1999) and Gilbert (1999) both offer such a treatment in the context of general texts on retailing. Neither presents linkages between the (marketing/retail management) approach they take and the wider geographic or cultural studies literature. This serves to emphasize further the point that, for contemporary retail management, where the desire to 'manage consumption' is present, further integrative effort is required.

Area Analysis and its Derivatives

The treatment of area analysis in the main rests on the neo-classical approaches (Brown, 1992). The three conceptualizations in this tradition that Brown identifies are central place theory, bid rent theory and the principle of minimum differentiation (pp. 36–89). The importance of central place theory in shaping the theoretical considerations in this arena is considerable, though as Brown shows, its place has also been much contested. Central place theory, and the other neo-classical approaches, address the key question relating to the spatial distribution of shops. The original emphasis may have been on the regional, but such approaches (and derivatives of them) have been applied at the area (and also site) level.

The neo-classical approaches grew from largely theoretical roots. Clarke et al. (1997) identify the growing use of data and techniques for locational analysis as the second major strand of research (after the neo-classical) within the geographical tradition. They see this strand as deriving from techniques used by practitioners, both within retailing and the land-based professions such as surveying. The contributions from this strand include interaction modelling and geographical information systems. The third strand that they identify is the work dealing with land use, public policy and planning issues. This work they see as forming the basis for the policy frameworks and policy implementation. These three strands co-exist, but are not much inter-twined.

The desire for an effective framework within which to articulate decision-making (both private and public) about planned retail location is widespread. Davies, and Clarke, (Davies 2000; Davies and Clarke, 1994) devised an inte-grating framework for locational positioning and strategy from the retailers perspective. The framework delineates different tiers of corporate decision making in relation to location, and also relates the tiers to broader environ-mental issues at each level. Their framework combines elements of the geographic/spatial with an explicit recognition of the need to link this to an understanding of the customer from a behavioural perspective. The framework (which is focused on the network planning requirements of operators of chains of outlets) uses descriptors of types of retail agglomera-tion and dispersion (retail park, solus site, parade and high street), in conjunction with characteristics of goods and of consumer behaviour. What it does not explicitly incorporate is the consideration of the consumption aspects of that purchase behaviour. The application of the model is very much a marketing one. The authors emphasize that retailers lack a vocabu-lary to articulate perceptions about sites and locations. Their hope is that models, of the type they present, contribute to the processes of articulation for an important aspect of many retail businesses.

Behavioural Treatments

The behavioural perspective on location is also given extended treatment by Brown (1992, pp. 90–162). A (particular) behavioural perspective can, most appropriately, be brought to bear at the area or site levels, where aggregation of related behaviours by similar customers can be used, either to explain the

existing spatial arrangement of retail facilities, or determine the specific benefits of a particular site. These types of observation lend support to the request
by Clarke (2000) above for a further stage of development of approach in the
consideration of retail markets local to a consumer base.

Macro-Level Considerations

The macro level in this schema relates to the choice of which (regional/
national) market to operate in or enter (from the retailer's perspective) and
the contextual set for the everyday exercise of choice by consumers. A recent
issue of the International Marketing Review (17/4–5, 2000) provides an interesting set of papers on retail internationalization issues. Alexander and
Myers (2000) offer a perspective on the process of retail internationalization
that brings together the corporate and market (but not consumer or consumption) elements. They also present a review of the research activity in this field
in the last 15 years. This is in part synthesized in a model of the process (from
a corporate perspective) of the pattern of the internationalization of firms.

In their model, firms move from a market of origin (country), driven by
concept or technological forces and the possession of facilitating competencies, such as leadership and experience. This gives rise to: locational decisions
(which other countries); the choice of entry method (acquisition, organic
growth, franchising etc.), and the selection of an overt strategy (global, multinational etc.) for the deployment of financial assets. These choices are again
facilitated (or not) by the possession of internal competencies (functional
coordination, perceptions and attitudes etc.). The learning that organizations
gain through involvement in the process feeds back into their internal competencies, and the cycle may be repeated.

The corporate perspective that is developed in this way then has a major
role to play in the pattern of market extension adopted. Alexander and Myers
(2000) suggest that this interplay leads to one of four conditions: proximal
development, with an ethnocentric perspective and a low desire for market
extension; transnational forms, where market extension desire is low and the
perspective of the firm is geocentric; multinational forms, where ethnocentr-
ism is combined with high market extension; and finally, the global firm,
combining a geocentric perspective with high market extension.

Consumer Issues

Burt and Carralero-Encinas (2000) focus on an aspect of retail presence that
contends intimately on consumers image. They conclude that, within their
narrow ambit, image is 'weaker' in a 'foreign' country other than the home

one. This result does however suggest that there are non-location issues that connect to the ability of (relatively) mass market operators to develop in international markets. For those retailers that appeal to more 'exclusive' consumer segments, image may be held by consumers within the segments served, without the need for a specific grounded familiarity. It is this interplay and contrast between segments, retailers and locational policies that has led to concerns with the 'McDonaldization' of culture (Ritzer, 1993). In those mass markets where such an approach is successful, the loss of the sense of place to which concentrations of international retailers may give rise is a concern for some commentators. These concerns have been most acute for those writing in the consumption studies literature.

In the same issue, Godley and Fletcher (2000) point out that the growth in international investment by retailers reflects growth in consumer purchasing power in national markets. That is, explanations at the level of the firm are essentially second-order effects. Where consumer purchasing power is growing, retail firms will be tempted to enter the new (foreign) national market.

Considered research that focuses on the consumer as the unit of analysis in retail internationalization is much rarer. This may be because of the difficulties with such studies more generally (Nasif et al., 1991), or because of particular sectoral impediments in retailing (Davies and Flemmer, 1995). There is however a suggestion in the literature that the focus may have shifted to questions of consumer perception and retailer image because of the relative failure of central place theory to explain observed patterns of provision. The explanatory power of central place theory (a key neo-classical approach) would, of course, not extend upwards to this macro level.

Observations on Theory Development in Retail Location

There is a clear need to develop a theory or theories relating to retail location that forms an encompassing framework. At present, such a framework is not available. Any such framework must contain a series of explanatory devices germane to each of the four discernible levels or tiers (store, mall or locality, area, region); some devices might pertain to more than one level. Secondly, the framework must incorporate a range of disciplinary perspectives: geography, marketing, consumption studies. Thirdly, the framework should consider both supply (retail management) and demand (consumer) issues. Fourthly, there should be an attempt to build on the various theoretical foundations available to us in the different existing traditions, coupled with the newer methods of analysis available.

Managing Spaces and Places of Consumption

There are two areas where the management of spaces and places occurs, to an increasing degree, that are not stores. The first is the shopping centre or mall, the second the town centre. There has been some consideration of the management of mall space in the sections above, but little in reference to town centre management. The growth of town centre management (TCM) imports into the real, idiosyncratic space some of the concepts and approaches that inform retail management more generally. This development has had particular strength in the UK, as town and cities 'positioned' themselves to compete more effectively with the growth in out-of-town retailing provision.

The expressed British government view about the need to 'preserve' city centres, supports the economically-related desires of the businesses located in town centres. The government's view is important, because of the particular structure of land use and planning regulation in the UK. The policy desire was for a 'true urban renaissance' (Jones and Hillier, 1998), of which TCM might be a 'humble manifestation'.

The practice of TCM in the UK differs little in its intent from schemes elsewhere, though there is, as always, a strong contingent element in the precise nature of particular schemes and their objectives. Concern to introduce identifiable areas, replete with signs and signifiers; desire to introduce 'branding' elements; coherent visual treatments; pedestrianization; influence on the mix of provision; delivery of consumer desiderata, such as safety; all of these may form part of the approach of TCM. What is striking in many schemes (in the UK at least) is the extent to which they may emphasize the historic components of place. This emphasis (also seen in some district redevelopment schemes) is one of the causes of concern about the rise of the 'inauthentic' in issues of urban space and place.

Jones and Hillier (1998) also identified a concern that the focus of schemes could be seen as 'cosmetic', but there was evidence that they were starting to make a contribution to the continued vitality of centres, presumably through trade retention and increased footfall. Medway et al. (2000) uncovered a number of reasons for retailer involvement in TCM, which extended from economic self-interest, to a perspective on the social desirability of retaining town centres as accessible centres of shopping for the widest sections of the community. These retailers' concerns showed a social or community dimension that extended beyond the narrowly private, corporate sphere.

The links between the private sector and public provision in terms, for example, of car parking, street furniture, public space, street maintenance, are crucial in securing appropriate funding from private sector participants.

The extent to which retailers in Britain contribute to the costs of TCM was investigated by Medway et al. (1999). They found that, in general, a low proportion of retailers contributed to defray costs and that issues of participation raised wider debates about urban governance and the concept of stakeholders. This was despite the fact that retail promotion was a key ingredient of town centre management schemes.

Consequences of Managed Town Centres

If the managed town centre is taken as the type of space that further contributes to the elision of public and private space, then there are consequences for retailers. Within a managed town centre, the staging of retail drama may be simplified, at least in terms of the ability of a (participating) retailer to influence the nature of the 'created space'. Such created spaces can be set alongside the 'mediated symbolic materials' of modern societies (Thompson, 1995) as elements in the repertoire that can be used to contribute to the formation of self without destroying the 'shared locale' (p. 207).

Retailers exist within the schema of TCM alongside other stakeholders with commercial interests: property developers and owners, service providers, and the public authorities. The interplay between their commercial desires and the overarching social perspective infrequently includes a place for the representation of involved communities. Incorporating the community perspective (and possibly an individuated consumer one) is a necessary task, if the sense of 'sharing in the locale' is to be maintained. Where the sense of sharing at any fundamental level is lost or absent, then the experience of the managed town centre for the consumer is somehow unauthentic, merely a surface phenomenon. "Though on the surface our towns and cities appear to provide a consumerist escape from the harsh realities and resource divisions that characterize consumer society, in reality all they do is reinforce the very problems, stresses, not to say environmental strains, that they purport to resolve" (Miles, 1998, pp. 68–69).

The concern that Miles identifies in the production of 'consumerist escape' is at the heart of the tensions that TCM may generate. There is a balance to be struck between the control of space, to ensure the possibility of 'delivery' of the intended story or script, and the consequences for those actors who, in the minds of some (many?) have no part in the drama. The urban space is not one that can be (should be) entirely 'sanitized' to conform to any one narrow definition of desirable. The maintenance of a plurality of uses, plays and players is a key component in sustaining the urban tradition in the contemporary context.

Conclusions

The development of increasing numbers of larger-scale retail places, such as the mega-malls and managed (synthesized) shopping districts and urban centres, places renewed pressure on the framework for locational analysis and management in retailing. Four tiers or levels (store, mall or local district, area and region) can de identified in current structures, though being distinguishable does not imply that they are entirely distinct. There are three main academic traditions which have, each in their separate (though in the case of marketing, related) ways provided a perspective on retail location and the effects that give rise to its current forms (geography, marketing, consumption studies).

Evidence from studies amongst retailers suggests that they utilize only a part of the range of perspectives and tools available. The policies for location to which this gives rise may exhibit some analytical sophistication, at a given tier or level, but there is little evidence of articulation across all levels. The policies of retailers could be improved through a more explicit engagement with a wider range of concerns. Policies may also need to address more directly the immediate external (mall or micro-level) concerns for the management of space, as well as area (meso) level concerns in urban centres.

References

Alexander, N. and Myers, H. 2000 The retail internationalisation process. *International Marketing Review*, 17(4–5), 334–353.

Bocock, R. 1993. *Consumption*. London: Routledge.

Brown, S. 1992. *Retail Location: a Micro-Scale Perspective*. Aldershot: Avebury (Ashgate Publishing).

Burt, S. and Carralero-Encinas, J. 2000. The role of store image in retail internationalization. *International Marketing Review*, 17 (4–5), 433–453.

Clarke, D. 1996. The limits to retail capital. In Wrigley, N. and Lowe, M. (Eds). *Retailing, Consumption and Capital*. Harlow: Longman.

Clarke, I. 2000. Retail power, competition and local consumer choice in the UK grocery market. *European Journal of Marketing*, 34(8), 975–1002.

Clarke, I., Bennison, D. and Pal, J. 1997. Towards a contemporary perspective of retail location. *International Journal of Retail and Distribution Management*, 25(2–3), 59–69.

Davies, B.J. and Flemmer, M. 1995. Consumer behaviour convergence in the European Union. *The Service Industries Journal*. 15(4), 177–190

Davies, B.J. and Ward, P.J. 2000. Space allocation in the UK grocery sector. *British Food Journal*, 102(5), 406–419.

Davies, M. 2000. Location Network Presentation, at Contemporary Issues in Retailing Conference (CIRM), Manchester.

Davies, M. and Clarke, I. 1994. A Framework for Network Planning. *International Journal of Retail and Distribution Management*, 22(6), 6–10.

Ferguson, H. 1992. Watching the world go round. In Shields, R. (Ed). *Lifestyle Shopping: the Subject of Consumption*. London: Routledge.

Jones, P. and Hillier, D. 1998. Changing the balance – the 'ins and outs' of retail development. *Property Management*, 18(2), 114–126.

Gilbert, D. 1999. *Retail Marketing Management*. Harlow; Pearson Education.

Godley A. and Fletcher S. 2000. Foreign entry into British retailing, 1850–1994. *International Marketing Review*, 17 (4–5), 392–400.

Guy, C. 1994. *The Retail Development Process* London: Routledge.

Hernandez, T., Bennison, D. and Cornelius, S. 1998. The organisational context of retail location decision-making. *Geojournal*, 45(4), 295–308.

Jackson, P. and Thrift, N. 1995 Geographies of Consumption. In Miller, D. (Ed). *Acknowledging Consumption: A Review of New Studies*. London: Routledge.

Jones, K. and Simmons, J. 1990. *The Retail Environment*. London: Routledge

Lee, M. 1993. *Consumer Culture Reborn: the Cultural Politics of Consumption*. London: Routledge

Lowe, M. and Wrigley, N. Towards the new retail geography. In Wrigley, N. and Lowe, M. (Eds). *Retailing, Consumption and Capital* Harlow: Longman.

Medway, D., Alexander, A., Bennison, D., and Warnaby, G. 1999. Retailers' financial support for town centre management. *International Journal of Retail and Distribution Management*, 27(6)), 246–255.

Medway, D., Warnaby, G., Bennison, D. and Alexander, A. 2000. Retailers' financial support for town centre management. *International Journal of Retail and Distribution Management*, 28(8), 368–378.

Miles, S. 1998. *Consumerism – as a Way of Life* London: Sage Publications.

Nasif, E., Daeaj, H., Ebrahimi, B. and Thibodeaux, M. 1991. Methodological problems in cross-cultural research: an up-dated review Management International Review, 31(1), 79–91.

Omar, O. 1999. *Retail Marketing*. London: Financial Times Management.

Pine, B.J. and Gilmore, J. 1999 *The Experience Economy*, Boston, MA: Harvard Business School Press.

Ritzer G., 1993. *The McDonaldization of Society*. Newbury Park, CA: Pine Forge.

Shields, R. (Ed). 1992. *Lifestyle Shopping: the Subject of Consumption*. London: Routledge.

Storey, J. 1999. *Cultural Consumption and Everyday Life*. London: Arnold.

Thompson, J., 1995. *The Media and Modernity: a Social Theory of the Media* Cambridge: Polity Press.

16

The Social and Ecological Context

The focus of concern here is on those broader aspects of retail policy, effectively beyond management's control (albeit subject to some influence), which embed the firm in its environment:

- Political;
- Economic;
- Social;
- Technical; and
- Legal.

However, these are used only to place the following issues in context:

- Retailer responsibility, and the consideration of the social consequences of firm-level activity – the politics of choice;
- Ethical retailing and fair trade;
- The ecological impact of retail decisions; and
- Considerations of corporate ethics.

Introduction

Just as customers' interaction with the Servuction arena (see Chapter 6) is mediated by their particular personal and cultural context, so the actions of a retailer are bounded by the social and ecological environment in which it operates. These factors provide a set of implicit or explicit parameters that find expression in the political, legal, economic, social and technological aspects of the wider macro-environment within which retailers must trade. Each of these environmental factors obviously impacts the decisions that retailers make. However, to consider them fully at the individual level would extend the discussion beyond issues purely concerned with social and ecological concerns. In this chapter therefore, whilst these macro-economic factors are considered, this is only done where there is a direct social or ecological aspect.

Social and ecological concerns themselves can also be placed against a wider theoretical backdrop – that of business ethics. This area of interest brings with it a range of potential problems – the first being its definition. The debate about what ethics are, in the widest possible context, is one that has stretched over thousands of years and has developed into distinct areas of study including, for example moral philosophy. For many people, when asked what ethics is about, the answer provided is based around the difference between right and wrong. This would seem to suggest that there are potential 'absolutes' of ethical behaviour; or at the least, a clear demarcation. However, this is not the case. There is a degree of 'relativism' – as what constitutes 'right or 'wrong' in one social or cultural context may not be the case in another. This is reflected in the results of Burns and Brady (1996): who found different perceptions of retail ethics between students in Malaysia and the United States.

The issue of what ethics concerns is further complicated by the difficulty of reducing the set of constructs, attitudes and behaviours that are used to a simple bipolar position – that of right and wrong. Here, there are elements of 'acceptability', of 'interpretation' and of 'degree'. For some, given these problems, rather than attempting to provide an encompassing definition of ethics (even simply within a business context), the focus instead moves to consider process. Hunt and Vitell (1986) focus on 'ethical judgement', which they consider to be the mechanism that is used when an individual evaluates potential courses of action against the perceived probability and desirability of the consequences. Others display a similar perspective: considering probability of occurrence of an act weighted by the potential of the consequences to either do harm or provide benefit (Jones, 1991).

So, whilst it is difficult within the scope of this chapter to provide a definition of ethics that is acceptable to all that study the subject, it can be seen as being a set of social and individual guidelines that shape the nature of choices made, decisions taken and responses to them. These guidelines, which may not be constant and context-specific, therefore provide a lens through which action can be taken and evaluated.

As Schlegelmilch (1998) notes, the prominence of this particular lens increased throughout the 1990s – displayed, in part, by the increasing number of courses offered by universities, and the increasing attention paid to the subject by journals. Schlegelmilch (1998) also points out that there have been concomitant increases in both consumers' and investors' concerns about unethical practices. In the case of investors however, a degree of caution must be exercised. Balabanis et al. (1998), in a UK-based study, found that capital markets were indifferent to companies that undertook socially responsible activities and, in fact, disclosure of such activity had a *negative* impact; although companies have themselves placed greater stress on developing programmes and strategies that are 'ethical'. This level of corporate concern provides a starting point for examining the social and ecological contexts that impact retailers' strategies and operations.

Corporate Ethics and the Impact of Macro-Economic Factors

At the corporate level, the overall position of the company is set, not only in relation to the direction of business strategy, but also to its ethical stance. The company does not however operate in a vacuum – the decisions made by companies at the corporate level are clearly influenced by macro-environmental forces. This is also true for those decisions that either have an clear 'ethical' component (although it could be argued that all decisions taken at the corporate level have an ethical component); or relate to issues that are seen as being ethically sensitive. Singhapakdi et al. (2001), in their cross-cultural study, consider each of the macro-environmental factors in turn. However, the way that individual macro-environmental elements impinge on such decisions is primarily contingent upon the cultural (or social) context in which these decisions are made.

Social Impact on Ethical Decisions

Singhapakdi et al. (2001) suggest that differences in the underlying values of a culture result in managers in different countries displaying distinct attitudes to the importance of ethics and social responsibility in corporate decision-making. They use the typology based on the five dimensions developed by Hofstede (1980) and Hofstede and Bond (1988) to classify cultures:

- Individualism;
- Uncertainty avoidance;
- Power distance;
- Masculinity; and
- Confucian dynamism.

A rank is established for each dimension, which enables predictions to be made about the behaviour of individuals from any particular culture, based on their relative scores. Examples of the potential impact of different cultures can be seen between those cultures that are individualistic and those that are collectivist. In collectivist cultures, the greater dependence that individuals display would lead managers to place more emphasis on maintaining organizational effectiveness as a result of the loyalty that they are likely to feel to their employer. Equally, where a culture is 'masculine' – placing high value on ambitiousness and competitiveness – managers are also more likely to make decisions that are aimed to bolster their careers, rather than favouring ethics and social responsibility.

There is in these examples however, an implicit assumption that making decisions that are ethical and socially responsible means making decisions that do not maximize the efficiency of the company. This perhaps also highlights a cultural effect: that ethical and social responsible decisions are perceived as being 'extra'. This can be seen both in terms of the approach taken to decision-making itself i.e. ethics and social responsibility are primarily 'bolt-on' concerns, that will negatively impact corporate performance and efficiency and secondly, that in addressing such concerns the company will have to bear additional costs. In those countries with a Confucian perspective (e.g. China), this might not be the case. Here, the focus on the future might lead managers to see ethics and social responsibility as a primary concern in decision-making, rather than an adjunct. Although if a manager's future focus is centred on the *firm*, this may lead to behaviour at the other end of the spectrum.

Singhapakdi et al. (2001) found that mangers from countries with different rankings did indeed display distinct attitudes to ethics and social responsibility in relation to corporate efficiency in their decision making. Whilst this highlights the impact of culture and social context, it also emphasizes an area of potential difficulty for those companies trading internationally. In the retailing context, this provides potential concern at a number of levels.

Firstly, given the global nature of product-sourcing and the varying attitudes unearthed, there is the potential for culturally-generated 'conflict'. In countries displaying different attitudes to ethics and social responsibility, the decisions taken by either party (supplier or buyer) may lead to tension. Whilst such tension may be managed between the companies themselves, problems can occur when these 'differences' are displayed publicly. The criticisms levelled at some retailers for the practices of their international suppliers might be one such case in point. Secondly, when a company itself expands internationally, there may be tension generated between the stance of the company entering the country and that of the country itself. However, this conflict need not be readily apparent. For example, Marks and Spencer traded in France without apparent conflict for years. Although when it announced its intention to cease trading internationally and focus on its UK operation, subtle differences in attitudes towards ethical treatment and social responsibility in relation to employees came to the surface. These differences were additionally supported by the legal protection of employees' rights in France – which also illustrates that cultural differences can manifest themselves in the *legal* environment. This relationship is expressed by Beauchamp and Bowie (1993), who state that "Law is the public's agency for translating morality into explicit social guidelines and practices and stipulating offences" (p. 4).

Legal/Political Impact on Ethical Decisions

The impact of the legal/political environment on ethical decisions and social responsibility is directed by the social context. Legislative regulation indicates those areas of ethical concern and social responsibility within a culture that have a strength of feeling attached to them, which, in turn, precipitates 'formal' action. For example, there are differences in the culpability of firms in the USA and UK in relation to claims for personal damages as a result of 'harm' caused by product usage. This illustrates again that there are considerable differences to be found internationally. These distinctions can also extend to the degree of law enforcement (Singhapakdi et al., 2001).

Differences also arise as a result of political frameworks and agendas, which are again bounded by the cultural dimension. For example, the stance taken by American President George W. Bush on emissions and corporate adherence to internationally-agreed quotas, displays a stronger concern for the economic viability of the country rather than the suggested long-term health of the planet. This contrasts with the attitudes espoused by many of his European counterparts – where global ecological concern apparently outweighs the economic consideration of their respective countries. This also begins to highlight the potential of economic factors to play a role in the development of attitudes to ethical concerns in decision making.

Economic Impact on Ethical Decisions

Perhaps the most important consideration here is the 'type' of economic system within which a company operates. The predominant global form is now that of capitalism. The capitalist system has historically been criticized by those subscribing to a Marxist or socialist perspective for its exploitative nature. Nevertheless, the market has become the single most 'successful' economic form. Despite this success:

> Capitalism is not self-justifying as an economic system merely because it emerges spontaneously from the free exchanges that individuals may legitimately make under the rule of law (encompassing crime, contact, tort, and property) but has to be licensed by moralists using extra-market criteria....

Free trade, exchange and the search for profit are not intrinsically moral even when they are conducted within the confines of conventional ethics… [and] It is not enough for business to satisfy the wants of members of the community for better and cheaper products, more jobs and higher standards of living; it must also meet standards, which are not related to profit and economic progress. These standards, if too rigorously pursued, will ultimately undermine capitalism's capacity for satisfying what many of its critics call the 'baser' human instincts.

Barry, 2000, p. 5

Barry's underlying proposition rests on a distinction between two basic levels of morality in relation to companies: generic morality and supererogatory moral duties. Generic morality concerns 'the basic rules of the game' that are followed daily in order that business can take place, e.g. respect for property, sanctity of contract, and the promotion of trust and reliability in business dealings. Without such basic 'moral' propositions, the transaction of business would be difficult at best. These moral conditions, Barry refers to as "conventional ethics"; and this term encompasses issues related to the practice of business and the relationships within that business.

The second level, of supererogatory moral duties, relates to non-compulsory displays of social virtue e.g. donations to 'good' causes. Barry (2000) highlights that those companies that are best placed to take this kind of action are *private* companies (where profits belong to the owners, who can decide which social elements to support) and monopolies (where profits are likely to be large enough to satisfy shareholder obligations whilst funding such activity). Monopolies, are however, 'economically immoral' – which sets up a potential dichotomy. Barry goes on to suggest the such 'moral duties' are beyond the normal scope of business, and, in fact, begin to potentially undermine the very fabric of many organizations by making them resemble political organisms.

For many, it is as much the *generic* morality of companies under capitalism that causes concern. Barry (2000) specifically considers the Anglo-American form of capitalism, and states that transgressions of generic morality often become apparent as a result of the relative transparency of companies operating under this system. He suggests that this transparency is one of the strongest elements in ensuring that companies remain 'moral'. Where transgressions occur, the company concerned often suffers economically and therefore – in the long term such actions are often as harmful to the well-being of the company as they are to society. His overall contention is that companies in capitalist systems are subject to the best regulator of all – competition; and that, to survive, they cannot cross the generic moral code. This proposition is also supported by Takala and Uusitalo (1996), who, in discussing the nature of the economic environment in most European countries, state that the

> ...system can endure only if it operates in such a way that the majority of people believe that at least some amount of justice prevails in it. If the system lacks legitimacy, it is likely to fail.

The nature of the economy is, however, only one factor. Other pressures on both corporate generic morality and supererogatory moral duties come from economic drivers.

Where a country is seeking economic growth as a primary driver, there may be less emphasis on ethics and social responsibility, as the impetus is for the development of profit within the corporate sector. This again displays an underlying assumption that adopting an ethical perspective to business decisions inhibits maximization of profit. Economic drivers can stem from the nature of the business environment itself. Singhapakdi et al. (2001) suggest that, in economies that are characterized by powerful businesses, there is an expectation that companies will behave ethically. They also note that in developing countries, as business and economic environmental forces are still evolving, the importance of business ethics and social responsibility may be lower than those displayed by companies in developed economies. However, they also propose that these factors could also precipitate the opposite effect – leading companies to actually be more ethical and socially responsible to provide the company with competitive advantage. This proposition raises further questions: Is it possible for managers within a company to make ethical decisions and display social responsibility simply as a competitive tool? And, if this is the case, then what are the implications? Should such actions be condoned and encouraged? Or, should such behaviour be accepted, whatever its motivation?

Technological Impact on Ethical Decisions

Unlike the other macro-environmental factors, the impact of technology on ethics and social responsibility is less 'directive' in its effect. Rather than impacting beliefs, or providing a strong attitudinal stimulus for or against 'ethical' activity, technology removes potential obstacles, or, sometimes, creates new problems.

For example, if supply takes place at an international level, technology facilitates communication and travel – thereby removing barriers such as physical distance, that previously precluded buyers verifying and monitoring the practices of suppliers. In other circumstances, technological advancement can provide solutions to ethical problems: for instance, limiting the amount of ecological damage that results from transporting goods, by using more efficient engines or catalytic converters in distribution fleets. The use of such technologies will obviously be moderated by the combined effect of the other macro-economic factors.

Technology can also create problems with ethical and social implications. If, for example, Internet retailing is considered, this can raise the issue of social exclusion. Only those that have access to the appropriate technology can derive the 'benefits' of Internet shopping. This means that those that do not have access – often those who are considered disadvantaged or vulnerable – are effectively precluded from gaining these benefits. At the same time, the Internet has the potential to be 'inclusive', as it gives easy access to retail provision to those customers with mobility problems (Morganosky and Crude, 2000).

The Internet also provides a mechanism for disseminating information; and this has been used to highlight areas of concern over the practices of retailers and other businesses, as well as providing a platform for the publishing of 'good works' (Whysall, 2000). Again, though, there are issues related to the ability to access this information.

Technology, therefore, alongside other macro-environmental factors, develops a framework of values, regulation, competitive pressures and potential problems and solutions within which managers must operate in relation to business ethics and social responsibility. The combination of these elements therefore creates a setting in which choices are made.

The Broadening of Ethical Issues

The macro-environmental factors outlined above impact the way in which choices can be made, as well as providing a complex framework for decision-making. However, the range of 'specific' areas in which such decisions need to be taken has broadened. This is true for all corporations, but perhaps especially for retailers – stemming from their unique position in the distribution channel. Retailers need to consider a wide range of issues in relation to their own practices; as well as the practices of their suppliers, and the perceptions of both their customers and shareholders, where applicable.

Current ethical concerns facing retailers based in western countries can therefore cover a broad spectrum of subjects:

- Fair trade policies (e.g. Strong, 1996; Strong, 1997; Dennis et al., 1998).
- Product safety and purity (for example, the concern over the use of genetically-modified foodstuffs (e.g. Jones et al., 2000; Pearce and Hanson, 2000)).

- Animal husbandry and welfare (including animal testing (e.g. Dennis et al., 1998)).
- Worker exploitation and child labour (Christian Aid Reports, 1999; Christian Aid Reports, 1996).
- Production methods and practices.
- The provision of honest and easily understood information – including labelling and promotion claims (e.g. Pearce, 1999; Dennis et al., 1998).
- Environmental issues – including obtaining materials from sustainable sources; trading in products derived from protected species; the use of packaging; the use of chemicals in production; the disposal of waste, and the location of stores (Dennis et al., 1998; Jones, 1996; Strong, 1995).
- Social exclusion – including lack of access due to non-car ownership, rural locations or income (Williams and Windebank, 2001; Clarke, 2000; Ellaway and Macintyre, 2000; Jones, 1996).
- Pricing issues – including selling at supernormal profits, and deceptive pricing.
- The targeting of 'vulnerable' groups – in particular, children.
- The invasion of privacy – primarily through the (mis)use of information technology (Whysall, 2000; Whysall, 1995).
- Staff selection, work practices (Broadbridge, 2000) and remuneration.
- The provision of ethical practices in the workplace – including policies on harassment and bullying (Broadbridge, 2000).
- Treatment of suppliers.
- Industrial espionage and sabotage.
- Responsibility to shareholders.
- Adherence to high standards of corporate governance i.e. issues of disclosure and propriety.

Decisions made in relation to each concern have implications for the retailer, the consumer and for society in general. There are also extensive interrelationships between individual concerns; and actions taken in relation to one issue may impact another concern – either negatively or positively. This means that decisions cannot be made in isolation, and that the politics of choice need extensive and careful consideration. For example providing organic produce may mean charging prices that exclude some members of society; or by opening a large out-of-town store offering lower prices, smaller neighbourhood retailers (who tend to charge higher prices) may be forced to close – potentially limiting competition and choice.

Given this list, and the possible interrelationships, it is impossible to provide a detailed discussion of each topic within a single chapter. Therefore two major topics from the list have been selected – fair trade and environmental issues – because both have received considerable attention in the academic and public arenas. However, before considering the specifics of these two issues, it would seem appropriate to consider the emergence of ethical retailing in a 'modern' sense.

The Dawn of Ethical Retailing

One of the oldest retailer organizations in the UK that is closely aligned to taking an ethical approach – and indeed societal responsibility more generally – is the Co-operative Movement. From its very inception, the Co-operative Movement has had a strong ethical component. The impetus for its creation stemmed from a strong belief that a new form of society was needed to address the social problems of the late nineteenth century (see also Chapter 2). It was founded on a 'socialist' creed that sought brotherhood rather than selfishness, and unity rather than competition (Baren, 1996). The Movement's founding principles identified:

> … open membership; democratic control… payment of limited interest on capital; political and religious neutrality, cash trading and promotion of education.
>
> Birchall, 1994, p. 54

The co-operative model of retailing is to be found across much of Europe. The development and extent of its rise is however, distinct in many countries. What does provide a common thread is their "advocacy of morality in trade" (Purvis, 1999).

However, co-operative societies were not the first stirrings of a collectivist ethic in the provision of goods. Bamfield (1999) documents the development of consumer-owned community flour and bread societies in England, which flourished between the mid-eighteenth and mid-nineteenth centuries. These organizations, in line with the principles of the Victorian Co-operative Movement, provided low-priced goods and 'pure' food; traded on cash and not credit; limited the role of capital; had wide membership, and in some cases, were democratic (Bamfield, 1999). As Bamfield also highlights, many of these organizations stated that they operated for the benefit of the poor (although the poorest members of society were probably unable to participate, due to their lack of equity). These early co-operative enterprises laid the seeds for a socially responsible organizational form of retailing and trading practices that would be adopted by later retail societies.

Co-Operative Retail Societies

The most well-known of the early UK co-operative societies is that of the

Rochdale Society of Equitable Pioneers established in 1844. The aims and 'ethical' stance of the Society also extended well-beyond supplying goods at affordable prices, and included the building or purchasing of houses to improve members' social and domestic conditions, as well as promoting sobriety. These broader societal aims were augmented by a key decision regarding the way that the Society would be structured and run.

The Society's founders resolved to distribute profit to its members in proportion to the amount of money that they spent in the store. This decision displays not only a particular ethical stance, but was also taken with a clear 'business' goal in mind. It also reflects the fact that both co-operative societies and their members were equally motivated by practical and principled concerns (Purvis, 1999). The distribution of what was termed 'dividend' also helped to ensure that, not only was there an incentive to become a member of the Society, but that members were also more likely to shop in the store as it provided them with positive benefits – increasing their propensity to be loyal. This practice became a common component of co-operative societies' offers: further accentuating that these organizations were run for the 'benefit' of their many members – who also constituted, in part at least, their customers.

This approach was markedly different to the ethos of most retail companies at the time, who were run to benefit an owner or small group of owners – many of whom were not necessarily those companies' customers. The issue of ownership through membership, and the ultimate management of the organization by these members, means that co-operative societies have remained distinct in many ways from other retail operations. The founding principles have also meant that the stance taken by co-operative societies has remained somewhat distinct from many other retailers.

The Ethical Position of Modern Co-operative Retailing

The 'principled' beginnings of the Co-operative Movement have continued to play a role in the development of retail societies to the present day. For example, the CWS – one of the UK's largest societies – commissioned research on consumers' attitudes to food safety in 2000 (Gordon-Seymour and Beddall, 2000). The results suggest that three-quarters of UK consumers have concerns regarding the production of the food that they purchase, and highlight what have been termed seven 'food crimes' by the Society:

- Blackmail – the use of corporations' substantial backing to promote products that fail to comply with advice on healthy eating.

- Contamination – the unnecessary use of 'chemicals' on land and in live-stock.
- Grievous bodily harm – the disregard for animal welfare in an attempt to minimize costs.
- Vandalism – the negative ecological impact of mass farming methods.
- Cannibalism – the practice of feeding animals with the remains of their own (or related) species.
- Pillage – exploitation of countries, cultures and creeds by multinationals.
- Fraud – the deliberate 'assault' on the taste and appearance of food.

The language used is emotive, and the report itself was heavily criticized by others in the trade, as well as by the Food and Drink Federation, who suggested that the report was aimed solely at achieving competitive gain. However, it was suggested by a senior manager of the Society that…

> The Co-op cannot ignore the overwhelming sense of unease among shoppers towards the food industry. The way the world rears its animals, grows its crops and markets food is beginning to sicken the public. It's time to take action.
>
> Gordon-Seymour and Beddall, 2000, p. 6

The authenticity of the stance taken by the Society is perhaps enhanced by the nature and history of the organization and the wider Movement. The Co-operative Movement was established with supererogatory moral duties at its core. Its corporate form is different from the vast majority of retailers – and therefore its duties are also distinct. The stance taken does not seem to be as unlikely as that adopted by other retailers. So, whilst it could be suggested that this view has been projected to create competitive advantage, it is this very type of value system that originally spurred the rise of such organizations – be it the consumer-owned community flour and bread societies of England, or the rise of the Victorian Co-operative Societies themselves.

The issue related to 'pillage' is perhaps the most modern – in that increasing international trade and the economic distance between the retailer's operating countries and the countries within which its suppliers operate, has brought this concern to a higher level of prominence. The ethics of international supply perhaps did not manifest themselves to the same degree in the early Co-operative Movement, for two primary reasons: the level of international supply was more limited; but perhaps more controversially, attitudes to exploitation were less well developed. These factors have, however, both changed significantly recently, making issues of fair trade much more prominent.

Fair Trade

The concept of fair trade was established to promote equitable trade between the First and Third Worlds (Strong, 1997), and involves co-operative, rather than competitive, trading principles – ensuring fair price and fair working conditions for the producers and suppliers (Strong, 1996). It became an issue that received considerable attention, particularly in the 1990s, with the 'success' of companies such as the Body Shop and Oxfam Trading and Trade-craft. The impetus for fair trade stems from:

- The evolving caring consumer of the 1990s;
- Pressure group support for fairer trading practices with the Third World;
- Increasing media interest in fair trade issues;
- Increasing corporate responsibility;
- Increasing supplier power in the marketplace.

Strong, 1997

The nature of the fair trade concept, and a number of the reasons for its stated elevation in importance, can be considered within the definition of generic morality provided by Barry (2000). Poor treatment of suppliers and unscrupulous practices will damage the reputation of a company, and this warrants 'fair trade' from a 'purely business perspective' as well as a moral one. The potential for such practices, in their own right, to provide sustainable competitive advantage, however, is less clear. The Body Shop provides an example of these potential difficulties.

The company, and its founder, Anita Roddick, have always been associated with ethical trading and the application of 'high' moral principles to the business – not only in relation to 'trade not aid', but also in relation to their refusal to use substances tested on animals in products, as well as in relation to human rights issues. The company enjoyed a high degree of success until the mid-1990s, when it experienced a drop in the price of its stock. This was partly as a result of the increasing scrutiny of the Body Shop's business methods, and its moral sincerity, which placed the company under an exacting and revealing investigation (Barry, 2000). This detailed examination of the company was damning – all the claims made by the company were examined, and it was suggested that they were potentially "deceptive" and "little more than publicity stunts" (Dennis et al., 1998).

The Body Shop's 'trade not aid' programme was among the areas of business practice examined. The company did not disclose, or respond to requests for information regarding the percentage of its raw materials that were actually sourced through this programme (Dennis et al., 1998), and there is little evidence to support the claim that the programme has delivered the benefits proposed to the producers involved. Such concerns were also accompanied by increased competition from rivals, who took on many of the 'ethical' practices of the company for themselves. This combination of examination and appropriation of practice acted as the foundation for the company's problems. The advantage, both moral and competitive, had been effectively eroded.

What this example also begins to illustrate is that the 'rules of the game' are subject to change. The generic morality that guides business dealings is itself not static, nor is it purely defined by the economic nature of the market that a company operates within. It is as much part of the wider issue of the underlying generic morality of the society within which the company is based. For instance, when society as a whole no longer accepts the use of animals for the testing of cosmetics, or when it rejects slavery or child labour, these moral values become as much part of the 'game' as is the honouring of contracts. These socially-defined morals are often displayed not simply in terms of general attitude, but are also expressed through the consumption behaviour of individual consumers. There has already been the suggestion that consumers are now much more concerned with the business ethics applied by industry. However, the most powerful mechanism through which they can voice their concerns is by modifying their purchasing behaviour – applying the most vital part of the regulatory power of competition. Here, there are issues related to the attitude voiced by consumers and the behaviour that they display. (These concerns are discussed later in the chapter.)

Given that the rules of the business game are inextricably bound-up with those of the specific society the 'game' operates in, this serves to reinforce that such rules are likely to vary between countries. This in turn can create difficulties in putting into practice principles such as fair trade. For example, a US-based retailer uses a programme of fair trade to import cocoa from a South American country. The prices paid are 'fair'; the cocoa is produced with due regard for the care of the workforce and for the environment. However, the cocoa producer employs some children aged thirteen – a practice that is within the rules of the game in that country. This is clearly at variance, though, with the rules of the game as played in the United States. So, does this mean that the retailer is acting unethically, or that it is the producer – or is it both organizations? If it can be judged that there is unethical behaviour taking place, what are the implications for fair trade? For instance, if it is determined that the retailer is at fault, and it then stops its trading association with the producer, does this create more harm than if they had continued to trade? These questions have no single best or right answer – the decisions taken are guided by the underlying ethical standard of the individual, the corporation and society.

As part of the consideration of fair trade, there has also been examination of the related issue of 'sustainable development', which encompasses issues of economic, self-sustained and supportable growth. The final element here begins to highlight the importance of ensuring that as a result of fair trade, there is no adverse environmental impact that, in the end, will precipitate more harm than good – not only for those directly involved, but also on a much broader basis. Such environmental concerns have also received wide-scale attention from governments, the public and organizations alike.

Environmental Issues

The large-scale growth in environmental concern within organizations was evident in the early 1970s in America, where federal government passed a raft of new environmental laws (Meyer, 2000). The period between the mid-1960s and early 1970s (see Chapter 3) has been accredited as the beginning of what it is suggested will, in the final analysis, be seen as a defining element of the of twentieth century – environmentalism (Caldwell, 1997). There has been a steady increase in the number of consumers who state that they are at least 'concerned' about the state of the environment – although not activists in the environmental movement (Dunlap, 1997). This is mirrored by an increase in the number of corporations that have expressed that they are wherever possible, taking action to modify their business practices to ones that are environmentally responsible (Grove et al., 1996; Meyer, 2000). This means that a vast range of organizational issues have come under examination from an environmental perspective. Grove et al. (1996) suggest that this broad range of considerations can be summarized by examining the underlying nature of an activity in relation to its proposed environmental impact. They suggest three categories of action: re-using, recycling and reducing – sometimes referred to as the '3 Rs' formula for environmental management. The aim here is to control the unnecessary and detrimental wasting of natural resources in the pursuit of corporate activity, by applying (at least) one of the categories of action.

Re-Using

For example, a retailer might re-use packaging materials by offering containers that can be refilled. The Body Shop is an obvious example of a retailer that has such a policy. However, such practices have actually existed for centuries e.g. the re-use of glass bottles for drinks, or the Roman practice of simply replenishing their amphorae with olive oil. This practice can be seen in door-step deliveries of milk, where bottles are used, returned, refilled and used again and again – the milk bottle remaining the property of the supplying company and the customer deriving additional benefit by not having to dispose of the packaging. It can also be seen in the selling of other fresh foods such as eggs through markets and local stores, where empty egg cartons are taken and re-filled. This re-use extends to carrier bags, many of which are re-used by customers for their original purpose. This activity has led many supermarkets to offer 'a bag for life' – customers' purchasing much stronger bags that have a considerably longer life-expectancy. (Once the bag 'dies', the customer can take it to the store and 'swap' it for a new one.)

One of the other less obvious areas is the 're-use' of merchandise. There are those retailers that sell second-hand merchandise and in so doing, could be seen as 're-using' it. These retailers have made a fundamental decision regarding their market position and merchandise – that even though not necessarily taken with an underlying environmental concern, has ecological implications. To bring second-hand merchandise to market uses significantly less resources than supplying new ones. This means therefore – just as with re-using packaging, but on a much larger scale – that natural resources are not unduly wasted.

Recycling

Where straight re-use is not feasible, then there is the possibility of recycling. For retailers, this can come both from the products sold themselves and from the by-products of the process of getting them to market e.g. paper and card from the boxes used by suppliers in distributing goods.

Retailers not only have the potential to look inside their own businesses for opportunities to recycle, but can also influence the practices of both their suppliers and customers. In fact, to make the full use of recycling opportunities, the co-operation of these groups is necessary. For example, customers returning 'unwanted' refrigerators, which are then passed back to suppliers for recycling. In this instance, the retailer acts as a member of a chain of both purchase and disposal that provides a positive environmental impact, compared to the alternative of normal disposal.

In the UK grocery market, retailers also frequently offer 'recycling points' for customers. These often include the provision of paper, glass, clothing and fabric and shoe recycling points. However, there is significantly less provision for the recycling of plastics and metal. The 'need' for retailers to offer such facilities is also partially dependent on the recycling provision of the country or area itself. Where consumer recycling is actively managed through government agencies or provision e.g. in Germany, then there is less 'benefit' to be gained by retailers duplicating these arrangements. Whilst recycling provides a clear environmental benefit – irrespective of who organizes it – there is perhaps the potential to derive even more benefit by not unnecessarily using resources wherever possible.

MANAGING RETAIL CONSUMPTION

Reducing

In the first instance, reducing the level of impact that business has on natural resources is perhaps the 'purest' form of corporate environmentalism. This can be done in a number of ways. One of the easiest is the reduction of energy consumption, waste, and pollution. Such activity may have positive economic benefits for the company, although "…it is very difficult to isolate the impact of the environmental work on the overall profitability of the company" (Pujari and Wright, 1996). It is also often readily achievable, making it a popular starting point for companies in their environmental efforts (Meyer, 2000). For example, retailers and manufacturers have reduced the amount of packaging used. There has also been increased interest in developing products that are themselves needed in reduced amounts e.g. concentrated detergents – or that use reduced inputs such as energy-efficient electrical goods. Those products that are 'concentrated' also often require less packaging, again helping to reduce the resources associated with them.

The service aspect of a product offer can also be reduced. This may, though, involve the 're-engineering' or reworking of service processes to lessen environmental impact, rather than a simple reduction of the materials involved (Grove et al., 1996). For example, rather than simply replacing towels each day in a hotel, guests are asked to indicate their desire for clean towels by placing them in a distinct location. Housekeeping staff then 'read' the signs and act accordingly: either providing clean towels, or not – the purpose being to reduce the environmental impact of laundering towels daily and perhaps unnecessarily.

The three issues of re-using, recycling and reducing, provide a basic framework for considering environmental issues in relation to retailing – or indeed any business. However, these issues serve to primarily highlight the 'actions' taken, rather than to consider the extent to which these actions are truly motivated by ethical concerns or a sense of social responsibility. Whilst on a surface level there is clear environmental benefit, the question is: Has this been prompted by ethical concern, or is it a manifestation of some other motivational force?

The Reality of Ethical and Social Responsibility in Retailing

The preceding discussion highlights that for retailers, there is a wide range of ethical considerations that can affect the choices made in terms of both strategic and operational issues. It could be suggested that such issues are becoming increasingly part of the rules of the game; so to what extent do they actually impact retailers' decisions?

Piacentini et al. (2000) investigated the motivation of retailers in relation to actions that could be seen as displaying a degree of social responsibility. Their study, although limited in geographic coverage, but specific in its context, concludes, after discussion with retail decision-makers, that the actions taken are the result of customer orientation rather than social responsibility. Seeing that customers' perceptions of the rules of the game have shifted, retailers then work to realign their practices within these new boundaries. However, as Piacentini et al. (2000) also note, many retailers – particularly smaller ones – do not take actions that could be deemed socially responsible: suggesting that, not only are they not acting in this manner, they also show little market orientation.

It would seem that for some, especially the larger retailers, the impetus for taking what could be deemed socially responsible action *is* the customer. This would seem to accord with Schlegelmilch's (1998) comment that the rise in the importance of business ethics is in part due to changing patterns of moral value in consumers themselves, and that for retailers, these values are expressed through purchasing behaviour (Whysall, 1995).

The Key Role of the Customer

In research conducted for Retail Week in 1996 within the UK, ethical considerations were not identified as the predominant concerns for product choice in the majority of the six retail sectors examined – grocery, clothes, shoes, electrical/electronics, DIY and liquor (Wills, 1996). The most important issues were price, style and quality – however, there was increasing awareness of ethical considerations: ranging from child labour to environmental concerns. This is echoed in the findings of Schlegelmilch et al. (1996), who identified that environmental consciousness may impact purchasing, but that such decisions are also influenced by other moderating factors.

However, where customers have taken a united and obvious stance on ethical issues – e.g. the use of CFCs in packaging and aerosols or child labour usage by the suppliers of Levi and Wal-Mart (The Economist, 1995) – there has been swift action on the part of business to address these concerns. Jones (1996) highlights that it is in the role of consumer that there is, for many, the most effective outlet for expressing dissent and exerting influence – through their 'wallets'. Customers are willing to punish unethical behaviour by withdrawing their support, and are also willing to reward ethical behaviour by paying higher prices (Creyer and Ross, 1997). However, customers' willingness to undertake either of these actions is influenced by the importance placed on the ethical behaviour, and, to a lesser degree, by their expectations of how a firm should behave (Creyer and Ross, 1997).

These concerns also extend to the degree of sophistication that customers display in terms of their knowledge of the marketplace. Titus and Bradford (1996) suggest that choice in modern western markets, allied with increasingly pressured lifestyles, leads customers to exhibit less knowledge than might be assumed. This, in turn, can lead to their displaying a concomitant lack of sophistication in relation to ethical considerations. This is described by Strong (1997), who comments that, whilst a customer may purchase Café Direct, they could conceivably pay for it with money taken from a wallet produced by a workforce in a Third World location under conditions of extreme exploitation.

So, the suggestion is that, whilst consumers provide a central element in determining the ethical behaviour of firms, their influence is perhaps at best selective and inconsistent. This, Titus and Bradford (1996) state, highlights the need for intervention on the part of government to provide guidelines that constitute the 'rules of the game'. They also suggest that the influence of competition is not enough to shape ethical behaviour, as it rests ultimately on the level of customer sophistication displayed in any particular market. Given the inconsistencies emphasized previously, competition alone is not sufficient to ensure ethical behaviour by firms – necessitating the use of other macro-environmental factors.

Conclusions

The macro-economic factors listed at the beginning of the chapter are of key importance in forming the basis for a firm's approach to ethical concerns – especially those related to the legal, political, economic, and social (in the shape of both consumers' attitudes and the larger framework of social values that these are located within). The nature of the relationship between these factors and the relative merits and extent to which intervention, competition and customer power act as regulators of ethical behaviour in firms, will continue to generate extensive debate. However, it is unlikely that there will be a definitive understanding of the complexities of their impact on corporate ethics.

However, what is evident is that the issues of social responsibility and ethics are unlikely to decrease in importance – both for customers and thereby for companies. The issues are also widening in their scope, and whilst the exact extent to which the actions taken are motivated by true ethical concern or by other issues, such as customer orientation, and the seeking of competitive advantage is difficult to determine, the likelihood is however, that such actions will continue also to rise in number.

Retailers cannot ignore these concerns, and must develop appropriate actions in response. In doing this, there is a need to consider the implications of such actions beyond their immediate scope, and to examine the interrelationships that exist. Only by doing this can retailers take actions that can be truly described as ethical. The adoption of such thinking has implications for the company and its culture. Whilst not explicitly explored in this chapter, the corporate culture of an organization also has a part to play in influencing the decisions made by those inside the firm and the ethical component of that choice (Carter, 2000). Retailers must therefore balance the requirements of the macro-environmental factors with the creation of appropriate corporate context.

References

Balabanis, G., Phillips, H.C. and Lyall, J. 1998. Corporate social responsibility and economic performance in the top British companies: are they linked? *European Business Review*, 98(1), 25–44.

Bamfield, J. 1999. Consumer-owned community flour and bread societies in the eighteenth and early nineteenth centuries. In Alexander, A. and Akehurst, G. *The Emergence of Modern Retailing, 1750–1950*. London: Frank Cass, pp. 16–36.

Baren, M. 1996. *How It All Began: Up The High Street*. London: Michael O'Mara Books Limited.

Barry, N. 2000. *Respectable Trade: the Dangerous Delusions of Corporate Social Responsibility and Business Ethics*. London: Adam Smith Research Trust.

Beauchamp, T.L. and Bowie, N.E. 1993. *Ethical theory and Business*. Englewood Cliffs, NJ: Prentice Hall.

Birchall, J. 1994. Co-op: the people's business. Manchester: Manchester University Press.

Broadbridge, A. 2000. Stress and the female retail manager. *Women in Management Review, 15(3), 145–156*.

Burns, D.J. and Brady, J.T. 1996. Retail ethics appraised by future business personnel in Malaysia and the United States. *Journal of Consumer Affairs*, 30(1), 195–217.

Caldwell, L.K. 1997. Globalizing environmentalism: threshold of a new phase in international relations. In McDonagh, P. and Prothero, A. (Eds.). *Green Management: a Reader*. London: Dryden Press, pp. 40–54.

Carter, C.R. 2000. Precursors of Unethical behavior in global supplier management. *Journal of Supply Chain Management*, 36(1), 45.

Christian Aid Reports, 1999. *A Sporting Chance: Tracking Child Labour in India's Sports Goods Industry*. London: Christian Aid.

Christian Aid Reports, 1996. *The Global Supermarket: Britain's Biggest Shops and Food from the Third World*. London: Christian Aid.

Clarke, I. 2000. Retail power, competition and local consumer choice in the UK grocery sector. *European Journal of Marketing*, 34(8), 975–1002.

Creyer, E.H. and Ross, W.T. Jr. 1997. The influence of firm behavior on purchase: do consumers really care about business ethics? 14(6), 421–432.

Dennis, B., Neck, C.P. and Goldsby, M. 1998. Body Shop International: an exploration of corporate social responsibility. *Management Decision*, 36(10), 649–653.

Dunlap, R.E. 1997. Trends in public opinion toward environmental issues 1965–1990. In McDonagh, P. and Prothero, A. (Eds.). *Green Management: a Reader.* London: Dryden Press, pp. 40–54.

Ellaway, A. and Macintyre, S. 2000. Shopping for food in socially contrasting localities. *British Food Journal*, 102(1), 52–59.

Gordon-Seymour, N. and Beddall, C. 2000. Crimes? This is a stunt! – FDF. *Grocer*, 223(7456), 6.

Grove, S.J., Fisk, R.P., Pickett, G.M. and Kangun, N. 1996. Going green in the service sector: social responsibility issues, implications and implementation. *European Journal of Marketing*, 30(5), 56–66.

Hofstede, G. 1980. National cultures in four dimensions: a research based theory of cultural differences among nations. *International Studies of Management and Organization*, 13(1/2), 46–74.

Hofstede, G. and Bond, M.H. 1988. The Confucius connection: from cultural roots to economic growth. *Organizational Dynamics*, 16(4), 5–21.

Hunt, S.D. and Vitell, S. 1986. A general theory of marketing ethics. Journal of Macromarketing, 6(1), 5–16.

Jones, J. 1996. Polling in the aisles. *New Statesman*, 127(4377), 32–34.

Jones, P., Clarke-Hill, C., Hillier, D. and Shears, P. 2000. Food retailers' responses to the GM controversy within the UK. *British Food Journal*, 102(5/6), 441–448.

Jones, T.M. 1991. Ethical decision-making by individuals in organizations: an issue-contingent model. *Academy of Management Review*, 16(2), 366–395.

Meyer, H. 2000. The greening corporate America. *Journal of Business Strategy*, 21(1), 28.

Morganosky, M.A. and Crude, B.J. 2000. Consumer response to online grocery shopping. *International Journal of Retail and Distribution Management*, 28(1), 17–26.

Pearce, R. 1999. Social responsibility in the marketplace: asymmetric information in food labelling. *Business Ethics: A European Review*, 8, 26–36.

Pearce, R. and Hanson, M. 2000. Retailing and risk society: genetically modified food. *International Journal of Retail and Distribution Management*, 28(11), 450–459.

Piacentini, M., MacFadyen, L. and Eadie, D. 2000. Corporate social responsibility in food retailing. *International Journal of Retail and Distribution Management*, 28(11), 459–469.

Pujari, D. and Wright, G. 1996. Developing environmentally conscious product strategies: a qualitative study of selected companies in Germany and Britain. *Marketing Intelligence and Planning*, 14(1), 19–28.

Purvis, M. 1999. Stocking the store: co-operative retailers in north-east England and systems of wholesale supply, circa 1860–77. In Alexander, N. and Akehurst, G. *The Emergence of Modern Retailing, 1750–1950.* London: Frank Cass, pp. 55–78.

Schlegelmilch, B.B. 1998. *Marketing Ethics: an International Perspective.* London: International Thompson Business Press.

Schlegelmilch, B.B., Bohlen, G. and Diamantopoulos, A. 1996. The link between green purchasing and measures of environmental consciousness. *European Journal of Marketing*, 30(5), 35–55.

Singhapakdi, A., Karande, K., Rao, C.P. and Vitell, S.J. 2001. How important are ethics and social responsibility? – A multinational study of marketing professionals. *European Journal of Marketing*, 35(1/2), 133–152.

Strong, C. 1997. The problems of transplanting fair trade principles into consumer purchase behaviour. *Marketing Intelligence and Planning*, 15(1), 32–38.

Strong, C. 1996. Features contributing to the growth of ethical consumerism – a preliminary investigation. Marketing Intelligence and Planning, 14(5), 5–13.

Strong, C. 1995. Are grocery retail buyers making greener purchasing decisions? *Greener Management International*, 11, 103–112.

Takala, T. and Uusitalo, O. 1996. An alternative view of relationship marketing: a framework for ethical analysis. *European Journal of Marketing*, 30(2), 45–60.

The Economist. 1995. Human rights: ethical shopping. *The Economist (US)*, 335(7917), 58–59.

Titus, P.A. and Bradford, J.L. 1996. Reflections on consumer sophistication and its impact on ethical business practice. Journal of Consumer Affairs, 30(1), 170–194.

Whysall, P. 2000. Retailing and the Internet: a review of ethical issues. *International Journal of Retail and Distribution Management*, 28(11), 481–489.

Whysall, P. 1995. Ethics in retailing. *Business Ethics: a European Review*, 4, 150–156.

Williams, C.C. and Windebank, J. 2001. Acquiring goods and services in lower income populations: an evaluation of consumer behaviour and preferences. *International Journal of Retail and Distribution Management*, 29(1), 16–24.

Wills, J. 1996. How ethical is your shopper? *Retail Week*, 19th January, 12–14.

Part 4

The Retail Future

17

CONCLUSIONS AND PROGNOSIS

This chapter provides specific consideration of a number of emerging themes identified throughout the book, and that can be discerned as operating in much of retailing. The merchandise and services that western consumers need, want and desire, are placed in the context of both developments in retailing, and in consumption. The following, sometimes competing, themes are highlighted:

- The diverging of retail into pleasure-oriented centres of consumption and utilitarian loci of supply – a division however, not solely based on the ability to pay, as it was historically.
- The prospect of the return of manufacturing to the site of retail – against the clear trend of retailing attached to manufacturing (such as factory outlets).
- Retail internationalization and consumption convergence.
- Identification through material wealth – the limits of sustainability, and the rise of the spiritual (post-materialist?) consumer.

Introduction

The central approach of this book has been the consideration of retailing from the consumer's perspective – encompassing a wide assortment of issues, that includes:

- The impact of location and the physical environment;
- The selection of merchandise;
- The nature of retail strategy; and
- The effects of interpersonal contact.

This wide range reflects the fundamental premise that retailing can be more than just a simple mechanism for the distribution of goods, but can also be a social activity – both as a point of interaction, and as part of the very fabric of our society.

This viewpoint parallels the suggestion that the act of consumption itself is not solely based on an economic-materialist rationale, but is, in fact, one that necessarily has a psychological-cultural dimension (Campbell, 1995).

The retail store therefore fulfils a number of roles. This requires that retailers look beyond managing the store from a purely economic perspective to acknowledging that the space that they operate is one where more than material exchanges take place (which is already reflected in the practices of a growing number of contemporary retailers). In adopting such a view, there is of course, a probability that the economic performance of the business will be increased. However, to fully capitalize on this, managing the retail store needs to be approached as a holistic endeavour that takes account of the varied nature of retail provision and its potential role in the wider social context.

Managing the Consumption Arena

The retail store has acted as the focus of this text, as it is the main form of retail provision in the majority of situations, and acts as the primary 'space' in which the consumption of goods, services and experiences takes place. Therefore, the management of this 'consumption arena' is – and always has been – of central importance to the retailer. However, the approach taken when conducting this role is one that now, perhaps more than ever, calls for balance – of efficiency and effectiveness, of conception and execution, and of the roles of retailers and consumers themselves.

One of the major reasons for this rests in the development of a postmodern society and the associated practices and concerns that denote such cultural movement. Most important among these shifts, for the retail sector, are:

- Fragmentation – both at the wider social level and that of an individual's self-concept(s);
- The centrality of image; and
- The elevation of consumption to the chief mechanism for identity creation.

This latter shift in particular, places the retailer in an unparalleled, central position – locating them not only between producer and customer as the primary element within the 'sphere of circulation'; but also connecting consumers and their acts of identity formation. In this way, retailers are a creative resource, providing both the 'material' and the 'space' for such activity. This pivotal role reinforces the notion that the key concern of the modern retailer should be one of balance.

Balancing Efficiency and Effectiveness

This notion of balance can be considered at a number of levels. The first relates to one of the central threads of this text, and concerns the balance between the elements of efficiency and effectiveness as expressed by the Servuction model. Here, the functional requirements of operating the retail store must be aligned with the need to provide a 'theatrical' space for the creation and enactment of consumption. Both elements therefore need to be present to develop a retail offer that provides an appropriate environment to stimulate customer satisfaction and fulfil the requirements of retail management – again reflecting the notion that consumption is based on both economic and social requirements. It is simply not enough for a retailer to develop an offer that provides maximum efficiency (thereby focusing on economic issues) if in so doing, they inhibit or curtail the potential for providing a space with which customers can engage (i.e. ignoring the social aspect of consumption).

This however, does not mean that for every retailer there is a need to construct an overtly 'theatrical' offer; but rather that there needs to be a much clearer consideration of the nature of the drama to be enacted. The motive here should be to generate an offer that does not merely apply theatrical devices at the surface level. Instead, retail strategy should construct a 'deeper meaning' that forms the basis for the provision of a cohesive plot (or strategy). This must of course, be tempered by a consideration of efficiency, which cannot simply be ignored, as it is an important factor that must be included in the development of any retail strategy.

In developing such a retail 'story', balance is not simply about creating a strategy with an equal measure of both efficiency and effectiveness, but is rather about achieving equilibrium, thereby generating the 'right' blend in terms of the company and its customers. If the development of successful retail strategy hinged on providing 'equal measure', then this approach would inevitably mean that *all* retailers inhabited a 'middle-ground'. This would lead to a retail market where there was little differentiation.

What appears to be a more credible proposition is that in developing their stories, retailers would choose to focus primarily on either a *functional* or a *pleasurable* experience (whilst understanding the importance of both). This suggests therefore, that retail provision is likely to diverge. At one end of the spectrum will be those retailers that focus on presenting a story that hinges on the provision of a 'utilitarian' locus of supply. At the other will be those that create 'pleasure-oriented' consumption experiences.

Each end of this spectrum has its own 'theatricality', and its own issues related to both efficiency and effectiveness. Take for instance, the differences between a discount operator such as T.K. Maxx (providing a plot clearly focused on utility – to customers in terms of price, and to the retailer in terms of operational concerns); and up-market clothing retailer such as Jaeger (that constructs a story that rests on creating a pleasurable shopping experience). Although the approaches taken are clearly distinct (even if the merchandise can be similar in many ways), both retailers have created their own plots – ones that balance efficiency and effectiveness, as well as functionality and experience – which they communicate clearly (albeit in different ways).

For consumers, the choice of which store to frequent is no longer driven solely by their economic circumstances. The decision to visit one store or the other may stem from the requirements of the customer at that particular moment – and there is no reason why one customer could not use and derive benefit from both offers above. This reflects the increasing fragmentation of consumers' identities, and their happiness to use a variety of resources for the creation of these self concepts. It also indicates the pluralism that is present in the retail sector and in the society that surrounds it. The provision of environments that are distinct and that have a comprehensible image, clearly hinges on retailers' abilities to create cohesive stories. However, it also necessitates that such plots are executed in a consistent and appropriate manner.

Balancing Conception and Execution

To enable a retail story to be 'performed' clearly, in a manner that depicts its key propositions as intended, it is necessary to establish mechanisms for the management of what is essentially a creative environment. This means considering the elements depicted in the Servuction system not as isolated factors, but as interconnecting structures that provide a framework for the retail drama. (Such an approach would be consistent with one of the very earliest, and most enduring, metaphors used in marketing: that of the original, integrative marketing mix.) Where the plot is based on a 'utilitarian locus of supply', then the physical environment, service personnel and the facilitating of customer-to-customer interaction, all need to be managed in concert to present the consumer with a 'legible' story across all elements. The retail manager therefore essentially becomes a director: interpreting the plot provided by the retail strategy, and then orchestrating its performance. If this alignment is not present, then one of either two basic situations will occur. The development of a clear and consistent retail strategy will be impeded by poor implementation; or good execution will be hindered by a lack of clear direction.

To ensure that such situations are avoided, it is necessary to provide a communication framework that facilitates the expression of the underlying 'actants' in the retail plot. This framework must also indicate the degree of improvisation that can be accommodated. Improvisation clearly relates to the 'people' aspects of the retail offer, but it also affects *all* the elements of the Servuction arena. For example, how much will individual store managers, or their staff, be allowed to create or modify the nature of the service arena itself? Is it central to the plot that all stores in the chain are the same; or does the deeper meaning that is to be communicated rest on flexibility, individuality and variety?

Irrespective of the approach taken by the individual retailer, what appears paramount is that a cohesive drama is delivered, and that for this to take place there needs to be a clear understanding by *all* involved – everyone within the retail organization, the customers, as well as those that constitute the wider social context. This is not to suggest that there will not be any variation of interpretation – clearly, this will always be present. The issue here is to create a retail offer where the deeper meaning developed at the core of the story is transmitted to all concerned. Whether those people *outside* the organization can develop a sense of these meanings – in essence, whether they can *read* them – is the underlying question. Not all that is read in each retail story will be consistent. This of course, will depend on their own attitudes, tastes and preferences. Those that find the story of interest should, however, have a clear understanding of that, deeper meaning.

Balancing the Roles of Retailer and Consumer

This does not imply that the retailer can ever impose meaning on the totality of the customer's reading of a retail story. To do so would be to ignore that a theatrical performance is an act of co-production between those that stage the drama and those that form the audience. This is no difference in the retail context. In fact, here the concept of co-production is strengthened by the very nature of postmodern consumption which stresses that consumers adopt a 'creative' function when constructing their desired identities. In this context, the customer does not simply 'take' the meanings attached to products by those producing and retailing goods, services and or experiences; there is instead a (re)negotiation of the meanings, signs and symbols between buyer and seller. Varying patterns can be seen – at times customers creating their own distinct and very different meanings to those proposed by the retailer; at others, the consumer simply choosing to adopt the meaning presented by the seller. There is also a large middle ground where various positions between these two extremes can be seen. The development of the meanings attached to consumption and the very patterns of consumption itself are therefore being continually constructed, deconstructed and reconstructed.

The creation of consumption patterns is also therefore an issue for balance – one between the role of the retailer and the role of the consumer. Again, given the varied nature of the 'meaning patterns' that can exist, balance cannot be seen as a simple equality of role, or in particular, of power. If this were the case, then meaning would be generated in equal measure by consumer and retailer within each shopping event. However as stated above, this is not the case.

In the final analysis, 'control' and 'power' rest with the consumer – the retailer is not able to dictate these patterns. The consumer can choose to accept, reject, modify – or simply ignore – the meanings and messages that the retailer attempts to convey. The retailer can therefore develop the deeper meaning that underlies the plot; fashion its story, and then direct performance, however it is in the minds and actions of those who are the audience where the elements will either coalesce to create an effective reading, or fail. This reinforces the notion expressed throughout the book that retailers must attend not only to the aesthetics of *production* (constructing and staging their story) but also, more importantly, to the aesthetics of *reception* (the reading of this story by the audience).

To adequately attempt such considerations, retailers must actively seek feedback from customers in relation to their customers' 'reading' of the retail offer. This goes deeper than examining issues such as satisfaction or service quality and aims to monitor and observe whether a retailer's customers perceive the intended 'actants' that underlie the totality of that retail offer. If they do not, then the retailer must consider whether what customers perceive provides a credible basis for a retail offer. If it does, then maybe this should provide a new set of 'actants'. However, if customers are unable to discern the deeper meaning of the plot at all, then the retailer faces an even bigger challenge and has potentially failed to engage its audience at any meaningful level. The necessity for the audience to provide response and criticism helps to reinforce that customers are *participative* – providing a point of co-production, as well as, through their understanding, helping to shape the very deeper meaning that may be developed for a retail offer.

Balancing Public and Private Space

The audience therefore acts as primary co-producer. However, in the retail context, there are other 'actors' that also impact the nature and staging of the drama. Of specific importance are those that manage the 'physicality' of the space in which retailing is enacted e.g. the shopping centre developers and local authorities (and even in cyberspace, those that administer 'gateway' sites and other virtual points where a customer may come seeking access to retail provision). In 'private' spaces, those operated and controlled by a private corporation, there is a natural tendency for those managing it to want control: both in terms of who is allowed to trade, and in relation to what 'visitors' can do. This can mean that there is less room for the delivery of the intended retail story, as 'direction' given by the manager of the private retail space can impose constraints. Such space can also inhibit the actions of customers – who are not as free to act in the variety of ways that might be seen in 'public' environments. Private spaces therefore, have constraints that result from the desire of their managers to control; even if they are often viewed in large part as 'public' spaces – providing a focus for the development of community, and as places where consumers can simply 'be' outside their homes or their work.

The development of the use of private spaces for such 'public' activities has perhaps been the result of the increasing preference of consumers for clean and controlled environments, aided by increased access to such spaces for the majority of consumers. This has resulted in those responsible for public spaces seeking in some ways to emulate private environments. This has primarily been through the employment of town centre managers, whose role it is to control the 'direction' of public space – often with the aim of establishing a clear identity (or even 'meaning') for the environments that they preside over. Such actions have provided public spaces that are in a sense, 'policed', and which therefore begin to share some of the restraining features typical of their private counterparts. Both locations are therefore subject to similar characteristics – including a level of control and yet at the same time, providing a space that is communal and capable of acting as the backdrop for self-expression.

This creates a tension that once more, is a focus for the notion of balance. If the consumption environment becomes too rigid by being overly controlled, managed or policed, then there is the potential to deny the creation of a setting focused on self-expression. Given the importance of the retail environment in providing a location for such action and enactment, then hampering its development presents the retailer with severe problems. Equally, if the environment does not exhibit the 'signs' of being a 'managed space', this may itself deter consumers from either visiting or remaining in the location. This is perhaps not only an issue of balance, but again of pluralism. Consumers want safe, clean, warm, controlled, exciting, surprising, uninhibiting and expressive environments. To meet such a range of requirements presents those that manage retail spaces, and retailers themselves, with a number of challenges.

One mechanism for potentially contending with this task is to provide mass customization. This customization can occur in a number of ways. Perhaps, most importantly, it can be considered in relation to the experience that consumers develop as a result of their interaction with retailing. The provision of the 'space' for consumers to construct their own experience – in a sense involving them as audience and utilizing the co-productive and participatory nature of the customer-retailer relationship – offers a means of customizing the experience. (This is of course, necessarily reliant on the customer as the point where customization occurs.) This approach would utilize the suggested nature of retailing presented throughout the text and would, in essence, see the audience as ultimately in charge of creating an experience that affords them with satisfaction. The retailer is clearly in this sense the 'director' – providing the framework and performance that enables consumers to generate such personalized experiences.

The Future of Retail Provision

There is also scope for customization in relation to the goods sold. This can be seen in the increasing number of retailers that have returned to an historical form – that of retail-manufacturer. The resurgence of such a union between the point of production and circulation enables retailers to offer customers such customization at a more palpable level. This trend can be set against the propensity of many manufacturers to provide retail provision – often in the form of the 'factory shop'. Here, customization is not always as possible as it is for the retail-manufacturer. In this context, 'customization' stems from customers' ability to access and use products with symbolic qualities that they may otherwise have been unable to purchase.

Customers may also increasingly be able to access a broader range of products as a result of the rise in retail internationalization. The current trend towards international and even global retail operators is unlikely to decrease – as successful retailers seek new markets. The ability of retailers to transfer their offers has been in part supported by the broad-scale convergence of consumption patterns. This can be seen in the growth of 'super-brands' such as McDonalds, Nike, Coca-Cola and Levi's, which are consumed over a large part of the world. However, in what seemingly suggests convergence, there is in fact, customization – both in terms of the product itself, and in what the product symbolizes in different contexts. This means that, rather than having a single clear meaning, offers are moulded by the audiences in each country, just as they are by each individual member of the audience *within* a country. Therefore, whilst there may well be a degree of shared meaning in relation to international brands and offers, there is also likely to be variation and customization. This presents retailers attempting such expansion with an additional level of co-production to consider.

An additional challenge is presented by the rise of what has been termed the 'post-materialist consumer' (McLarney and Chung, 1999). This new 'breed' of consumer has not let go totally of more mainstream materialist values related to the acquisition and retention of economic goods. These have however, been displaced in their supremacy by the need for belonging, as well as aesthetic and intellectual needs. These notions also serve to emphasize the increased importance of experience, rather than the simple purchase of goods, in many retail contexts. For retailers, the development of the story of the retail drama that they offer is thereby again brought into stark relief. These shifts are in part responsible for the growing interest displayed by consumers in ethical and social issues, and the growing numbers of customers that are driven by a particular cause or even spiritual belief.

As a result of the issues of balance and the shifts identified, retailers must consider the development of retail plot and the management of the service arena as interconnected, interdependent and inseparable elements, which are the basis of the discourse between consumer and retailer. Without understanding this proposition and recognizing that customers are active – and in fact the deciding component of retail consumption – management of this complex social process is undermined.

References

Campbell, C. 1995. The sociology of consumption. In Miller, D. (Ed.). *Acknowledging Consumption. A Review of New Studies*. London: Routledge, pp. 96–126.

McLarney, C. and Chung, E. 1999. Post-materialism's 'silent revolution' in consumer research. *Marketing Intelligence and Planning*, 17(6), 288–297.

INDEX

Public Limited Companies 32–3
public space 131
punk 76
purchase deferral, time availability and 222–3
pure-play operators 38
Puritanism 51–2, 54

quality measurement 291–4

Rainforest Café 83
rational-comprehensive perspective 265
Realism 59
Recreational Equipment 83
recycling 332
reducing 333
regional centres 44
relationship markers 198
retail brand intent 234–6
retail buying, merchandise and 153–6
retail classification technology matrix 288–9
retail development, conditions for 19–20
retail forms 104–5
retail networks 30–2
retail parks 44
retail staff 210–12
    see also service employees
retail strategy review and development 269
retailing history 17–46
re-using 331–2
risk associated with goods and services,
    understanding 242–3
risk-reduction strategies 243–7
Roberts of London 30
Rochdale Society of Equitable Pioneers 31,
    327
Roddick, Anita 329
Romanticism 58–9
root method 267
Ruskin, John 62

Safeway 32
Sainsbury's 31, 32, 155
satisfaction, customer 297–8
ScrewFix 35
Sears 42, 277
second-hand stores 44
self-concept, store image and 184–5, 186
self-identity 58
self-knowledge, store knowledge and 185–6
self-service retailing 122
service characteristics 282–6
    heterogeneity 285

inseparability 285
intangibiity 282–5
perishability 285–6
service employees 120–1, 204–12
    behavioural classifications 206
    behavioural impacts 205
    non-verbal aspect 207–9
    retail staff 210–12
    venue staff 209–10
service encounter 205, 285
service factories 291
service quality, customer satisfaction and
    297–8
service quality measurement 294–7
    instruments 295–6
    in retailing 296–7
    service shops 290
service type classification 290–1
services classification 286–90
services marketing, growth of 115–17
servicescape 120, 146
SERVPERF 296
SERVQUAL approach 295–6, 297
Servuction model 107–9, 111–26
    concept 117–22
    creating benefit 119
    customer 121–2
    development of 112–17
    extensions to 122–5
        antecedents 123–4
        technology 124
    inanimate environment 119–20
    line of visibility 118
    locating merchandise within 152
    service personnel 120–1
Seven Ps approach 115
shared identity 75–6
Shaw, George Bernard 63
shopping centres 42–4
shops, history of 24–5
signification 88
Simmel, Georg 61
Singer Sewing Machine Company 31
Smiles, Samuel 57
Smith, Adam: *Wealth of Nations* 54
social capital 75
social change 63–4
social class
    consumption as demarcator of 73–5
    middle class 57, 59–60
    working class 59–60
social interaction, space and 135–6

Veblen, Thorstein: *Theory of the Leisure Class, The* 60–1
venue staff 209–10
verbal communication 198–200
Vertbaudet 35
virtual merchants 38–9
visibility 273–5
    product attractiveness and 158–9
visible inanimate environment 134
Vision Express 42
visitors 202–4
visual sense 141–2, 147

Wal-Mart 32, 42, 334
Warsaw Pact 65
wayfinding 148
Weber: *Protestant Ethic, The* 51–2
Wedgwood 51

weekend, origin of 60
West Edmonton Mall 44
Whiteaway Laidlaw 40
Wilde, Oscar 63
window displays 30, 157
Woolworth, Frank Winfield 40
Woolworth's 31, 32, 40, 105, 190, 261
work ethic 57
    middle-class 60
    Protestant 51–2
working class 59–60
working hours 60

youth subculture 76
Yuppies 65, 66

Zoo York 49